The Miniature Schnauzer Handbook

BY

LINDA WHITWAM

ISBN: 979-8388330857

This book is dedicated to Max

Copyright

Acknowledgements

My sincere thanks to the dedicated breeders, owners and canine experts for sharing their extensive knowledge and passion for the (in my opinion) **wonderful** Miniature Schnauzer! This book would not have been possible without them.

Breeder Contributors

WADE BOGART

STEVE MATTHEWS

ANDREW & GAYNOR RAY

LESLEY MYERS

BETH RAILTON

DR LISA SARVAS

Owner Contributors

REBECCA MAKDAD

YOLANDE

CHLOE DONG & JACKY ZOU

GARY BLAIN

VIVIAN WILLIAMS

YVONNE & SIMON SONSINO

CHRIS LEE

LEAH DUMMER

Sincere thanks also to Dr Lisa Skiwski and Dr Samantha Goldberg, Aaron Bailey and Les Chant

Table of Contents

Author's Notes

The Miniature Schnauzer Handbook uses British English, except where Americans have been quoted, when the original US English has been preserved.

I have alternated between "he" and "she" in chapters to make this book as relevant as possible.

This book has been printed in black and white to make it affordable for all new owners. The FULL COLOUR edition is also available from Amazon.

1. Meet The Miniature Schnauzer

The Miniature Schnauzer is a dog with universal appeal and the most popular of the three Schnauzer breeds. These intelligent dogs are alert, playful and affectionate with a sense of fun.

This striking breed has a rectangular shape, trademark beard and beautiful brown eyes that look right at you, melting your heart. Instantly recognisable, they combine elegance with a certain robustness and a jaunty gait.

They approach life with cheerfulness and enthusiasm. Like all Schnauzers, they love being with their humans, forming very deep emotional bonds.

And once you've been owned by a Miniature Schnauzer, no other breed seems quite the same...!

....

A Small Package Bursting with Character

There are hundreds of breeds registered with the Kennel Clubs and all of them are different, but the Miniature Schnauzer is truly unique. These spirited dogs approach life full-on. Not quite Terrier, much more than a companion dog, and bright as a button, this dog refuses to be pigeonholed.

Minis are classed in the Utility Group in the UK and the Terrier Group in the US. There's no denying they have a lot in common with Terriers, with their inquisitive nature, perkiness, love of chasing small furry and feathered critters, and fondness for the sound of their own voices.

But as I and other Mini owners will tell you; they are so much more. They are creatures of contrast. Many are wusses when it comes to going out in the rain, but will bravely fight for their lives if threatened.

They will play for hours in the snow, but a Mini that enjoys swimming is hard to find - most don't even like getting their paws wet!

They will chase the neighbour's cat out of the yard or garden, but live happily alongside the family feline - especially if introduced at a young age. They bark their heads off at visitors to your house. But if they decide they like you, they'll be laid at your feet 10 minutes later enjoying a belly rub.

Photo: Rommey (Wundia Just A Rumour JW Sh.CM), aged 14 months, courtesy of Lesley Myers.

Minis are loyal, highly intelligent and quick to learn new things. Their eagerness to please you, love of treats and desire to show off all make them easy to train - provided you put the time in.

Make sure you do, as many have a stubborn streak and if you don't train them, you could end up with a 'Little Emperor' or 'Little Princess' ruling your house!

Don't let their innocent expressions lull you into falsely believing that you are the boss, Minis soon spot your weaknesses and will twist you around their little paws - if you let them. Be strong!

Living With a Mini

With their loving and amusing personalities, Miniature Schnauzers are a joy to live with - they will never bore you. And when they trot along jauntily at the side of you on a walk, they attract attention from admiring passers-by, something that Minis lap up, provided they feel comfortable in their surroundings.

Miniature Schnauzers can have a reputation for being highly strung. I feel this is somewhat unfair as it's usually down to a lack of socialisation - which is essential for Minis to feel relaxed. Take your young Mini out and about to encounter lots of other dogs, humans, situations and sounds (some Minis can be noise-sensitive), for a well-adjusted adult dog.

Mini Schnauzers are true 'people dogs' who thrive on being in the midst of family life. They often have a favourite, to whom they show very deep affection, but are usually very loving with other family members as well.

When trained to respect each other, Minis and children get along famously. Add to the mix their size and non-shedding coat, and it's no wonder the Mini is such a popular breed across the world.

Like all Schnauzers, Minis love to play with their owners; in fact, some prefer human company to that of other dogs. They do well with other Miniature Schnauzers, which is why many owners have two.

They are not naturally aggressive dogs, although can bark or lunge at other dogs when fearful. If they are not comfortable around other dogs, it's often due to a lack of early opportunities to mix with other dogs in different locations...socialisation, socialisation, socialisation!

Minis like to be at the centre of things and develop to their fullest potential when treated as part of the family - although it's sometimes difficult to remember that they're dogs and not humans.

When those beautiful brown eyes stare straight into your soul, it's obvious they know everything you're thinking!

A couple of nicknames are *'Velcro dog'* and *'Shadow'* as they become very attached to their owners and like to be with you - even following you to the toilet!

Photo: Special Delivery! Rebecca Makdad's Rosie and Navy en route with the Christmas tree, courtesy of Camie Stouck-Phiel.

They are quite vocal, with a range of sounds. It may not surprise you to learn that many owners, including several contributors to this book, have regular two-way conversations with their Minis.

And if you have a Mini, you don't need a doorbell! Their senses of hearing and smell are highly developed and they are always on alert. They will bark when anyone approaches the house - although if it's friendly burglars armed with treats, the family silver will soon be gone...

To get the best out of these highly-rewarding companions, they should be at the heart of the family with lots of interaction with their humans. These busy little dogs are not usually placid or lazy, either mentally or physically.

They do well in canine sports such as Agility, where they get a chance to exercise their minds as well as their compact, athletic bodies. Training classes and schemes like Canine Good Citizen are excellent ways of keeping them occupied and giving them a chance to shine.

A Miniature Schnauzer involved in his owner's daily life, getting regular exercise and playtime is a happy dog.

Photo: An American Mini with cropped ears.

The AKC (American Kennel Club) says: "The Miniature Schnauzer, the smallest of the three Schnauzer breeds, is a generally healthy, long-lived, and low-shedding companion. Add an outgoing personality, a portable size, and sporty good looks, and you've got an ideal family dog.

"Stocky, robust little dogs standing 12 to 14 inches, Miniature Schnauzers were bred down from their larger cousins, Standard Schnauzers. The bushy beard and eyebrows give Minis a charming, human-like expression. Created to be all-around farm dogs and ratters, they are tough, muscular, and fearless without being aggressive.

"The Miniature Schnauzer is a bright, friendly, trainable companion, small enough to adapt to apartment life, but tireless enough to patrol acres of farmland. They get along well with other animals and kids. Minis are sturdy little guys and enjoy vigorous play. Home and family oriented, they make great watchdogs."

The One and Only...!

Here's a short story about our Mini. Max loved chasing squirrels on his walks and had no road sense, so we only let him off the lead away from traffic. He also enjoyed rolling in fox and cow excrement!

One day my Dad, who was in his mid-80s, was walking near a field of cows when Max suddenly limbo-danced his way under the fence and headed off at top speed. Max was in his element, rolling in big, sloppy pats of cow dung. Dad started shouting at him, which drew a crowd of fellow dog walkers.

Spurred on by the audience and Dad, who had by now climbed the fence and was giving chase, Max proceeded to run from one cow pat to the next, eating as much of the stuff as he could, tossing it in the air and dashing on to the next one before my elderly father caught up with him.

One of the younger dog walkers managed to stop laughing long enough to catch Max, who was promptly taken home in disgrace for an early bath!

Photo: Dad and Max.

Here are some more affectionate stories from owners and breeders that sum up the unique personality of the Miniature Schnauzer, starting with Wade Bogart, AKC

Breeder of Merit and Breed Mentor, Sumerwynd Miniature Schnauzers, New York State: "I purchased fettuccine alfredo for my evening meal and had been savoring the thought of eating this dish for an entire day. My Miniature Schnauzer Tara had free run of the house. I put my fettuccine alfredo on the dining room table and walked into the kitchen, about 15 feet away, for a beverage.

"Seconds later, to my astonishment, I saw Tara on the table enjoying my dinner! She had hopped on a chair and then onto the table. All I could do was laugh. Her sneaky actions illustrated the athleticism and inelegance characteristic of the breed.

"Tara frequently greeted my arrival from work with a 25ft-long stream of toilet paper behind her - she was happy to see me! Once again the joke was on me. Her gesture showed the loyalty and love typical of the Miniature Schnauzer toward their owner."

Yolande has a similar tale of greed: "I was making a special lunch for the family and left four fillet steaks marinading on the kitchen table. All the chairs were pushed in securely around the table, or so I thought.

"A little while later, I checked on the steaks and found there were only three... Mayzy had managed to push a chair out, worm her way onto the kitchen table and eat a steak marinaded in olive oil, fresh garlic and rosemary - and by now was sleeping it off on one of our armchairs! The moral of the story is never underestimate the guile of a Miniature Schnauzer!"

Leah Dummer, owner of Freddie (3) and puppies Leelo and Lily: "One thing we did notice was how protective Freddie was of me when I was pregnant. He would often lay on my stomach as if listening to the baby. Our daughter Ellie was born in July and Freddie bonded with her extremely well.

"A short while later we got our black and silver girl, Leelo, and our salt and pepper girl, Lily. We'll always remember the day Lily entered the room for the first time, because our daughter Ellie crawled for the first time.

"It still amazes us now how Ellie and the three dogs get on so well together." *Photo: Ellie and Freddie.*

Rebecca Makdad: "I chuckle as I remember how Rosie chewed a book on Schnauzers - she already knew everything there was to know about herself! Rosie spent many hours visiting with nursing home residents. She was always very gentle and entertaining; the residents knew her name, but not mine!"

Aaron and Sally Bailey, Assured Breeders of Lakesidekelb Miniature Schnauzers, Herefordshire, UK: "Something that happens nearly every day with our pack of Schnauzers is their excitement to see you when you get back from popping out of the house. You may have been gone for one hour or one minute, it makes no difference!

"They are always like: "Where have you been? We are so pleased you are back, we thought you had gone forever." This always brings a smile to our faces. It is fantastic to be needed!"

Simon and Yvonne Sonsino: "When we were having our house renovated, there was a lot of tradespeople coming and going, and Bu was a firm favourite. He especially liked it when the packed lunches came out and started sitting on the drive waiting for them.

"Now the renovation is finished, we sometimes find him sitting in the same place waiting, or lying on the windowsill with a clear view of the front gate!"

Chris Lee: "Betsy is very vocal, very varied and expressive in her sounds. I am trying to learn Schnauzer language and have so far identified the following: the Bark (of course), the Roo-Roo, the

slow loud yawn called the Auoo, and the quiet grunt known as the Uh-uh-uh-uh, which often precedes food."

Show judge and former breeder Lesley Myers: "Rommey was able to pick your pocket without you feeling anything, It was mostly tissues, but one day she pinched a £5 note from my coat pocket; it must have been her as I eventually found it buried in the garden.

"She genetically passed this trick on to her daughter Ziska; she could do the same without you knowing."

Chloe Dong: "Oslo's desire for physical affection is welcome, most of the time. He sleeps with us almost every night and has a habit of pressing his body against you until it becomes uncomfortably warm. Sometimes he falls asleep in my arms.

"He doesn't hesitate to move spots in the middle of the night, often walking over you without a second thought. One morning I was slowly awakened by an increasing sense of pressure on my chest. I opened my eyes to Oslo standing on my chest, snout an inch away from my face, staring at me with his deceptively innocent, wide eyes."

Photo: Oslo looking like butter wouldn't melt in his mouth...

Chloe adds: "Oslo's ears are completely natural. He went from one ear pointing down to both of them standing up at around three months of age."

And finally, here's how they sum up their Minis:

- Joyful Family Companion
- Loving, Shadow, High-Spirited, Alert
- Loyal, Clingy, Stubborn, Affectionate
- Yappy, Friendly, Good Companion
- Loyal, Playful, Loving
- Strong-Willed, Purposeful, Funny, Characterful
- Ambassador to Senior Citizens
- Exuberant, Alert, Loyal, Vocal
- Loving, Loyal, Manageable
- Alert, Spirited, Loyal, Handsome!
- Loving, Cute, Independent, Talkative
- Loyal and Loving Companion

Whether you're a growing family, a single person working from home, or a retiree, the Miniature Schnauzer is a true friend and canine companion second to none.

Read on to learn how to understand, train and take the best care of your Mini for the rest of his or her life, and how to successfully build a deep bond that will become one of the most important things in your life - and certainly theirs.

2. Schnauzer History

The exact history of the breed we know today as the Schnauzer has been lost in the ancient mists of time. In the absence of precise historical records, dog breed experts have discussed many theories over many decades - but nobody knows just how and when the first Schnauzer appeared.

We do know that the Schnauzer has one of the longest histories of all breeds, dating back over 500 years, and it's packed with surprising facts. After much research, here is what we believe to be the most credible version of the Schnauzer's origins.

....

Birth of the Breeds

The Schnauzer originated in Southern Germany in the 14th or 15th century. In those days farmers and tradespeople travelled around the countryside with heavily-laden carts selling their produce and skills at markets.

They needed a medium-sized, versatile dog, strong enough to guard the cart and livestock, with enough stamina to drive animals, but small enough to easily fit into the same cart. These practical men also wanted a good ratter to keep down the vermin back at home.

Those involved in the creation of the Schnauzer probably crossed the following breeds to create the first Schnauzer:

- ❖ Black German Poodle
- ❖ Grey Wolfspitz
- ❖ Wire-Haired Pinscher, *pictured*, also known as the Rough Pinscher

This medium-sized 'prototype' most closely resembled today's Standard Schnauzer and established the breed as a working dog.

The reason it's impossible to be precise about the foundation breeds is that before the late 1800s, there were no official 'breeds'.

There were simply 'types' of dogs, which were usually bred to do a job, e.g. Retrievers, Setters, Pointers, Hounds (all bred for the hunt) and Terriers (bred to catch and kill vermin), etc.

In 1859, the first dog show was held (alongside a cattle show!) in the north of England and the situation was quite chaotic, with different-looking dogs of various sizes being entered as the same type. Dog shows became very popular with the Victorians, but there was no conformity of size or appearance. Dogs were simply entered into classes according to what their owners thought they were.

There were no official records of specific dog breeds; owners would mate their dogs with another dog they liked the look of, or which had some attribute they admired.

A group of 13 Englishmen decided something had to be done to restore order. So in 1873 they set up The Kennel Club to lay down a consistent set of rules for the popular new activities of dog showing and field trials.

A year later the Stud Book was introduced to register the name of successful competition dogs alongside the breed. Today pedigree registration documents are issued with every purebred Schnauzer. They trace a puppy's lineage back through five generations.

More Than a Pinch of Pinscher

Shown courtesy of the American Kennel Club, the Schnauzer Family Tree outlines the different dog breeds used to develop the three types of Schnauzer. It's interesting that although they look nothing alike now, modern Schnauzers and Pinschers share the same ancestors.

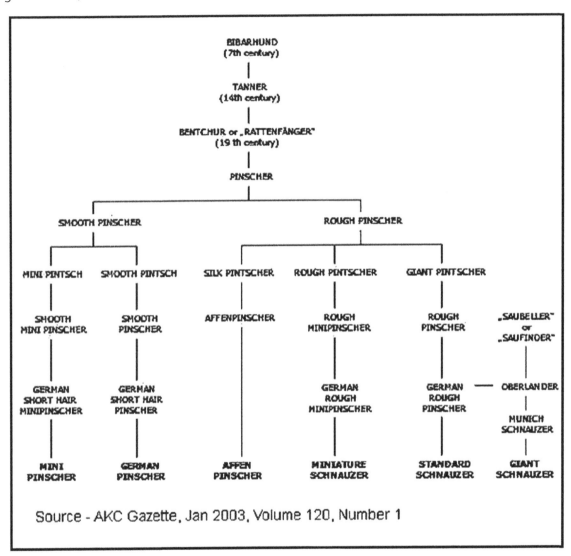

Image: The Schnauzer Family Tree according to the AKC Gazette.

As working dogs, German Pinschers were prized for their vermin-hunting skills and instinct to protect the home and family. In the early days, Schnauzers were referred to as Wire-Haired Pinschers.

The two breeds were once so closely intertwined in Germany that smooth pups (we today call Pinschers) and rough-haired pups (Schnauzers) often appeared in the same litter. In the late 19th century, the two breeds had the same breed club in Germany: The Pinscher-Schnauzer Klub, which is still active today. The Klub's first Stud Book listed Standard Schnauzers, Smooth-Coat Pinschers, Miniature Pinschers and Wire-Haired Miniature Pinschers (now known as Miniature Schnauzers).

At the 3rd German International Show in 1879, three Wire-Haired Pinschers, owned by C. Berger from Württemberg, were entered. The winner was a dog called *"Schnauzer."* And from then on, all dogs of this breed were called Schnauzers.

 The Schnauzer is unique in that it is the only breed named after a specific dog.

The original Smooth-Coated Pinschers were bred with each other to give the sleek coat of today's Miniature and Doberman Pinschers. The Wire-Haired Pinschers were specifically bred to give the rough coat of modern Schnauzers.

Image: Wire-haired Pinscher illustration by Ludwig Beckmann, 1895.

The German Pinscher was not as popular as the Schnauzer and the breed became almost extinct by 1950. Numbers have since increased due to a concerted effort and imports by some breed fanciers.

It is interesting to see how selective breeding, albeit over a long period, can produce such different dogs in terms of appearance, temperament and size; i.e. the Pinschers and the Schnauzers.

In his book **"Dogs Of All Nations"** published in 1915, author W.E. Mason describes:

The Wire-Coated German Terrier (Schnauzer or Rattler)

Color: Pepper and salt, iron-gray, silver-gray, dull black with yellow or tan markings on head and legs, rust-yellow and gray-yellow. A bright red is objectionable.

Height: 18 in. Weight: 28 lbs.

This is a strongly-built cobby dog, of a rather nervous temperament, yet he is gay, watchful, very intelligent and courageous, without being quarrelsome. He is a first-rate rat dog.

The head is strong, fairly long, with a flat skull rather narrow between the ears, and the occiput is well developed. The ears are set on high and are cropped with rounded tips. The oval eyes convey an intelligent and vivacious expression, with eyebrows well developed and covered with rough upstanding hair.

His back is strong and straight and rather flat sided in rib. The tail is set on high, is docked very short and if a bob-tail, is much appreciated. The coat is as hard, rough and wiry as possible, of the stand-off variety and though it is shorter on the head, it is not softer. On the muzzle we find a characteristic short beard and whiskers.

This breed has worked himself into popular favor in Germany by his indefatigable industry as a worker and as a good friend of the horse, hence he is much appreciated in the stable.

Certainly he is very intelligent, a very apt pupil, as quick as lightning in his movements and unfailing in his fidelity, courage, endurance and muscular strength. He is a rare good dog for bad weather purposes.

The correct German-like pronunciation of word Schnauzer is **Sh-now-tser,** with the German **Z** sounding like **TS** - as in Mozart, which is spoken "Mowtsart." In fact, many people pronounce it **Sch-now-zer** or **Sh-now-sser.**

It comes from the German word "Schnauze" meaning snout. This refers to the wonderfully-whiskered muzzle, usually described as the beard and moustache - the Schnauzer trademark which gives them such a unique appearance. It's thought the heavy whiskers gave protection from vermin bites.

Standard Schnauzer

The Standard Schnauzer is the original. It is the oldest of the three distinct Schnauzer breeds and the one from which Miniatures and Giants originate. The breed is known as the *Mittelschnauzer* (Middle Schnauzer) in its native Germany, and simply as the Schnauzer in the UK.

The mid to late 19th century was a time of great excitement and experimentation in the dog world, with Victorian dog fanciers adding a little bit of this dog and a hint of that one to create new breeds. It is when the foundations were laid for many of today's modern breeds.

Photo: The different types of Pinscher that existed in 1895.

German dog breeders began to show an interest in this versatile native breed. Wire-Haired Pinschers, as the Standard Schnauzer was then called, were first exhibited at the Hannover show in 1879.

Dog Fanciers were so impressed with these versatile, medium-sized dogs, that they began crossing them with other breeds to create smaller and later larger versions. We now recognise these as the Miniature and Giant Schnauzer.

Although there may have been an occasional earlier one, the first Schnauzers were imported into

the UK and America around 1900. They were probably brought to England and the New World as beloved pets of immigrant families as well as by travellers and traders returning home.

During World War I, Standard Schnauzers were used as guard dogs by the German Army and dispatch carriers by the Red Cross. And it was soldiers returning from the war who brought back Schnauzers in greater numbers. The fighting men greatly admired the courage and spirit of these dogs.

Photo: Standard Schnauzer Ch Brodrick Castle Romper, born 1936.

Miniature Schnauzer

The first Miniature Schnauzer was recorded in Germany in 1988 - a black bitch called Findel. Of the eight Miniature Schnauzer bitches first registered in the Pinscher-Schnauzer Klub Stud Book, there were three blacks, three yellows, one black and tan and one pepper and salt!

(Interestingly, fans of the white Schnauzer point to the fact that *'gelb'* or yellow was a natural colour for the Schnauzer dating back to the earliest records).

There was still much crossbreeding at the end of the 19th century, when it seems that the named breed depended more on outward appearance than genetic makeup. One Miniature Pinscher is registered as having a Standard Schnauzer dam, while another dog registered as a Miniature Schnauzer had a Miniature Pinscher sire.

It's generally agreed that the Miniature Schnauzer derived from breeding the smallest of Standard Schnauzers with Affenpinschers, grey Spitz (possibly the Toy Spitz or Pomeranian) and black Poodles in a highly selective breeding programme.

The Standard and Miniature Schnauzer (*Zwergschnauzer* or Dwarf Schnauzer in Germany) were considered to be variants of the same breed and were shown together at early dog shows.

It wasn't until 1899 that they were classed and shown as separate breeds in Germany.

Photo: Miniature prizewinner, Jocco-Fulda Lilliput, 1899.

Mrs Marie Slattery of the Marienhof Kennels provided the foundation stock for the miniature Schnauzer in America when she imported four of them.

Originally a German Shepherd breeder, she read about Miniature Schnauzers and abruptly switched breeds in 1923, never having seen one until her imports arrived from Germany.

Miniature Schnauzers were first registered as a separate breed in the US in 1926. The following year the first American champion was Mrs Slattery's Ch. Moses Taylor. This was an honour shared with Don v. Dornbusch, since both won on the same day - but at different shows.

Despite frequently moving for her husband's army career, her breeding programme thrived, ultimately breeding over 60 champions in its 40-year history.

Photo: Marie Slattery with Joshua, Hosea, Ch. Marko, Ch. Josiah, Arbecci, Kathleen of Marienhof, Heidy Anfiger, and Ch. Mehitabel of Marienhof III.

Both Standards and Miniatures were moved to the Terrier Group in 1927, and it wasn't until 1945 that the Standards moved back to the Working Group. In the UK, both the Standard and Miniature are in the Utility Group.

 The only two countries in the world to place the Miniature Schnauzer in the Terrier Group are the United States and Canada. In all other countries they are in the Utility or Non-Sporting Group.

Since those early days, the Miniature Schnauzer has gone from strength to strength. Its reputation as a cheerful, entertaining and devoted pet has placed this spirited little dog at the heart of families across the United States and Europe, where it is consistently in the top 10 to 20 most popular breeds.

Giant Schnauzer History

Some reports say that a dog similar to the Giant Schnauzer was known as long as a thousand years ago. There is no way we will ever know if this is true. We do know, however, that the Giant was the last of all three Schnauzer breeds to be created.

Its modern origins lie in the 17ᵗʰ century. Bavarian farmers admired the tenacity and versatility of the Standard Schnauzer, but wanted a bigger dog to guard as well as drive their cattle (and sheep) to market. Indeed, the first Giants were known as **Munich Schnauzers** (Munich is the capital of the German state of Bavaria).

There is some difference of opinion regarding exactly WHICH breeds were involved in the Giant's DNA, but there is general agreement that the Standard Schnauzer, of course, and the black Great Dane were foundation breeds. The Great Dane gave strength and power to the Giant, as well as the instinct to protect.

Some say that the French sheepdog, the Bouviers de Flanders *(pictured)*, also went into the genetic makeup, along with the Rottweiler, but others dispute this. (The Bouviers is related to the Old German Shepherd Dog).

In the 1928 book on German dog breeds, E. von Otto says the father of the Giants was the great *"bear Schnauzer"* of Munich.

Early German breeders excelled in producing new dog breeds with consistent conformation and temperament. They were also *"fit for function."* There were no dog shows in the 17ᵗʰ and 18ᵗʰ centuries; these men were producing a dog to fulfil a specific purpose.

They excelled with the Giant Schnauzer, creating a strong, imposing yet beautifully proportioned, athletic dog. He had a huge heart, a strong desire to work and protect, and fierce loyalty to his owners - traits which have been carried through to today's Giants.

News of this powerful new breed and excellent guard dog spread from the Bavarian hills to the towns and villages of southern Germany, and the Giant became popular with tavern owners, breweries and butchers.

Just before World War I the Giant Schnauzer began to be recognised nationally in Germany as an excellent police dog. He showed a natural aptitude for the job, being intelligent, courageous yet calm, with a strong work ethic and devotion to his handler. But the breed was still virtually unknown internationally.

Eventually, the first Giants were imported into the USA in the 1930s, although until the 1960s there were still fewer than 50 Giants a year registered in the US. In 1969, the Odivane Kennel of Mary Moore was one of the first UK importers with the arrival of Odivane Marcus, who was the first Giant to grace the big ring at Crufts.

The Giant has since excelled at police work in various countries, as well as in many canine competitions. And with selective breeding, imports from successful kennels and word of mouth, the popularity of the Giant Schnauzer has increased considerably over the last few decades.

3. The Breed Standard

The Breed Standard is a blueprint not only for the ideal appearance of each breed, but also for character and temperament, how the dog moves and what colours are acceptable.

In other words, it ensures that a Miniature Schnauzer looks and acts like a Miniature Schnauzer, ensuring he or she is "fit for function, fit for life." Good breeders strive to breed their dogs to the Breed Standard.

If you are looking to buy a puppy, have a good look at the mother and father - or at least the mother. Purebred puppies usually resemble their parents.

The Breed Standard is administered by the Kennel Club in the UK. In the USA it is written by the national breed club, the AMSC (American Miniature Schnauzer Club), and approved by the AKC (American Kennel Club).

The Kennel Clubs then keep the register of purebred, or pedigree, dogs. Dogs entered in conformation shows run under Kennel Club and AKC rules are judged against the Breed Miniature.

Breeders approved by the Kennel Clubs agree to produce puppies in line with the Breed Miniature and maintain certain welfare conditions.

 **Responsible breeders select only the finest dogs for reproduction, based on the health, look and temperament of the parents and ancestors.**

The Miniature Schnauzer is in the *Terrier Group* in the US and *Utility Group* in the UK, which covers a wide range of breeds that don't naturally fit into other groups.

The UK Kennel Club says: "This group consists of miscellaneous breeds of dog mainly of a non-sporting origin, including the Bulldog, Dalmatian, Akita and Poodle.

"The name 'Utility' essentially means fitness for a purpose and this group consists of an extremely mixed and varied bunch, most breeds having been selectively bred to perform a specific function not included in the Sporting and Working categories.

"Some of the breeds listed in the group are the oldest documented breeds of dog in the world."

The AKC says this about the Terrier Group: "Feisty and energetic are two of the primary traits that come to mind for those who have experience with Terriers. In fact, many describe their distinct personalities as "eager for a spirited argument."

"Bred to hunt, kill vermin and to guard their families home or barn; sizes range from fairly small, as in the Norfolk, Cairn or West Highland White Terrier, to the larger and grand Airedale Terrier.

"Prospective owners should know that terriers make great pets, but they do require determination on the part of the owner because they can be stubborn, have high energy levels, and require special grooming (known as "stripping") to maintain a characteristic appearance."

Cropping and Docking

In North America, Miniature Schnauzers may have cropped ears and docked tails, *pictured.* This accentuates the Schnauzer's sharp, square appearance, a look preferred by many owners and breeders.

Cropping is the removal of part of the external flaps of the ear, which sometimes involves bracing and taping the remainder of the ears to train them to point upright.

Docking is the removal of the majority of the tail while a puppy is a few days old.

Cropping and docking are now banned in most of Europe and the rest of the world, where it is generally considered "cruel and unnecessary."

The exception is working dogs, such as working Spaniels, where the tail may be docked to prevent it from getting caught in the undergrowth and causing injury.

The American Kennel Club (AKC) describes docking and cropping as: "Acceptable practices integral to defining and preserving breed character and/or enhancing good health."

The National Animal Interest Alliance in the US adds: "Ear cropping has been a common practice throughout the centuries and developed according to the type of work a breed was expected to do.

"Guard dogs were cropped to enhance their alertness and make their appearance more threatening to potential criminals. Smaller versions of guard dogs were also cropped to achieve the alert look of their larger cousins.

"Today's pet owners and breeders like the look that upright ears present and many believe that cropped ears allow their dogs to hear better and prevent or reduce the potential for infections that sometimes plague drop-eared dogs."

It is true, however, that many North American vets now refuse to crop and dock, while natural ears and tails are becoming more acceptable in the US show rings.

Some US breeders have their Schnauzers docked and/or cropped, while others don't; yet others will ask the potential owner for their preference.

....

Schnauzer Colours

As you will read in the Breed Standard, the range of colours accepted by the Kennel Clubs is very small:

- ❧ Pepper and Salt (also called Salt and Pepper)
- ❧ Black and Silver
- ❧ Solid Black
- ❧ White (now accepted in the UK but not by the North American Kennel Clubs)

However, if you are looking for a Miniature Schnauzer puppy, you will see them advertised in all sorts of colours, including: wheaten, platinum, platinum silver, liver, liver pepper, liver tan, chocolate, and chocolate phantom.

Then there are all the parti options. *"Parti"* comes from the French word for divided and means two colors - like piebald or skewbald (pinto) for a horse. All parti Schnauzers have patches of white on them, such as: black parti, salt and pepper parti, liver parti, liver tan parti, liver pepper parti, and black and silver parti.

There are even more, but you get the picture - there are Miniature Schnauzer puppies currently being bred in many different colors. If people love the look of a parti, chocolate, or any other colour of Mini - and many do – and these puppies have Kennel Club, KC or CKC (Canadian Kennel Club) pedigree certificates, why do the Miniature Schnauzer breed clubs and so many respected breeders object to them?

One of the main aims of the Kennel Club and breed clubs, most notably the AMSC, is to protect the integrity and health of the Miniature Schnauzer by producing puppies that conform to the Breed Standard.

These so-called 'rare colours' have led to a big increase in Miniature Schnauzer puppy farms and people with little knowledge of Minis breeding dogs primarily for colour, with scant regard for the genetics, health or welfare of the pups.

 **FACT** ⟩ Parti, chocolate, merle, phantom, etc. do not occur naturally in Miniature Schnauzers, so another breed has been introduced somewhere along the line to get the 'new' colour.

Even if a coloured Schnauzer has pedigree papers, he or she may not be entered into conformation shows under AKC or AMSC rules. However, dogs of all colours can compete in local dog shows and canine events such as Agility, Canine Good Citizen, Obedience and Earth Dog Trials.

Although white Minis are not accepted in shows run by the North American breed and Kennel Clubs, they are accepted in the UK and all FCI (Fédération Cynologique Internationale) countries, including Germany, where the Miniature Schnauzer originated.

AKC Breeder of Merit with 40 years' experience Wade Bogart, who is also an AKC Breed Mentor, says: "These non-Schnauzer colors are a big problem in the US. Colors not accepted in the Breed Standard usually indicate that the dog is not pure bred. My recommendation to prospective Miniature Schnauzer owners is to do your homework. A great resource is https://amsc.us/"

Here's what AKC Licensed Show Judge Marcia Feld has to say about Breed Standards: "This definition is what makes a Great Dane a Great Dane, a Poodle a Poodle, a Dalmatian a Dalmatian, etc.

"It is not up to each of us to decide that we would like to change each of these breeds because we like it or find it appealing. Adhering to these definitions is what retains the individuality of the breed. Breeding to the definition is the challenge for the breeder.

"A brown Dalmatian might be cute - but he is no longer a Dal; a tiny Great Dane would be more

easily kept - but he is no longer a Great Dane, and a hard-coated Poodle would be easier to groom, but he wouldn't be a Poodle.

"And in that same light, a white or colored Schnauzer is no longer a Schnauzer; he is disqualified because he does not meet the definition of that breed."

NOTE: One of the original colours in Germany, where Schnauzers originate, was *'gelb'* - literally yellow - but more commonly taken to mean white. However, none of the other 'unaccepted' colours have any historical base.

We strongly recommend you stick to the Breed Standard if you are looking for a Miniature Schnauzer, but if you are desperate to have a different colour, then do your time and research to find the right breeder – too many people realise too late that they have bought from a puppy farm.

See **Chapter 5. Finding Your Puppy** for lots of practical tips on finding a good breeder.

USA Breed Standard

As is customary, the USA Breed Standard is far more detailed than that of the UK, where breeders are less concerned with exact measurements and more concerned with the overall look, structure and temperament of the dog.

General Appearance:

The Miniature Schnauzer is a robust, active dog of terrier type, resembling his larger cousin, the Standard Schnauzer, in general appearance, and of an alert, active disposition.
Faults - Type - Toyishness, ranginess or coarseness.

Size, Proportion, Substance: Size - From 12 to 14 inches. He is sturdily built, nearly square in proportion of body length to height with plenty of bone, and without any suggestion of toyishness.
Disqualifications - Dogs or bitches under 12 inches or over 14 inches.

Head:

Eyes - Small, dark brown and deep-set. They are oval in appearance and keen in expression.
Faults - Eyes light and/or large and prominent in appearance.

Photo: Wade Bogart's show champion Am Can Ch Sumerwynd Still Sizzlin.

Ears - When cropped, the ears are identical in shape and length, with pointed tips. They are in balance with the head and not exaggerated in length. They are set high on the skull and carried perpendicularly at the inner edges, with as little bell as possible along the outer edges.

When uncropped, the ears are small and V-shaped, folding close to the skull.

Head - strong and rectangular, its width diminishing slightly from ears to eyes, and again to the tip of the nose. The forehead is unwrinkled. The topskull is flat and fairly long.

The foreface is parallel to the topskull, with a slight stop, and it is at least as long as the topskull.

The muzzle is strong in proportion to the skull; it ends in a moderately blunt manner, with thick whiskers which accentuate the rectangular shape of the head.

Faults - Head coarse and cheeky. The teeth meet in a scissors bite. That is, the upper front teeth overlap the lower front teeth in such a manner that the inner surface of the upper incisors barely touches the outer surface of the lower incisors when the mouth is closed.
Faults - Bite - Undershot or overshot jaw. Level bite.

Neck, Topline, Body:

Neck - Strong and well arched, blending into the shoulders, and with the skin fitting tightly at the throat.

Body - Short and deep, with the brisket extending at least to the elbows. Ribs are well sprung and deep, extending well back to a short loin. The underbody does not present a tucked-up appearance at the flank.

The backline is straight; it declines slightly from the withers to the base of the tail. The withers form the highest point of the body. The overall length from chest to buttock appears to equal the height at the withers.

Faults - Chest too broad or shallow in brisket. Hollow or roach back.

Tail - set high and carried erect. It is docked only long enough to be clearly visible over the backline of the body when the dog is in proper length of coat. A properly presented Miniature Schnauzer will have a docked tail as described; all others should be severely penalized.
Fault - Tail set too low.

Forequarters: Forelegs are straight and parallel when viewed from all sides. They have strong pasterns and good bone. They are separated by a fairly deep brisket which precludes a pinched front. The elbows are close, and the ribs spread gradually from the first rib so as to allow space for the elbows to move close to the body. *Fault* - Loose elbows.

The sloping shoulders are muscled, yet flat and clean. They are well laid back, so that from the side the tips of the shoulder blades are in a nearly vertical line above the elbow. The tips of the blades are placed closely together. They slope forward and downward at an angulation which permits the maximum forward extension of the forelegs without binding or effort. Both the shoulder blades and upper arms are long, permitting depth of chest at the brisket.

Feet - short and round (cat feet) with thick, black pads. The toes are arched and compact.

Photo: Wade's handsome champion Woody (Ch Sumerwynd Stiff Competition).

Hindquarters - The hindquarters have strong-muscled, slanting thighs. They are well bent at the stifles. There is sufficient angulation so that, in stance, the hocks extend beyond the tail.

The hindquarters never appear overbuilt or higher than the shoulders. The rear pasterns are short and, in stance, perpendicular to the ground and, when viewed from the rear, are parallel to each other. *Faults* - Sickle hocks, cow hocks, open hocks or bowed hindquarters.

Coat - Double, with hard, wiry, outer coat and close undercoat. The head, neck, ears, chest, tail, and body coat must be plucked. When in show condition, the body coat should be of sufficient length to determine texture. Close covering on neck, ears and skull.

Furnishings are fairly thick but not silky.

Faults - Coat too soft or too smooth and slick in appearance.

Color:

Allowed colors: salt and pepper, black and silver and solid black. All colors have uniform skin pigmentation, i.e. no white or pink skin patches shall appear anywhere on the dog and the nose must be solid black.

Salt and Pepper - The typical salt and pepper color of the topcoat results from the combination of black and white banded hairs and solid black and white unbanded hairs, with the banded hairs predominating. Acceptable are all shades of salt and pepper, from the light to dark mixtures with tan shadings permissible in the banded or unbanded hair of the topcoat.

In salt and pepper dogs, the salt and pepper mixture fades out to light gray or silver white in the eyebrows, whiskers, cheeks, under throat, inside ears, across chest, under tail, leg furnishings, and inside hind legs. It may or may not also fade out on the underbody. However, if so, the lighter underbody hair is not to rise higher on the sides of the body than the front elbows.

Black and Silver (pictured) - The black and silver generally follows the same pattern as the salt and pepper. The entire salt and pepper section must be black. The black color in the topcoat of the black and silver is a true rich color with black undercoat. The stripped portion is free from any fading or brown tinge and the underbody should be dark.

Black - Black is the only solid color allowed. Ideally, the black color in the topcoat is a true rich glossy color with the undercoat being less intense, a soft matting shade of black. This is natural and should not be penalized in any way. The stripped portion is free from any fading or brown tinge.

The scissored and clippered areas have lighter shades of black. A small white spot on the chest is permitted, as is an occasional single white hair elsewhere on the body.

Disqualifications - Dogs not of an allowed color or white striping, patching, or spotting on the colored areas of the dog, except for the small white spot permitted on the chest of the black.

The body coat color in salt and pepper and black and silver dogs fades out to light gray or silver white under the throat and across the chest. Between them there exists a natural body coat color. Any irregular or connecting blaze or white mark in this section is considered a white patch on the body, which is also a disqualification. Nose any color other than solid black.

Gait:

The trot is the gait at which movement is judged. When approaching, the forelegs, with elbows close to the body, move straight forward, neither too close nor too far apart. Going away, the hind legs are straight and travel in the same planes as the forelegs.

Note - It is generally accepted that when a full trot is achieved, the rear legs continue to move in the same planes as the forelegs, but a very slight inward inclination will occur. It begins at the point of the shoulder in front and at the hip joint in the rear. Viewed from the front or rear, the legs are straight from these points to the pads.

The degree of inward inclination is almost imperceptible in a Miniature Schnauzer that has correct movement. It does not justify moving close, toeing in, crossing, or moving out at the elbows.

Viewed from the side, the forelegs have good reach, while the hind legs have strong drive, with good pickup of hocks. The feet turn neither inward nor outward.
Faults - Single tracking, sidegaiting, paddling in front, or hackney action. Weak rear action.

Temperament:

The typical Miniature Schnauzer is alert and spirited, yet obedient to command. He is friendly, intelligent and willing to please. He should never be overaggressive or timid.

....

UK Breed Standard

The UK Kennel Club says: "A breed standard is the guideline which describes the ideal characteristics, temperament and appearance including the correct colour of a breed and ensures that the breed is fit for function. Absolute soundness is essential.

"From time to time, certain conditions or exaggerations may be considered to have the potential to affect dogs in some breeds adversely... If a feature or quality is desirable it should only be present in the right measure."

General appearance - Sturdily built, robust, sinewy, nearly square, (length of body equal to height at shoulders). Expression keen and attitude alert. Correct conformation is of more importance than colour or other purely 'beauty' points.

Characteristics – Well-balanced, smart, stylish and adaptable.

Temperament - Alert, reliable and intelligent. Primarily a companion dog.

Head and Skull - Head strong and of good length, narrowing from ears to eyes and then gradually forward toward end of nose. Upper part of the head (occiput to the base of forehead) moderately broad between ears. Flat, creaseless forehead; well-muscled but not too strongly developed cheeks.

Medium stop to accentuate prominent eyebrows. Powerful muzzle ending in a moderately blunt line, with bristly, stubby moustache and chin whiskers. Ridge of nose straight and running almost parallel to extension of forehead. Nose black with wide nostrils. Lips tight but not overlapping.

Eyes - Medium sized, dark, oval, set forward, with arched bushy eyebrows.

Ears - Neat, V-shaped, set high and dropping forward to temple.

Mouth - Jaws strong with perfect, regular and complete scissor bite, i.e. upper teeth closely overlapping lower teeth and set square to the jaws.

Neck - Moderately long, strong and slightly arched; skin close to throat; neck set cleanly on shoulders.

Forequarters - Shoulders flat and well laid. Forelegs straight viewed from any angle. Muscles smooth and lithe rather than prominent; bone strong, straight and carried well down to feet; elbows close to body and pointing directly backwards.

Body - Chest moderately broad, deep with visible strong breastbone reaching at least to height of elbow rising slightly backward to loins. Back strong and straight, slightly higher at shoulder than at hindquarters, with short, well-developed loins.

Ribs well sprung. Length of body equal to height from top of withers to ground.

Hindquarters - Thighs slanting and flat but strongly muscled. Hindlegs (upper and lower thighs) at first vertical to the stifle; from stifle to hock, in line with the extension of the upper neck line; from hock, vertical to ground.

Feet - Short, round, cat-like, compact with closely arched toes, dark nails, firm black pads, feet pointing forward.

Tail - Previously customarily docked.
Docked: Set on and carried high, customarily docked to three joints.
Undocked: Set on and carried high, of moderate length to give general balance to the dog. Thick at root and tapering towards the tip, as straight as possible, carried jauntily.

Gait/Movement - Free, balanced and vigorous, with good reach in forequarters and good driving power in hindquarters. Topline remains level in action.

Coat - Harsh, wiry and short enough for smartness, dense undercoat. Clean on neck and shoulders, ears and skull. Harsh hair on legs. Furnishings fairly thick but not silky.

Colour: Pepper and salt – shades range from dark iron grey to light grey. Hairs banded dark/light/dark. Dark facial mask to harmonise with corresponding coat colour.

Pure Black

Black and silver – solid black with silver markings on eyebrows, muzzle, chest, brisket, forelegs below point of elbow, inside of hindlegs below stifle joint, vent and under tail.

White

Good pigmentation essential in all colours.

Size - Ideal height: dogs: 36 cm (14 in); bitches: 33 cm (13 in). Too small, toyish appearing dogs are not typical and undesirable.

Faults - Any departure from the foregoing points should be considered a fault and the seriousness with which the fault should be regarded should be in exact proportion to its degree and its effect upon the health and welfare of the dog and on the dog's ability to perform its traditional work.

Note: Male animals should have two apparently normal testicles fully descended into the scrotum.

> **Author's Note:** If you live in the USA, you may see **'Teacup Schnauzers'** advertised. These have been bred down from full-size Miniature Schnauzers and do not conform to the Breed Standards of any country.
>
> Breeding miniature versions compromises the skeleton and these dogs may be prone to muscular-skeletal issues as they age.
>
> There are some unscrupulous breeders cashing in on the trend for tiny Miniature Schnauzers and producing dogs of poor quality. We advise anyone buying a Mini to get one that conforms to the Breed Standard - it's there for a reason.

Glossary:

Cow Hocks - knock-kneed appearance (although the hock corresponds to the human ankle)

Dewclaw - the extra nail on the upper, inner part of a dog's foot - usually on the front legs

Crabbing - moving with the body at an angle to the line of travel

Croup - where the back meets the tail

Furnishings - longer facial hair around the eyebrows, moustache and beard

Hackney Gait - high stepping front action with exaggerated flexion of the wrist

Paddling - the front feet thrown out sideways when moving, often in a loose, uncontrolled manner

Roach Back - arched back

Sickle Hocks - acute angulation of the hock joint, which can cause weakness in the back legs

Withers - the ridge between the shoulder blades

4. Schnauzers for Allergy Sufferers

Hypoallergenic

The Miniature, Standard and Giant Schnauzer are all '*hypoallergenic*' breeds. The official definition of the word hypoallergenic is *"having a <u>decreased</u> tendency to provoke an allergic reaction."*

In other words, there is no cast-iron guarantee that an allergy sufferer won't suffer a reaction to an individual dog - although choosing a hypoallergenic breed will reduce the overall risk.

 **FACT** Every dog is an individual and every person's allergies are different. It is well documented that a person can be allergic to one or more puppies in a litter and not to the others - even with a hypoallergenic breed.

Because of this, some breeders will not allow their puppies to go to homes where there are allergies. They don't want the heartbreak - for them, the family and the puppy - of things not working out and the dog having to be returned.

In this chapter we look at what people with allergies can do to successfully share their lives with a Schnauzer.

From personal experience and numerous comments on our website, we can say that many people with allergies live perfectly happily and sneeze-free alongside Schnauzers. My partner is allergic to horses, cats and usually dogs, but had no reaction to our Miniature Schnauzer.

Amazingly, more than 50 million Americans suffer from allergies, according to the Asthma and Allergy Foundation of America. One in five of these - 10 million people – is a pet allergy sufferer.

Most people think that people are allergic to animal hair, but that's not true. What they are allergic to are proteins - or allergens. These are secreted by the animal's oil glands and then shed with the *dander*, which is actually dead skin cells like dandruff.

NOTE: These proteins are also found in dog saliva and urine, which all dogs of all breeds produce.

The AKC (American Kennel Club) says: "The truth is, there are no 100% hypoallergenic dogs, dog breeds, or mixed breeds, but there are many dog breeds that are less allergenic for people with dog allergies.

"Dander, which is attached to pet hair, is what causes most dog allergies in people, and these (hypoallergenic) dog breeds have a non-shedding coat that produces less dander."

The UK Kennel Club: "All dogs shed their hair, but some breeds shed their coat less than others.

"This is something to consider if you have dog allergies, live with someone who does, or don't want to deal with large amounts of dog hair. If you do have an allergy, you should consult a medical professional before getting a dog."

....

BEFORE You Get A Puppy

Pet allergy sufferers can enjoy living with a dog without spending all of their time sneezing, wheezing, itching or breaking out in rashes. Countless people all over the world are living proof.

Indeed, many people choose Schnauzers either because someone in their household has an allergy or because these dogs are mostly non-shedding and don't leave hair all over the house.

However, it is not completely straightforward and you DO have to put in extra time to make sure that you pick the right dog and maybe make a few adjustments to your home as well. Let's clear up a couple of points right away:

- ❖ **No dog is totally non-shedding**
- ❖ **No dog is totally hypoallergenic**

And remember:

- ❖ **People's pet allergies vary greatly**
- ❖ **People with allergies react differently to different breeds, as well as to individual dogs within that breed or litter**

All Schnauzers are considered to be non-shedding and hypoallergenic. They might lose the occasional little fur ball, but they generally do not shed. If a Schnauzer brushes up against you or the furniture, not a lot of hair will fall out.

This is largely due to the double coat. The outer coat is hard and wiry and the undercoat is softer and close to the skin. The outer coat traps the inner coat and the dander.

This type of coat sheds only when the dog is left ungroomed for several months.

FACT ❯ All dogs - even so-called "hairless" breeds, like this American Hairless Terrier, have hair, dander, saliva and urine. Therefore all dogs can cause allergic reactions.

...But not all dogs do.

Here are our tips to maximise your chances of choosing a puppy you won't be allergic to:

1. **Choose a hypoallergenic breed** like all three types of Schnauzer.
2. **Choose a GOOD breeder.** In the US, look for AKC Breeders of Merit, Bred With Heart and/or members of a breed club. In the UK, look for a Kennel Club Assured Breeder or a member of one of the three main breed clubs.
3. **Beware of "guarantees"** that the puppies in a litter are non-shedding or won't cause allergies. No responsible Schnauzer breeder would **ever** give a guarantee because it's impossible to know every person's allergies.

4. **Be prepared to pay a high price** for a Schnauzer puppy from a good breeder. You get what you pay for – a lot of time, effort and money go into each litter and the breeder knows her dogs.

5. **Speak to the breeder** before you visit a litter and discuss your allergies.

6. **Take a cloth with you** when you visit a litter, and rub the puppies with it. When you return home, rub your face with the cloth and wait 48 hours to see if you have any reaction.

7. When you visit a litter, **spend time playing on the floor** with the puppies and allow them to lick your hands and face.

8. If the breeder has a particular puppy in mind for you, **visit only that puppy** and keep away from the other puppies. Repeat the steps above.

9. Ask the breeder if you can **visit the puppy a second time** and repeat the above process.

10. **Ask the breeder what the policy is** if you develop allergies some time after the dog is home.

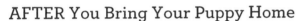

AFTER You Bring Your Puppy Home

Allergies are all about the allergen load. Once you reach your tolerance limit, your eyes itch, your nose runs and the sneezing starts; you might also come out in a rash or start wheezing.

If you can keep the allergen level BELOW your tolerance level, you will have no reaction - and hopefully live happily ever after with your Schnauzer!

Here are our tips for doing just that:

❧ **Keep your Schnauzer clean** - bathe him regularly (using a dog shampoo, not human). This varies from dog to dog but may be every one to four weeks

❧ **Keep his coat short** - either by stripping and trimming yourself or by regular trips to the groomer every six weeks

❧ **Brush (or get a family member) to brush your Schnauzer regularly**, preferably outside the house

❧ **Consider using a product such as Allerpet Dog Dander Remover**, *pictured*, on your dog. A once or twice-weekly wipe-over with Allerpet, or similar, and a damp cloth should help to reduce dander – it is guaranteed safe for pets and humans

❧ **Don't allow your Schnauzer to sleep in the bedroom,** this will definitely increase the allergen load

❧ If you have air vents and/or air conditioning, **close air registers in the bedroom** or room you spend a lot of time in to reduce the amount of dander circulating in the air

❧ **Keep him off the furniture** and on the floor. What little hair he does shed may get trapped on soft surfaces such as cushions, sofas and beds

❧ **Wash your dog's bedding regularly** - avoid using harsh detergents

❧ **Wash hands and face** after playing with or touching the dog

- **Don't let him lick your face** - and try and avoid him licking you altogether
- **If your dog travels in the car,** use seat covers and wash them regularly
- **Reduce the number of rugs and carpets** in your home; have more hard floors - they are 'on trend!'
- **Keep your house clean!** Dust adds to the allergen load
- **Use a HEPA (High Efficiency Particulate Air) vacuum cleaner**, it's claimed they remove 99.97% of dust, pollen, mould, bacteria and other airborne particles
- **Use an air purifier** to capture dust, pollens, dander, etc. around the home
- If you still have a slight reaction, try **inexpensive off-the-shelf antihistamines** like Piriton for flare-ups - or visit an allergist if the problem persists
- If the situation becomes unmanageable, always **contact the breeder in the first instance**. All responsible breeders will either take the dog back or help to find a new forever home

What The Breeders Say

All three types of Schnauzer are considered hypoallergenic and here we include comments from breeders of Miniatures, Standards and Giants.

Wade Bogart, AKC Breed Mentor, of Sumerwynd Miniature Schnauzers, New York State: "Over my 40-plus years in the breed, I have placed a few Miniature Schnauzer puppies into households with an allergic family member.

"My only policy is that I will take the puppy back, with no questions asked, if an allergy issue arises. In my experience, if a reaction is going to happen it will do so almost immediately.

"My brother Brian and I have bred our Miniature Schnauzers side by side for all those years. He is also an American Kennel Club judge. Believe it or not, Brian is allergic to dogs!!

"A few tips he uses to keep the dog dander down, thus keeping his reactions down, is to bathe dogs weekly. Brian also does not allow his dogs to lick him, as proteins in their saliva can cause problems."

Photo: Cash (Sumerwynd Cash Up Front) bred by Wade.

Beth Railton, professional groomer, specialising in Schnauzers, and breeder of Lefenix (Standard) Schnauzers, Derbyshire, UK: "I had someone buy a dog who was allergic to dogs. She spent four hours in my house with the house full of Schnauzers before the puppies were born. She then repeatedly visited during the eight weeks running up to their leaving.

"She did not have a reaction; it was decided that it was more the coat type than the dogs she was allergic to. She took the puppy home at eight weeks and found that over the years she has become less allergic to other coat types.

"I groomed the dog for her and would strip the coat until it was kinder to clip due to age. We found that stripping helped. Some people buy a dog and then find out they are allergic afterwards. If you do your research properly, the outcome can be very productive."

Over the last 30 years, Steve Matthews has bred Miniature and Giant Schnauzers with the Silbertraum prefix in Dorset, UK. Steve says: "I wouldn't generally place a Schnauzer in a home where person(s) have allergies, fearing that the dog may eventually be rehomed.

"That said, people's allergic reactions vary with different stimulants, so if they are unsure I ask them to come and spend time with the dog to see how they react. If they find no issues and successfully acquire a puppy or dog, I always offer the option of returning it if things don't work out."

Photo: Miniature Schnauzer Theo (Templarshome Back to Black, bred by Steve's wife, Sue) relaxing in front of the fire at home with Giant pal Greta (Silbertraum Spirit of Zeus).

Andrew and Gaynor Ray, Minnienoom Schnauzers, Derbyshire, UK: "We encourage all new potential Schnauzer owners to give us as much information regarding family life as possible – including on health.

"It's not uncommon for someone to inform us that the reason for choosing a Schnauzer is because they are hypoallergenic. We do clarify that just because Schnauzers don't moult seasonally, they do shed some hair and this could cause an issue,

"We advise and invite the potential new owner to come and visit us at our home and sit in the room that all our three sizes of Schnauzer share with us and this would provide a good footing of how they will react to the dogs and how it may affect their allergies.

"We are happy to repeat this process several times over a few weeks in order for the new potential owner to be happy with the situation and hopefully go on and invest in a new companion in the form of a Schnauzer."

5. Finding Your Puppy

Finding a good puppy can be a minefield. If you haven't got yours yet, read this chapter before you commit to anything; it will increase your chances of finding a healthy, happy Miniature Schnauzer with a good temperament.

The best way to select a puppy is with your HEAD - not your heart! You'll soon find dozens of Schnauzer puppies advertised, but it requires a bit more time and research to find a first-rate breeder.

If you already have your puppy, skip to the next chapter.

....

It's a fact: a Miniature Schnauzer puppy is the cutest thing on Earth! If you go to view a litter, the adorable pups are sure to melt your heart and it is extremely difficult - if not downright impossible - to walk away without choosing one.

If you haven't yet chosen your pup and take only one sentence from this entire book, it is this:

FIND AN ETHICAL, KNOWLEDGEABLE BREEDER WHO PRODUCES HEALTHY PUPPIES WITH GOOD TEMPERAMENTS

 – even if that means waiting longer than you'd like. It will be worth it in the long run. And if you're looking for a Mini in a colour not recognised by the Kennel Clubs (parti, etc.) make sure the breeder meets the standards recommended in this chapter.

 Although the Miniature Schnauzer is considered to be a relatively healthy breed, there are still genetic disorders that can be passed down. So, look for a breeder who health tests. See <u>Chapter 13. Mini Schnauzer Health</u> for details.

Find a breeder who knows Schnauzers inside out and who does not offer lots of different breeds.

After all, apart from getting married or having a baby, getting a puppy is one of the most important, demanding, expensive and life-enriching decisions you will ever make.

Your Schnauzer will love you unconditionally - but there is a price to pay. In return for their devotion - you have to fulfil your part of the bargain.

In the beginning, you have to be prepared to devote much of your day to your new puppy. You have to feed her several times a day and housetrain virtually every hour, you have to give her your attention and start to gently introduce the rules of the house.

You also have to be prepared to part with hard cash for regular healthcare and pet insurance.

Puppies are high energy and hard work! If you are unable to devote the time and money to a new arrival, if you have a very young family, a stressful life or are out at work all day, then now might not be the right time for a puppy.

Mini Schnauzer puppies are very demanding of your attention and thrive on being involved. They are not couch potatoes, nor do they like being shut away from people or left alone for extended periods.

Pick a healthy Schnauzer pup and they should live for 12 or more years, so this is certainly a long-term commitment. Before taking the plunge, ask yourself some questions:

....

Do I Have Enough Time for a Puppy?

Even a strong-willed puppy will feel a bit lonely after leaving his mother and littermates for the first time. Spend time with your new arrival to make them feel safe and sound. Ideally, for the first few days, you will be around most of the time to help yours settle and to start bonding.

If you work, book time off if you can - although this is more difficult for some of our hardworking American readers who get short vacations - but don't just get a Schnauzer puppy and leave her all alone in the house a couple of days later.

Housetraining (potty training) starts the moment your pup arrives home and swallows up time if you do it right. Then, after the first few days, make time for short sessions of a few minutes of behaviour training. Most Mini Schnauzer puppies are lively, curious, playful, cheeky and greedy - and these traits need channelling positively.

FACT ❯ Socialisation is a very important part of training, so you need to make time for it. Start as soon as possible, as that critical window up to four or five months of age is when your puppy is at her most receptive to all things new. Good breeders will have already started the process.

Gently introducing her to different people will help her to become more relaxed around people. Initially, get people to sit on the floor.

Make time right from the beginning to get your pup used to being handled by all the family and dog-friendly visitors, gently brushed, ears checked, and later having their teeth touched and cleaned – which is also important but most Minis hate it if they are not used to being handled.

Photo: Eight-week-old Giant Schnauzer Arthur greets four-week-old Miniature Schnauzer with a friendly lick, courtesy of Steve Matthews.

You'll have to take your pup for a short walk every day - five minutes once fully vaccinated, increasing gradually to around 10 minutes at four months.

While the garden or yard is fine, new surroundings stimulate interest, help with socialisation and stop puppies from becoming bored.

 We recommend you have your pup checked out by a vet within a couple of days of arriving home - many good breeders insist on it - but don't put your puppy on the clinic floor where she can pick up germs from other dogs.

How Long Can I Leave My Puppy?

This is a question we get asked a lot and one that has to be considered before you get a puppy. All dogs are pack animals; their natural state is to be with others. So being alone for long periods is not normal for them - although some have to get used to it.

Another issue is the toilet; Schnauzer puppies have very tiny bladders. Forget the emotional side of it, how would you like to be left for eight hours without being able to visit the bathroom? So how many hours can you leave a dog alone?

In the UK, rescue organisations will not allow anybody to adopt if they regularly leave the dog alone for more than four hours a day.

And the UK's Code of Practice for the Welfare of Dogs states: "Experts recommend four hours as the maximum time period... No dog should routinely be left on its own for prolonged periods. If the time alone is excessive, you can expect behavioural problems that are distressing for both you and your dog."

 A general rule of thumb is that a puppy can last without urinating for one hour or so for every month of age.

So, provided your puppy has learned the basics, a three-month-old puppy should be able to last for around three hours without needing to go. If the breeder has done a lot of housetraining, the puppy will be able to last longer. But until housetraining kicks in, young puppies just pee at will!

....

Minis and Children

Mini Schnauzers really do make excellent family pets, with one proviso: You have to be willing to devote enough time to meet your Schnauzer's needs in terms of attention, training, grooming and - once she is grown - exercise. Schnauzers can and do form very strong and loving bonds with children, once both have learned respect for each other.

However, a new puppy may not be suitable for all families with very young children. Small kids' coordination skills are not fully developed and there can be an accidental risk of injury - or a puppy nipping a pestering child, if left unsupervised.

 Children (and adults) should be taught how to correctly handle a Miniature Schnauzer puppy so as not to damage her small, delicate skeleton. Encourage youngsters to interact with the dog on the floor, rather than picking her up to cuddle.

Puppies regard children as playmates - and a child regards a puppy as a playmate. Both are playful and excitable and need to learn the boundaries of play, and Mini puppies have needle-sharp teeth. A Schnauzer puppy wouldn't intentionally harm a child, or vice versa, but either could cause injury if they get over-excited.

A puppy nipping the kids (or adults) is not aggression; she is doing what comes naturally. But all puppies need to be taught right from the beginning that this is not acceptable; humans are not toys! Take time to train them out of this habit - and teach your children not to run away from your

Mini, as this will only encourage them to chase and nip even more. See **Training chapters 10 and 11** for more detailed information.

Your dog's early experiences with children should all be positive. If not, a dog may become nervous or mistrustful - and what you want around children is most definitely a relaxed Schnauzer that does not feel threatened by a child's presence.

 Teach your children to be gentle with your Mini and your Mini to be gentle with your children.

Approached in the right manner, a Miniature Schnauzer will form a deep, lifelong bond that your children will remember throughout their lives.

NOTE: Minis who are not used to being around children can be uncomfortable or fearful when they do come across them. They may be wary of young children's unpredictability, and no Miniature Schnauzer likes being teased or handled roughly. Look for signs that your Mini isn't comfortable, which may include the ears sitting flat or back on the head, barking, retreating or even growling.

If your Mini lives in a house with no children, but you have young visitors, get them used to each other slowly in a positive manner until both be comfortable with the other.

 Regardless of how well young children and dogs get on, they should never be left together unsupervised.

Breeders' and Owners' Thoughts

Wade Bogart, breeder of Sumerwynd Miniature Schnauzers, New York State, since 1979: "Yes, I would place a puppy with a family with children and have done so over the years. However, I make it clear to the grown-ups that all interactions with the kids are to be supervised by an adult.

"Miniature Schnauzers react positively when the interaction is supervised by an adult. Unfortunately, many children do not understand that a puppy is a living breathing thing. Pups don't appreciate beard pulling, ear yanking, serious roughhousing and the like - and will respond in kind when these occur."

UK Kennel Club Assured Breeder of Miniatures and Giants, Steve Matthews: "It depends on the children. Children who have grown up with dogs are generally fine and Miniature Schnauzers that have been socialised with small children will get on fine. Both dogs and children need to respect each other, and children need to recognise that the dog is not a toy and needs a break sometimes."

Fellow Assured Breeder Andrew Ray, Minnienoom Schnauzers Derbyshire, England (who breeds all three types) says: "Miniature Schnauzers and Giant Schnauzers make excellent family pets and interact and bond really well with young children. However, I would recommend getting a young puppy (rather than an older dog) and letting the puppy fit in and grow with the family.

"Standard Schnauzers are more challenging and although make excellent family pets, I personally don't advise people with young children to take on a Standard Schnauzer puppy until the child is older. I have always been cautious of placing any adult Schnauzer with a family who has young children, more so if the adult dog has not had involvement with young children.

"We feel really blessed that we had all three sizes of the Schnauzer family living peacefully within our family home. The children adored the dogs and the dogs adored the children."

Here are some comments from owners. Rebecca Makdad, owner of Rosie and Navy: "I think Minis get on well with children if they are socialised early." Gary Blain: "Jamie is quite relaxed around most people and children. Evie is very timid around people, although OK with them."

One couple took on a one-year-old Mini who didn't get on well with their small children so, after an agreed trial period, she was returned to the breeder. They then got a young male puppy from the same breeder and this has worked out very well. The couple is "amazed" at how well the children and dog get on.

Chris Lee: "Betsy has met small children and is friendly and somewhat withdrawn around them - until they take the initiative." Yvonne and Simon Sonsino: "Our Minis Bu and Wilf are good with anyone - as long as they're not poked and prodded too much."

Vivian Williams: "Bogart has limited experience with children, but we have not observed problems with him. Recently, we've had a five-month-old regularly visiting us. Bogart is both interested in and respectful of the infant; he is allowed to sniff the baby's feet and belongings under supervision."

Yolande: "Our grandchildren came to stay with us over the holidays and initially Mayzy, *pictured,* was nervous with them and backed away. I could see her nervous response to the five-year-old who was noisy and unpredictable - as young children are!

"The girls have their own dog back home and were disturbed by Mayzy's reaction. By the time they left after two weeks, they were all the best of friends.

"Our rural location makes socialising with children difficult. I took Mayzy out from puppyhood as often as I could to meet friends or go down to the local pub, and she is very friendly with adults."

Single People

Many singles own dogs, but if you live alone, getting a puppy will require a lot of dedication on your part. There is nobody to share the responsibility, the exercise or the bills, so taking on a social dog like the Schnauzer requires commitment and a lot of time if the dog is to have a decent life.

If you are out of the house all day, a Miniature Schnauzer is NOT a good choice. They love time spent with their humans, so being alone all day is not much of a life for them.

However, if you are around for much of the time, then he or she will undoubtedly become your best friend.

A Miniature Schnauzer can be a good choice for older people, provided the owner(s) can meet the Mini's need for regular exercise. Both parties will love having a constant companion.

Other Pets

However friendly your puppy is, other pets in your household may not be too happy with a new arrival. Well-socialised Minis get on well with other animals, but it might not be a good idea to leave your pet hamster or rabbit running loose...Originally, one of the Schnauzer's jobs was to hunt rodents, and Minis have quite a bit of Terrier ancestry, and some still have quite a bit of prey drive (chase instinct).

If an animal or bird stands its ground, most Minis will not attack, but if they try to get away, some Schnauzers' prey drive may well take over. As with any breed of dog, the rules go out of the window when there is more than one dog and pack instinct kicks in.

Some Schnauzers live very well with cats - especially if introduced when still a puppy - but this may not stop them from chasing small animals outdoors. Our Mini Max was the only animal in our household and would tolerate being in a friend's house with her cat, but wouldn't hesitate to chase the aforementioned cat - as well as squirrels and birds - if he came across them outdoors.

While we could never stop him from chasing squirrels when out on a walk, he was trained very quickly from an early age to walk among sheep off the lead and not chase them.

Introduce other pets slowly to your Schnauzer. Puppies are naturally extremely curious and playful and will sniff and investigate other pets; they may even chase them inside the house.

Depending on how lively your pup is, you may have to separate them initially, or put the pup into a pen or crate for short periods to allow the cat to investigate without being pestered by a hyperactive pup who thinks chasing the cat is a great game.

This will also prevent your puppy from being injured. If the two animals are free and the cat lashes out, your pup's eyes could get scratched. A timid Schnauzer might need protection from a bold cat - or vice versa.

A bold cat and a timid Mini Schnauzer will probably settle down together quickest!

If things seem to be going well after one or two supervised sessions, let them loose together. Take the process slowly; if your cat is stressed or frightened, he may decide to leave. Our feline friends are notorious for abandoning home because the board and lodgings are better down the road...

More than One Dog

Well-socialised Miniature Schnauzers have no problem sharing their home with other dogs - particularly other Schnauzers. Introduce your puppy to other dogs in a positive, non-frightening manner that will give her confidence. Supervised sessions help everyone get along and the other dog or dogs to accept your new pup.

If you can, introduce them for the first time outdoors on neutral ground, rather than in the house or in an area that one dog regards as her own. You don't want the established dog to feel she has to protect her territory, nor the puppy to feel she is in an enclosed space and can't get away.

If you are thinking about getting more than one pup, consider waiting until your first puppy is a few months old or an adult before getting a second. Waiting means you can give your full attention to one puppy; get housetraining, socialisation and the basics of obedience training out of the way before getting your second.

Another benefit is that an older well-trained dog will help teach the new puppy some manners. Owning two dogs can be twice as nice; they will be great company for each other, but bear in mind that it's also double the training, food and vet bills.

Think carefully before getting two puppies from the same litter. Apart from the time and expense involved, you want your new puppy to learn to focus on YOU, and not her littermate.

Plan Ahead

Choosing the right breeder is one of the most important decisions you will make. Like humans, your puppy will be a product of her parents and will inherit many of their characteristics.

 Appearance, natural temperament, size and some health traits are all influenced by genetics.

Responsible breeders check the health history and temperament of the parents, carry out health tests where necessary and only breed from good, healthy stock with suitable temperaments.

Since Covid, price is no longer a reliable indication of the quality of the pup, but beware of *"bargain"* puppies, these are not top-quality pups. Instead, spend the time to find a reputable breeder and read **Chapter 13. Mini Schnauzer Health** to discover what health issues to be aware of before buying.

 BE PATIENT. Start looking months or even a year before your planned arrival. Good Schnauzer breeders with quality dogs often have a waiting list for their pups. Phone or email your selected breeder(s) to find out about future litters and potential dates, and ask lots of questions.

Visit the breeder personally at least once before picking the puppy up – this should be an absolute must in the UK.

> NOTE: Some American breeders do not allow the public on to their properties when they have unvaccinated pups. Also, when vast distances are involved, personal visits are not always possible.

In these cases speak at length on the phone to the breeder, video call, ask lots of questions and ask to see photos and videos of the pups from birth to the present day. Reputable breeders will be happy to answer all your questions - and will have lots for you too.

All Schnauzer puppies should be **at least eight weeks old** before they leave the breeder; Giants and Standards may be eight to 10 weeks old. Puppies need this time to physically develop and learn the rules of the pack from their mothers and littermates. In the UK and some US states it is illegal to sell a puppy younger than eight weeks.

....

Buyer Beware

Good breeders do not sell their dogs on general-purpose websites, Gumtree, Pets4Homes, Craig's List or Freeads, in car parks or somebody else's house.

In 2020, the UK Government passed *Lucy's Law* saying: " *'Lucy's Law'* means that anyone wanting to get a new puppy or kitten in England, Scotland or Wales must now buy direct from a breeder, or consider adopting from a rescue centre instead.

"Licensed dog breeders are required to show puppies interacting with their mothers in their place of birth. If a business sells puppies or kittens without a licence, they could receive an unlimited fine or be sent to prison for up to six months. The law is named after Lucy, a Cavalier King Charles Spaniel who was rescued from a puppy farm."

Unfortunately, in practice, there are lots and lots of people breeding for profit in the UK who are not licensed, and there is no such law in the US.

If you are looking at dogs on Pets4Homes in the UK, follow their guidelines carefully, see the pup with the mother and check what test certificates the parents have.

There is a difference between *a hobby breeder* and a *backyard or backstreet breeder*. Both may breed just one or two litters a year and keep the puppies in their homes, but that's where the similarity ends.

In the UK there are many good *hobby breeders*. They often don't have a website and you will probably find out about them via word of mouth. Good hobby breeders are usually breed enthusiasts or experts; sometimes they show their pedigree dogs. They usually carry out health tests and lavish care and love on their dogs. They are not professional dog breeders.

NOTE: While it is often a good sign in the UK, the term "*hobby breeder*" can have negative implications in the USA.

Backyard breeders are often breeding their own pets. They have less knowledge about the breed, pay little attention to the health and welfare of their dogs and are doing it primarily for extra cash. They may be very nice people, but avoid buying a dog from them.

 All GOOD breeders, professional or hobby, have in-depth knowledge of the Miniature Schnauzer. They take measures to prevent potential health issues from being passed on to puppies, and are passionate about the breed.

Here are four reasons for buying from a good breeder:

1. HEALTH: Like all breeds, Schnauzers have potentially inheritable health issues. The way to improve breed health is for breeders to test their breeding dogs and NOT mate two dogs whose combined results mean there's a significant risk of passing on genetic disorders.

2. SOCIALISATION: Scientists and dog experts now realise that the critical socialisation period for dogs is up to the age of four months. An unstimulated puppy is likely to be less well-adjusted and more likely to have fear or behaviour issues as an adult. Good breeders start this process, they don't just leave the puppies in an outbuilding for two or three months.

3. TEMPERAMENT: Good breeders select their breeding stock based not only on sound structure and health, but also on temperament. They will not breed from an aggressive or overly timid dog.

4. PEACE OF MIND: Most good breeders agree to take the dog back at any time in her life or rehome her if things don't work out - although you may find it too hard to part with your beloved Schnauzer by then.

Avoiding Bad Breeders

Getting a puppy is such an emotional decision - and one that should have a wonderfully positive impact on you and your family's life for many years. Unfortunately, the high price of puppies has resulted in unscrupulous people producing litters primarily for the money.

This section helps you avoid the pitfalls of getting a puppy from a puppy mill or farm, a puppy importer, dealer or broker (somebody who makes money from buying and selling puppies) or a backyard breeder.

You can't buy a Rolls Royce or a Corvette for a couple of thousand pounds or dollars - you'd immediately suspect that the *"bargain"* on offer wasn't the real deal. No matter how lovely it looked, you'd be right – well, the same applies to Schnauzers.

Become Breeder Savvy

Websites have become far more sophisticated and it's getting harder to spot the good, the bad and the ugly. Here are some tips if you're looking for a puppy:

- Avoid websites where there are no pictures of the owner's home or kennels or the dogs in the home

- If the website shows lots of photos of cute puppies with little information about the family, breeding dogs, health tests or environment, click the **X** button

- Don't buy a website puppy with a shopping cart symbol next to her

- **See the puppies with their mother face-to-face -** always in the UK. If not possible in the US, speak at length on the phone with the breeder, ask lots of questions and ask to see videos of the puppies in their surroundings and beds

- Be wary if the mother is not with the puppies, but brought in to meet you

- Is the pup interacting with the "mother" or do the two dogs appear to have no connection? If the pups are really hers, she will interact with them

- You hear: "You can't see the parent dogs because......" ALWAYS ask to see the parents or, as a minimum, the mother

- Be wary if the puppies look small for their stated age

- See where the puppy is living - either in person or via Facetime, etc. Miniatures should always be in the house, not an outbuilding

- Make sure there is a genuine litter - see the littermates when you visit or Facetime

- Good breeders are happy to provide lots of information. If the breeder is reluctant to answer your questions, look elsewhere

- **Check all paperwork relating to the puppy,** and if the breeder says that the dam and sire are Kennel Club or AKC registered, ask to see the registration papers

- Ask for at least one reference from another puppy owner before you commit

- Pressure selling: the breeder doesn't ask you many questions and then says: "There are only X many puppies left and I have several other buyers interested." Walk away

- You hear "Our Miniature Schnauzer puppies are cheaper because...." Walk away

- Photographs of so-called "champion ancestors" do not guarantee the health of the puppy

Look beyond the cute, fluffy exterior. The way to look INSIDE the puppy is to see the parents – or at least the mother - and check what health tests have been carried out. NOTE: *"Vet checked"* does NOT mean the pup or parents have passed any health test

- The person you are buying the puppy from did not breed the dog themselves. Deal with the breeder, not an intermediary

- The only place you meet the puppy seller is a car park, somebody else's house or a place other than the puppies' home. Walk away

- The seller tells you that the puppy comes from top, caring breeders from your own or another country. It is now illegal in the UK to buy a puppy from a third party - i.e. anyone other than the breeder

- Ask to see photos of the puppy from birth to the present day

- Beware of "rare colours" or "rare markings" as it probably means that the puppy you are looking at is not pure Schnauzer

Photo: A litter of white Miniature Schnauzers. White is an acceptable Kennel Club colour for Minis in the UK, but not in North America.

- Price – if you are offered a very cheap puppy, there is usually a reason

- Familiarise yourself with the Breed Standard and what an eight to 10-week-old Mini Schnauzer should look like. Make sure the puppy you are interested in looks and acts like a Mini Schnauzer

- Google the name of the breeder and prefix (kennel name), and see if any comments come up

- Go on to Schnauzer Facebook groups and ask if anybody has had a puppy from this breeder and if so, ask if the dog is still healthy and would they recommend buying from the breeder

- NEVER buy a puppy because you feel sorry for it; you condemn other dogs to a life of misery

- If you have any doubt, go with your gut instinct and WALK AWAY - even if this means losing your deposit. It will be worth it in the long run

- If you get a rescue Schnauzer, make sure it is from a recognised rescue group and not a "puppy flipper" who may be posing as a do-gooder, but is getting dogs (including stolen ones) from unscrupulous sources

 Bad breeders do not have two horns coming out of their heads! Most will be friendly when you phone or visit - after all, they want to make the sale. It's only later that problems may develop.

Personal Experiences

This was owner Chris Lee's experience of getting his Mini, Betsy, having previously owned Boxers (Chris lives in the UK): "We decided to go for a smaller breed - and one less likely to dislocate a shoulder when pulling! We thought the Schnauzer looked attractive, was the right size and everyone wrote that they were intelligent and full of character.

"We spent time doing our research, and what was important was that the breeder said: 'Come and visit anytime.' This meant a journey of just under two hours, but each visit was very worthwhile.

"**Visit 1** led to meeting the very-pregnant Mum and two of her companions. We spent a lot of time talking with the breeder and learning about how she brings up her dogs. Her advice proved invaluable.

"**Visit 2** was an opportunity to be amongst the nine young pups and their wonderful Mum. It gave us a chance to see how cute they all were and the challenges we might face several weeks later. We discussed gender, which was not an issue for us but, given there were eight females and one male, ours was a girl.

"**Visit 3** was to choose your pup, as they had been microchipped. We made our choice with no real set criteria in mind. The most chilled pup seemed very happy to be picked up and was also playful - so Betsy was chosen. Once again, lots of advice was offered by the breeder.

"**Visit 4** was 'Gotcha Day' and anxious owners picked up their not-very-anxious pup. The journey saw Betsy sleep for the majority of it.

"Much of the cautious planning for her homecoming was unnecessary and Betsy ran around the garden and throughout the house as if she owned it! What a great first day, which set the tone for what was to follow.

"My advice is to research the breeder and visit them if you are allowed to. Listen to what they say if they are experienced breeders but, in the end, go with your own experience and knowledge.

"Don't be too anxious and over-prepared, but do be prepared for some wonderful times as your pup grows and fits in with your life."

Photo: A confident Betsy, aged 20 months, watching out for the postman! Courtesy of Chris.

Chris's experience also highlights the fact that puppies from good breeders are generally less anxious and better prepared for their new lives, as the breeder has already spent time socialising and training them.

Yolande adds: "My advice is do not buy from the internet; Pets4Homes being such a website. Cute pictures, but little in the way of lineage. Prospective owners need to meet and visit the breeder, the sire and dam and the litter ahead of collecting the puppy at eight weeks.

US owner of Navy and Rosie, Rebecca Makdad, says: "The first step should be to research the breed thru the Breed Club or a reputable site, such as the AKC. I'd recommend you contact several breeders, then you can compare their willingness to help you purchase a puppy and also your comfort level with the breeder.

"I have called and emailed breeders, only to have them NEVER return my inquiry. If a breeder does not want to take time to return your call, then I would look for another. Frequently, very high-quality breeders have a "wait list" for puppies. Others may have them listed on their kennel website.

"Once you have established contact with a breeder, the dialogue should begin. The breeder should ask you as many questions as you ask them. So beware if they do not inquire as to the type of home their puppy will be joining."

If you live in the USA Rebecca Makdad also advises asking if any of the females are *'co-owned:'* "This is where the female lives with her primary owner until it's time to welp, then she lives with the breeder. Once her breeding time is over, the primary owner keeps her - they get the dog much cheaper. So in reality, the home you see when selecting a puppy is not the dog's true home nor family."

Chloe Dong and Jacky Zou: "When we first started looking for a Miniature Schnauzer, our main goal was to avoid puppy mills. We started with the AMSC registry for breeders. One obstacle we constantly encountered was the long waitlists or lack of available puppies from the breeders on the registry.

"One experience that stood out involved a breeding group from the southeast region. Before the birth, the breeder mainly discussed what physical features we were looking for in our Miniature Schnauzer. However, on the weekend of the litter's birth, the breeder contacted us stating the mother had had a C-section and unfortunately the whole litter didn't make it.

"The day after, they stated the mother had passed away too. In hindsight, this was probably a puppy mill that euthanized the mother due to her inability to produce sellable litters.

"Another thing we noticed about these puppy mills was how sly they can be. We're based in New York and there are laws and standards in place to deter puppy mills. We found a breeder in New Jersey who immediately threw up a red flag.

"In comparison to NY, NJ also has licensing and inspections, but no substantive standards of care. The NJ breeder stated: "Your puppy is arriving at the kennel next week." When asked where the puppy was coming from, they stated, "Missouri, we're driving the puppies up."

Missouri is a state with absolutely no regulations in place to prevent puppy mills."

"We also cold-called Wade Bogart at Sumerwynd Schnauzers. I had reached out to Wade in the past, but he had no puppies available. Lucky for us, he picked up his phone that afternoon and that led to a series of events resulting in us getting our new furry family member, Oslo," *pictured here just after he arrived home.*

"We'd advise potential owners to be patient - even if the wait is one year, it'll save you lots of headaches and heartache in the years to come.

"Research, research and research! Puppy mills are constantly trying to appear to be something they aren't. They'll provide visually-pleasing websites and be your "yes-man" when you inquire about their puppies anything to get you to buy a puppy from them. If the process is too good to be true, take a step back and take a breather."

Licences and Imports

Licences

If your potential breeder is licensed, DO YOUR RESEARCH. Holders of dog breeding licences in North America and the UK range from excellent, responsible breeders to puppy farms.

Minimum requirements vary from state to state in the US; it can be anything from five to 30 breeding dogs - and legal minimum standards of care vary wildly. Many of them just cover the basics, such as adequate food, water and paperwork. This does not make for a good puppy. Responsible licensed breeders put a great deal more time and effort into their puppies than this.

In some US states, licence holders are not even visited by an inspector. Personally, I would not consider buying a dog from anybody who has more than about half a dozen breeding dogs, preferably less. And then only if the breeding dogs were living in the house with the breeder.

Establishments with 20 or 30 breeding dogs are, in my book, puppy farms. The licence holders cannot possibly know so many individual dogs and then properly socialise, stimulate and interact with many hundreds of puppies every year.

In the UK, anybody breeding three or more litters a year or who is "breeding puppies and advertising a business of selling them" should be licensed. This latter part is abused as there are many unlicensed people regularly breeding puppies for five-figure profits.

There is something to help UK buyers navigate this minefield and that is the licensing star system: **One Star** - Minor Failings, **Two or Three Stars** - Minimum Standards have been met, **Four or Five Stars** - Higher Standards have been met. **Look for a breeder who meets the higher standards.**

Imports

Occasionally Schnauzers are imported, usually by experienced breeders to improve their bloodlines. Another scenario is that a top exhibitor might import a Schnauzer with show potential or an excellent track record in the show ring.

If a Schnauzer is imported, these are the official documents required: UK - a pet passport with all the inoculations listed; Rabies done 21 days prior to import. If the puppy travels with a courier he or she will need paperwork from DEFRA. USA: if the puppy travels as excess luggage, he or she will need a pet passport and paperwork to be filled in by the courier.

 Pet Schnauzers are not normally imported. Be aware there are puppy factories in some Eastern European and other countries producing and exporting poorly-bred puppies by the hundreds.

Be very wary if offered a Schnauzer from another country. Only buy if you are 100% sure the dog's home and ancestry are genuine and if all the above paperwork is in order, with the relevant certificates accompanying the puppy.

Puppy Mills and Farms

Unscrupulous breeders are everywhere. That's not to say there aren't excellent Schnauzer breeders out there; there certainly are. You just have to do your research.

While new owners might think they have bagged a cheap or a quick puppy, it often turns out to be false economy and emotionally disastrous when the puppy develops health problems or behavioural problems due to poor temperament or lack of socialisation. The UK's Kennel Club says as many as one in four puppies bought in the UK may come from puppy farms - and the situation is no better in North America.

The KC Press release states: "As the popularity of online pups continues to soar:

* ❧ Almost one in five pups bought (unseen) on websites or social media die within six months
* ❧ One in three buys online, in pet stores and via newspaper adverts - outlets often used by puppy farmers - this is an increase from one in five in the previous year
* ❧ The problem is likely to grow as the younger generation favours mail-order pups, and breeders of fashionable breeds flout responsible steps

"We are sleepwalking into a dog welfare and consumer crisis as new research shows that more and more people are buying their pups online or through pet shops, outlets often used by cruel puppy farmers, and are paying the price with their pups requiring long-term veterinary treatment or dying before six months old." The KC research found that:

* ❧ One-third of people who bought their puppy online or over social media failed to experience "overall good health"
* ❧ Some 12% of puppies bought online or on social media end up with serious health problems that require expensive ongoing veterinary treatment from a young age

The Kennel Club said: "Whilst there is nothing wrong with initially finding a puppy online, it is essential to then see the breeder and ensure that they are doing all of the right things.

"This research clearly shows that too many people are failing to do this, and the consequences can be seen in the shocking number of puppies that are becoming sick or dying."

Marc Abraham, TV vet and founder of Pup Aid, added: "Sadly, if the *"buy it now"* culture persists, then this horrific situation will only get worse.

"There is nothing wrong with sourcing a puppy online, but people need to be aware of what they should then expect from the breeder.

"For example, you should not buy a car without getting its service history and seeing it at its registered address, so you certainly shouldn't buy a puppy without the correct paperwork and health certificates and without seeing where it was bred.

"However, too many people are opting to buy directly from third parties, such as the internet, pet shops, or from puppy dealers, where you cannot possibly know how or where the puppy was raised. Not only are people buying sickly puppies, but many people are being scammed into paying money for puppies that don't exist."

Cautionary Tales

As a canine author, I hear these stories all the time. A good friend of mine recently lost a £350 ($420) deposit on an internet puppy scam. Then there are people breeding puppies who are not fraudsters, but who have no clue how to do it properly, resulting in third-rate puppies.

Here's another: An intelligent, well-educated friend and her husband lost their beloved dog of 13 years and shortly afterwards answered an advert for a puppy on Pets4Homes - rather than contacting a good breeder and waiting.

They visited the "breeder's" house, which had five different dogs of different ages and breeds, none of them interacting with the family. They asked to see the puppy's mother, who was allowed into the room and promptly ran around like crazy before pooping on the sofa. She had not been out of the house all day.

My friends felt sorry for the attractive puppy and bought her. She was 13 weeks old and had only been out of the house twice in her life - once to the vet's and once into the garden! Now she's home the puppy is very timid - especially with men, whom she barks at loudly.

Nearly one year - and a lot of behaviourist training bills - later, the dog is still nervous and the jury is out on whether, temperament-wise, she will ever truly overcome this. She also has weak hindquarters and has hydrotherapy sessions at the vet clinic.

My friends regret their hasty decision and still have a lot of hard work ahead if the dog is to have a chance of meeting their expectations. All credit to them for sticking with her.

One of our contributory breeders said: "We have had at least two to three people every litter who had already put a deposit on a fake puppy. One couple even "bought" one of our puppies from someone else; a scammer who pulled our pictures off Facebook and used them."

 Resist the urge to rush out and get a Miniature Schnauzer puppy NOW! Be patient, pick the right puppy from a good breeder and look forward to many happy years with a healthy, well-bred, well-adjusted dog.

If you really care about Schnauzers, avoid buying from a breeder-for-profit. Ultimately, they are damaging the breed by introducing dogs that are not fit for purpose into the Schnauzer gene pool. Visit the UK Kennel Club's *Buying a Dog* section for more tips: www.thekennelclub.org.uk or type *UK Kennel Club buying a dog* into a search engine.

In the US, search for *AKC Tips for Finding and Working With a Responsible Breeder.*

Where to Find a Good Breeder

1. The Kennel Club in your country. In the US look for an AKC Breeder of Merit or a Bred with H.E.A.R.T. breeder, and Kennel Club Assured Breeders in the UK.

2. National and regional breed clubs.

3. Visit dog shows or canine events where Schnauzers are participating and talk to owners and breeders.

4. Get a recommendation from somebody who has a Schnauzer that you like - check that the breeder health screens her dogs.

5. Ask your vet for details of local, ethical Schnauzer breeders.

6. Search the internet - there are lots of breeders out there; use the advice in this chapter to find the right one.

7. If you are in the UK, visit the Schnauzer stands breed stand at **Discover Dogs** during the annual Crufts dog show in early March, or Discover Dogs at Excel in London, normally held during November. See the Events and Activities section on the Kennel Club website for dates.

Details of these organisations can be found in **Useful Contacts** at the back of this book.

Questions to Ask a Breeder

Here's a list of the questions you should be asking:

1. **Can I see the litter with the parents** - or at least the mother? It's important to see the pup in his or her normal surroundings, not brought out of a building and shown to you.

2. **How many dogs do you have**?

3. **Do they all live in the house**?

4. **What documents come with the puppy?** These should include health certificates and pedigree registration.

5. **What veterinary care have the pups had so far?** First wormings and usually first vaccinations and microchipping.

6. **Are you registered with the US AKC or UK Kennel Club or a member of a Schnauzer club?** Not all good breeders are, but it's a good place to start.

7. **How long have you been breeding Schnauzers?** You are looking for someone with a good track record with the breed.

8. **How many litters has the mother had?** Females should be at least 18 months to two years old. The UK Kennel Club will not register puppies from a dam under one year old, had more than four litters or is over the age of eight.

9. **What happens to the mother once she's finished breeding?** Are they kept as part of the family, rehomed in loving homes or sent to animal shelters? Do you see any old Schnauzers at the breeder's home?

10. **What made you want to breed Schnauzers?**

11. **Do you breed any other types of dogs?** Buy from a specialist, preferably one who does not have lots of other breeds.

12. **What are you looking for in an owner?**

13. **How socialised and housetrained is the puppy?** Good breeders start these processes.

14. **How would you describe the parents' characters?** Temperament is extremely important; try to interact with both parents, or at least the mother.

15. **Do you provide a written Sale or Puppy Contract**? And will you take the pup back if things don't work out?

16. **How old will the puppy be when I collect her**? And what is the procedure?

17. **Do you send anything home with the puppy**? Most good breeders supply a Puppy Pack.

18. **Can you put me in touch with someone who already has one of your puppies?** ALWAYS contact at least one owner.

19. **Why aren't you asking me any questions?** If he or she doesn't, then walk away.

Rebecca also advises asking if any of the females are *'co-owned'* if you live in the USA: "This is where the female lives with her primary owner up until it's time to welp, then she lives with the breeder. Once her breeding time is over, the primary owner keeps her - they get the dog much cheaper. So in reality, the home you see when selecting a puppy is not the dog's true home nor family."

Choosing a Healthy Mini Puppy

Once you've selected your breeder and a litter is available, you then have to decide WHICH puppy to pick, unless the breeder has already earmarked one for you after asking lots of questions. Here are some pointers on puppy health:

1. **The pup's eyes should be bright and clear** with no discharge or tear stain. Steer clear of a puppy that blinks a lot. Bordetella and Kennel Cough vaccines can sometimes cause runny eyes and nose for up to 10 days - ask when the litter was vaccinated for these.

2. A Schnauzer puppy should have **a well-fed appearance.** She should not, however, have a distended abdomen (pot belly) as this can be a sign of worms or other illnesses. The ideal puppy should not be too thin either - you should be able to feel, but not see, her ribs.

3. **Her nose should be cool, damp and clean** with no discharge.

4. **The pup's ears should be clean** with no sign of discharge, soreness or redness and no unpleasant smell.

5. **Check the puppy's rear end** to make sure it is clean and there are no signs of watery poop.

6. **The pup's coat should look clean,** feel soft, not matted - and puppies should smell good! The coat should have no signs of ticks or fleas. Red or irritated skin or bald spots could be a sign of infestation or a skin condition.

   Also, check between the toes of the paws for signs of redness or swelling.

7. **Schnauzers are lively, alert dogs and puppies should be the same.** They should not be timid or frightened by you. Be wary if the breeder makes excuses for the puppies' behaviour.

8. **Gums should be clean and pink.**

9. **Choose a puppy that moves freely** without any sign of injury or lameness.

10. When the puppy is distracted, clap or make a noise behind her - not so loud as to frighten her - to **make sure she is not deaf.**

11. Finally, **ask to see veterinary records** to confirm your puppy has been wormed, possibly had her first vaccinations and a vet check.

 Take your puppy to a vet to have a thorough check-up within 48 hours of purchase. If your vet is not happy with the pup's condition, return her - no matter how painful it may be. Keeping an unhealthy puppy will only lead to further distress and expense.

Puppy Contracts

Most good breeders provide their puppy parents with an official Puppy Contract, also called a Sale Contract. This protects both buyer and seller by providing information on the puppy until he or she leaves the breeder. A Puppy Contract will answer such questions as whether the puppy:

❧ Is covered by breeder's insurance and can be returned if there is a health issue within a certain period

- ❖ Has been micro-chipped (compulsory in the UK) and/or vaccinated and details of worming treatments
- ❖ Has been partially or wholly toilet-trained
- ❖ Has been socialised and where he or she was kept
- ❖ What health conditions the pup and parents have been screened for
- ❖ What the puppy is currently being fed and if any food is being supplied
- ❖ Was born by Caesarean section (C-section)
- ❖ And details of the dam and sire

It's not easy for caring breeders to part with their puppies after they have lovingly bred and raised them, and so many supply extensive care notes for new owners, which may include details of:

- ❖ The puppy's daily routine
- ❖ Feeding schedule
- ❖ Vet and vaccination schedule
- ❖ General puppy care
- ❖ Toilet training
- ❖ Socialisation

The Royal Society for the Prevention of Cruelty to Animals (RSPCA) has a free downloadable puppy contract, *pictured,* endorsed by vets and animal welfare organisations; you should be looking for something similar from a breeder. Visit https://puppycontract.org.uk/about-us or type *"AKC Preparing a Puppy Contract"* if you're in the US.

....

★ A good course of action would be something like this:

1. Decide which size of Schnauzer would best suit your lifestyle.
2. Decide on a male or female.
3. Do your research and find a good breeder with healthy Schnauzers.
4. Register your interest, keep in touch with the breeder for updates - and WAIT until a litter becomes available.
5. Pick a puppy with a suitable temperament - a good breeder will help you choose.
6. Enjoy a decade or longer with a beautiful, healthy Schnauzer.

Some people pick a puppy based on how the dog looks. If coat colour, for example, is very important to you, make sure the other boxes are ticked as well.

6. Bringing Puppy Home

Getting a new puppy is so exciting; you can't wait to bring him home. Before that happens, you probably dream of all the things you are going to do together: going for walks, playing games, travelling, snuggling down at home together, and maybe even taking part in canine competitions.

Your pup has, of course, no idea of your big plans, and the reality when he arrives can be a BIG shock! Puppies are wilful little critters with minds of their own and sharp teeth. They leak at both ends, chew anything in sight, constantly demand your attention, nip the kids or anything else to hand, cry and don't pay a blind bit of notice to your commands... There is a lot of work ahead before the two of you develop that unique bond!

Your pup has to learn what you require from him before he can start to meet some of your expectations - and you have to learn what your pup needs from you.

....

Once your Mini Schnauzer puppy lands in your home, your time won't be your own, but you can get off to a good start by preparing things before the big day. Here's a list of things to think about getting beforehand - your breeder may supply some of these:

Puppy Checklist

- ✓ A dog bed or basket
- ✓ Bedding – a Vetbed or Vetfleece is a good choice
- ✓ A piece of cloth (remove buttons, etc) that has been rubbed on the puppy's mother to put in the bed
- ✓ A puppy gate or pen
- ✓ A crate if you decide to use one
- ✓ A collar or puppy harness with an ID tag and a lead (leash)
- ✓ Food and water bowls, preferably stainless steel
- ✓ Puppy food – find out what the breeder is feeding and stick with that to start with
- ✓ Puppy treats, healthy ones, carrot and apple pieces are good, no rawhide
- ✓ Newspapers or pellet litter and a bell if you decide to use one for housetraining
- ✓ Poo(p) bags
- ✓ Toys and chews suitable for puppies
- ✓ A puppy coat if you live in a cool climate or it's winter
- ✓ Old blanket for cleaning and drying and partially covering the crate

AND PLENTY OF TIME!

Later, you'll also need grooming brushes, flea and worming products and maybe a car grille or travel crate. Many good breeders provide Puppy Packs, which contain some or all of these items:

- ✓ Pedigree certificate
- ✓ Puppy contract
- ✓ Information pack with details of vet visits, vaccinations and wormings, parents' health certificates, diet, breed clubs, etc.
- ✓ Puppy food
- ✓ ID tag/microchip info
- ✓ Blanket that smells of the mother and litter
- ✓ Soft toy that your puppy has grown up with, possibly a chew toy as well
- ✓ A month's free insurance

FACT › By law, all UK puppies have to be microchipped and registered BEFORE they leave the breeder. New owners are legally bound to ensure their puppy's microchip registration is updated with their own details and also to register any change of address or ownership.

Puppy Proofing Your Home

Some adjustments will be needed to make your home safe and suitable. Schnauzer puppies are small bundles of curiosity, instinct and energy when they are awake, with little common sense and even less self-control.

They have bursts of energy before running out of steam and spending much of the rest of the day sleeping. As one breeder says: "They have two speeds – ON and OFF!"

They also have an excellent sense of smell and love to investigate with their noses and mouths. Fence off or remove all poisonous or low plants with sharp leaves or thorns, such as roses, that could cause eye injuries.

There are dozens of plants harmful to a puppy if ingested, including azalea, daffodil bulbs, lily, foxglove, hyacinth, hydrangea, lupin, rhododendron, sweet pea, tulip and yew.

The Kennel Club has a list of some of the most common ones, type "*Kennel Club poisons in your garden*" into Google. The ASPCA has an extensive list for the USA if you Google *"ASPCA poisonous plants."*

Make sure any fencing planks are extremely close together and that EVERY LITTLE GAP has been plugged; Schnauzer puppies can get through almost anything and they have no road sense whatsoever. Don't leave your puppy unattended in the garden or yard in the beginning.

FACT › Dognapping is on the increase. Over 2,000 dogs are now being stolen each year in the UK. The figures are much higher for the US, where the AKC reports increasing dog thefts and warns owners against leaving dogs unattended.

Puppies are little chew machines and puppy-proofing your home involves moving anything sharp, breakable or chewable - including your shoes.

- Lift electrical cords, mobile phones and chargers, remote controls, etc. out of reach and block off any off-limits areas of the house with a child gate or barrier, especially as he may be shadowing you for the first few days.

- Create an area where your puppy is allowed to go, perhaps one or two rooms, preferably with a hard floor that is easy to clean. Keep the rest of the house off-limits, at least until the pair of you have mastered potty training.

- This area should be near the door to the garden or yard for toileting. Restricting the puppy's space also helps him to settle in. He probably had a den and a small space at the breeder's home. Suddenly having the freedom of the whole house can be quite daunting - not to mention messy!

- You can buy a purpose-made dog barrier or use a sturdy baby gate, which may be cheaper, to confine a puppy to a room or prevent him from going upstairs. Choose one with narrow vertical gaps or mesh, and check that your puppy can't get his head stuck between the bars, or put a mesh over the bottom of the gate initially.

- You can also make your own barrier, but bear in mind that cardboard, fabric and other soft materials will definitely get chewed. Don't underestimate your puppy! Young Schnauzers are lively and determined - they can jump and climb, so choose a barrier higher than you think necessary.

- You'll then need a bed and/or a crate. A rigid moulded bed that's more difficult for a puppy to damage is a good option initially, with Vetbed or blankets inside for comfort. A luxury soft bed could prove to be an expensive mistake while puppies are still at the chewing stage! Some owners also like to create a penned area for their pups.

....

Collecting Your Puppy

Let the breeder know what time you will arrive and ask her not to feed the pup for a couple of hours beforehand - unless you have a very long journey, in which case the puppy will need to eat something. He will be less likely to be car sick and should be hungry when he lands in his new home. The same applies to an adult dog moving to a new home.

Ask for an old blanket or toy that has been with the pup's mother – you can leave one on an earlier visit to collect with the pup, or take one with you and rub the mother with it to collect her scent and put this with the puppy for the first few days. It will help him to settle.

Get copies of any health certificates relating to the parents and a Contract of Sale or Puppy Contract – see **Chapter 5. Finding Your Puppy** for details. It should also state that you can return the puppy if there are health issues within a certain time frame. The breeder will also give you details of microchip registration, worming and any vaccinations, as well as an information sheet.

Find out exactly what the breeder is feeding and how much; dogs' digestive systems cannot cope with sudden changes in diet - unless the breeder has deliberately been feeding several different foods to her puppies to get them used to different foods. In the beginning, stick to whatever the pup is used to; good breeders send some food home with the puppy.

The Journey Home

Steve Matthews, breeder of Silbertraum Miniature Schnauzers has this advice for transporting puppy home: "When you first collect your new puppy it is important to provide safe and suitable transport arrangements. One of the best ways to do this is by using a purpose-built dog crate to keep your puppy secure.

"The crate needs to be anchored securely to your vehicle to prevent movement when you accelerate or brake. This can be done using bungees.

"Put bedding on the floor of the crate to provide a non-slip and comfortable resting place - and in sufficient quantity that it cannot slide around. The door of the crate needs to be securely fastened so that the puppy cannot escape."

Photo: Posing for the camera, courtesy of Steve.

"On anything more than a very short journey, your puppy will need water and toilet breaks and, if the journey is long, food. You will need to take a lead and a small puppy collar so that you can prevent the puppy from running free during toilet stops.

"If more than one person is travelling, you may prefer to do parts or all of the trip with the puppy on the passenger's lap."

 Have an old towel between your travel companion and the pup as he may quite possibly pee, drool or be sick - the puppy, not the passenger! Kitchen towel is useful and a large plastic bag for any soiled items. And if your puppy is not fully vaccinated, avoid toilet breaks on ground where there are other dogs.

NOTE: UK law states that any dog travelling in a car must have a "suitable restraint." While a crate is ideal, we believe it's acceptable for a pup to be held firmly on a person's knee for this first journey.

....

Settling In

These first few days are critical in getting your puppy to feel safe and confident in his new surroundings. Spend time with the latest addition to your family, and talk to him often in a reassuring manner. Introduce him to his den and toys, slowly allow him to explore and show him around the house – once you have puppy-proofed it.

If you've got other animals, introduce them to each other slowly and in supervised sessions on neutral territory - or outdoors where there is space so neither feels threatened - preferably once the pup has got used to his new surroundings, not as soon as you walk through the door.

Gentleness and patience are the keys to these first few days, so don't overwhelm your pup.

 Have a special, gentle puppy voice and use his new name frequently - and in a pleasant, encouraging manner. Never use his name to scold or he will associate it with bad things. The sound of his name should always make him want to pay attention to you as something good is going to happen - praise, food, playtime, and so on.

We receive emails from worried new Mini Schnauzer owners. Here are some of their most common concerns:

- My puppy won't stop crying or whining
- My puppy is shivering
- My puppy won't eat
- My puppy is very timid
- My puppy follows me everywhere, he won't let me out of his sight
- My puppy sleeps all the time, is this normal?

These behaviours are quite common at the beginning. They are just a young pup's reaction to leaving his mother and littermates and entering into a strange new world. It is normal for puppies to sleep most of the time, just like babies. It is also normal for some puppies to whine during the first couple of days.

 If you constantly pick up a crying pup, he will learn that your attention is the reward for his crying. Wait until your puppy STOPS crying before giving him your attention.

If your puppy is shivering, check that he's warm enough, as he is used to the warmth of his siblings. If he's on the same food as he was at the breeder's and won't eat, then it is probably just nerves. If he leaves his food, take it away and try it later, don't leave it down all of the time or he may get used to turning his nose up at it.

Make your new pup as comfortable as possible, ensuring he has a warm (but not too hot), quiet den away from draughts, where he is not pestered by other pets or children. Handle him gently, while giving him plenty of time to sleep. Avoid placing him under stress by making too many demands. If your puppy whines or cries, it is usually due to one of the following reasons:

- He is lonely
- He is hungry
- He is cold
- He needs to relieve himself
- He wants attention from you

If it is none of these, then physically check him over to make sure he hasn't picked up an injury. Try not to fuss too much! If he whimpers, reassure him with a quiet word.

If he cries and tries to get out of his allotted area, he may need to go to the toilet. Take him outside and praise him if he performs.

FACT Schnauzer puppies from breeders who have already started socialisation and training are often more confident and less fazed by new things. They often settle in quicker than those reared with less human contact and new experiences.

A puppy will think of you as his new mother, and if you haven't decided what to call him yet, "Shadow" might be apt as he will follow you everywhere! But after a few days start to leave your pup for periods of a few minutes, gradually building up the time.

A puppy unused to being left alone can grow up to have Separation Anxiety.

Helping a new pup to settle in is virtually a full-time job. If your routine means you are normally out of the house for a few hours during the day, get your puppy on a Friday or Saturday so he has at least a couple of days to adjust to his new surroundings.

A far better idea is to book time off work to help your puppy to settle in, if you can. (Easier to do in the UK than in the US). If you don't work, leave your diary free for the first couple of weeks.

 Your puppy's arrival at your home coincides with his most important life stage for bonding, so the first few weeks are very important.

Breeders' Advice

Andrew and Gaynor Ray, Minnienoom Miniature Schnauzers: "When your puppy first arrives home, try not to leave him or her alone for too long. Your puppy will miss mum and siblings; everything is new and overwhelming, so it is important that you increase the length of time he or she spends alone gradually.

"If your puppy is very distressed for the first few nights, let them sleep in their crate in your bedroom. Then gradually move the crate to where you want them to spend the night. Before bedtime, give your puppy a play session and ensure they have been to the toilet.

"It is very important that your puppy has their own crate, box or playpen which is their own personal and safe space. Place this in a warm, draught-free position away from anything that can be chewed. Puppies tire easily so let him or her sleep peacefully as and when they want.

"A new puppy is very inquisitive, like a toddler, so make sure the environment is safe. A few particular hazards include: medicines and cleaning products, small objects like marbles, coins, stones, toys that could be a choking hazard and plastic bags which could lead to suffocation."

Photo: Settling in nicely. Eight-week-old Tillie (Minnienoom Dark Princess), courtesy of Andrew and Gaynor.

They added: "Be extra vigilant with electric and telephone cables as (s)he will have needle-like teeth and be inclined to chew when teething. Keep your puppy safe from garden ponds and be aware of the dangers of large birds of prey and rivers when out.

"We strongly recommend you supervise your new puppy in your garden until (s)he becomes confident in their new surroundings."

Steve Matthews: "Puppies are similar to babies; they like to explore everything with their mouths, so you need to be careful not to leave small objects lying around and also exposed electrical cables. I recommend crate training so that you can leave the puppy alone for a while without the worry of chewing when they go through the chewing stage. I also tell all owners not to overfeed, especially with treats."

 These early days and weeks are also a critical time for developing a relationship with your new puppy.

The most important factors in bonding with your new arrival are TIME and PATIENCE, even if he makes a mess in the house or chews something. Spend time with your Schnauzer pup and you will have the most loyal lifelong friend. This emotional attachment may grow to become one of the most important aspects of your life - and certainly his.

Where Should the Puppy Sleep?

Just as you need a home, so a puppy needs a den - a haven where your pup feels safe. One of the most important things you can do for your young Schnauzer puppy is to ALLOW HIM LOTS AND LOTS OF SLEEP – as much as 18 or 20 hours a day!

Your puppy doesn't know this and will play until he drops, so make sure you put him in his quiet place regularly during the day - even if he doesn't want to go, he will fall asleep and get the rest he needs.

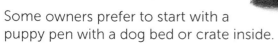 **The importance of pups getting enough sleep cannot be overstated. Lack of sleep can lead to over-excitement and naughtiness, which will make him harder to train.**

Steve Matthews: "Before you collect your puppy, you need to arrange somewhere for your puppy to sleep and where it won't get into trouble or wreck your house if it wakes during the night.

"Once again, a dog crate provides an ideal and safe environment. You need to place bedding and a water bowl in the dog crate so the puppy has somewhere comfortable to sleep and can have a drink during the night.

"Be aware that your puppy may bark or whine during the night. This is understandable as it has been removed from its mother, siblings and familiar environment. It will soon settle down once it becomes acquainted with its new home."

While it is not acceptable to shut a dog in a cage all day, you can keep your puppy in a crate at night until housetrained, and many adult Schnauzers prefer to sleep in a crate - with the door open.

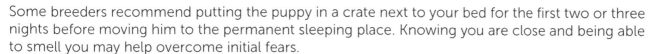

Some owners prefer to start with a puppy pen with a dog bed or crate inside.

Some breeders recommend putting the puppy in a crate next to your bed for the first two or three nights before moving him to the permanent sleeping place. Knowing you are close and being able to smell you may help overcome initial fears.

Others recommend biting the bullet and starting the puppy off in his permanent sleeping place; he will quieten down after a few nights.

Ask your own breeder's advice on this one.

 It's normal for most puppies to cry for the first night or two. Resist the urge to get up to hold and comfort your pup, who learns that crying equals attention. Invest in a pair of silicone earplugs; puppies soon settle down.

Young puppies can't go through the night without needing to pee (and sometimes poo); their bodies simply aren't up to it.

Many breeders recommend putting newspapers or pellets in the pup's confined area – but away from his bedding – so he can relieve himself during the night until he can last for six or seven hours.

Set your alarm for an early morning wake-up call and take him out first thing, even before you are dressed. As soon as he wakes, he will want to pee.

Alternatively, we set our alarm and get up with a puppy once in the middle of the night for the first week - lights off, no fuss, a quick trip outside - to speed up housetraining. Again, ask your breeder what she recommends for your puppy.

We don't advise letting new puppies sleep on the bed. They are not housetrained. They need to learn their place in the household and have their own quiet place for resting. See **Chapter 7** for more information on night housetraining.

It's up to you whether to let yours on the bed or not once housetrained. Schnauzers can sleep almost anywhere and anyhow. They don't need your comfy bed!

And be aware that Minis have a range of nocturnal noise - we know, we shared our bedroom with one for 13 years (big mistake if you're a light sleeper!).

They snuffle, snore, fart and - if not in a crate - pad around the bedroom in the middle of the night and come up to the bed to check you are still there - or to try and get stroked!

None of this is conducive to a good night's sleep...

 A Schnauzer puppy used to being on his own every night (i.e. not in your bedroom) is less likely to develop Separation Anxiety, so consider this when deciding where he should sleep.

While it is not good to leave a dog alone all day, it is also not healthy to spend 24 hours a day together, as a dog can become too dependent.

Although this is very flattering for you, it actually means that the dog is nervous and less sure of himself when you are not there. The last thing you want on your hands is an anxious Mini.

It may surprise American readers to learn that it's not uncommon practice in the UK to contain the puppy in the kitchen or utility room until he's housetrained, and then allow him to roam around the house at will. Some owners do not allow their dogs upstairs, but many do.

 Studies have shown that pups who regularly run up and down stairs, or jump on and off furniture, before their growth plates are fully formed may be more likely to develop joint problems later in life.

The time any young children spend with the puppy should be limited to a few short sessions a day and supervised. You wouldn't wake a baby every hour or so to play, and the same goes for puppies.

Wait a day or two before inviting friends around to see your beautiful new puppy... and even then, don't inundate the pup with constant visitors. However excited you are, your new arrival needs a few days to get over the stress of leaving mother and siblings and start bonding with you.

While confident, well-socialised Minis may settle in right away, others may feel sad and a little afraid. Make the transition as gentle and unalarming as possible.

After a few sleep-deprived nights followed by days filled with entertaining your little puppy and dealing with chewed shoes, nipping and a few housetraining "accidents," your nerves might be a tiny bit frayed!

Try to remain calm and patient... your puppy is doing his best. Miniatures are quick learners, it just takes a little time for you both to get on the same wavelength.

......

Personal Experiences

Starting in the USA with Chloe Dong and Jacky Zou: "During the first few days (and weeks) when Oslo arrived home, we were his personal attendants 24/7! He hardly went a minute without one pair of eyes on him.

"One tip I would give to new owners is to constantly watch what he puts in his mouth. To Oslo, everything is a first and if it fits in his mouth, he'll try to ingest anything under the sun. Whenever his mouth made a chewing movement, one of us would hurry over to open his jaws.

"Although unrelated, another emotion I felt was relief. Not from the puppy arriving home, but from knowing whom I got him from. Prior to meeting my breeder, Wade Bogart, I went through a multitude of other breeders with various qualifications.

"One concerning pattern I noticed across many of them was the lack of interest in the living environment their puppies were going to. The majority asked similar questions about color, budget, timeframe of litters, and discounts right off the bat.

"To anyone looking for a Mini Schnauzer, even after doing your research, don't let impatience and external details like color preference cloud your judgment.

"We were extremely lucky to have avoided those puppy mills and that Wade decided to pick up the phone on a whim that day to talk to us."

Photo: Oslo, aged eight weeks, in his playpen before his crate arrived.

Vivian Williams: "Bogart came to us crate-trained and nearly housetrained. He never whined or cried in the crate. We carefully introduced him to our Standard Poodle and they became good companions and playmates.

"Bogart sleeps in his crate each night. He associates the crate with comfort; after all, dogs are den animals. There is a dog bed inside for him; each day he eats his meals in the crate and he receives an occasional treat there."

Rebecca Makdad: "Navy was extremely well adjusted. My first Schnauzer, Rosie, was eight years old and wonderful with her. I paid very close attention, initially, to their interactions. Very early on the puppy was following all the older dog's behavior. It was a very easy transition.

To begin with, I crated Navy at night in the bedroom with me and Rosie. Once she was housetrained, she transitioned to the human bed!"

Simon and Yvonne Sonsino, owners of Bu (14) and puppy Wilf: "We've been very lucky, as the first few days (with both boys) were relatively calm. The only tip at this stage is to be strong when putting the pup into the crate for its rest and not give in to the crying. It only lasts 20 seconds (well it did for us).

"Our old boy sleeps on a sheepskin rug in our bedroom at night and Wilf is in his crate downstairs. For the first few nights, we had Wilf in the bedroom with us but still in his crate."

Now some comments from UK owners. Gary Blain agrees with Simon and Yvonne's advice - but it's easier said than done. Mini Schnauzers are notorious for getting you to do what THEY want to do if they spot a chink in your armour!

Andrew: "I've had puppies before, a long time ago though, so I'd forgotten how it would be when Jamie (7) and Evie (4) came home for the first time, both as puppies. Evie was easier as she had Jamie to keep her company.

"I'm a big softy. Jamie hated being put in a crate, so when he cried the first few nights, I slept with him.... It didn't last; he soon had me wrapped around his little paw. Although Jamie started in a crate as I intended, it lasted two nights before he was sleeping on my bed, where he sleeps now.

"In fact, both my Minis sleep on my bed. Who knew such small dogs could spread so much and take up so much space?!

"My advice is before you get your puppy make your plan to decide what you will and won't let your puppy do - and stick to it. It's hard if you are a softy like me..."

Leah Dummer: "We had three young children (one nine months old) when our puppies Leelo and Lily arrived, and we already had an older Mini, three-year-old Freddie.

"We found that our household was full of lots of child energy and toys. So we had to be on our toes that our child Ellie wasn't chewing the puppies' toys and the puppies weren't chewing Ellie's toys.

"We were expecting to have to reassure the puppies, as they had come into a new home and left their mum. However, they found comfort in Freddie and followed what he was doing.

"All three of our dogs sleep in the kitchen together on dog beds. This is where they have always slept. However, Leelo likes to sleep inside their toy basket."

Photo: Ellie and Leelo, the best of friends, courtesy of Leah.

Yolande: "Mayzy settled in very quickly with the family, no whimpering or howling. I used a furry toy puppy with a heartbeat in her sleeping crate so she wouldn't miss her siblings too much. I took her out onto the grass often to get her used to the idea that this was where she would relieve herself.

"She slept in a crate covered with a blanket. I created a dark snug place for her to sleep at night within the crate. I always keep the crate door open, but the utility room door shut. Mayzy sleeps there still."

Chris Lee: "We had prepared well, we thought. We put bricks on the step from the garden to the house to make it less of a problem for the little pup to get in and out. On the first day after a two-hour car journey, Betsy entered the garden and ran around as if she owned the place. The worries about the step were unfounded as she leapt over the supportive bricks!

"As for the crate, she had been surrounded by them at the breeder's; she walked right into it without any persuasion and settled. Initially, we had a few disturbed nights and early mornings, but this lasted no more than a few weeks.

"In terms of advice - prepare for a bright dog that will fit in well to your home, and give a consistent and loving welcome."

....

Treats and Toys

Pups explore the world with their noses. Once they have found something interesting, they usually put it in their mouths, so chews and toys are a must. Don't scold a pup for chewing; it's natural.

Instead, put objects you don't want to be chewed out of reach and replace them with chew toys. There are some things you can't move out of puppy's way, like kitchen cabinets, doors, sofas, fixtures and fittings, so try not to leave your pup unattended for any length of time where he can chew something difficult or expensive to replace.

Tip Avoid giving old socks, shoes or slippers, or your pup will naturally come to think of your footwear as fair game!

You can give a Miniature Schnauzer puppy a raw bone to gnaw on - NEVER cooked bones as these can splinter. Avoid poultry and pork bones. Ribs - especially pork ribs - are too high in fat. Knuckle bones, *pictured,* are a good choice and the bone should be too big for the puppy to swallow.

Puppies should ALWAYS BE SUPERVISED and the bone removed after an hour or so. Don't feed a puppy a bone if there are other dogs around, it could lead to food aggression.

FACT ⟩ Raw bones contain bacteria, and families with babies or very young children shouldn't feed them indoors. Keep any bones in a fridge or freezer and always wash your hands after handling them.

Alternatives to real bones or plastic chew bones include natural *reindeer antler* chew toys which have the added advantage of calcium, although they are hard and have been known to crack teeth.

Natural chews preferred by some breeders include ears, dried rabbit pelt and tripe sticks – all excellent for teething puppies - once you have got over the smell!

Tip Rawhide chews are not recommended as they can get stuck in a dog's throat or stomach, but bully sticks *(pictured)* are a good alternative.

Made from a bull's penis(!) they can be a good distraction and help to promote healthy teeth and gums. *Bully sticks* are highly digestible, break down easily in the stomach and are generally considered safe for all dogs. Made from 100% beef, they normally contain no additives or preservatives, come in different sizes - and dogs love 'em.

NOTE: Puppies should be supervised while eating bully sticks or any other treats.

Dental sticks are good for cleaning your dog's teeth, but contain preservatives and quite a lot of calories - and don't last very long with a determined chewer.

One that does last is the *Nylabone Dura Chew Wishbone, pictured,* made of a type of plastic infused with flavours appealing to dogs. Get the right size and throw it away if it starts to splinter with sharp edges.

Another long-lasting treat option is the *Lickimat (pictured),* which you smear with a favourite food. This inexpensive mat will keep your puppy occupied for some time – although they can leave a bit of a mess.

Other choices include *Kong toys,* which are pretty indestructible, and you can put treats - frozen or fresh - or smear peanut butter inside (one without Xylitol, which is highly toxic to dogs) to keep your dog occupied while you are out. All of these are widely available online, if not in your local pet store.

As far as toys go, the *Zogoflex Hurley* and the *Goughnut* are both strong and float, so good for swimmers – and you'll get your money back on both if your Schnauzer destroys them!

For safety, the Goughnut has a green exterior and red interior, so you can tell if your dog has penetrated the surface - as long as the green is showing, you can let your dog "goughnuts!"

A *natural hemp* or cotton tug rope is another option, as the cotton rope acts like dental floss and helps with teeth cleaning. It is versatile and can be used for fetch games as well as chewing.

FACT ❯ Puppies' stomachs are sensitive, so be careful what goes in. Even non-poisonous garden plants can cause intestinal blockages and/or vomiting. Like babies, pups can quickly dehydrate, so if your puppy is sick or has watery poop for a day or two, seek veterinary advice.

Vaccinations and Worming

We recommend having your Schnauzer checked out by a vet soon after picking him up. Some Puppy Contracts stipulate that the dog should be examined by a vet within a couple of days.

This is to everyone's benefit and, all being well, you are safe in the knowledge that your puppy is healthy, at least at the time of purchase.

 Keep your pup on your lap away from other dogs in the waiting room as he will not yet be fully protected against infectious diseases.

Vaccinations

Puppies are covered by immunity from their mum until around eight weeks. Then all puppies need immunisation, and currently the most common way of doing this is by vaccination. They receive their first dose at around eight weeks old - although it can be any time from six to nine weeks old.

 When you collect your puppy from the breeder, check whether he has had his first round of vaccinations.

The second vaccination is done two to four weeks later, typically at 11 to 13 weeks. Puppies are considered to be fully protected one to two weeks after their second vaccination (depending on the brand).

Intranasal Kennel Cough vaccine, when given, provides protection after three weeks. A booster is then required at six to 12 months.

 An unimmunised puppy is at risk every time he meets other dogs as he has no protection against potentially fatal infectious diseases – and it is unlikely a pet insurer will cover an unvaccinated pup.

It should be stressed that vaccinations are generally safe and side effects are uncommon. If your Schnauzer is unlucky enough to be one of the *very few* that suffers an adverse reaction, here are some signs to look out for; a pup may exhibit one or more of these:

MILD REACTION - Sleepiness, irritability and not wanting to be touched. Sore or a small lump at the place where he was injected. Nasal discharge or sneezing. Puffy face and ears.

SEVERE REACTION - Anaphylactic shock. A sudden and quick reaction, usually before leaving the vet's, which causes breathing difficulties. Vomiting, diarrhoea, staggering and seizures.

A severe reaction is rare. There is a far greater risk of your Schnauzer either being ill or spreading disease if he does not have the injections.

BSAVA (British Small Animal Veterinary Association) recommends the following core vaccinations in the UK:

- ❧ CDV (Distemper)
- ❧ CPV (Parvo)
- ❧ CAV (Adenovirus or Infectious Canine Hepatitis)
- ❧ Leptospirosis (often called *Lepto*)

The Leptospira vaccine is not always considered to be a core vaccination as its use depends on veterinary advice in different parts of the UK.

Risk factors include exposure to, or drinking from, rivers, lakes or streams, exposure to wild or farm animals, and contact with rodents or other dogs. Owners should discuss Lepto with their vet.

Many vets also recommend vaccinating against Kennel Cough (Bordetella). Rabies is very rare in the UK; it's more commonly seen in some US states and Europe. When deemed necessary, Rabies vaccines start at 12 weeks.

Some vets also recommend puppies have at least one course of Fenbendazole (marketed in the UK as Panacur) as it also covers Giardia, which is commonly found in puppies with diarrhoea.

Google *"AKC puppy shots"* for a list of recommended vaccinations. In-depth information on core vaccinations for the US can be found on the World Small Animal Veterinary Association website, search online for *"WSAVA dog vaccinations"* or visit: https://wsava.org/wp-content/uploads/2020/01/WSAVA-Vaccination-Guidelines-2015.pdf (skip to Page 17).

WSAVA states: "Core vaccines for dogs are those that protect against canine distemper virus (CDV), canine adenovirus (CAV) and the variants of canine parvovirus type 2 (CPV-2)... with the final dose of these being delivered at 16 weeks or older and then followed by a booster at six or 12 months of age."

Puppies in the US also need vaccinating separately against **Rabies** after 16 weeks, but this varies by state. There are optional vaccinations for **Coronavirus (C)** and - depending on where you live and if your dog is regularly around woods or forests - **Lyme Disease.**

Bordetella (Kennel Cough) is another non-core vaccine. It can be given intranasally, by tablet or injection, with boosters recommended for dogs deemed to be at high risk, e.g. when boarding or showing.

- ❧ Boosters for Distemper, Parvo and Canine Hepatitis are recommended no more often than every three years
- ❧ Boosters for Leptospirosis are every year

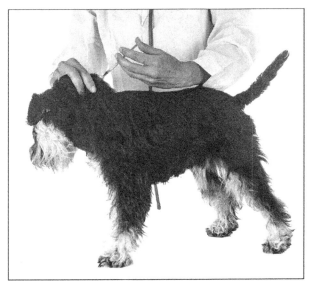

The current Lepto vaccine only protects against certain types of the many different variants of the Leptospira bacteria.

However, having your dog vaccinated does decrease their risk of becoming sick with Lepto. The Lepto vaccination should not be given at the same time as Rabies.

NOTE: Some dogs have been known to have bad reactions to the Lepto 4 vaccine, although Schnauzers are not a particularly susceptible breed.

Diseases such as Parvo and Kennel Cough are highly contagious and you should not let your new arrival mix with other dogs - unless they are your own and have already been vaccinated - until a week after his last vaccination, otherwise he will not be fully immunised.

Parvovirus can also be transmitted by the faeces of many animals, including foxes.

Tip Avoid taking your new puppy to places where unvaccinated dogs might have been, like the local park. This does not mean that your puppy should be isolated - far from it.

This is an important time for socialisation. It is OK for the puppy to mix with other dogs that you absolutely know are up-to-date with their vaccinations and appropriate boosters. Perhaps invite a friend's dog round to play in your garden or yard to begin the socialisation process.

The vet should give you a record card or send you a reminder when a booster is due, but it's also a good idea to keep a note of the date in your diary.

Tests have shown that the Parvovirus vaccination gives most animals at least seven years of immunity, while the Distemper jab provides immunity for five to seven years. In the US, many vets now recommend that you take your dog for *a titre test* once he has had his initial puppy vaccinations and six or 12-month booster.

The Diseases

Vaccinations protect your puppy and adult dog against some nasty diseases, so it's important to keep your Schnauzer up to date with protection.

Canine Distemper (CDV) is a contagious disease affecting different body parts, including the gastrointestinal and respiratory tracts, spinal cord and brain.

Common symptoms include a high fever, eye inflammation, eye and/or nose discharge, struggling for breath, coughing, vomiting, diarrhoea, loss of appetite and lethargy, and hardening of nose and footpads. It can also result in bacterial infections and serious neurological problems.

Canine Parvovirus (CPV) is a highly contagious viral disease that causes acute gastrointestinal illness in puppies commonly aged six to 20 weeks old, although older dogs are sometimes also affected. Symptoms include lethargy, depression and loss or lack of appetite, followed by a sudden onset of high fever, vomiting, and diarrhoea. Sadly, it is often fatal.

Infectious Canine Hepatitis (ICH), also called Canine Adenovirus or CAV, is an acute liver infection. The virus is spread in the poop, urine, blood, saliva, and nasal discharge of infected dogs, and other dogs pick it up through their mouth or nose.

The virus then infects the liver and kidneys. Symptoms include fever, depression, loss of appetite, coughing and a tender abdomen. Dogs can recover from mild cases, but more serious ones can be fatal.

Rabies is a fatal virus that attacks the brain and spinal cord. All mammals, including dogs and humans, can catch rabies, which is most often contracted through a bite from an infected animal. Rabies usually comes from exposure to wild animals like foxes, bats and raccoons.

Leptospirosis (Lepto) is a bacterial disease that causes serious illness by damaging vital organs such as the liver and kidneys. Leptospirosis bacteria can spread in urine and can enter the body through the mouth, nose or open wounds.

Symptoms vary but include fever, jaundice (yellow gums and eyes), muscle pain and limping, weakness, reduced appetite, drinking more, vomiting, bloody diarrhoea, mouth ulcers and difficulty breathing. An infected dog may quickly become restless and irritable, even showing aggression, or being excessively affectionate. One of the most well-known symptoms is foaming at the mouth, a sign that the disease is progressing.

Bordetella (Kennel Cough) - Dogs catch Kennel Cough when they breathe in bacteria or virus particles. The classic symptom is a persistent, forceful cough that often sounds like a goose honk (and is different from a reverse sneeze).

Some dogs may show other symptoms, including sneezing, a runny nose or eye discharge, but appetite and energy levels usually remain the same. It is not often a serious condition and most dogs recover without treatment.

Lyme Disease gets into a dog's or human's bloodstream via a tick bite. Once there, the bacteria travel to different parts of the body and cause problems in organs or specific locations such as joints. These ticks are often found in woods, tall grasses, thick brush and marshes – all places that Schnauzers love.

Lyme Disease can usually be treated if caught early enough. It can be life-threatening or shortening if left untreated.

Giardia is an infection caused by a microscopic parasite that attaches itself to a dog's intestinal wall causing a sudden onset of foul-smelling diarrhoea. It may lead to weight loss, chronic intermittent diarrhoea, and fatty poop.

The disease is not usually life-threatening unless the dog's immune system is immature or compromised. Treated dogs usually recover, although very old dogs and those with compromised immune systems have a higher risk for complications.

Titres (Titers in the USA)

Some breeders and owners feel that constantly vaccinating our dogs is having a detrimental effect on our pets' health, especially as many vaccinations are now effective for several years.

Vets recommend boosters every three years for the core vaccines; however, one alternative is titres. The thinking behind them is to avoid a dog having to have unnecessary repeat vaccinations for certain diseases as he already has enough antibodies present. Known as a *VacciCheck* in the UK, they are still relatively uncommon, but more widespread in the USA.

Not everybody agrees with titres. One vet I spoke to said that the titre results were only good for the day on which the test was taken. Other disadvantages are:

❧ Titres may be more expensive than booster shots, and

❧ They may not be accepted by boarding kennels, nor when travelling internationally with your dog

To *'titre'* is to take a blood sample from a dog (or cat) to determine whether the animal has enough antibodies to provide immunity against a particular disease, particularly Parvovirus, Distemper and Adenovirus (Canine Hepatitis).

If so, then a booster injection is not needed. Titering is NOT recommended for Leptospirosis, Bordetella or Lyme Disease, as these vaccines provide only short-term protection. Many US states also require proof of a Rabies vaccination.

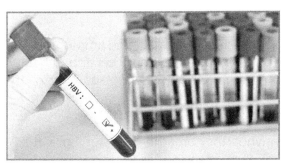

The vet can test the blood at the clinic without sending off the sample, thereby keeping costs down for the owner. A titre for Parvovirus and Distemper currently costs around $100 in the US, sometimes more for Rabies, and a titre test in the UK costs as little as £40.

Titre levels are given as ratios and show how many times blood can be diluted before no antibodies are detected. So, if blood can be diluted 1,000 times and still show antibodies, the ratio would be 1:1000, which is a 'strong' titre, while a titre of 1:2 would be 'weak.'

A *strong (high) titre* means that your dog has enough antibodies to fight off that specific disease and is immune from infection.

A *weak titre* means that you and your vet should discuss revaccination - even then your dog might have some reserve forces known as *'memory cells'* that will provide antibodies when needed.

If you are going on holiday and taking your dog to kennels, check whether the kennel accepts titre records; many don't.

In the UK, not many dog breeders use titres as yet, it is far more common in the US. But here's what some who do titre said: "I titre test periodically rather than do automatic boosters. They have all still had a full level of immunity on the tests - that's after their initial puppy vaccinations."

Another said: "When my puppies go to their new homes, I tell all my owners to follow their vet's advice about worming and vaccinating, as the last thing new owners require is to be at odds with their vets. All dogs must have their puppy vaccinations; it is now thought that the minimum duration of immunity is between seven and 15 years.

"However, a few owners do express concern about all the chemicals we are introducing into our puppies' lives and if they do, I explain how I try to give my dogs a chemical-free life, if possible, as adult dogs.

"Instead of giving my adult dogs their core vaccinations for Canine Distemper, Parvovirus and Adenovirus (Hepatitis) every three years, I just take my dogs down to the local vet and ask them to do something called a titre test, also known as a VacciCheck.

"They take a small amount of blood and check it for antibodies to the diseases. If they have antibodies to the diseases, there is no reason to vaccinate dogs. However, you should note that there is a separate vaccination for Leptospirosis and Canine Parainfluenza, which is given annually.

"Leptospirosis is more common in tropical areas of the world and not that common in England. To make a decision about whether to give this to your dog annually, you need to talk to your vet and do some research yourself so you can make an informed decision.

"We vaccinate our children up to about the age of 16. However, we don't vaccinate adults every one to three years, as it is deemed that the vaccinations they receive in childhood will cover them for a lifetime.

"This is what is being steadily proved for dogs and we are so lucky that we can titre test our dogs so we don't have to leave it to chance."

Another added: "I do not vaccinate my dogs beyond the age of four to five years, I now have them titre tested. Every dog I have titre tested aged five to 10 years has been immune to the diseases vaccinated against when younger. I believe many vets over-vaccinate."

The (UK) Kennel Club now includes titre testing information in its Assured Breeder Pack but has yet to include it under its general information on vaccines on its website.

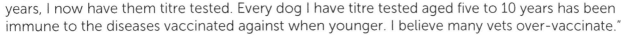

Worming

All puppies need worming (technically, deworming). A good breeder will give the puppies their first dose of worming medication at around two weeks old, then probably again at five and eight weeks before they leave the litter – or even more often.

Get the details and inform your vet exactly what treatment, if any, your pup has already had.

The main worms affecting puppies are roundworms and tapeworms. In certain areas of the US, the dreaded *heartworm* can also pose a risk. If you live in an affected area, discuss the right time to start heartworm medication when you visit your vet for puppy vaccinations – it's usually from a few months old.

The pill should be given every month when there is no heavy frost (frost kills mosquitos that carry the disease); giving it all year round gives the best protection. The heartworm pill is by prescription only and deworms the dog monthly for heartworm, round, hook, and whipworm.

Roundworm can be transmitted from a puppy to humans - often children - and can in severe cases cause blindness or miscarriage in women, so it's important to keep up to date with worming.

Worms in puppies are quite common, usually picked up through their mother's milk. If you have children, get them into the habit of washing their hands after they have been in contact with the puppy – lack of hygiene is the reason why children are susceptible.

Most vets recommend worming a puppy once a month until six months old, and then around every two to three months. If your Schnauzer is regularly out and about running through woods and fields, it is important to stick to a regular worming schedule, as he is more likely to pick up worms than one who spends more time indoors.

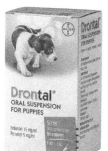 Fleas can pass on tapeworms to dogs, but a puppy would not normally be treated unless it is known for certain he has fleas - and then only with caution. You need to know the weight of your puppy and then speak to your vet about the safest treatment to get rid of these parasites.

NOTE: Buy age-appropriate worming treatments.

Breeders must worm their puppies. However, there are ways to reduce worming treatments for adult dogs.

Following anecdotal reports of some dogs experiencing side effects with chemical wormers, more owners are looking to use natural wormers on their dogs. If you go down this route, check exactly which worms your chosen herbal preparation deals with – it may not be all of them.

A method of reducing worming medication by testing your dog's stools is becoming more popular. You send a small sample of your dog's poo(p) in an envelope every two to three months. If the result is positive, your dog needs worming, but no treatment is necessary if negative.

In the UK this is done by veterinary labs like Wormcount www.wormcount.com and similar options are available in the USA – there is even a *"fecal worm test"* available at just over $20 from Amazon.com.

7. Crate and Housetraining

Crates are becoming more popular year after year. Used correctly, they speed up housetraining (potty training), give you and your puppy short breaks from each other and keep him safe at night or when you are out.

Some owners also crate their adult Schnauzers for short periods, although most breeders involved in this book only use crates for puppies and young dogs. Trainers, behaviourists and people who show, compete or train dogs all use crates.

....

Using A Crate

A crate should always be used humanely. If you decide to use one, spend time getting your puppy or adult dog used to it, so he comes to regard the crate as his own safe haven and not a punishment cell or prison.

Crates may not be suitable for every dog - or owner. Dogs are social animals; they thrive on interaction. Being caged for long periods is a miserable existence for any dog, but particularly for people-loving breeds like Miniature Schnauzer.

However, they are very useful for puppies and can help speed up housetraining. We prefer a wire crate that allows air to pass through.

Andrew Ray, who has bred Schnauzers for over 30 years, says: "We encourage all new pet owners to crate train their new pup for safety reasons, but are strongly against dogs being kept in cages for any length of time."

Mini Schnauzers thrive on being with their humans. A crate should NEVER be used as a means of confinement while you are out of the house for six, eight or more hours every day.

 Before leaving your dog unattended in a crate, always remove his collar - dogs will panic if their collars get caught - and make sure he has fresh water during the day.

Non-spill water bowls are available from pet shops and online, as are bowls to attach to the bars.

Crates are ideal for giving you or the puppy some downtime. You cannot watch a puppy 24/7; a crate is a safe place for him while you do other things. Schnauzer puppies need LOTS OF SLEEP - but they don't know this, so a crate (or puppy pen) is an excellent place for resting without distractions.

Your puppy first has to get used to the crate so he looks forward to going in there - some breeders may have already started the process.

NOTE: An eight-week-old puppy should not be in a crate for longer than two hours at a time during the day.

Not every owner wishes to use a crate, but used correctly they:

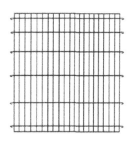

- ❧ Are a useful housetraining tool
- ❧ Create a canine den
- ❧ Give you a break
- ❧ Limit access to the rest of the house until potty trained
- ❧ Are a safe place for the dog to nap or sleep at night
- ❧ Provide a safe way to transport your dog in a car

Another very good reason to crate train is that if your dog has to visit the vet or be confined for an illness, he will not have the added stress of getting used to a crate. Confining a Miniature Schnauzer NOT used to a crate is very stressful for both dog and owner.

What Size Crate and Where?

Crate size will vary according to the size of your Miniature Schnauzer - even within the breed there is variation, with males generally being bigger than females, and some Schnauzers are naturally stockier than others, depending on bloodlines.

A broad recommendation for average-sized Minis is a 30" to 36" crate, which should give them room to stand up, turn around and stretch out to sleep, as well as space for a small water bowl. If you're in the US, Midwest Crates get good reviews for their crates and pens.

If you're only intending to buy one crate, it will be too big for your pup, which can slow down housetraining. You can buy a crate divider *(pictured above)* or make a sturdy panel to block off part of the crate while the pup is growing (don't use anything chewable). A smaller area also helps him to feel more secure.

 Partially covering the crate with an old blanket creates a den for your new puppy at night. Only cover on three sides - leave the front uncovered and a gap around the bottom on all sides for air to flow. You can also just cover half or part of the crate to make it cosier for the pup.

Place the crate in the kitchen or another room where there are people during the day, preferably one with a hard, easy-to-clean floor. Puppies are curious pack animals and like to see and smell what is going on. If you have children, strike the balance between putting the crate in a place where the pup won't feel isolated, yet allowing him some peace and quiet away from the kids.

Avoid putting the crate behind a closed door away from everybody, or he will feel lonely and sad. If you are using a room off the kitchen, allow the pup free run of the room and use a pet gate or baby gate with narrowly-spaced bars so his head can't get stuck but he can still see what's going on.

If you've got the space, a playpen is great to use in addition – or as an alternative – to a crate.

The chosen location should be draught-free, not too hot and not in bright sunshine.

Opinions vary, but some owners put the crate right next to the bed for the first night or two - even raised next to the bed - to help the puppy settle in quicker. Some even sleep downstairs on the sofa or an air mattress next to the crate for the first couple of nights. Others believe in putting the crate in its permanent place from day one.

Put the following items inside the crate during the day:

* Bedding – Vet Bed (pictured) or other bedding your puppy won't destroy in a few days

* A blanket or item that has been rubbed with the mother's scent

* A non-spill water bowl

* A healthy chew to stop him from gnawing the crate and bedding

* Possibly a toy to keep him occupied

Tip The washable *'Vet Bed'* is a good choice. Made from double-strength polyester, it retains extra heat, allows air to flow through and is widely used in vets' clinics to make dogs feel warm and secure.

It also has drainage properties, so your pup will stay dry if he has an accident. Vet Beds are also a good option for older dogs, as the added heat is soothing for aging muscles and joints. You can buy "Vet Bedding" by the roll, which keeps costs down. One breeder added: "Don't use beds with stuffing at this age, as once they learn to de-stuff a bed, it may become a lifelong habit and possibly graduate into de-stuffing furniture or pillows later!"

At night, remove the water and chew. Add an extra blanket if you think he might get cold overnight; he has been used to the warmth of his littermates and mother.

Whining

If your puppy is whining, whimpering or howling in the crate, make sure:

A. **He doesn't need the toilet.**

B. **He is warm.**

C. **He is physically unharmed.**

If none is the case, then the reason is that he doesn't want to be left alone. He has come from the warmth and security of his mother and litter, and the Brave New World can be a very daunting place for an eight-week-old puppy all alone in a new home.

He is not crying because he is in a cage. He would cry if he had the freedom of the room - he is crying because he is separated. Dogs are pack animals and being alone is not a natural state for them. With patience and training, he will get used to being alone and being in the crate. Some owners make the crate their dog's only bed, so he feels comfortable and safe in there.

If the breeder has done lots of socialisation and crate training, your puppy should settle in quickly. If he is nervous, here are some tips to help him settle in a crate:

* **Leave a ticking clock next to the crate,** or

* **A Snuggle Puppy,** *pictured,* **or other dog toy with a heartbeat. If you think he might destroy it, remove it when you're not there.** Contributing owner Yolande used a furry puppy toy with a heartbeat and her pup Mayzy settled in very well

* **Leave a radio on softly nearby** ...make sure it's not tuned to a heavy metal music station or news channel reporting from a war zone!

* **Lightly spray DAP on a cloth or small towel and place it in the crate**

 DAP, or Dog Appeasing Pheromone, is a synthetic form of the pheromone that nursing females give off after giving birth, and then again after weaning, to reassure their puppies that everything is fine.

DAP has been found to help reduce fear in young puppies, as well as Separation Anxiety, phobias and aggression caused by anxiety in adult dogs. According to one French study: "DAP has no toxicities or side effects and is particularly beneficial for sick and geriatric dogs." Google *"Canadian Veterinary Journal Dog Appeasing Pheromone"* for more details about the study.

 The ADAPTIL Junior collar, *pictured,* with slow-release DAP, is designed to reduce fear in anxious puppies. There's also an Adaptil Calming collar for adult dogs, which gets good reports from many, not all, owners.

Travel Crates and Harnesses

Special travel crates, *pictured,* are useful for the car, or for taking your dog to the vet's, a show or on holiday. Choose one with holes or mesh in the side to allow free movement of air rather than a solid one, in which a dog can soon overheat. Your normal size crate may be too big for travelling, unless you block off part of it.

Put the crate on the shady side of the interior and make sure it can't move around; put the seatbelt around it. If it's very sunny and the top of the crate is wire mesh, cover part of it so your dog has some shade and put the windows up and the air conditioning on.

If you have more than one dog, another option is to buy a metal grille/dog guard to keep your dogs confined to the back of the car. Some use a *Ventlock* on the car boot/trunk to keep it open slightly, allowing air to flow.

Dogs can also be safely transported using a seat belt harness, *pictured.* Make sure it's the right size and fitted properly.

Allowing your dog to roam freely inside the car is against the law and not safe, particularly if you - like me - are a bit of a "lead foot" on the brake and accelerator!

And try to avoid letting your Schnauzer ride with his head out of the window - even if he does look like Easy Rider! Wind pressure can cause ear infections or bits of dust, insects, etc. to fly into unprotected eyes. Your dog will also fly forward if you suddenly hit the brakes.

 Schnauzers have double coats. Don't leave yours unattended in a vehicle for more than a few minutes; they can overheat alarmingly quickly.

How To Crate Train

Many breeders will have already started the process but, if not, here's a tried-and-tested method of getting your dog firstly to accept a crate, as recommended by Miniature Schnauzer owner and Mary E. Falls, of Classic Giant Schnauzers of Easentaigh, Wisconsin. Mary has over 40 years' experience with Mini Schnauzers.

Phase One

1. **Bring them over to the crate and talk to them in a happy tone of voice.** Make sure the crate door is open and secured so that it won't hit your dog and frighten them.

2. **Drop a few puppy treats around and then inside the crate.**

3. **Put their favourite toy in there**, and keep the door open.

4. If they refuse to go all the way in at first, **don't force them to enter. Be patient.**

5. **Continue tossing treats into the crate** until your dog will walk calmly all the way into the crate to get the food.

6. If not interested in treats, **toss a favourite toy in the crate.** This step may take a few minutes or as long as several days.

 Place a chew or treat INSIDE the crate and close the door while they are OUTSIDE the crate. They will be desperate to get in! Open the door, let them in and praise them for going in - keep the door open

Phase Two

1. **Feed meals inside the crate.** Again, keep the door open.

2. If they are readily entering the crate to eat, **place the food dish or interactive puzzle toy stuffed with food all the way at the back of the crate.**

3. If they remain reluctant to enter, **put the dish only as far inside as they will readily go** without becoming fearful or anxious. Each time you feed, place the dish a little further back in the crate.

4. Once they are standing comfortably in the crate to eat their meal, **close the door while they're eating.** The first time you do this, open the door as soon as they finish the meal.

5. With each successive feeding, **leave the door closed a few minutes longer** until they stay in the crate for 10 minutes after eating.

6. **If they begin to whine to be let out, you may have increased the length of time too quickly.** Next time, try leaving them in the crate for a shorter period.

Phase Three

Practise with longer crating periods. After your dog is eating regular meals in the crate with no sign of fear or anxiety, you can confine them there for short periods while you're home.

1. **Call them over to the crate and give them a treat.**

2. **Give them a voice cue to enter, such as "crate."** Encourage them by pointing to the inside of the crate with a treat in your hand.

3. **After they enter the crate, praise them,** give them the treat and close the door.

4. **Sit quietly near the crate for five to 10 minutes** and then go into another room for a few minutes. Return, sit quietly again for a short time and then let them out.

5. **Repeat this process several times a day,** gradually increasing the length of time you leave them in the crate and the length of time you're out of sight.

6. **Once your dog will stay quietly in the crate for about 30 minutes with you mostly out of sight,** you can begin leaving them crated when you're gone for short periods and/or letting them sleep there at night. This may take several days or weeks.

Phase Four - Daytime

After your dog can spend about 30 minutes in the crate without becoming anxious or afraid, you can begin leaving them crated for short periods when you leave the house.

1. **Put them in the crate using your regular command and a treat.** You might also want to leave them with a few safe toys in the crate.

2. **Vary the moment during your "getting ready to leave" routine** that you put your dog in the crate. Although they shouldn't be crated for a long time before you leave, you can crate them anywhere from five to 20 minutes before leaving.

3. **Don't make your departures emotional and prolonged** - they should be matter-of-fact. Praise your dog briefly, give them a treat for entering the crate and then leave quietly.

4. **Put your dog in his crate at regular intervals during the day - maximum two hours.** Use it as a *"sleep zone"* or *"safe zone."*

   By using the crate both when you are home and while you are gone, your dog becomes comfortable there and is not worried that you won't come back, or that you are leaving him alone. This helps to prevent Separation Anxiety.

 If your pup is not yet housetrained, make sure he has relieved himself BEFORE you put him in the crate. Putting him in when he needs to eliminate will slow down training.

Phase Four – Night-Time

Initially, it may be a good idea to put the crate in your bedroom or nearby in a hallway, especially if you have a puppy. Puppies often need to go outside to eliminate during the night and you'll want to be able to hear your puppy when they whine to be let outside. Older dogs should also initially be kept nearby so they don't associate the crate with social isolation.

Once your dog is sleeping comfortably through the night with the crate near you, you can begin to gradually move it to the location you prefer, although time spent with your dog - even sleep time - is a chance to strengthen the bond between you and your pet.

Further Tips

1. **If you are leaving your dog unattended in a crate,** give him a chew and remove his collar, tags and anything else that could become caught in an opening or between the bars.

2. **Make it very clear to any children that the crate is NOT a den for them,** but a *"special room"* for the dog.

3. **Although the crate is your dog's haven and safe place, it must not be off-limits to humans.** You should be able to reach inside at any time.

4. **The crate should ALWAYS be associated with a positive experience in your dog's mind.**

5. **Try and wait until your dog is calm before putting him in the crate.** If he is behaving badly and you grab him and shove him in the crate straight away, he will associate the crate with punishment. Try not to use the crate if you can't calm him down, instead either leave the room or put the dog in another room until he calms down.

6. **Don't let your dog out of the crate when he is barking or whining**, or he'll think that this is the key to opening the door. Wait until he has stopped whining for at least 10 or 20 seconds before letting him out.

    ✓ During the day the crate door should not be closed until your pup is happy with being inside.

    ✓ At night-time it is OK to close the door.

    ✓ If you don't want to use a crate, use a pet gate, section off an area inside one room, or use a puppy pen to confine your pup at night.

Housetraining

You have five major factors in your favour when it comes to toilet training a Miniature Schnauzer:

1. **They are intelligent.**

2. **They learn very quickly.**

3. **They respond well to rewards - treats, praise, toys or games.**

4. **They are very eager to please you.**

5. **They love showing off!**

Puppies naturally want to keep their space clean; it's instinctive. From when he can first walk, a pup will move away from his mother and sleeping area to eliminate.

The aim of housetraining is to teach the puppy exactly WHERE this space starts and finishes.

When a puppy arrives at your home, he may think that a corner of the crate, the kitchen, your favourite rug or anywhere else in the house is a good place for him to pee or poop.

Through housetraining, you teach him that the house is his and your "space" and therefore not OK for him to mess it up.

 The speed and success of housetraining depend to a degree on the individual dog and how much effort the breeder has already put in. However, the single most important factor in success is undoubtedly YOU.

The more vigilant you are during the early days, the quicker your Mini will be housetrained. How much time and effort are you prepared to put in at the beginning to speed up housetraining? Taking the advice in this chapter and being consistent with your routines and repetitions is the quickest way to get results. Clear your schedule for a week or so and make housetraining your No.1 priority – it'll be worth it.

I get complaints from some American readers when I write: "Book a week or two off work and housetrain your dog!" I know Americans get much shorter vacation time than most Europeans, but honestly, if you can take a few days off work to monitor housetraining at the beginning, it will speed the process up no end.

If you're starting from scratch or if yours is a rescue Schnauzer who has arrived with some bad habits, then time, patience and vigilance will be needed.

Miniature Schnauzers, like all dogs, are creatures of routine - not only do they like the same things happening at the same times every day but establishing a regular routine with your dog also helps to speed up obedience and toilet training.

 **To keep things simple in a pup's mind, have a designated area in your garden or yard that the pup can use as a toilet. Dogs are tactile creatures, so they pick a toilet area that feels good under their paws.**

Dogs often like to go on grass - but this will do nothing to improve your lawn, so think carefully about what area to encourage your puppy to use.

Perhaps consider a small patch of crushed gravel in your garden - but don't let your puppy eat it - or a particular corner of the garden or yard away from any attractive or spiky plants.

Opinion is divided on puppy pads. Many breeders advise against using them as they can slow down potty training, and some say that newspapers can also encourage a pup to soil inside the house.

Because dogs are tactile and puppy pads are soft and comfy, dogs like going on them. When you remove the pads, the puppy may be tempted to find a similar surface, like a carpet or rug.

A general rule of thumb is that puppies can last for one hour per month of age without urinating. So:

- An eight-week pup can last for two hours
- A 12-week-old pup can last for three hours
- A 16-week pup can last for four hours
- A six-month-old can last for six hours

NOTE: If the breeder has started the housetraining process early, puppies can often last longer.

 **If a puppy is active or excited, he will urinate more often, and if he is pleased to see you, he may urinate with excitement.**

To speed up the process even more, consider setting your alarm clock to get up in the night to let the pup out to relieve himself for the first week. Don't switch the lights on or make a fuss of the pup, just take him outside. You might hate it, but it can shorten the overall time spent housetraining.

We didn't use a crate when we housetrained Max, but we did set the alarm and get up once in the night to let him into the garden for the first few nights, and we were vigilant during the day. Schnauzers are really smart dogs and he got the hang of it in no time. Max was housetrained in less than two weeks (with the help of lots of tiny treats). After that he only had a couple of 'accidents,' but that was our fault really; we should have taken him out sooner.

Housetraining Tips

...speed up housetraining:

...essential for the first week or two if you are to housetrain your ...dy is there, he will learn to pee or poop inside the house.

...e at the following times:

...he wakes – every time
...ter each feed
...rink
...e gets excited
...xercise or play
...ing at night
...ly every hour or two - whether or not he looks like he wants to go

...e above list is an exaggeration, but it isn't! Housetraining a pup is almost a full-...ining. If you are serious about toilet training your puppy quickly, then clear your diary ...two and keep your eyes firmly glued on your pup...learn to spot that expression or circling motion just before he makes a mess on your floor.

1. Take your pup to **the same place** every time, you may need to use a lead (leash) in the beginning - or tempt him there with a treat. Some say it is better to only pick him up and dump him there in an emergency, as it is better if he learns to take himself to the chosen toilet spot.

   Dogs naturally develop a preference for going in the same place or on the same surface. Take or lead him to the same patch every time so he learns this is his toilet area.

Photo: Max, aged eight weeks, getting distracted by a yoghurt pot during a wintry toilet trip to the garden.

2. **No pressure – be patient. Schnauzers do not perform well under pressure.** You must allow your distracted little darling time to wander around and have a good sniff before performing his duties – but do not leave him, stay around a short distance away. Unfortunately, Miniature Schnauzer puppies are not known for their powers of concentration, so it may take a while for them to select the perfect bathroom spot!

 Housetraining a Mini should ALWAYS be reward-based, never negative or aggressive. Give praise and/or a treat IMMEDIATELY after he has performed his duties in the chosen spot. Persistence, praise and rewards are best for quick results.

3. **Share the responsibility.** It doesn't have to be the same person who takes the dog outside all the time. In fact, it's easier if there are two of you, as this is a very time-demanding business. Just make sure you stick to the same principles, command and patch of ground.

4. **Stick to the same routine.** Sticking to the same times for meals, exercise, playtime, sleeping and toilet breaks will help settle him into his new home and housetrain him quicker.

5. **Use the same word** or command when telling your puppy to go to the toilet – or while he is in the act. He will gradually associate this phrase or word with toileting.

6. **Use your voice ONLY if you catch him in the act indoors.** A short sharp sound is best - **ACK! EH!** It doesn't matter, as long as it is loud enough to make him stop.

   Then either pick him up or run enthusiastically towards your door, calling him to the chosen place and wait until he has finished what he started indoors. Only use the ACK! sound if you actually catch him MID-ACT.

7. **No punishment, no scolding, no smacking or rubbing his nose in it.** Your Mini will hate it. He will become either stubborn or afraid to do the business in your presence, so may start going secretly behind the couch or under the bed.

   Accidents will happen. He is a baby with a tiny bladder and bowels and little self-control. Housetraining takes time - remain calm, ignore him (unless you catch him in the act) and clean up the mess.

 Mini Schnauzers have a keen sense of smell. If there's an "accident" indoors, buy a special spray or use a hot washing powder solution to get rid of the smell, which discourages him from going there again.

8. **Look for the signs.** These may be:
   a. Whining
   b. Sniffing the floor in a determined manner
   c. Circling and looking for a place to go
   d. Walking uncomfortably - particularly at the rear end!

   Take him outside straight away, and try not to pick him up all the time. He has to learn to walk to the door himself when he needs to go outside.

9. **Use a crate at night-time.**

Schnauzers love being with you and young puppies certainly won't pee or poop outside on their own when it's pouring down. One breeder advises new owners to invest in a good umbrella and be prepared for lots of early mornings in the first few weeks!

Troubleshooting

Don't let one or two little accidents derail your potty training - accidents WILL happen! Here is a list of some possible scenarios and actions to take:

* **Puppy peed when your back was turned** - Don't let him out of his crate or living space unless you are prepared to watch his every move

* **Puppy peed or pooped in the crate** - Make sure the crate isn't too big; it should be just enough for him to stand up and turn around, or divided. Also, make sure he is not left in the crate for too long

* **Puppy pooped without warning** - Observe what he does immediately beforehand. That way, you'll be able to lead him outside next time before an accident happens

- **Puppy pees on the same indoor spot daily** - Make sure you get rid of the sm~~e''~~ and don't give your puppy too much indoor freedom too soon

- **Puppy not responding well** - Increase the value of your treats for h~~r~~ else. Give a tiny piece of meat, chicken etc. ONLY when your Sch~~ ~~ in the chosen spot

Some breeders use *"tethering"* where the puppy is fastened to the ~~ ~~ead indoors~~.~~ they can watch the puppy like a hawk and monitor his behaviour. It's a huge commitment, ~~b~~ only do this for a short time - a week or so - and it speeds up housetraining no end

Even after all your hard work, occasionally some dogs continue to eliminate indoors, often male~~s~~ even though they understand housetraining perfectly well. This is called "marking" and they do it t~~o~~ leave a scent and establish your home as their territory. This can take time to cure.

Apartments and Indoor Housetraining

Miniatures can be indoor housetrained. Access to outdoor space may not be so easy If you live in an apartment, so you may wish to consider indoor housetraining.

Most Minis can be trained with this method fairly easily, especially if you start early. Stick to the same principles already outlined, the only difference is that you will be placing your Schnauzer on puppy pads or newspaper instead of taking him outdoors.

Start by blocking off a section of the apartment for your pup. Use a baby gate or make your own barrier. You will be able to keep a better eye on him than if he has free run of the whole place, and it will be easier to monitor his "accidents."

Select a corner away from his eating and sleeping area that will become his permanent bathroom area — a carpeted area is to be avoided if at all possible.

At first, cover a larger area than is needed, about a meter square, or 3x3 to 4x4 feet, with puppy pads or newspapers and gradually reduce the area as training progresses.

Take your puppy there as indicated in the **Housetraining Tips** section.

Praise him enthusiastically when he eliminates on the puppy pad or newspaper. If you catch him doing his business out of the toilet area, pick him up and take him back there. Correct with a firm voice - never a hand. With positive reinforcement and close monitoring, he will learn to walk to the toilet area on his own.

FACT Owners attempting indoor housetraining should be aware that it generally takes longer than outdoor training. Some dogs will resist. Also, once a Mini learns to go indoors, it can be difficult to train them to go outdoors on their walks.

If you don't monitor your puppy carefully enough in the beginning, indoor housetraining will be difficult. The first week or two is crucial to your puppy learning what is expected of him.

Bell Training

Bell Training is a method that works well with some dogs. There are different types of bells, the simplest are inexpensive and widely available, consisting of a series of adjustable bells that hang on a nylon strap from the door handle.

Another option is a small metal bell attached to a metal hanger that fixes low down on the wall next to the door with two screws. As with all puppy training, do bell training in short bursts of five to 10 minutes or your easily distracted little student will switch off!

1. Show your dog the bell, either on the floor, in fact it is fixed anywhere, or by holding it up. Point to it and give the command *"Touch," "Ring,"* or whatever word you decide.

2. Every time he touches it with his nose, reward him with praise.

3. When he rings the bell with his nose, give him a treat. You can rub something tasty on the bell, like peanut butter, to make it more interesting.

4. Take the bell away between practice sessions.

5. Once he rings the bell every time you show it to him, move on to the next step.

6. Take the bell to the door you use for housetraining. Place a treat just outside the door while he is watching. Then close the door, point to the bell and give the command.

7. When he rings the bell, open the door and let him get the treat outside.

8. When he gets to the stage of ringing the bell as soon as you place a treat outside, fix the bell to the door or wall.

9. The next time you think he needs to relieve himself, walk to the door, point to the bell and give the command. Give him a treat or praise if he rings it, let him out and reward him again with enthusiastic praise when he performs his duty.

 In between training sessions, ring the bell yourself EVERY time you open the door to let him outside.

Some Minis can get carried away by their own success and ring the bell any time they want your attention, fancy a wander outdoors or see a passing squirrel!

Make sure that you ring the bell every time your puppy goes out through the door to relieve himself, but DON'T ring the bell if he is going out to play. And if he starts playing or dawdling around the garden or yard, bring him in!

....

Advice from Breeders

Here are some views from people who have spent decades with Schnauzers, starting with three Kennel Club Assured Breeders in England. Steve Matthews, Silbertraum Schnauzers, Dorset: "Crate training is what I recommend to all new owners. Puppies don't generally like to toilet in their bed space - there will be a few 'accidents' over the first few weeks, but this is all part of puppy ownership.

"Start the puppy in a crate (their own safe space). Don't let them sleep on your bed unless you plan to continue this for the rest of their lives. Put them out last thing at night and first thing in the morning and praise them when they toilet outside.

"I never recommend puppy pads as they tend to think that it's just another plaything to drag around.

"It should only take a couple of weeks to get the hang of it, and it's much easier if there is already an older dog present, as the puppy will copy the older dog."

Photo of this handsome, lively litter with their white Miniature Schnauzer mother courtesy of Steve.

 White Minis are accepted by the UK Kennel Club. And white Mini mothers do not always have white puppies; it depends on genetics, as you can see from this photo.

Andrew Ray, Minnienoom Schnauzers, Derbyshire: "We start housetraining from four weeks of age when we move the puppies from whelping box to puppy run. We place newspaper or puppy pads for toilet training just away from the puppy bed; at this age puppies want the toilet as soon as they start to move from their beds. By the time the puppies are six to eight weeks of age, the pads have been moved further away and out of the door.

"I try and enter the puppy run at least hourly and will call the puppies to me as I do. This is the start of Recall and it's lovely to see several puppies following you like the 'Pied Piper!' Praise is given to every puppy that manages to get out the door into the garden for the toilet."

Andrew has this advice: "Puppies have very poor bladder control and need to urinate frequently, so take them out every one to two hours initially, after a sleep or meal. He'll also need to be taken out after playing or any excitement, first thing in the morning and last thing at night.

"Take him outside, stay with him and when he begins, say a chosen phrase then praise him enthusiastically. Use different words for urination and defecation. Be patient, there are many distractions outside. At night, place newspaper on the floor as he will not be able to go through without wanting the toilet.

"Ignore any housetraining accidents you find, but clean the area with an odour eliminator or biological powder. However, if you catch him in the act, shout to stop him mid-flow - but not too loud so he runs for cover. Then go towards the back door encouraging him to follow and go outside.

"Wait until he has relaxed and finishes what he started earlier. Say your chosen phrase and praise him. DO NOT punish or get angry. The distress your puppy feels will inhibit the learning process and he could start sneaking off to go to the toilet.

"During the times in the day when you cannot watch your puppy, confine him to an area like a playpen where any accidents can be cleaned up easily. Be patient - some puppies take longer than others to learn."

"On crates Andrew says: "I personally do not think a dog requires long periods in a crate. If one is to be used, set it up as an indoor kennel somewhere safe and quiet in your home. Puppy pads or old newspaper can be placed away from crate and feeding area for puppy to use as a toilet if required, for example at night.

"Over the years I've discovered that if you keep going to your new puppy throughout the night when he cries or barks to get your attention, the process of puppy getting used to being left alone takes far longer.

"However, not all puppies settle and a few can get themselves into such a state that intervention is inevitable. As a last resort, I would recommend that one person either sleeps alongside the puppy crate or, as a very last option, take the puppy in the crate to your bedroom for a couple of nights.

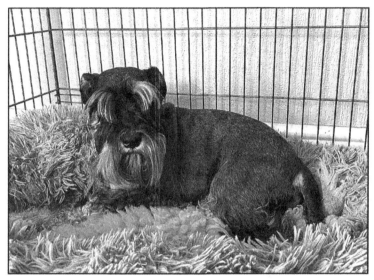

"I remember a lady once calling for advice. She had a Miniature Schnauzer that became 'a monster' during the night. She wasn't able to get any sleep for several nights, which was taking a toll on her health.

"When I asked what the puppy was doing at the time of her call (late morning) she said it was fast asleep on her lap!

"My advice was to place the pup in its own bed and get some sleep herself. Her tiredness and giving in to her new puppy were placing her in a situation where she'd probably make herself ill. (I'd just like to add the puppy was not one of ours and no advice was given from the breeder she obtained the puppy from)."

Photo: Andrew's two-year-old Reggie (Valentino Silver Grand Calvera At Minnienoom) relaxing in his crate.

Now for the USS, starting with Wade Bogart, AKC Breed Mentor and breeder of Sumerwynd Miniature Schnauzers, New York State, since 1979: "My puppies are housebroken prior to going to their new homes.

"One tip I could offer is to take them to the exact same spot every time, do so frequently and offer praise generously when the deed is done. It takes only a very few days for pups to pick up housetraining in the new environment.

"Crates are great and I feel puppies should be crated when not being supervised by an adult. Miniature Schnauzers have good hygiene and usually don't soil their beds.

"Crates can also be used as a time-out to modify negative behaviour. I believe puppies should sleep in their crates from Day One. Miniature Schnauzers are good housekeepers and they will alert their owner if a potty trip is necessary."

Dr Lisa Sarvas DVM BSA, veterinarian and breeder of Beauideal Schnauzers, North Carolina, since 1987, says: "By the time they are in their new homes, our puppies may be sleeping six or seven hours at night.

"However, if they wake up and are restless or whining, then they may need to go outside to potty. Plan to take your puppy to the same place outside each time you take them out. Stay quiet and let them focus on their business. Praise them consistently for pottying outside."

She added: "I've found that the key to successful housetraining is to stay consistent for the first 30 days. At first, you will be trained - and then so will your puppy! Dogs may need to do something 100 times in order to display the learned behavior consistently.

"This means about 30 days of you being consistent with their potty schedule and preventing any accidents in the house. Kennel (crate) your puppy when you are unable to watch them closely; it will keep them safe as well as prevent potty accidents in the house."

Dr Sarvas added this on how long a puppy should be in a crate: "My rule of thumb is the number of months old the puppy is, plus one, is equal to the number of hours they will typically be OK in a kennel (crate).

"So, a two-month-old puppy may be OK for three hours in a crate. At three months old, they should be able to be left for four hours. By five months old they may be OK for a full six hours."

Photo of this lovely litter of blacks and salt and peppers, courtesy of Lisa.

I should add here that there is a cultural difference between the USA and the UK. Crates are more widely used and for longer periods in the US, compared with Europe. In the UK, for example, the general rule is never to leave a dog in a crate for longer than four hours - regardless of age.

Confining a puppy in a crate for six hours would not be acceptable to most British breeders or owners, who often use crates in puppyhood and then stop using them - except if the dog sleeps there, usually with the door open. We prefer our dogs to have the run of the house - or at least a room - here in the UK.

What the Owners Say

UK

Chris Lee: "Betsy's crate is her sleeping accommodation now and she sleeps all through the night, every night. She will wake to have a drink of water, but settles down right away after that.

"In terms of housetraining, she had a few accidents with poos over the first few weeks, but then preferred the garden as her place of relief. Her weeing took a bit longer and she found places that were not obvious to do it.

"My advice here is not to tell the pup off as she will quickly adapt to what is needed - provided, of course, she has an outside space and/or plenty of walks. The latter was not on the agenda until she was fully vaccinated."

Leah Dummer: "We have three Minis but do not use a crate. It took a few weeks to housetrain our two puppies Lily and Leelo. If the older dog Freddie went outside, the puppies would follow him. Because I was on maternity leave and in the house, I would open the back door every 30 minutes and say 'wee wees' to try to encourage them to go outside. I followed them outside and when they did do their business, I gave them lots of praise."

Gary Blain: "I tried to use a crate for Jamie, but failed miserably as he cried and I'm too soft-hearted. My dogs are part of my family and are treated so. It might not necessarily be the right thing to do, but it's how I am.

"Jamie was very good with housetraining, it took about a month to six weeks maximum before he was clean indoors, Evie was even quicker - within a couple of weeks - as she had Jamie to follow.

"My top tips are to have plenty of puppy training pads set on the floor in one area. Make sure after eating and drinking you put your puppy outside to allow them to learn to go to the toilet. Use a happy tone of voice to encourage them to do their business, and praise them when they have done it.

"Persevere, don't get angry when they have an accident indoors; you don't want to frighten them."

Photo: Jamie (front) and Evie managing to relax perfectly well without a crate, courtesy of Gary.

Yolande: "Apart from the night sleeping crate, I have a playpen in the kitchen with a day bed with a canopy over the bed end to create shade. It also has Mayzy's toys in it and a bowl of water.

"This was a safe space for her when I was away from the room and Mayzy was shut in as a puppy whenever I was elsewhere in the house or people called at the door. The day pen is still used today and is a convenient place to store her toys and for a nap, but the door is always open.

"Mayzy was brought up with her siblings to relieve herself on the kitchen floor, a habit which took me a month to break! I kept her in the kitchen during the day, where I am most often. This was also the best place for the inevitable 'accidents' to be cleared up. I tried the puppy mats for her to pee on, but she ignored them.

"She was dry at night straight away, mainly because I got up very early in the morning to take her out. I took her onto the grass frequently and gave the command 'quickie' for a pee or 'hurry up' for the other and reinforced with praise when she performed.

"These phrases were co-opted from Barbara Woodhouse's (a famous British trainer) dog training and work for me and my previous dogs. Mayzy knows these commands and responds to them when we are out for our lead walk in the morning or last thing at night."

USA

Simon and Yvonne Sonsino: "We use a crate with our puppy, Wilf. His naps during the day can be anything from 30 minutes to two hours - he needs a lot of sleep. When we can see he's getting a bit over-excited and 'nippy,' we'll take him out for a wee and then put him in for a nap, even if he doesn't want to go.

"He's learned that crying doesn't get him out, so goes down very quickly. We don't bother with a crate for our older Mini, Bu, who has free access to all areas.

"We were lucky with Bu's housetraining as one of us was always at home, so could work regularly with him. Wilf's is still ongoing, but again we're able to be here all the time. The important things are consistency and repetition and being aware of the pup at all times.

"Even if you're not interacting with him, you need to know where he is and what he's doing so you can gauge his needs. If there are accidents, it's not his fault."

Rebecca Makdad: "I brought Navy home mid-May when the weather was perfect for potty training. I would allow Rosie (then eight years old) to potty first and then take Navy to the same spot...success! And, as always, reward and praise. I never used pee pads or newspaper."

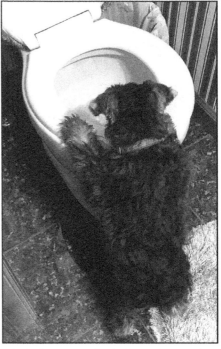

Photo: Three-month-old Navy getting to grips with potty training! Courtesy of Rebecca.

She added: "As for crates, I view crate training almost as important as potty training. It is not cruel or punishment to crate train a dog; think of it as a den or doggie hotel.

"Actually, you are protecting your Mini - when a puppy is crated, you know where it is. It cannot run away, destroy anything more than the items in the crate, or harm itself by eating something it should not. Like training, if kept fun and made a game, the dog will find the crate a place to relax. The crate should never be used as punishment.

"Most Mini Schnauzers will likely be required to be crated many times in their life. I travel with my girls, Rosie and Navy, and when we stay with family and friends, I travel with crates. Groomers briefly crate their four-legged clients, as well as the veterinarian, especially if the Mini requires surgery - and of course at most canine events. My girls are frequently crated, as we participate in companion canine sports. Part of the Agility Foundation course was the proper use and training of a crate."

Chloe Dong and Jacky Zou: "For the first few nights, Oslo slept on a dog bed in a medium-sized playpen that we had on hand for another pet (a hedgehog). He progressed to sleeping in a crate a few weeks later. By the end of the second month with us, Oslo was sleeping on our bed almost every night.

"We bought a crate and use it sparingly - approximately two to three hours at most. He is vocal when bored (and we live in an apartment in the city), so we puppy-proof our room and let him roam freely when we're not home.

"When starting off with a crate, it's best accompanied with treats and a verbal command. Time in the crate should start with just a few minutes with the door open. Slowly test boundaries by closing the door and keeping the puppy inside for longer periods. If the puppy is vocal and cries, it's best to wait until they're quieter before returning to take them out.

"The owner should try their best not to use the crate as a form of punishment, instead establishing it as the dog's personal space for when they need to decompress."

"Housetraining took approximately two months. Besides a couple of accidents due to a case of giardia and prolonged absences on our end, we were able to quickly learn how often Oslo needed to go and established a routine.

"One of the main tips we took from our breeder was "When you first get your puppy, they decide your schedule. You get your turn later on." Therefore, if our puppy whined and woke us up at 6am, it meant taking him outside to relieve himself without question. After he got used to only going outside to pee/poop, we began to slowly edge the times towards our preferences."

Vivian Williams: "We use a crate each day for Bogart to eat or sleep in and then we close the door. That is to provide security and prevent midnight strolls through the house. We've had friends whose dog had diarrhea throughout their house...walls, floors, carpets, sofa and so on. What a mess! Talk about a bad day on poop patrol!

"With every dog we've owned, we've followed our veterinarian's recommendation about limiting time in a crate to the pup's age in months plus one to calculate the number of hours a pup could be left in a crate.

"If we are away, we make arrangements for our dogs to be let out. If we are at home and awake, our dogs are not crated. No matter their age, we limit the areas of the home where our dogs can roam for their safety - and our sanity...

"Bogart is not spoiled - despite owning a padded mat in his crate, a MyPillow dog bed in the great room, and a thick orthopedic bed in the kitchen. He also has a choice of chairs, a sofa, or a comfortable lap!"

Photo: Bogart and Rabies chilling out at home, courtesy of Vivian. (Her previous dogs were called Mange and Parvo!)

Vivian added: "Bogart was fully and reliably housetrained within a couple of weeks. Again, he came to us fully crate-trained and nearly housetrained. He is bright and eager to please.

"We keep Bogart and Rabies, our Standard Poodle, on a regular meal-time and fresh-air schedule, which makes housetraining easier."

....

Opinions may vary on whether to carry the pup outside or whether it's important for him to walk there, and whether to use puppy pads or not.

However, breeders and owners all agree that if you're vigilant and pay very close attention to your puppy in the first few days or weeks, you'll speed up housetraining.

Schnauzers are intelligent and quickly get the hang of it once they know what's expected of them - especially when they get a reward.

Photo: "Spoiled, me? Never!" This Mini's dedicated owner has converted an old TV set into a luxury dog bed - the Mini jumps in and out through the 'screen!'

....

8. Feeding a Mini

We are what we eat! The right nutrition helps to keep your dog in excellent working order throughout his or her life - it can even extend lifespan. As you'll read in the Holistic section of Chapter 14, a healthy gut is the foundation of good health.

Good nutrition and maintaining a healthy weight can also delay or lessen the effects of joint issues such as hip dysplasia and arthritis. Some Miniature Schnauzers have sensitive stomachs or skin issues; the right food can reduce or eliminate problems.

....

The topic of feeding can be something of a minefield; owners are bombarded with advertisements and numerous choices.

There is not one food that gives every single Schnauzer the strongest bones, the most energy, the healthiest coat, the best digestion, the least gas and the longest life.

You could feed a high-quality food to a group of Schnauzers and find that most of them thrive on it, some do not do so well, while a few might get an upset stomach or itchy skin.

The question is: *"Which food is best for MY Mini Schnauzer?"*

Puppies

Puppies get all their nutrients from their mother's milk and then are gradually weaned (put on to a different food by the breeder) from three or four weeks of age.

Some breeders feed their puppies a variety of foods to build up a tolerance, but most feed a single puppy food. Continue feeding the same food and at the same times as the breeder when you bring your puppy home. You can investigate other options later.

If you switch foods, do so gradually, as dogs' digestive systems work differently to ours and they cannot tolerate sudden changes in diet - although if you stick to the identical brand, you can change flavours in one go. These ratios are recommended by Doctors Foster & Smith Inc:

- 🐾 Days 1-3 add 25% of the new food
- 🐾 Days 4-6 add 50%
- 🐾 Days 7-9 add 75%
- 🐾 Day 10 feed 100% of the new food

Feed your puppy three or four times a day up to the age of 12-16 weeks. If at any time your puppy starts being sick, has loose stools or is constipated, slow the rate at which you are switching the food. Puppies soon dehydrate, so seek veterinary advice if vomiting or watery poop continues for more than a day.

If you live far away from the breeder, fill a large container with water from the breeder's house and mix it with your own water back home. Different types of water, e.g. moving from a soft to a hard water area or vice versa, can upset a sensitive pup's stomach.

Giving your puppy more or less food will not affect adult size, it will only affect the rate of growth.

 If fed too much or the diet is too rich, puppies can actually grow TOO quickly. Their bodies become larger quickly, but their skeletons don't have time to catch up.

Life Stages

There are three **Life Stages** to consider when feeding:

- 🐾 Puppy
- 🐾 Adult
- 🐾 **Senior**, also called **Veteran**

Some manufacturers also produce a Junior feed for adolescent dogs. Each represents a different physical stage of life. If you decide on a commercially-prepared food, choose one approved either for **Puppies** or for **All Life Stages**.

How long your dog stays on Puppy food will depend on the size of your Schnauzer. Big dogs usually switch to an Adult food earlier. Seek your breeder's advice on timing.

An **Adult** feed won't have enough protein, and the balance of calcium and other nutrients will not be right for a pup. Puppy food is very high in calories and nutritional supplements.

Some manufacturers offer foods specifically formulated for Minis, such as the Royal Canin Miniature Schnauzer Adult Dry Dog Food. They may be worth considering, but read the label first, they may be similar to general adult feeds.

NOTE: Feeding older Minis is covered in **Chapter 18. Caring for Seniors**

Reading Dog Food Labels

A NASA scientist would have a hard job understanding some manufacturers' labels, so it's no easy task for us lowly dog owners. Here are some things to look out for on the manufacturers' labels:

- 🐾 **The ingredients are listed by weight and the top one should always be the main content,** such as chicken or lamb. Don't pick one where grain is the first ingredient; it is a poor-quality feed. If your Schnauzer has a food allergy or intolerance to wheat, check whether a food is gluten-free; all wheat contains gluten

- 🐾 **Chicken meal (dehydrated chicken) has more protein than fresh chicken, which is 80% water.** The same goes for beef, fish and lamb. So, if any of these "meals" are No. 1 on the ingredient list, the food should contain enough protein

- 🐾 Anything labelled *"human-grade"* is of higher quality than normal dog food ingredients. E.g. Human-grade chicken includes the breast, thighs and other parts of the chicken suitable for human consumption. Human-grade chicken complies with United States Department of Agriculture (USDA) welfare standards

- Flavourings can make a food more appetising for your dog. **Choose a food with a specific flavouring,** like *"beef flavouring"* rather than a general *"meat flavouring,"* where the origins are not so clear

- **Find a food suitable for the Schnauzer breed and your dog's age and activity level.** Talk to your breeder or vet, or visit an online Schnauzer forum to ask other owners' advice

- **Natural is best.** Food labelled *'natural'* means that the ingredients have not been chemically altered, according to the FDA in the USA. However, there are no such guidelines governing foods labelled *'holistic'* – so check ingredients and how they have been prepared

- In the USA, dog food that meets American Feed Control Officials' (AAFCO) minimum nutrition requirements has a label that states: *"[food name] is formulated to meet the nutritional levels established by the AAFCO Dog Food Nutrient Profiles for [life stage(s)]"*

 If you live in the USA, we recommend looking for a food "as fed" to real pets in an AAFCO-defined feeding trial. The AAFCO label is the gold standard, and brands that do costly feeding trials indicate so on the package.

Dog food labelled *'supplemental'* isn't complete and balanced. Unless you have a specific, vet-approved need for it, it's not something you want to feed your dog long term.

The *Guaranteed Analysis* listed on a sack or tin legally guarantees:

- Minimum percentages of crude protein and crude fat, and

- Maximum percentages of crude fibre and moisture

GUARANTEED ANALYSIS	
Crude protein (min.)	28.00 %
Crude fat (min.)	12.00 %
Crude fiber (max.)	4.50 %
Moisture (max.)	11.00 %
Docosahexaenoic acid (DHA) (min.)	0.05 %
Calcium (min.)	1.20 %
Phosphorus (min.)	1.00 %
Omega-6 fatty acids* (min.)	2.20 %
Omega-3 fatty acids* (min.)	0.30 %
Glucosamine* (min.)	500 mg/kg
Chondroitin sulfate* (min.)	500 mg/kg
* Not recognized as an essential nutrient by the AAFCO Dog Food Nutrient Profiles.	

While it is a start, don't rely on it too much. One pet food manufacturer made a mock product with a guaranteed analysis of 10% protein, 6.5% fat, 2.4% fibre, and 68% moisture (similar to what's on some canned pet food labels) – the ingredients were old leather boots, used motor oil, crushed coal and water!

- **Protein** – found in meat and poultry, protein should be the first ingredient and is very important. It helps build muscle, repair tissue and contributes to healthy hair and skin

  According to the National Research Council, a growing puppy requires a diet that is about 29% protein (by weight). This should provide about 20-25% of his dietary calories. Adults need about 18% dietary protein. Too little protein results in underdevelopment and too much can lead to weight gain and increased stress on the kidneys and liver

- ❦ **Fats** – these are a concentrated form of energy that give your dog more than twice the amount of energy that carbohydrates and proteins do. Common fats include chicken or pork fat, cottonseed oil, vegetable oil, soybean oil, fish oil, safflower oil, and many more. They are highly digestible and are the first nutrients to be used by the body as energy. AAFCO recommends 8% fat for Schnauzer puppies and 5% for adults

- ❦ **Fibre** – found in vegetables and grains. It aids digestion and helps prevent anal glands from becoming impacted. The average dry dog food has 2.5%-4.5% crude fibre, but reduced-calorie feeds may be as high as 9%-10%

- ❦ **Carbohydrates** typically make up anywhere from 30%-70% of a dry dog food. They come mainly from plants and grains, and provide energy in the form of sugars

- ❦ **Vitamins and Minerals** – have a similar effect on dogs as humans. Glucosamine and chondroitin are good for joints

- ❦ **Omegas 3 and 6** – fatty acids that help to keep Schnauzers' skin and coat healthy. Also good for inflammation control, arthritic pain, heart and kidneys

Well-formulated dog foods have the right balance of protein, fat, carbohydrates, vitamins, minerals and fatty acids. If you're still not sure what's best, look at our breeders' comments and check out these websites: https://www.dogfoodadvisor.com run by Mike Sagman in the USA and www.allaboutdogfood.co.uk run by UK canine nutritionist David Jackson. (I have no affiliation with these websites).

....

How Much Food?

The right amount of food depends on several factors:

- ❦ Breed
- ❦ Gender
- ❦ Age
- ❦ Natural energy levels
- ❦ Metabolism
- ❦ Amount of daily exercise
- ❦ Health
- ❦ Environment
- ❦ Number of dogs in the house
- ❦ Quality of the food
- ❦ Whether your Mini is taking part in Agility or other active events

Dogs that have been spayed may be more likely to put on weight, and growing puppies and young dogs need more food than senior dogs with a slower lifestyle. Maintaining a healthy body weight for dogs – and humans – is all about balancing calories taken in with calories burned.

Certain health conditions, e.g. underactive thyroid, diabetes, arthritis or heart disease, can lead to dogs putting on weight, so their food has to be adjusted accordingly. And just like us, a dog kept in a very cold environment will need more calories to keep warm than a dog in a warm climate, as he burns extra calories in keeping warm.

 **FACT** > A dog kept on his own is more likely to be overweight than a dog kept with other dogs, as he receives all of the food-based attention.

Manufacturers of cheap foods may recommend feeding more than necessary, as a major ingredient is cereal, which is not doing much except bulking up the weight of the food – and possibly triggering allergies. The daily recommended amount listed on dog food sacks or tins can be too high – after all, the more your dog eats, the more they sell!

Canine Calorie Counter

This is an AVERAGE. If you can't get your dog to lose or put weight on, seek veterinary advice.

If your dog is overweight, start by targeting the highest acceptable weight of his breed class. On the other hand, if your Schnauzer is underweight, target the lowest acceptable weight of his breed class. Then gradually work toward the middle of the range, bearing in mind your dog's natural energy levels and amount of exercise.

BREED	WEIGHT	ENERGY
Miniature	10 lb / 4.5 Kg	341 - 411 Kcal
Schnauzer	15 lb / 6.8 Kg	463 - 556 Kcal
5 – 9 kg	20 lb / 9.0 Kg	575 - 690 Kcal
	25 lbs / 11.3 Kg	680 - 816 Kcal
Standard	30 lbs / 13.6 Kg	779 - 935 Kcal
Schnauzer	35 lbs / 15.8 Kg	875 - 1050 Kcal
20 – 27 kg	40 lbs / 18.1 Kg	965 - 1158 Kcal
	45 lbs / 20.4 Kg	1056 - 1267 Kcal
	50 lbs / 22.6 Kg	1143 - 1327 Kcal
	55 lbs / 24.9 Kg	1228 - 1437 Kcal
	60 lbs / 27.2 Kg	1310 - 1537 Kcal
	65 lbs / 29.5 Kg	1392 - 1670 Kcal
Giant	70 lbs / 31.7 Kg	1471 - 1766 Kcal
Schnauzer	75 lbs / 34.0 Kg	1549 - 1859 Kcal

36 – 50 kg	80 lbs / 36.27 Kg	1626 - 1951 Kcal
	85 lbs / 38.6 Kg	1701 - 2042 Kcal
	90 lbs / 40.8 Kg	1776 - 2132 Kcal
	95 lbs / 43.1 Kg	1850 - 2220 Kcal
	100 lbs / 45.3 Kg	1922 - 2307 Kcal
	110 lbs / 49.8 Kg	2065 - 2478 Kcal
	120 lbs / 54.4 Kg	2204 - 2645 Kcal

Feeding Options

Here are the main options explained:

Dry dog food - also called kibble, is a popular and relatively inexpensive way of providing a balanced diet. Millions of dogs thrive on kibble. It comes in a variety of flavours and with different ingredients to suit the different stages of a dog's life. Cheap kibble is often false economy with Schnauzers.

Canned food - dogs love the taste and it generally comes in a variety of flavours. Some owners feed kibble mixed with some canned food. These days there are hundreds of options, some are high quality; others not.

As with dry food, read the label closely. Generally, you get what you pay for and the origins of cheap canned dog food are often somewhat dubious. Some Schnauzers can suffer from stomach upsets with too much tinned or soft food. Uneaten canned food should be removed from your dog's bowl after a couple of hours to prevent bacteria. Open cans should be stored in the refrigerator and consumed within two days.

Home-Cooked - this can be a very good option for fussy eaters and some dogs with digestive issues or allergies. You'll know EXACTLY what your dog is eating, but a home-cooked diet can be time-consuming and expensive.

The downsides - as with a raw diet - are a) it's time-consuming and expensive, b) knowing if you're getting the balance right and c) sticking to it once you have started with the best of intentions - but your dog will love it and he won't be eating preservatives or fillers. Some high-end dog food companies now provide boxes of freshly-prepared meals with natural ingredients.

Dehydrated - this lightweight food is only minimally processed. It offers many of the benefits of raw feeding, including lots of nutrients, but with none of the mess or bacteria found in raw meats.

Gentle heating slowly cooks proteins and helps start the digestive process, making it easier on the digestive tract of older Schnauzers, or those with sensitive stomachs. Owners just add water and let it stand for a minute or two to reconstitute the meal.

Freeze-Dried - this is usually raw, fresh food that has been freeze-dried by frozen food manufacturers. It's a more convenient, hygienic and less messy option than raw, and handy if you're going on a trip. It contains healthy enzymes but no preservatives.

It is highly palatable and keeps for six months to a year. It says *"freeze-dried"* on the packet, but the process bumps up the cost and it is not available from every pet store – although it is widely available online. A good option for owners who can afford it.

Semi-Moist – semi-moist dog food is a relatively new type of dog food, about 60%-65% water, that's soft and chewy and doesn't have to be refrigerated. At its best, it is natural ingredients slow-baked to retain the goodness in vitamins and minerals. It may also be suitable for older dogs or those with dental issues, but some brands have a high salt and sugar content, check the label.

Semi-moist treats are shaped like pork chops, bacon *(pictured),* salamis, burgers, etc. They are the least nutritional of all dog foods, full of sugars, artificial flavourings and colourings, so avoid giving them regularly.

The Raw Diet

Opinions are divided on a raw diet. There is anecdotal evidence that some dogs thrive on it, particularly those with food intolerances or allergies, although scientific proof is lagging behind. Claims made by fans of the raw diet include:

- Reduced symptoms of - or less likelihood of - allergies, and less scratching
- Better skin and coats
- Easier weight management
- Improved digestion
- Less flatulence, and drier and less smelly stools, more like pellets
- Higher energy levels
- Can help fussy eaters
- Reduced risk of Bloat
- Fresher breath and improved dental health
- Overall improvement in general health and less disease
- Most dogs love a raw diet

Manufactured dog foods may contain artificial preservatives, grains and excessive protein and fillers – causing a reaction in some dogs. Dry, canned and other styles of processed food were mainly created as a means of convenience – for humans, not dogs!

 If your Mini is not doing well on kibble, has skin issues or loose poop, etc., consider a more natural diet. Raw is one option, but there are several others nowadays, as you've just read.

Some nutritionists believe there are inherent beneficial enzymes, vitamins, minerals and other qualities in meats, fruits, vegetables and grains in their natural, uncooked state.

However, critics of a raw diet say that the risks of nutritional imbalance, intestinal problems and food-borne illnesses caused by handling and feeding raw meat outweigh any benefits.

It is true that owners must pay strict attention to hygiene when preparing a raw diet and it may not be a suitable option if there are children in the household. The dog may also be more likely to ingest bacteria or parasites such as Salmonella, E. Coli and Echinococcus - although freeze-dried meals reduce the risk.

 Raw is not for every dog; it can cause loose stools, upset stomach and even vomiting in some, and other dogs simply don't like the taste.

There are two main types of raw diet, one involves feeding raw, meaty bones and the other is known as the BARF diet (*Biologically Appropriate Raw Food* or *Bones And Raw Food)*, created by Dr Ian Billinghurst.

Raw Meaty Bones

The diet is:

- ❧ Raw meaty bones or carcasses form the bulk of the diet. **Cooked bones should NOT be fed, as they can splinter**

- ❧ Table scraps both cooked and raw, such as vegetables

Australian veterinarian Dr Tom Lonsdale is a leading proponent of the raw meaty bones diet. He believes the following foods are suitable:

- ❧ Chicken and turkey carcasses, after the meat has been removed for human consumption

- ❧ Poultry by-products, including heads, feet, necks and wings

- ❧ Whole fish and fish heads

- ❧ Sheep, calf, goat, and deer carcasses sawn into large pieces of meat and bone

- ❧ Other by-products, e.g. pigs' trotters, pigs' heads, sheep heads, brisket, tail and rib bones

- ❧ A certain amount of offal can be included in the diet, e.g. liver, lungs, trachea, hearts, tripe

- ❧ Table scraps and some fruit and vegetable peelings, but should not make up more than one-third of the diet

Low-fat game animals, fish and poultry are the best sources of food. If you feed meat from farm animals (cattle, sheep and pigs), avoid excessive fat and bones too large to be eaten. It depends on price and what's available locally - start with your local butcher or farm shop.

 **Dogs are more likely to break their teeth eating large knuckle bones and bones sawn lengthwise than when eating meat and bone together.**

You'll also need to think about WHERE and WHEN you are going to feed. A dog takes some time to eat a raw bone and will push it around the floor, so the kitchen may not be the most hygienic place. Outside is one option, but what do you do when it's raining? If you live in a hot climate, evening feeding may be best to avoid flies.

Establishing the right quantity to feed is based on your dog's activity levels, appetite and body condition. A very approximate guide of raw meaty bones for the average dog is:

15%-20% of body weight per week, or 2%-3% a day.

So, if your Mini Schnauzer weighs 18lb (8kg), he requires 2.7lb-3.6lb (1.2-1.6kg) of carcasses or raw meaty bones weekly.
These figures are only a rough guide for adult dogs in a domestic environment.

Dr Lonsdale says: "Wherever possible, feed the meat and bone ration in one large piece requiring much ripping, tearing and gnawing. This makes for contented pets with clean teeth." More information is available from www.rawmeatybones.com

NOTES: Pregnant or lactating females and growing puppies need more food. This diet may not be suitable for old dogs used to a processed diet or those with dental issues, or in households with children, due to the risk of bacterial infection from raw meat.

- ❖ Monitor your dog whilst eating, especially in the beginning

- ❖ Don't feed bones with sharp points, and remove any bone before it becomes small enough to swallow

- ❖ Raw meaty bones should be kept separate from human food and any surface the uncooked meat or bones have touched should be thoroughly cleaned afterwards

 Puppies can and do eat diets of raw meaty bones, but this needs careful monitoring so consult your breeder or vet before embarking on raw with a young dog.

The BARF diet - A variation of the raw meaty bones diet is the BARF created by Dr Ian Billinghurst, who owns the registered trademark "Barf Diet."

A typical BARF diet is made up of 60%-75% of raw meaty bones - with about 50% meat, such as chicken neck, back and wings - and 25%-40% of fruit and vegetables, offal, meat, eggs or dairy foods. Bones must not be cooked or they can splinter inside the dog. There is lots of information on the BARF diet on the internet.

Top Tips for Feeding Your Mini Schnauzer

1. If it ain't broke, don't fix it! If your Mini is thriving on his current diet, don't change it (until he moves into an older phase of life).

2. If you choose a manufactured food, pick one where meat or poultry (or meat or poultry meal) is the first item listed. Many Minis do not do well on foods with lots of cheap cereals or sugar.

3. The longer the shelf life, the more a food has been processed.

4. Some Minis can have sensitive skin, 'hot spots' or allergies. A cheap food bulked up with grain will only make this worse. A dry food described as *"hypoallergenic"* on the sack means *"less likely to cause allergies."*

5. Consider feeding a probiotic, such as a spoonful of natural, live yoghurt, to your Schnauzer's meals to help maintain healthy gut bacteria.

6. Feed your adult dog twice a day, rather than once. Smaller feeds are easier to digest, and reduce gas and the risk of Bloat, although this more commonly affects larger breeds.

7. Establish a feeding regime and stick to it. Dogs like routine. Stick to the same times, morning and late afternoon/early evening. Feeding too late won't give your dog's body time to process the food before bed. Feeding at the same times also helps your dog establish a toileting regime.

8. Don't feed an hour before or after vigorous exercise as this can cause Bloat or digestive issues.

9. Remove the bowl after 15 to 20 minutes - even if there is some left. Most Schnauzers love their food, but any dog can become fussy if food is constantly available. A healthy, hungry dog will look forward to the next meal and should soon stop leaving food. If he's off his food for a couple of days or more, it could be a sign of illness.

10. Always put fresh food down, never top up old food. It encourages bacteria and your dog to go off his food.

11. Feeding time is a great training opportunity - particularly for the commands **SIT** and **STAY** followed by the release.

12. Leave your puppy or adult dog in peace while eating. Taking the bowl away while he is eating can cause anxiety and lead to food aggression.

13. Use stainless steel or ceramic bowls. Plastic bowls don't last as long and can trigger an allergic reaction around the muzzle in some sensitive dogs. Ceramic bowls are best for keeping water cold, but can crack.

14. Use apple or carrot slices, or other healthy alternatives, as training treats for puppies.

15. Don't feed cooked bones, as these can splinter and cause choking or intestinal problems. And avoid rawhide, as a dog can gulp it without chewing, causing an internal blockage.

16. The following items are poisonous to dogs: grapes, raisins, chocolate, onions, Macadamia nuts, any fruits with seeds or stones, tomatoes, avocados, rhubarb, tea, coffee and alcohol.

17. Check your dog's faeces (aka stools, poo or poop)! If the diet is suitable, the food should be easily digested and produce dark brown, firm stools. If your dog is producing lots of gas, soft, light-coloured or watery poop, his diet may need changing. Consult your vet or breeder for advice.

18. Too many tidbits and/or treats between meals cause obesity, which is life-shortening. Feed leftovers in the bowl as part of a meal. Feeding from the table also encourages attention-seeking behaviour, begging and drooling.

19. And finally, always make sure that your dog has access to clean, fresh water. Change the water and clean the bowl every day or so – it gets slimy!

Andrew and Gaynor Ray have bred all three sizes at Minnienoom Schnauzers, Derbyshire, England, for 30 years. Andrew adds: "At feeding times, the temperaments of all the dogs living in the pack alter and the 'Survival of the Fittest' mentality kicks in. Noise levels raise and stand-offs happen.

"We feed all our dogs separately to ensure no dog is 'robbed' of its feed; this also stops intimidation from the stronger dogs. Lastly, by feeding separately I can monitor feed intake and ensure that each dog is getting the correct nutritional intake."

 If your dog isn't responding well to a particular family member, get that person to feed the dog every day. The way to a Mini Schnauzer's heart is often through his stomach!

Breeders' Advice on Feeding

When a Miniature Schnauzer puppy leaves Steve Matthews' Silbertraum Schnauzers, Dorset, England, they are being fed four times a day, at 8am, 12 noon, 5pm and 10pm. Steve says: "For breakfast we feed Purina Beta Small Breed Puppy complete food soaked with boiling water until absorbed and allowed to cool. We follow this with a drink of goat's milk with an egg yolk mixed in - we do not give cow's milk as this will upset the puppy's stomach.

"Lunch and dinner are the same without the milk drink. The last meal of the day is the same as dinner. However, it is normally more satisfying if followed by a milk drink with or without an egg yolk. This will help your puppy to sleep."

Once the puppy leaves, Steve advises new owners: "Feed your puppy four times a day until it is 12 weeks old at which point this can be reduced to three. Puppy feed products can be purchased at any reputable pet store or supermarket.

"Your puppy has been fed on Purina Beta Small Breed Puppy and we recommend a quality Junior feed such as Royal Canin Junior as the next step."

Photo of this lively Silbertraum litter courtesy of Steve.

"Puppies can be greedy or picky with their food, so it can sometimes be difficult to gauge how much to give them. Care should be taken not to over or underfeed.

"Mini puppies can often appear 'chubby,' especially after they have eaten, but under normal circumstances they should have a defined waist. If in any doubt about your puppy's weight or diet, consult your vet when you next visit for a puppy check-up.

"Please remember that stability in the diet will help maintain good digestion. Any change in diet should be made very gradually over at least a week to avoid upset, and you should try a new diet for at least 10 days before making any further changes."

"I now feed all my adult dogs a good quality kibble mixed with a little canned food. They also get daily raw chicken wings and occasional raw minced beef. I have fed raw tripe in the past - which they love - but it does make their beards smell, especially in summer!"

Andrew and Gaynor's puppy feeding times are 6.30am, 12.30pm, 6.30pm and 11pm. They have this feeding advice for their new owners: "Growing puppies require two times more protein and three times more calcium and phosphorus each day than an adult dog, so he or she must be fed the correct food for his or her age. A complete dog food causes less stress to your puppy's digestion and internal organs."

He tells new puppy owners: "Your puppy requires regular and small meals. Up to three months feed a Miniature Schnauzer puppy three meals a day and then reduce this to two meals. As your puppy matures into adulthood it is recommended to continue feeding two meals a day.

"Your puppy has been weaned on Royal Canin Puppy complete dried puppy food soaked in boiled water and cooled. If you wish to change to another make, gradually mix in the new food. The

information on the packaging will guide you on how much food to give your puppy daily - however, puppy appetites vary enormously.

"The right amount should produce firm, dark brown stools - firm stools that get softer towards the end are an indication of overfeeding."

Photo: Six-weeks-old Leelo (Minnienoom Angel Grace) ready to explore the world, courtesy of Andrew and Gaynor.

"If your puppy loses appetite, try mashing a little puppy meat, fish or chicken in with the soaked food or add a little warmed goat's milk.

"This lactose-free milk suits a puppy's digestion (never feed cow's milk). Gradually wean them off soaked food and feed dry instead. Fresh water should always be available.

"If your puppy suffers from diarrhoea soon after (s)he arrives, it could be due to the stress of moving to the new home, but it can also be a sign of overfeeding, so consider reducing the amount of food offered at the next meal."

AKC Breed Mentor Wade Bogart, Sumerwynd Miniature Schnauzers, New York State, and breeder since 1979: "I feed Fromm Classic Recipe Adult Chicken and Hill's Science Diet Puppy Chicken Meal and Barley Recipe dry dog food. My dogs do well on it."

Dr Lisa Sarvas DVM BSA, Beauideal Schnauzers, North Carolina, and breeder of numerous show champions over the last 35 years: "We feed Purina Pro Plan with small amounts of extra foods for exposure to a variety of foods."

What Owners Feed Their Minis

Here are some comments on feeding, starting with American owners. **Rebecca Makdad**: "I feed all dry kibbles. My girls, Rosie and Navy, and I travel (RVing and visiting friends and family) and it is much easier. Plus, we've never had any issues with allergies or intolerances."

Chloe Dong and Jacky Zou: "We feed Oslo a mix of kibbles from Hill's Science and food toppers from Farmer's Dog. We chose Hill's Science as his main food as it was recommended by our breeder. Later on, we added the food topper since we wanted him to eat warm food (as it was getting cold out too) with better variety in nutrition and flavor."

Simon and Yvonne Sonsino: "We've always fed a mixture of kibble and meat. We're not confident enough to use raw meat and bones and don't really have the facility to store it."

Photo: The couple's puppy Wilf, aged four months.

Chris Lee: "I feed kibble, sweet potato, cooked chicken and a carrot for lunch. Betsy just loves these foods, but I suspect there would be many other foods that she'd like. However, this works and she is fit and well."

Leah Dummer: "Freddie (three years old) is on Arkwright Complete. Leelo and Lily (10 months) are on Royal Canin Mini puppy food. We have started mixing that with the food Freddie is eating to wean them off the puppy food."

Vivian Williams: "We feed Bogart quality dry kibble with freeze-dried raw food as a topper in the evening. We limit the amount of food to a level half cup twice a day.

"Our breeder warned us that the amount of food recommended by dog food manufacturers is excessive; he is adamant that a full-grown Mini should weigh no more than 20 pounds." *Photo: Bogart.*

Vivian added: "We do not offer manufactured dog treats or bones to Bogart. His treats are limited to fresh fruits and vegetables suitable for dogs (blueberries, apple slices, carrots, lettuce, and bell peppers, for example). We occasionally use a bit of scrambled egg, plain yoghurt, or cottage cheese as a food topper."

Yolande: "Since Mayzy's spay operation, her appetite has increased, and she is less fussy. I have cut her calorie intake down by about 20%. I give her 80% good quality wet food and 20% dry complete twice a day. Mayzy's stools are inclined to be firm, so this is why I give her mostly wet food. How boring for a dog to only have dry food!

"I do cook chicken, turkey, lamb etc. with rice and vegetables for her from time to time, with a mineral supplement, and she also has some raw beef and a little raw liver or a cooked egg occasionally.

"She's spoilt rotten! For me, giving variety is the spice of life."

Photo: Mayzy contemplating her next snack, courtesy of Yolande.

She added: "Mayzy will also eat little treats of raw carrot, cucumber, cabbage stalks, watercress and fruit titbits, blueberry, banana, apple and orange or whatever I happen to be preparing.

"The only thing she spat out was celery - and who could blame her for that?!

"She has a good quality chew once a day, e.g. dried fish skin or a vegetable-based chew. I choose to avoid wheat cereals, mainly from experience, as this can cause skin problems."

Food Allergies

Dog food allergies are a reaction to food that involves the body's immune system and affect about one in 10 dogs. They are the third most common canine allergy after atopy (inhaled or contact allergies) and flea bite allergies.

While there's no scientific data as yet, stories from owners suggest that some Miniature Schnauzers can have adverse reactions to certain foods.

Food allergies affect males and females in equal measure as well as neutered and intact pets. They can start when your dog is five months or 12 years old - although the vast majority start when the dog is between two and six years old. It is not uncommon for dogs with food allergies to also have other types of allergies.

If your dog is not well, how do you know if the problem lies with his food or not? Here are some common symptoms to look out for:

- ❖ Itchy skin (this is the most common). Your dog may lick or chew his paws or legs and rub his face with his paws or on the furniture, carpet, etc.
- ❖ Excessive scratching or shedding
- ❖ Ear infections
- ❖ Hot patches of skin – "hot spots"
- ❖ Hair loss
- ❖ Redness and inflammation on the chin and face
- ❖ Recurring skin infections
- ❖ Increased bowel movements (maybe twice as often as usual)
- ❖ Skin or ear infections that clear up with antibiotics but recur when the antibiotics run out

The problem with food allergies is that the symptoms are similar to symptoms of other issues, such as environmental or flea bite allergies, intestinal problems, mange and yeast or bacterial infections. There's also a difference between dog food *allergies* and dog food *intolerance*:

ALLERGIES = SKIN PROBLEMS AND/OR ITCHING

INTOLERANCE = DIARRHOEA AND/OR VOMITING

Dog food intolerance can be compared to people who get an upset stomach from eating spicy curries. Symptoms can be cured by changing to a milder diet. With dogs, certain ingredients are more likely to cause a reaction than others. In order of the most common triggers across the canine world in general, they are:

Beef - Dairy Products - Chicken - Wheat - Eggs - Corn - Soy (Soya in the UK)

Unfortunately, these are also the most common ingredients in dog foods!

 A dog is allergic or sensitive to an ingredient, not to a particular brand, so it's important to read the label. If your Mini has a reaction to beef, for example, he will react to ANY food containing beef, regardless of how expensive or well-prepared it is.

AVOID corn, corn meal, corn gluten meal, artificial preservatives (including BHA, BHT, Propyl Gallate, Ethoxyquin, Sodium Nitrite/Nitrate and TBHQBHA), artificial colours, sugars and sweeteners, e.g. corn syrup, sucrose and ammoniated glycyrrhizin, powdered cellulose, propylene glycol.

Food Trials

The only way to completely cure a food allergy or intolerance is complete avoidance, which is not easy. First, you have to determine your dog DOES have an allergy to food - and not pollen, grass, etc. - and then you have to discover WHICH food is causing the reaction.

Blood tests are nowadays not thought to be reliable. Most people soldier on with trial and error, trying to eliminate certain foods and add others.

As far as I am aware, the only true way to determine exactly what your dog is allergic to, is to start a **food trial** or **exclusion diet**. This involves feeding one specific food for 12 weeks, something the dog has never eaten before. Food trials are a real pain-in-the-you-know-what. You have to be incredibly vigilant and determined, so only start one if you are prepared to see it through, or you're wasting your time.

The chosen food must be the **only thing** eaten during the trial. Don't give: treats, rawhide (not recommended anyway), pigs' ears, cows' hooves, flavoured medications (including heartworm treatments) or supplements, flavoured toothpastes or flavoured plastic toys.

A more practical, less scientific approach is to eliminate ingredients one at a time by switching diets over a period of a week or so. If you switch to home-cooked or raw, you know exactly what your dog is eating; if you choose a commercial food, a *hypoallergenic* one is a good place to start as they do not include wheat protein or soya and are often based around less common ingredients like venison, duck or fish.

Grain Intolerance

Although beef is the food most likely to cause allergies, grain can also be a problem. *"Grain"* is wheat or any other cultivated cereal crop. Some dogs also react to starch, found in grains and potatoes, as well as bread, pasta, rice, etc. Some breeds can be prone to a build-up of yeast in the digestive system, which crowds out the good bacteria allowing toxins to affect the immune system.

When this happens, the itchiness related to food allergies can cause secondary bacterial and yeast infections. These may show as hot spots, ear or bladder infections, excessive shedding, reddish or dark brown tear stains. You may also notice a musty smell, skin lesions or redness on the underside of the neck, belly or paws.

 **FACT** ❭ Drugs like antihistamines and steroids will help temporarily, but they do not address the root cause.

Before you automatically switch to a grain-free diet, a recent study by the University of California, Davis found a link between a form of heart disease called taurine-deficient dilated cardiomyopathy and some popular grain-free dog foods where legumes (e.g. beans, lentil, peas, soy) or potatoes were the main ingredients.

Lead author Joshua Stern said: "A well-researched dog food that has a healthy nutrient profile backed by expert formulation and research is of paramount importance." He added that while many owners may not want to see *"by-products"* listed in their dog's food, they often contain organ meat like heart and kidney, which are good sources of taurine.

Some of the symptoms of food allergies - particularly the scratching, licking, chewing and redness - can also be a sign of environmental allergies, caused by a reaction to pollen, grass, dust, etc. Some dogs are also allergic to flea bites. See **Chapter 1. Schnauzer Skin and Allergies** for more details.

Tip If your dog has poor skin or allergies, vomiting or watery poop, consider gradually changing to a more natural, less-processed food. If the problem persists, see a vet.

Remember that drugs only mask the problem and some vets promote specific brands of dog food, which may or may not be the best option for your Schnauzer. Do your research.

Bloat

Bloat occurs when there is too much gas in the stomach. It is known by several different names: *twisted stomach, gastric torsion* or *Gastric Dilatation-Volvulus (GDV)* and occurs mainly in larger breeds, particularly those with deep chests like the Giant Schnauzer. It is statistically more common in males than in females and in dogs over seven years old.

Although it is not common in Miniature Schnauzers, it is included here as any dog can get Bloat.

The stomach swells with gas and then twists, trapping air, food and water inside. The bloated stomach stops proper blood flow, leading to low blood pressure, shock and even damage to internal organs.

The causes are not fully understood, but there are some well-known risk factors. One is the dog taking in a lot of air while eating - either because he is greedy and gulping the food too fast, or stressed, e.g. where there are several dogs and food competition.

Exercising straight after eating or after a big drink increases the risk - like colic in horses. Another potential cause is diet. Fermentable foodstuffs that produce a lot of gas can cause problems for the stomach if the gas is not burped or passed into the intestines.

Symptoms - Swollen belly - Standing uncomfortably or hunched - Restlessness, pacing or looking for a place to hide - Rapid panting or difficulty breathing - Dry retching or excessive saliva or foam - White or colourless gums - Excessive drinking - Licking the air - General weakness or collapse.

Tips to Avoid Canine Bloat

- Buy a bowl with nobbles, *pictured,* and moisten your dog's dry food - both of these will slow down a gulper. Some owners buy a chest-high frame for food bowls, other experts believe dogs should be fed from the floor - do whichever slows your dog down

- Feed twice a day rather than once

- Avoid dog food with high fats or those using citric acid as a preservative, also avoid tiny pieces of kibble

- Don't let your dog drink too much water just before, during or after eating

- Stress can be a trigger, with nervous and aggressive dogs being more susceptible. Maintain a peaceful environment, particularly around his mealtimes

- Avoid vigorous exercise before or after eating, allow one hour either side of mealtimes before strenuous exercise

FACT ❯ Canine Bloat is one of the leading killers of dogs after cancer and can kill a dog in less than one hour. If you suspect your Schnauzer has it, get him off to the vet IMMEDIATELY. Even with treatment, mortality rates range from 10% to 60%. With surgery, this drops to 15% to 33%.

Overweight Dogs

Excess weight can shorten a dog's life. Don't be tempted to give in to those big brown eyes or turn your love for your Mini into food rewards. You are not rewarding him, you are contributing to his potential early demise if he becomes overweight!

It is far easier to regulate your dog's weight and keep it at a healthy level than to try and slim down a 'starving' Schnauzer when he becomes chubby. A Mini on a diet will pester the life out of you.

Overweight and obese dogs are susceptible to a range of illnesses, including:

Joint disease - excessive body weight increases stress on joints, triggering or worsening conditions such as Hip Dysplasia. It can also lead to a vicious cycle of reduced exercise and more weight gain.

Heart and lung problems - fatty deposits within the chest and excessive fat circulating can lead to cardio-respiratory and cardiovascular disease.

Diabetes – insulin resistance has been shown to occur in overweight dogs, leading to a greater risk of Diabetes Mellitus.

Tumours - obesity increases the risk of mammary tumours in female dogs.

Liver disease - fat degeneration may result in a liver deficiency.

Exercise intolerance - a common finding with overweight dogs.

Reduced Lifespan - one of the most serious proven findings in studies is that obesity in both humans and dogs reduces lifespan.

Schnauzers are extremely loyal and affectionate companions; they definitely become part of the family. However, beware of going too far.

FACT Studies show that dogs regarded as 'family members' by the owner (anthropomorphosis) are at greater risk of becoming overweight.

This is because all the attention given to the dog often results in food being given as well.

If you have to put your dog on a diet, be aware that a reduced amount of food will also mean reduced nutrients, so he may need a supplement during this time.

Remember that many of the problems associated with being overweight are reversible. Increasing exercise increases calories burned, which in turn reduces weight.

....

To Recap:

✓ Diet is extremely important, but no one food is right for every dog; you must decide on the best one for YOUR Mini Schnauzer

✓ Puppies need the right food in the right quantities

✓ The best test of a food is how well your dog is doing on it

If your Schnauzer is happy and healthy, interested in life, has lots of energy *(like the one in the photo above),* is not too fat and not too thin, doesn't scratch a lot and has dark brown, firm stools, then...

Congratulations, you've got it right!!

....

9. Mini Temperament

Many of us choose Mini Schnauzers because of their sheer beauty. Their perfect proportions combined with the cutest of faces, big brown eyes and bushy 'old men' beards are an irresistible combination. This is a striking breed.

But what makes this breed really special is not only the striking looks, but the personalities of each individual Miniature.

Schnauzers are unlike any other breed. Created to do a variety of jobs and with a mixture of breeds in their make-up, these beautiful dogs are hardy yet sensitive individuals with a lively intelligence, a playful spirit, a stubborn streak and a sense of humour.

You have to learn what makes a Schnauzer tick before you can develop a stress-free relationship that makes both of you happy. This chapter helps you to do just that, and to bring out the best in your Mini Schnauzer.

Just as with humans, a dog's personality is made up of a combination of temperament and character – or **Nature and Nurture.**

Temperament is the nature - or inherited characteristics - a dog is born with; it's the predisposition to act or react to the world around him. The amount of natural prey drive or protective instinct your Mini Schnauzer has is dominated by genetics and varies from one dog to the next.

The Miniature Schnauzer was bred down from the Standard Schnauzer, which protected the owner and possessions, guarded livestock and kept the vermin down - so don't be surprised if your Mini has prey drive (a desire to chase) and some watchdog instincts.

Character is what develops throughout the dog's life and is formed by a combination of temperament and environment. How you treat your Mini will have a huge effect on his personality and behaviour.

FACT > Plenty of early socialisation and training will help to curb any natural instincts to chase, bark indiscriminately or show suspicion towards other people, and help your Mini to take his place as a happy, relaxed member of your household.

Start out on the right foot with your puppy by establishing the rules of the house and good routines, while making time to teach the all-important Recall while your pup is very young and still wants to follow you. Treat him well and make lots of time for socialisation, training and, as his body matures, exercise.

FACT > Socialisation means "learning to be part of society." With dogs, it means helping them learn to be comfortable living within a human society which includes many different types of people, environments, sights, noises, smells and other animals.

Canine Emotions

As pet lovers, we are all too keen to ascribe human characteristics to our dogs; this is called *anthropomorphism* – "the attribution of human characteristics to anything other than a human being."

Most of us dog lovers are guilty of that, as we come to regard our pets as members of the family - and Miniature Schnauzers certainly regard themselves as members of the family!

An example of anthropomorphism might be that the owner of a male dog might not want to have him neutered because he will "miss sex," as a human might if he or she were no longer able to have sex. This is simply not true.

A male dog's impulse to mate is entirely governed by his hormones, not emotions. If he gets the scent of a bitch in heat, his hormones (which are just chemicals) tell him he has to mate with her. He does not stop to consider how attractive she is or whether she is *"the one"* to produce his puppies.

No, his reaction is entirely physical, he just wants to head on over there and get on with it!

It's the same with females. When they are in heat, a chemical impulse is triggered in their brain making them want to mate - with any male, they aren't at all fussy. So, don't expect your little Princess to be all coy when she is in heat, she is not waiting for Prince Charming to come along - the tramp down the road or any other scruffy pooch will do! It is entirely physical, not emotional.

Food is another issue. Most Schnauzers' greatest desire is to get that delicious treat or food - you have to count the calories.

Schnauzers are incredibly loyal and loving. They are amusing characters and if yours doesn't make you smile from time to time, you must have had a humour by-pass!

All of this adds up to one thing: a beloved family member that is all too easy to spoil.

 Miniature Schnauzers are intelligent and respond well to positive motivation - usually treats, combined with praise and/or a toy. Teach yours to respect the authority figure, which is you - not him! In the beginning, think of yourself as a kindly but firm teacher with a slightly wayward young student.

Learn to understand your Mini's mind, patiently train him to be comfortable with his place in the household, teach him some manners and household rules - like not jumping up or constantly barking - and you will be rewarded with a companion who is second to none and fits in beautifully with your family and lifestyle.

Dr Stanley Coren is well known for his work on canine psychology and behaviour. He and other researchers believe that in many ways a dog's emotional development is equivalent to that of a young child.

Dr Coren says: "Researchers have now come to believe that the mind of a dog is roughly equivalent to that of a human who is two to two-and-a-half years old. This conclusion holds for most mental abilities as well as emotions.

"Thus, we can look to human research to see what we might expect of our dogs. Just like a two-year-old child, our dogs clearly have emotions, but many fewer kinds of emotions than found in adult humans.

"At birth, a human infant only has an emotion that we might call excitement. This indicates how excited he is, ranging from very calm up to a state of frenzy. Within the first weeks of life the excitement state comes to take on a varying positive or negative flavour, so we can now detect the general emotions of contentment and distress.

"In the next couple of months, disgust, fear, and anger become detectable in the infant. Joy often does not appear until the infant is nearly six months of age and it is followed by the emergence of shyness or suspicion. True affection, the sort that it makes sense to use the label "love" for, does not fully emerge until nine or ten months of age."

So, our Schnauzers can truly love us – but we knew that already!

According to Dr Coren, dogs can't feel shame. So, if you are housetraining your puppy, don't expect him to feel ashamed if he makes a mess in the house, he can't; he simply isn't capable of feeling shame. But he will not like it when you ignore him when he's behaving badly, and will love it when you praise or reward him for relieving himself outdoors.

He is simply responding to you with his simplified range of emotions.

FACT Although Mini Schnauzers can sometimes be stubborn, they are also sensitive. They can show empathy - *"the ability to understand and share the feelings of another"* – and pick up on the mood and emotions of the owner.

One emotion that all dogs can experience is jealousy. It may display itself by being overly protective or possessive of humans, food or toys. An interesting article was published in the PLOS (Public Library of Science) Journal in 2014 following an experiment into whether dogs get jealous.

Building on research that shows that six-month-old infants display jealousy, the scientists studied 36 dogs in their homes and videoed their actions when their owners showed affection to a realistic-looking stuffed canine *(pictured).*

Over three-quarters of the dogs pushed or touched the owner when they interacted with the decoy. The envious mutts were more than three times as likely to do this for interactions with the stuffed dog, compared to when their owners gave their attention to other objects, including a book. Around a third tried to get between the owner and the plush toy, while a quarter of the put-upon pooches snapped at the dummy dog!

Professor Christine Harris from the University of California in San Diego said: "Our study suggests not only that dogs do engage in what appear to be jealous behaviours, but also that they were seeking to break up the connection between the owner and a seeming rival."

The researchers believe that the dogs thought that the stuffed dog was real. The authors cite the fact that 86% of the dogs sniffed the toy's rear end during and after the experiment!

Professor Harris said: "We can't really speak of the dogs' subjective experiences, of course, but it looks as though they were motivated to protect an important social relationship. Many people have assumed that jealousy is a social construction of human beings - or that it's an emotion specifically tied to sexual and romantic relationships.

"Our results challenge these ideas, showing that animals besides ourselves display strong distress whenever a rival usurps a loved one's affection."

Cause and Effect

There's no doubt that Schnauzers make wonderful canine companions. Once you've had one, no other dog seems quite the same. But sometimes they, just like other breeds, can develop behaviour problems. Poor behaviour or sadness may result from several factors, including:

- Lack of socialisation
- Lack of training
- Boredom, *pictured*
- Being left alone for too long
- Poor breeding
- Being badly treated
- A change in living conditions
- Anxiety, insecurity or fear
- Being spoilt

Bad behaviour may show itself in different ways:

- Excessive barking
- Chewing or destructive behaviour
- Constantly demanding your attention
- Becoming overly protective of their owner or home
- Becoming overly possessive of food, toys, etc. (resource guarding)
- Nipping, biting
- Soiling or urinating inside the house
- Stealing things
- Aggression, excitability or lunging on the leash
- Jumping up
- Suspicion or aggression towards people or other dogs
- Excessive digging

Tip Avoid poor behaviour by devoting lots of time early on to socialise and train your Schnauzer, and to nip any potential problems in the bud.

If you are rehoming a Mini Schnauzer, you'll need extra time and patience to help your new arrival unlearn some bad habits.

10 Ways to Avoid Unwanted Behaviour

Here are some tips to help you start out on the right foot:

1. **Buy from a good breeder**. They use their expertise to match suitable breeding pairs, taking into account factors such as good temperament, health and being *"fit for function."*

2. **Start socialisation right away.** Give a new puppy a couple of days to get used to his new surroundings and then start socialising him – even if this means carrying him places until the vaccination schedule is complete.

Socialisation does not end at puppyhood. While the foundation for good behaviour is laid down during the first few months, good owners reinforce social skills and training throughout a dog's life.

Dogs are social creatures that thrive on sniffing, hearing, seeing, and even licking. Socialisation helps them to learn their place in that universe and to become comfortable with it.

 Minis love to be at the centre of things, but it is important that they learn when young that they are not also the centre of the universe!

3. **Start training early** - you can't start too soon. Start teaching your puppy to learn his name as well as some simple commands a day or two after you bring him home.

4. **Basic training should cover several areas:** housetraining, chew prevention, puppy biting, simple commands like SIT, COME, STAY and familiarising him with collar and lead. Adopt a gentle but firm approach and keep training sessions short and FUN - start with five minutes a day and build up.

5. **Train with patience and kindness.** Miniature Schnauzers are sensitive and do not respond well to harsh treatment, such as being shouted at or hit.

6. **Puppy classes or adult dog obedience classes** are a great way to start; be sure to do your homework together afterwards. Spend a few minutes each day reinforcing what you have both learned in class - owners need training as well as dogs!

7. **Reward your dog for good behaviour.** All behaviour training should be based on positive reinforcement. Mini Schnauzers love treats and praise, and this trait speeds up the training process.

 The main aim of training is to build a good understanding between you and your Mini.

8. **Ignore bad behaviour**, no matter how hard this may be. If, for example, your dog is chewing his way through your kitchen, shoes, or couch, jumping up or chasing the kids, remove him from the situation and then ignore him. For most dogs, even negative attention is some attention.

Or if he is constantly demanding your attention, ignore him. Remove him or yourself from the room so he learns that you give attention when you want to give it, **not** when he demands it. If your pup is a chewer - and most are - make sure he has plenty of durable toys to keep him occupied.

9. **Take the time to learn what sort of temperament your Mini has.** Is he by nature confident or anxious? What was he like as a tiny puppy, did he rush forward or hang back? Does he

fight to get upright when on his back or is he happy to lie there? Is he a couch potato or a ball of energy?

Your puppy's temperament will affect his behaviour and how he reacts to the world. A nervous Schnauzer will certainly not respond well to a loud approach on your part, whereas an energetic, strong-willed one will require more patience and exercise, and a firm hand.

10. **Exercise and stimulation.** A lack of either is another reason for Schnauzers behaving badly. Regular daily exercise, games, toys, meeting up with other dogs and organised activities are all ways of stopping your dog from becoming bored or frustrated.

11. **Learn to leave your dog.** Just as leaving your dog alone for too long can lead to problems, so can being with him 100% of the time. The dog becomes over-reliant on you and then gets stressed when you leave; this is called *separation anxiety*. When your dog first arrives at your house, start by leaving him for a few minutes every day and gradually build it up so that after a while you can leave him for up to four hours.

12. **Love your Schnauzer – but don't spoil him,** however difficult that might be. You don't do your dog any favours by giving too many treats, constantly responding to his demands for attention or allowing him to behave as he wants inside the house.

....

First-Hand Experiences

We asked our contributing breeders and owners what first attracted them to the breed and to describe their Schnauzers' typical temperaments and traits. This is what they said:

Breeders

Steve Matthews, of Silbertraum Schnauzers, Dorset, UK, has bred Minis and Giants for well over a decade. He says: "I first owned a rescue Mini in 1997, I was attracted to the breed by its distinguishing features - beard, eyebrows, etc. I then took in three different Schnauzers as rehomes; I like their good looks and independent spirit.

"In my experience, Minis and Giants are quite similar in temperament, except for their size and exuberance - Standard Schnauzers are completely different."

"Both Giants and Minis are eager to please and like to be near people. I have never known a Miniature Schnauzer to be aggressive, although I have known Standard Schnauzers and Giants that have shown aggression towards other dogs.

"Minis are very sociable, intelligent dogs, full of energy, who are loyal to their owners. They can be quite vocal, especially around strangers. All Schnauzers are good watchdogs and protective of their family and/or territory - sometimes to the point of distraction, where the slightest noise or movement triggers a tirade of barking!"

Photo of this handsome black and silver pup courtesy of Steve.

Wade Bogart, AKC Breeder of Merit and Mentor for the Miniature Schnauzer breed, has bred Sumerwynd Miniature Schnauzers, New York State, for over 40 years and adds:

"The typical Miniature Schnauzer is alert and spirited, yet obedient to command. He is friendly, intelligent and willing to please."

Photo: Daisy and Beetle's litter of two boys and a girl, courtesy of Wade.

Andrew and Gaynor Ray have been breeding Minnienoom Schnauzers, Derbyshire, UK, since 1992. Today they breed all three sizes. Having previously owned Terriers, they started out with a female Mini called Boo-Boo and a growing family.

Andrew says: "What we liked most about the Miniature Schnauzer was how well this breed adapted to family life.

"It didn't moult, which was something fantastic as it meant our younger children didn't get covered in dog hair as they learned to crawl and walk around the family home. We discovered that the Miniature Schnauzer is an excellent house dog, a good protector, spirited and funny.

"All three sizes of the Schnauzer family are extremely good watchdogs and very intelligent. Before we entered the show world, we would attend obedience classes with our Giants - and one of our Miniatures (who was being trained by a family friend) was also present. Both the Mini and the Giant learned one-word commands very quickly and soon achieved their Bronze, Silver and Gold Good Citizen Awards.

"We feel really blessed that we have had all three sizes of the Schnauzer family living peacefully within our family home. The children adored the dogs, and the dogs adored the children.

"This breed is very intelligent and wants to please. Dogs of my breeding have excelled in all levels of Agility, Earthdog, Jumping, Obedience, Utility and Versatility competitions.

"Miniature Schnauzers are also fun-loving, outgoing, determined, focused, devoted, loyal, and observant and have a gentle spirit. Plus they are hardy and shed very little."

Dr Lisa Sarvas, veterinarian and breeder of Beauideal Schnauzers, North Carolina: "As a teenager, my 'shortlist' of favorite breeds included several smart-looking bearded terriers.

"Upon meeting a few Minis at a local show, their handsome, alert look, along with a strong (and sometimes demanding) character, attracted me immediately! The fact that they had flexible exercise needs and a non-shedding coat helped seal the deal with my parents. My future Mini would be the first indoor pet dog at our home.

"The Mini's confidence and loyal heart overshadow their moderate size. Indeed, I have many Minis that have taken it upon themselves to protect me when they felt the need."

Photo: Beauideal Direct From Hollywood, bred by Lisa, and awarded Best of Breed at her most recent US show outing.

Lisa added: "Miniature Schnauzers are alert, confident, loyal and loving. They truly fall in love with their owners! They enjoy meeting new people and dogs and will bark with excitement. They have a moderate prey drive, so many will enjoy playing with toys.

"However, while they get along with dogs of any size, their preference and priority is to be with their humans. They love their training time, and most are highly food-motivated. They excel at Obedience, Rally, Agility and Flyball. With positive training, they can be convinced to try most anything!

"Minis want to be part of the family, and bond very tightly with their caretakers. It is important to acclimate them to many experiences, sights, animals and noises while young. Otherwise they can be overly excited by novel experiences as adults. Minis love to learn and to please their owners - so start positive training early on."

Lesley Myers, former breeder with the Ersmy prefix and show judge, Berkshire, UK, who has also had considerable success in the show ring with her Minis: "I saw Ch Castilla Linajudo being awarded Crufts Reserve Supreme Champion on TV in 1980 and thought he looked like a little shire horse! I fell in love with the look of the breed.

"Whilst working in California in 1984, I saw all three sizes of Schnauzer and fell in love with the Mini all over again. A year later, I had my own Mini, who went on to live for 16 years and two weeks.

"The typical Mini Schnauzer is friendly with excitable greetings, loveable, keen, alert, reliable and intelligent, and a good watchdog.

"Minis are good with children. However, they and the children must be socialised. Some Minis can also be very wary of children and would prefer to go to another room out of the way.

"Minis can be loveable little rogues and loveable little goody-two-shoes all rolled into one!"

Photo: Lesley's Ziska (Ersmy Miss Congeniality JW Sh.CM) at 14 months old.

Owners

Yolande: "Our Labrador Retriever died aged 14-and-a-half and, given my advancing years, I looked for a breed that would be a companion dog, intelligent with the ability to do Agility or charity work, temperament allowing. I have done Agility previously and know how much my dogs have enjoyed the stimulation. I researched dog breeds via the internet, I also used The Schnauzer Handbook to research the breed.

"My black Mini Mayzy is loving and always ready for action, fun and games. She's inquisitive, stubborn and persistent. Having owned an obedient Labrador whose nature was to please, Mayzy will ask herself 'What's in it for me'? Usually, a treat overcomes this hesitation to a command! I love her intelligence, good memory and love of play.

"I don't think we have left her alone for more than three to four hours, but being left on her own doesn't seem to be a problem. We don't make a fuss about our exit and leave her with a chew and the door of her sleeping crate open in the utility room.

"Mayzy only barks at unfamiliar sounds, or strangers coming to the door. She has a whole vocabulary of funny noises to show how she is feeling and greets people she knows with '**Whooooooo,**' which amuses, once the recipient realises it is a friendly hello! Thank goodness she is not a persistent barker.

"As for anything unusual, apart from the extraordinary noises she makes - particularly when she is playing with my sons - I observe her trying to balance toys one on top of the other. We have a large cage ball that was a toy left over from my large Labrador, and I have watched her push toys inside the ball.

"Mayzy, *(pictured here looking very alert),* likes to play with frisbees thrown around the garden and I usually play with three at a time because 'retrieve' is not a command I have had much success with! She will collect the frisbees and stack them one on top of the other.

"Many socks, hats and gloves have also ended up at the bottom of the garden!"

Vivian Williams: "I grew up in a home with a host of outdoor dogs, primarily beagles and other hunting dogs, with a toy poodle kept inside during my teenage years.

"After I married, we had several dogs. When our Cockapoo died, we were looking for a dog small enough to enjoy as a lapdog but sturdy enough to play with our Standard Poodle, Rabies. After owning a variety of dogs, I was hooked on the non-shedding type and liked what I read about Minis.

We had a recommendation for well-known and respected breeder, Wade Bogart. Wade Bogart's genuine love of the breed, his champion bloodlines, and willingness to share his knowledge with others is impressive. In fact, we named our puppy W.B. Bogart after Wade and his brother Brian!

"Bogart, who is now three, is immensely loving, humorous, and playful. He is one of the sweetest-tempered dogs I've ever met. He also has a healthy prey drive. He's incredibly fast and when running full-tilt, reminds me of the nimble Rhosgobel rabbits that used to pull the sleigh in The Hobbit - An Unexpected Journey (2012, Peter Jackson film).

"Bogart chases field mice and voles as well as low-flying butterflies and the leaves that imitate them. He has an interest in toads, but mostly sniffs and observes them, and is respectful of horses and other large animals here on our farm.

"He gets along with other dogs when properly introduced because he has a less-than Alpha male mindset. Last summer we took him along when we attended an AKC dog show, where he behaved as the perfect canine gentleman.

"Bogart is an excellent watchdog. Miniature Schnauzers are noted for their alertness and suspicion of strangers, which is one of the reasons we were interested in the breed.

"For the first year or two, Bogart became overly excited when company arrived (he was a COVID-era puppy), and barked too long and shrilly. My husband and I worked on praising the initial barking and then giving him a "no bark" command.

"In the past year, we have more visitors in the home and his excess barking has drastically reduced."

Photo: Bogart leads Rabies on a merry chase around the yard.

Gary Blain: "I've had dogs in my life for most of my life. One of my friends had a Mini and I was taken by the breed as it doesn't shed hair like many dogs. Also, the Mini is a strong character, they are cheeky little dogs, happy to get out and about and enjoy a walk, but equally happy to curl up and keep your toes warm.

"My two are intelligent, clever little dogs, they are strong-willed, and like to have the last word (bark!). They are feisty characters, great house dogs, inquisitive (nosey), fearless, they love to play and cuddle and make lots of noise.

"Jamie has a teddy called Carsington, and if I say 'Jamie get Carsington,' he'll go find him! He loves his footie too; it's a full-size football and gets very excited dribbling with the ball and chasing it around; it's so funny.

"They like to chase everything from squirrels to cats and other dogs. If Jamie sees another dog he will move into stalk mode - he looks like a lion stalking his prey! As he gets close, he suddenly pounces and bounds past the other dog by a couple of feet.

"Evie different completely different. She will 'Wooo woo!' at the other dog before bounding on all four paws to within a few feet of them, then will run around them to take a look before running and hiding behind me! When on a lead, they can both be barking and growly.

"Jamie is quite relaxed around most people and children; Evie is timid around people but fine with them.

"Both Jamie and Evie are very vocal, whether in the street on a walk in the park or certainly when standing on the back of the sofa in the window barking at everything and anything that moves. They both like travelling in the car and campervan, and love to look out of the windows. When they see another dog, they will bark until I can get them to stop.

"They are well-travelled Minis, they've been to France, Belgium, Netherlands and Germany, and various parts of the UK.

"I'm a big softie; they have me wrapped around their little paws!"

Photo: Evie (left, aged five) and Jamie (eight) have got the measure of Gary!

Leah Dummer: "My partner always had Minis and when we set up home together, Winnie the black Mini Schnauzer came too. This is when I fell in love with the breed. I couldn't believe such an elderly dog got on so well with children aged two and five."

Winnie passed away and now Leah has another Mini, Freddie, three, and two puppies, Leelo and Lilly. She says: "I was surprised how good they all get on together, and also how good they are with the children. As they are small dogs, I thought they would yap a lot but they are all very chilled.

"Lily is very soft and gentle, and very laid back. Leelo can be stubborn and very cheeky, liking to run off with the children's toys and toilet rolls. Freddie is very loyal and follows me everywhere. I would also say he is like a guard dog to the house.

"The first thing he does when he goes out into the garden is run a lap of the perimeters to make sure it is all clear before he goes to play. He takes a bit of time to warm to people when they come into the house. He will bark at them first as if to say 'This is my house, who are you?' Once we have reassured him it's OK, he calms down and wants to be fussed.

None of our three like cats at all. If they see one in the garden, they will chase it and bark. We have a naughty cat in the street that likes to sit at the other side of our window, which really winds Freddie up. If a pigeon comes into the garden, they will chase that away. But they are quite happy to let smaller birds onto the bird table and bird bath in the garden.

"When we leave the house, they are all in the kitchen together. We always make sure we leave the radio on for them, and they are fine.

"The dogs are free to run around the garden as much as they like. The garden is very long and they love charging around the garden. We take them all for a walk once a day, usually late evening; we have found that this settles them for the night.

"We walk Leelo and Lily together and Freddie on his own. They will all cry for each other when the other walk is taking place. But once they are back, they are super excited to see each other!"

Photo: Growing up together. Ellie, aged one, with Freddie, two, and Leelo and Lily, both five months.

Separation Anxiety

Because Miniature Schnauzers get so attached to their beloved owners, Separation Anxiety can become an issue with some. And it's not just dogs that experience it, people do too! About 7% of adults and 4% of children suffer from this disorder.

Typical symptoms for humans are:

- Distress at being separated from a loved one
- Fear of being left alone

Our canine companions aren't much different. When a puppy leaves the litter, his owner becomes his new pack. It's estimated that as many as 10% to 15% of dogs suffer from Separation Anxiety, which is an exaggerated fear response caused by being apart from their owner.

Separation Anxiety affects millions of dogs and is on the increase. According to behaviourists, it is the most common form of stress for dogs. Even if your Schnauzer does not have Separation Anxiety, being over-reliant on you can lead to other insecurity issues, such as becoming:

- Too suspicious or fearful of other people or dogs
- Over-protective
- Too territorial
- Anxious

Separation Anxiety can be equally distressing for the owner - I know because our Max suffered from it. He howled whenever we left home without him. He'd also bark if one of us got out of the car - even if other people were still inside with him.

Fortunately, his problem was relatively mild. If we returned after only a short while, he was usually quiet. Although if we silently sneaked back and peeked in through the letterbox, he was never asleep. Instead, he'd be waiting by the door listening for our return.

Another example was when I took him to the Post Office and tied him up outside. Even though he could see me on the inside through the glass door, he frantically barked his head off. So much so that the postmistress couldn't hear a word anybody was saying at the counter.

She is a dog lover herself and despite the large "No Dogs Allowed" sign on the door, she took pity on him. She let Max in and he promptly sat at my feet, quiet as a mouse as though nothing had happened!

I work from home and Max got too used to being with us all the time – he also slept in his own bed in our bedroom. I should have structured more daily time where he and I were separated when he was a puppy, as he became very fixated on me, which became more apparent when he was elderly.

Tell-Tale Signs

Does your Schnauzer do any of the following?

- Follow you from room to room - even the bathroom - whenever you're home?
- Get anxious or stressed when you're getting ready to leave the house?
- Howl, bark or whine when you leave?
- Chew or destroy things he's not supposed to?
- Dig or scratch at the carpet, doors or windows trying to join you?
- Soil or urinate inside the house, even though he is housetrained? (This only occurs when left alone)
- Exhibit restlessness - such as licking his coat excessively, pacing or circling?

- Greet you ecstatically every time you come home – even if you've only been out to empty the bins?
- Wait by the window or door until you return?
- Dislike spending time alone in the garden or yard?
- Refuse to eat or drink if you leave him?
- Howl or whine when one family member leaves - even when others are still in the room or car?

If so, he may suffer from Separation Anxiety.

Causes

Schnauzers are pack animals and being alone is not a natural state for them. Puppies have to be taught to get used to periods of isolation slowly and in a structured way before they can become comfortable with being alone.

A Mini Schnauzer puppy will emotionally latch on to his new owner, who has taken the place of his mother and siblings. He will want to follow you everywhere initially and, although you want to shower him with love and attention, it's best to start leaving him, starting with a minute or two, right from the beginning. One or more of these can trigger it:

- ❧ Not being left alone for short periods when young

- ❧ Being left for too long by owners who are out of the house for most of the day

- ❧ Anxiety or lack of confidence due to insufficient socialisation, training or both

- ❧ Boredom

- ❧ Being given TOO MUCH attention

- ❧ All of the dog's attention is focused on one person – usually because that person spends time with him, plays, feeds, trains and exercises him

- ❧ Making too much of a fuss when you leave and return to the house

- ❧ Mistreatment in the past, a rehomed dog may well feel anxious when left alone

Adopted/rehomed dogs can be susceptible to Separation Anxiety. They may have been abandoned once already and fear it happening again.

FACT ⟩ It may be very flattering that your Schnauzer wants to be with you all the time, but Separation Anxiety is a form of panic that is distressing for your dog. Socialisation helps a dog to become more confident and self-reliant.

Most of the dogs in this book are fine when left, but a couple have experienced Separation Anxiety. Owner Chloe Dong: "Up to the age of six months, Oslo had pretty bad Separation Anxiety. We live in an apartment in Brooklyn, NY and our neighbor said she could hear him constantly cry when we were gone for work.

"Soon after, my fiancé and I restructured our work schedules so at least one of us was home with Oslo as often as possible. Now that he's older, we're more comfortable with leaving him home alone. Instead of crying, he tends to get bored and tries to find random things to chew on!"

Gary Blain says: "Jamie hates being left at home, he would be my constant shadow, bless him. When left at home, he would sit at the door and bark constantly until I returned home. Since I got Evie, he doesn't bark as much now.

"Although he waits at the door for me and when he hears the key going in the lock, he starts leaping up and down. I know this as I can see this silver blob bouncing up and down through the window!"

A different scenario is Separation Anxiety in elderly dogs. As dogs age, their senses, such as scent, hearing and sight, diminish. They often become "clingier" and more anxious when they are separated from their owners - or even out of view. You may even find that your elderly Schnauzer reverts to puppyhood and starts to follow you around the house again.

In these cases, it is fine to spend more time with your old friend and gently help him through his final years.

So, what can you do if your dog is showing signs of Canine Separation Anxiety? Every dog is different, but here are tried and tested techniques that have worked for some dogs.

Tips to Combat Separation Anxiety

1. This is extremely important:
    After the first couple of days at home, leave your new puppy or adult dog for short periods, starting with a minute, then two, then gradually increasing the minutes you are out of sight.

2. Use a crate. Crate training helps a dog to become self-reliant.

    NEVER leave your dog unattended in a locked crate for more than four hours maximum - or if he is frantic to get out, as it can cause physical or mental trauma.

3. Consider making his night-time bed NOT in your bedroom to get him used to being without you for a few hours a day.

4. Introduce your Schnauzer to other people, places and animals while young.

5. Get other members of your family to feed, walk and train the dog, so he doesn't become fixated on just one person.

6. Tire your Schnauzer out before you leave him alone. Take him for a walk, do an activity or play a game before leaving and, if you can, leave him with a view of the outside world, e.g. in a room with a patio door or low window.

7. Keep arrivals and departures low key and don't make a big fuss.

8. Leave him a *"security blanket,"* such as an old piece of clothing that still has your scent on it, a favourite toy, or leave a radio on softly in the room with the dog. Avoid a heavy rock station! If it will be dark when you return, leave a lamp on a timer.

9. Associate your departure with something good. Give him a rubber toy, like a Kong, filled with a tasty treat, or a frozen treat. This may take his mind off your departure. (Some dogs may refuse to touch the treat until you return home).

10. Structure and routine can help to reduce anxiety. Carry out regular activities, such as feeding and exercising, at the same time every day.

11. Dogs read body language very well and may start to fret when they think you are going to leave them. One technique is to mimic your departure routine when you have no intention of leaving. Put your coat on, grab your car keys, go out of the door and return a few seconds later. Do this randomly and regularly and it may help to reduce your dog's stress levels when you do it for real.

12. However lovable your Schnauzer is, if he is showing early signs of anxiety when separating from you, **do not shower him with attention all the time when you are there.** He will become too reliant on you.

13. If you have to regularly leave the house for a few hours at a time, try to make an arrangement so the dog is not on his own all day every day during the week. Consider dropping him off with a neighbour or doggie daycare if you can afford it.

14. There are many natural calming remedies available for dogs in spray, tablet or liquid form. Another option is to leave him with a Snuggle Puppy, which is warm and has a heartbeat - but not if you think he will destroy it and eat the mechanism!

15. Getting another dog to keep the first one company can certainly help, but can you afford double the food and veterinary bills? If you can, try and avoid getting two from the same litter as their first bond will be to each other - also an older dog can help to train a puppy.

Sit-Stay-Down

Another technique for helping to reduce Separation Anxiety is the *"sit-stay"* or *"down-stay"* exercises using positive reinforcement. The goal is to be able to move briefly out of your dog's sight while he is in the *"stay"* position.

Through this, he learns that he can remain calmly and happily in one place while you go about your normal daily life.

You have to progress slowly. Get your dog to sit and stay and then walk away from him for five seconds, then 10, 20, a minute and so on. Reward your dog every time he stays calm.

Then move out of sight or out of the room for a few seconds, return and give him a treat if he is calm, gradually lengthen the time you are out of sight.

If you're watching TV snuggled up with your dog and you get up for a snack, say *"Stay"* and leave the room. When you return, praise him quietly. It is a good idea to practise these techniques after exercise or when your dog is a little sleepy (but not exhausted), as he is likely to be more relaxed.

 **FACT** Canine Separation Anxiety is NOT the result of disobedience or lack of training. It's a psychological condition; your dog feels anxious and insecure.

NEVER punish your dog for showing signs of Separation Anxiety – even if he has pooped or peed in the house while you are out (when he knows not to), chewed your expensive rug or emptied the contents of your kitchen bin. This will only make him more anxious.

Separation Anxiety can be cured or lessened, but it does take time and commitment from the owner.

 Prevention is better than cure. Leave your Schnauzer for short periods from Day 1, don't let him sleep in your bedroom, and train and socialise him when young. He will gradually learn that the world is a safe place - even when you are not there.

10. Basic Training

Training a Miniature Schnauzer is like bringing up a child. Put in the effort early on and you will be rewarded with a well-mannered individual who will be a joy to spend time with for many years to come. But let your youngster do what he wants, allow him to think the world revolves around him and you could finish up with a noisy, stubborn adolescent!

All dogs are different and training should always be tailored to the individual. Miniatures are keen to please their owners, but natural temperament and energy levels vary from one to the next.

A well-trained dog doesn't magically appear overnight - it requires lots of time, effort and patience on your part. Miniature Schnauzers make super companions and family dogs; this chapter helps you to achieve that.

....

Be Firm But Kind

Mini Schnauzers are intelligent, some of them (including our Max) seem almost human; true members of the family. This is very endearing, but be careful. They are smart and, if not kept in their place, they can end up with *'Little Emperor Syndrome,'* ruling you and your household!

Your dog has to learn - through POSITIVE training - that you are pack leader, not playmate, otherwise he may push the boundaries. It's your house, you set the rules and, with kind and consistent training, your Schnauzer will learn to follow them.

Some Minis are naturally more confident and outgoing than others, but all are surprisingly sensitive. If you yell or are aggressive, you will frighten him and he won't like it. This could result in timidity or him switching off from you.

Mini Schnauzers are not aggressive by nature. If they do show aggression towards other dogs when on the lead, or shy away from people in your home, this is usually rooted in fear.

Confidence-building training is required and, most importantly, more socialisation. See **Chapter 12** for more information on socialising a puppy.

Miniature Schnauzers are not known for their powers of concentration – just throw a ball for one and see how long that lasts! You could never train a Mini to be a police dog; there are simply too many distractions.

When giving a command, you may see your Schnauzer torn between doing what you say or running after that dog/squirrel/human he has just spotted! Keep training short and fun, especially at the beginning.

Minis are also not like Border Collies, who hang on your every word, desperate to please you, even though they pick things up **extremely** quickly.

You have to persuade your Mini that what YOU want him to do is actually what HE wants to do, because good things will happen. In Mini Schnauzer terms this normally means bribing them with treats and lavishing them with praise!

Minis are also active, playful dogs, and most enjoy a challenge, activity or game, all of which help to keep them stimulated and improve their interest and receptiveness to training.

 Minis love to show off and be the centre of attention! Give yours a chance to shine; praise and reward him often until the particular training task becomes ingrained. You'll be giving a lot of treats, so try getting your pup used to a small piece of carrot or apple as a healthy treat.

The secret of good training can be summed up in four words:

- ❧ Consistency
- ❧ Reward
- ❧ Praise
- ❧ Patience

With Minis, it's always the carrot - never the stick - that persuades them to do the things you want them to do. Punishment or dominance has the opposite effect. Remember, you're a team.

The Intelligence of Dogs

Psychologist and canine expert Dr Stanley Coren has written a book called *The Intelligence of Dogs* in which he ranks the breeds. He surveyed dog trainers to compile the list and used *Understanding of New Commands* and *Obeying First Command* as his standards of intelligence. He says there are three types of dog intelligence:

- ❧ Adaptive Intelligence (learning and problem-solving ability). Specific to the individual dog and is measured by canine IQ tests
- ❧ Instinctive Intelligence. Specific to the individual dog and is measured by canine IQ tests
- ❧ Working/Obedience Intelligence. This is breed-dependent

He divides dogs into six groups and the brainboxes of the canine world are the 10 breeds ranked in the 'Brightest Dogs' section of his list. It will come as no surprise to anyone who has ever been into the countryside and seen sheep being worked by a farmer and his right-hand man (his dog) to learn that the Border Collie is the most intelligent of all dogs.

Number Two is the Poodle, followed by the German Shepherd, Golden Retriever, Doberman Pinscher, Shetland Sheepdog, Papillon, Rottweiler and Australian Cattle Dog. All dogs in this class:

- ❧ Understand New Commands with Fewer than Five Repetitions
- ❧ Obey a First Command 95% of the Time or Better

The eager-to-please and show-off Mini Schnauzer is a stellar performer, coming in at Number 12, near the top of the Excellent Working Dogs category, for dogs who:

- ❧ Understand New Commands with Five to 15 Repetitions
- ❧ Obey First Command: 85% of the Time or Better

The Mini is included in the Terrier Group in the US and Utility Group in the UK. Those of you who have read any of my previous articles on Minis will know that I agree with the Americans; Miniature Schnauzers have a lot of Terrier in them. As US contributor and Agility competitor Rebecca Makdad pointed out, The Miniature Schnauzer is rated the most intelligent of all the Terriers - and by some margin.

The full list can be seen here: https://en.wikipedia.org/wiki/The_Intelligence_of_Dogs

By Dr Coren's own admission, the drawback of this rating scale is that it is heavily weighted towards obedience-related behavioural traits found in working dogs, rather than the creativity and maverick minds found in other dogs, including some Schnauzers. As a result, breeds such as hounds and Terriers are ranked lower on the list due to their independent or stubborn nature.

FACT ❭ Miniature Schnauzers are intelligent and learn quickly. However, if yours has an independent or mischievous streak, you've got to use YOUR brain to think of ways to engage your Schnauzer and keep him interested and motivated.

Five Golden Rules

1. Training must be reward-based, not punishment based.
2. Keep sessions short or your dog will get bored.
3. Never train when you are in a rush or a bad mood.
4. Training after exercise is fine, but never train when your dog is exhausted.
5. Keep sessions fun.

More stubborn or independent-minded Minis may try to push the boundaries when they reach adolescence – any time between six months and two years old. They may start behaving badly, and some males may start "marking" or urinating in the house, even when they are housetrained.

In all cases, go back to basics and put the time in – sadly, there is no quick fix. You need to be firm with a strong-willed dog, but all training should still be carried out using positive techniques.

 Establishing the natural order of things is not something forced on a dog through shouting or violence; it is brought about by mutual consent and good training.

Schnauzers are happiest and behave best when they are familiar and comfortable with their place in the household.

 While it's tempting to madly praise your Mini, try not to be too excitable! Some Minis can be highly strung; you are aiming for a relaxed, confident dog.

If you have adopted an older dog, you can still train him, but it will take a little longer to get rid of bad habits and instil good manners. Patience and persistence are the keys here.

<u>Socialisation</u> is a very important aspect of training with Minis. A good breeder will have already begun this process with the litter and then it's up to you to keep it going when puppy arrives home. Young pups can absorb a great deal of information, but they are also vulnerable to bad experiences.

They need to be exposed - in a positive manner - to different people, animals and situations. If not, they can find them very frightening when they do finally encounter them later.

If they have a lot of good experiences with other people, places, noises, situations and animals before four or five months old, they are less likely to either be timid or nervous.

Tip Don't just leave your dog at home in the early days, take him out and about with you, get him used to new people, places and noises. Minis that are only socialised around the home and garden or yard tend to be less confident, more vocal and more likely to react on the leash when they are away from the home.

All pups are chewers. If you are not careful, some young pups and adolescents will chew through anything – wires, phone chargers, remote controls, bedding, rugs, etc. Train your young pup only to chew the things you give – so don't give him your old slippers or anything that resembles something you don't want to get chewed; he won't know the difference. Buy purpose-made long-lasting chew toys - see **Chapter 6. Bringing Puppy Home.**

A puppy class is one of the best ways of getting a pup used to being socialised and trained. Max and I loved our puppy classes - he got a chance to show off and I found the antics of the other puppies hilarious. If you're feeling a bit down, I highly recommend a puppy class to get you laughing again.

This should be backed up by short sessions of a few minutes of training every day back home.

Tip Do not give your young pup too much attention, and choose training times when he is relaxed, perhaps slightly tired, but not exhausted.

Despite what you may think, training a Mini can be a pleasure of toil - they are so keen to get that treat or praise, they will do anything - and they'll definitely make you smile. Properly done it is a rewarding experience, a learning curve and a lot of fun - for both of you.

NOTE: If you do need some professional one-on-one help (for you and the dog), choose a trainer registered with the Association of Professional Dog Trainers (APDT) or another <u>positive method</u> organisation; the old Alpha-dominance theories have gone out the window.

....

Miniature Schnauzer Basics

❧ Although Miniature Schnauzers share some character traits with Terriers, they are considered easier to train than Terriers.

❧ Miniature Schnauzers love to be at the centre of life. They are also enthusiastic and eager to please, two main reasons why they respond well to training.

❧ They are attention-seekers, so praise for a job well done has a powerful effect. But they don't respond well to negative reinforcement; it only increases stress and anxiety.

❧ No matter how eager to please your Mini is, obedience training is an absolute must. Most Minis are pretty smart and will try and push the boundaries - like barking their heads off at every blowing leaf, jumping up at people, begging for food, ignoring your call, or taking over your bed - if you let them.

❧ If you DO allow them to get away with bad habits, they will become ingrained - Minis soon work out what is and what is not permitted. Unless you want a cocksure little dog ruling your house, start your training early - and stick with it!

❧ If your Mini is behaving badly, once you have given him the "NO!" command and he has stopped, don't give him any more of your time - even bad attention is some attention for Minis.

In our experience, Minis have short attention spans. Try to get your Mini to focus on **you** for brief training sessions - see the next chapter for how to do this.

Tip The key to successfully training a Mini is a combination of variety with repetition and tons of praise. Minis love praise. Regularly change the location and command, and keep sessions short - too much repetition and they'll switch off.

Without discipline and guidelines, the Mini's energy and playfulness can occasionally turn to stubbornness. If you want to avoid having a 'Little Emperor' or 'Little Princess' on your hands, start training early, set your rules and stick to them.

We recommend signing up for local puppy classes. Not only will your Mini learn obedience, but he or she will also learn to socialise with other dogs and humans. Socialisation is a very important part of a dog's education - your Mini has to learn that he isn't the centre of the Universe. See **Chapter 12** for more information on Socialisation.

Once our Max was trained, I spent a few minutes regularly reinforcing that training on our walks. Occasionally, but not always, I rewarded him with a treat for sitting, staying or coming back - we decided not to bother with fancy tricks; he was happy to excel at the simple stuff!

Top Training Tips

1. **Start training and socialising straight away**. Like babies, puppies learn quickly and it's this learned behaviour that stays with them through adult life. Start with just a few minutes a day a couple of days after arriving home.

2. **Your voice is a very important training tool**. Your dog has to learn to understand your language and you have to understand him. Commands should be issued in a calm, authoritative voice - not shouted. Praise should be given in a happy, encouraging voice, accompanied by stroking or patting. If your dog has done something wrong, use a stern voice, not a harsh shriek.

3. **Avoid giving your dog commands you know you can't enforce** or he learns that commands are optional. Give your dog only one command - twice maximum - then gently enforce it. Repeating commands will make him tune out; telling your dog to *"SIT, SIT, SIT, SIT!!!"* is neither efficient nor effective. Say a single *"SIT,"* gently place him in the Sit position and praise him.

4. **Train gently and humanely.** Mini Schnauzers are sensitive and do not respond well to being shouted at or hit.

5. **Keep training sessions short and upbeat.** If obedience training is a bit of a bore, pep things up a bit by *"play training"* by using constructive, non-adversarial games.

6. **Do not try to dominate your dog.** Training should be mutual, i.e. your dog should do something because he WANTS to do it and he knows that you want him to do it. Miniature Schnauzers are not interested in dominating you - although they often try and push the boundaries, especially in adolescence.

7. **Begin training at home around the house and garden/yard**. How well your dog responds at home affects his behaviour away from the home. If he doesn't respond well at home, he certainly won't respond any better out and about where there are 101 distractions, e.g. interesting scents, food scraps, other dogs, people, small animals or birds.

8. **Mealtimes are a great time to start training.** Teach Sit and Stay at breakfast and dinner, rather than just putting the dish down and letting him dash over immediately.

9. **Use his name often and <u>in a positive manner</u>** so he gets used to the sound of it. He won't know what it means at first, but it won't take long before he realises you're talking to him.

10. <u>**DON'T use his name when reprimanding, warning or punishing.**</u> He should trust that when he hears his name, good things happen. He should always respond to his name with enthusiasm, never hesitancy or fear. Use words such as *"No," "Ack!"* or *"Bad Boy/Girl"* in a stern (not shouted) voice instead. Some parents prefer not to use "No" with their dog, as they use it so often around the kids that it can confuse the pup!

11. **In the beginning, give your dog attention when YOU want to – not when he wants it.** When you are training, give your puppy lots of positive attention when he is good. But if he starts jumping up, nudging you constantly or barking to demand your attention, ignore him. Wait a while and pat him when you are ready and AFTER he has stopped demanding your attention.

12. **You can give Schnauzers TOO MUCH attention in the beginning.** This may create a rod for your own back when they grow into needy or demanding adults that are over-reliant on you. They may even develop Separation Anxiety, which is stressful for both dog AND owner.

13. **Don't give your dog lots of attention (even negative attention) when he misbehaves.** Mini Schnauzers love your attention and if yours gets lots when he's naughty, you are inadvertently reinforcing bad behaviour.

14. **Timing is critical.** When your puppy does something right, praise him immediately. If you delay, he will have no idea what he has done right. Similarly, when he does something wrong, correct him straight away.

15. **If he has an "accident" in the house, don't shout or rub his nose in it; it will have the opposite effect with a Schnauzer.** He may start hiding and peeing or pooping behind the couch or in other inappropriate places.

    If you catch him in the act, use your *"No!"* or *"Ack!"* sound and immediately lead him to the door. Then back to basics with housetraining. If you find something but don't catch him in the act, ignore it. If your pup is constantly eliminating indoors, you are not keeping a close enough eye on him!

16. **Start as you mean to go on.** In terms of training, treat your cute little pup as though he were fully grown, i.e. introduce the rules you want him to live by as an adult.

17. **Make sure that everybody in the household sticks to the same set of rules.** If the kids lift him onto the couch or bed and you forbid it, your dog won't know what is allowed and what isn't.

FACT ❯ Many repetitions of a command over a few minutes with rewards for getting it right will reinforce the message and help it stick in your dog's mind.

Teaching Basic Commands

The Three Ds

The three Ds – **Distance**, **Duration** and **Distraction** – are the cornerstone of a good training technique.

<u>Duration</u> is the length of time your dog remains in the command.

<u>Distance</u> is how far you can walk away without your dog breaking the command.

<u>Distraction</u> is the number of external stimuli - such as noise, scents, people, other animals, etc. - your dog can tolerate before breaking the command.

Only increase one of the Three Ds at a time.

For example, if your new pup has just learned to sit on command, gradually increase the time by a second or two as you go along. Moving away from the dog or letting the kids or the cat into the room would increase the Distance or Distraction level and make the command too difficult for your pup to hold.

If you are teaching the Stay, gradually increase EITHER the distance OR the time he is in the Stay position; don't increase both at once.

Start by training your dog in your home before moving into the garden or yard where there are more distractions - even if it is quiet and you are alone, outdoor scents and sights will be a big distraction for a young dog. Once you have mastered the commands in a home environment, progress to the park.

 Implement the Three Ds progressively and slowly, and don't expect too much too soon. Work within your dog's capabilities, move forward one tiny step at a time and set your dog up to consistently SUCCEED, not fail.

The Value of Treats

Different treats have different values and using them at the right time will help you to get the best out of your dog:

1. **High Value Food** is human food - usually animal-based - such as sausage, ham, chicken, liver and cheese. All should be cooked if raw and cut into pea-sized treats - you're looking to reward your dog, not feed him! Place the tiny treats in a freezer bag in the freezer, which keeps them fresh, then you can grab a handful when you go out training. There's not much water content and they quickly thaw.

   When training, we want our dog to want more High Value Food. He smells and tastes it on his tongue but it is gone in a flash, leaving him wanting more. *So, all treats should be only as large as a pea - even if you're training a Giant Schnauzer!*

2. **Medium Value Food** such as moist pet shop treats or a healthy alternative like sliced apple or carrot.

3. **Low Value Food** such as kibble. Use your dog's own food if you feed dry, or buy a small bag if not.

IMPORTANT: Whenever you are asking your dog **to do something new,** make it worth his while. Offer a High Value treat like liver. Once your dog understands what you are asking, you can move down to a Medium Value treat.

When he does it every time use Low Value... reduce the frequency after a while and then only give it every other time... then only occasionally until you have slowly stopped giving any treat when asking for that task.

The aim at this point is to start getting you in control of your dog. And, most importantly, we want your dog to want to be controlled, as control brings good things.

....

The Sit

Teaching the Sit command to your Schnauzer is relatively easy. Teaching a young Mini to sit still for any length of time is a bit more difficult! If your little protégé is very distracted or high energy, it may be easier to put him on a leash to hold his attention.

1. **Stand facing each other and hold a treat between your thumb and fingers just an inch or so above his head** and let him sniff it. Don't let your fingers and the treat get much further away or you might have trouble getting him to move his body into a sitting position.

   If your dog jumps up when you try to guide him into the Sit, you're probably holding your hand too far away from his nose. If your dog backs up, you can practise with a wall behind him.

2. **As he reaches up to sniff it, move the treat upwards and back over the dog** towards his tail at the same time as saying *"Sit."* Most dogs will track the treat with their eyes and follow it with their noses, causing their noses to point straight up.

3. **As his head moves up toward the treat, his rear end should automatically go down towards the floor.** TaDa! (drum roll!).

4. **The second he sits, say** *"Yes!"* Give him the treat and tell your dog he's a good boy/girl. Stroke and praise him for as long as he stays in the sitting position.

5. **If he jumps up on his back legs** and paws while you are moving the treat, be patient and start all over again. At this stage, don't expect your bouncy little pupil to sit for more than a nanosecond!

NOTE: For positive reinforcement, use the words *Yes!, Good Boy!* or *Good Girl!*

Another method is to put one hand on his chest and with your other hand, gently push down on his rear end until he is sitting, while saying *"Sit."* Give him a treat and praise; he will eventually associate the position with the word "sit."

Once your dog catches on, leave the treat in your pocket (or have it in your other hand). Repeat, but this time your dog will just follow your empty hand. Say *"Sit"* and bring your empty hand in front of your dog's nose. Move your hand exactly as you did when you held the treat. When your dog sits, say *"Yes!"* and then give him a treat from your other hand or your pocket.

Gradually lessen the amount of movement with your hand. First, say *"Sit"* then hold your hand eight to 10 inches above your dog's face and wait a moment. Most likely, he will sit. If he doesn't, help him by moving your hand back over his head, like you did before, but make a smaller movement this time. Then try again. Your goal is to eventually just say *"Sit"* without having to move or extend your hand at all.

Once your dog reliably sits on cue, you can ask him to sit whenever you meet people (it may not work straight away, but it might help to calm him down a bit). The key is anticipation. Give your dog the cue before he gets too excited to hear you and before he starts jumping up on the person who just arrived. Generously reward him the instant he sits.

The Stay

This is a very useful command, but it's not so easy to teach a lively and distracted young Schnauzer pup - don't ask him to stay for more than a few seconds in the beginning.

The Stay requires concentration from your dog, so pick a time when he's relaxed and well-exercised, or just after a game - but not too exhausted to concentrate.

Mealtimes are a good opportunity to practise this, even if you have to physically (and gently) hold him during the Stay for a second or two; he will soon pick it up.

1. Tell your dog to sit.

2. Say *"Stay"* and instead of giving a treat as soon as he hits the floor, hold off for a couple of seconds. We find it useful to use a hand signal here, *pictured.*

3. After a second or two say your release word or phrase, **e.g.** *"Free!" "Here!"* or *"Come Here!"*

4. Give the treat when he comes towards you.

5. If he bounces straight up without staying, start over again. Give him one treat for the Sit and then keep a second for the Stay.

6. If your Mini pup finds it impossible to Stay, get someone to help you and gently hold the dog in position until your release command. Another good option is to practise at mealtimes. Hold the dog in the Stay position, looking at the food until you give the verbal release, then let him go.

7. Repeat the exercise a few times, gradually waiting a tiny bit longer before releasing the treat.

8. A common mistake is to hold the treat high and then give the reward slowly. As your dog doesn't know the command yet, he sees the treat coming and gets up to meet the food. Instead, bring the treat towards your dog quickly - the best place to deliver it is right between his front paws. If you're working on a Sit-Stay, give the treat at chest height.

9. When your dog can stay for several seconds, start to add a little distance. At first, you'll walk backwards, because your dog is more likely to get up to follow you if you turn away from him.

10. **Remember DISTANCE, DURATION, DISTRACTION.** Work on one factor at a time. Whenever you make one factor more difficult, ease up on the others then build them back up. So, when you add distance, cut the duration of the stay.

11. Once he's mastered the Stay with you alone, **move the training on so that he learns to do the same with distractions.** Have someone walk into the room, or squeak a toy or bounce a

ball once. A rock-solid stay is mostly a matter of working slowly and patiently to start with. Don't go too fast. If he does get up, take a breather and then give him a short refresher, starting at a point easier than whatever you were working on when he cracked.

 If you think he's tired or had enough, leave it for the day and come back later – just finish off on a positive note by giving one very easy command you know he will obey, followed by a reward.

Don't use the Stay command in situations where it is unpleasant for your dog. For instance, avoid telling him to stay as you close the door behind you on your way to work.

Finally, don't use Stay to keep a dog in a scary situation.

....

Down

There are several different ways to teach this command, which here means for the dog to lie down. (If you are teaching this command, then use the *"Off"* command to teach your dog not to jump up). This does not come naturally to a young pup, so it may take a little while to master.

Although you may gently push him down, don't make it a battle by physically forcing him down against his will; your Mini will not like it.

1. Give the Sit command.

2. When your dog sits, don't give him the treat immediately, but keep it in your closed hand. **Slowly move your hand straight down towards the floor, between his front legs.** As your Schnauzer's nose follows the treat, just like a magnet, his head will bend all the way down to the floor.

3. When the treat is on the floor between your dog's paws, start to move it away from him, like you're drawing a line along the floor. (The entire luring motion forms an L-shape).

4. At the same time say *"Down"* in a firm manner.

5. To continue to follow the treat, your dog will probably ease himself into the Down position. The instant his elbows touch the floor, say *"Yes!"* and immediately let him eat the treat. If your dog doesn't automatically stand up after eating the treat, just move a step or two away to encourage him to move out of the Down position.

Repeat the sequence above several times. Aim for two short sessions of five minutes per day.

If your dog's back end pops up, quickly snatch the treat away. Then immediately say Sit and try again. It may help to let him nibble on the treat as you move it toward the floor. If you've tried to lure your dog into a Down, but he still seems confused or reluctant, try this trick:

1. Sit down on the floor with your legs straight out in front of you. Your dog should be at your side. Keeping your legs together and your feet on the floor, bend your knees to make a 'tent' shape.

2. Hold a treat right in front of your dog's nose. As he licks and sniffs the treat, slowly move it down to the floor and then underneath your legs. Continue to lure him until he has to crouch down to keep following the treat.

3. The instant his belly touches the floor, say *"Yes!"* and let him eat the treat. If your dog seems nervous about following the treat under your legs, make a trail of treats for him to eat along the way.

4. Some dogs find it easier to follow a treat into the Down from a standing position. Hold the treat right in front of your dog's nose, and then slowly move it straight down to the floor, right between his front paws. His nose will follow the treat.

5. If you let him lick the treat as you continue to hold it still on the floor, your dog will probably plop into the Down position.

6. The moment he does, say *"Yes!"* and let him eat the treat (some Minis are reluctant to lie on a cold, hard surface. It may be easier to teach yours to lie down on a carpet). The next step is to introduce a hand signal. You'll still reward him with treats, though, so keep them nearby or hidden behind your back.

7. Start with your dog in a Sit and say *"Down."*

8. **Without** a treat in your fingers, use the same hand motion you did before. As soon as your dog's elbows touch the floor, say *"Yes!"* and immediately give him a hidden treat. **Important:** You want him to learn that he doesn't have to see a treat to get one.

9. Clap your hands or take a few steps away to encourage him to stand up. Repeat the sequence several times for a week or so. When he lies down as soon as you say the cue and use your new hand signal, you're ready for the next step.

Tip To stop bending down to the floor every time, you can gradually shrink the signal to a smaller movement. To make sure your dog continues to understand what you want him to do, progress slowly.

10. Repeat the hand signal, but stop when it's an inch or two above the floor and practise this for a day or two. Then reduce your movement by a few inches again.

11. Gradually stop your hand signal farther and farther from the floor; eventually, you won't have to bend over at all. You'll be able to stand up straight, say *"Down,"* and just point to the floor.

Your next job is harder: practise your dog's new skill in different situations and locations. Start with calm places, like different rooms in your house or your garden or yard when there's no one around. Then increase the distractions; so, do some sessions at home when family members are moving around, on walks and then at friends' houses, too.

Basic Recall

This basic command is perhaps the most important of all - and one of the hardest with many dogs, especially if you have a Mini Schnauzer with a lot of instinct. They soon get distracted by scents, small animals and birds - in fact, anything that's more interesting than following your command!

It will require lots of repetition and patience on your part, but you are limiting both your lives if you can't let your dog do what he was born to do; run free. A Schnauzer who obeys the Recall enjoys freedoms that other dogs cannot.

Make sure your Schnauzer has some grasp of the Recall before you allow him off-leash beyond fenced areas.

 Whether you have a puppy or an older dog, the first step is always to establish that coming to you is the BEST thing he can do. Any time your dog comes to you - whether you've called him or not - acknowledge that you appreciate it with praise, affection, play or treats. This consistent reinforcement ensures that your dog will continue to "check in" with you frequently.

Location is important; you don't want to compete with the surroundings for his attention. So start in the yard or garden where there are few distractions - or even inside the home. If you go to a new place, allow your dog time to sniff and settle down.

1. Start a short distance away from your dog.

2. Say your dog's name followed by the command *"Come!"* or *"Here!"* in an enthusiastic voice. You'll usually be more successful if you walk or run away from him while you call. Minis find it hard to resist chasing a running person, especially their owner.

3. He should run towards you!

4. A young dog will often start running towards you but then get distracted and head off in another direction. Pre-empt this situation by praising your pup and cheering him on when he starts to come to you and **before** he has a chance to get distracted.

    Your praise will keep him focused so that they'll be more likely to come all the way to you. If he stops or turns away, you can give him feedback by saying *"Oh-oh!"* or *"Hey!"* in a different tone of voice (displeased or unpleasantly surprised). When he looks at you again, smile, call him and praise him as he approaches you.

5. When your puppy comes to you, give him the treat BEFORE he sits down or he may think that the treat was earned for sitting, not coming to you.

6. Another method is to use two people. You hold the treats and let your dog sniff them while the accomplice holds onto the dog by his collar. When you are about 10 or 15 yards away, get your helper to let the dog go, and once he is running towards you, say *"COME!"* loudly and enthusiastically.

    When he reaches you, stop, bend down and make a fuss of him before giving a treat. Do this several times. The next step is to give the Come command just BEFORE you get your helper to release the dog, and by doing this repetitively, the dog begins to associate the command with the action.

NOTE: "Come" or a similar word is better than "Here" if you intend to use the "Heel" command, as "Here" and "Heel" sound very similar.

Progress your dog's training in baby steps. If he's learned to come when called in your kitchen, you can't expect him to do it straight away at the park, in the woods or on the beach when surrounded by distractions. When you first use the Recall outdoors, make sure there's no one around to distract your dog.

Initially consider using a long training leash - or do the training within a safe, fenced area. Only when your dog has mastered the Recall in different locations and in the face of various distractions can you expect him to come to you regularly.

Teaching The Recall With a Whistle

Some owners prefer to train their dogs to come back to a whistle. A small plastic whistle, such as the Acme Dog Whistle 210 series on a lanyard or keyring is ideal.

NOTE: Some Miniature Schnauzers are noise-sensitive. Initially, see how your Mini reacts to a whistle. If he puts his ears back, looks frightened or runs away, we don't recommend whistle training!

If you do decide to whistle train, start as soon as you can. The advantages are:

- A whistle is louder than your voice, especially when it's windy
- A whistle doesn't convey emotions such as frustration, anger or fear
- Different people can use the whistle, ensuring the dog returns to whoever is walking him
- Dogs respond well to a whistle; it sounds exciting to them
- If you're having trouble with voice commands or your teenage Schnauzer is regressing, a whistle might be the answer

 Whatever you may have read, dogs do NOT automatically know what a whistle means... they have to learn it!

1. Start using the whistle in the yard or garden to get him to come to you (and get your family to invest in some earplugs!).

2. You can even run away from him to encourage him to come.

3. Give two short peeps when you want him to come to you.

4. Reward and praise him when he does.

5. Progress in baby steps, if your Schnauzer is too distracted or otherwise not likely to come back to you, DON'T use the whistle. Set him up for success, not failure.

6. Once he starts to associate the whistle with really positive things and comes to you, increase the three D's gradually: **Distance, Duration and Distraction.**

7. You can also do this at mealtimes. Hold the dog's collar, give two sharp peeps on the whistle, release him and let him eat the food.

8. Give two sharp peeps before you leave the house for a walk. When he comes to you, reward and praise him.

9. Always associate the whistle with GOOD things and treats.

In the beginning reward your dog lavishly with treats, praise and/or a favourite toy. The aim is to get him to pay attention to you whenever you give the whistle command, knowing that something good lies in store for him.

Once you have mastered the Recall, you can use different peeps to convey other commands, such as Sit, Stay, down, etc.

Before you know it, your Mini will be giving the local Border Collies a run for their money!

Tips from Breeders

Andrew and Gaynor Ray, of Minnienoom Schnauzers, are UK Assured Breeders with decades of experience: "As soon as your puppy joins your family he or she can learn simple words like his or her name, 'Sit' and 'Come.'

"Reward with a titbit when he or she responds well and ensure the whole family use the same words of praise to avoid confusion.

"Make training enjoyable, and remember that you are laying the foundations for good behaviour. Puppies respond to cheerful, rather than threatening, voice tones and they will sense any stress or impatience on your part.

"Ask your vet to recommend a good puppy socialisation/training class and sign up if the sessions are well-controlled and planned, the class size is small (up to 10), they are run only for young puppies, and the puppies and owners look as though they are enjoying it and learning too.

"Alternatively, contact the Kennel Club and find your nearest dog training club, ideally one that offers obedience training and participates in the Kennel Club Good Citizen Dog Training scheme.

"If you want to show your puppy, Ring Craft classes will show you how to prepare and present him or her at their best and train them how to stand and show off."

UK Assured Breeder **Steve Matthews**, Silbertraum Schnauzers, Dorset: "Training your puppy begins at home and should start immediately with toilet training. Getting it right is fairly simple and will make life much more enjoyable. All Schnauzers like to please their owners, therefore constant praise rewarding good behaviours is the best training tip.

"We strongly recommend that you take your pup to puppy classes, as this not only offers an excellent start, but provides a safe environment in which it can socialise with other dogs of a similar

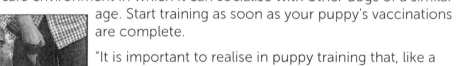

age. Start training as soon as your puppy's vaccinations are complete.

"It is important to realise in puppy training that, like a child, a puppy has a short attention span, so training is best delivered little and often. Bad habits learned early can lead to problems that take weeks or even months to resolve, so they are best nipped in the bud."

AKC Breeder of Merit **Wade Bogart,** of Sumerwynd Miniature Schnauzers, New York State: "The Miniature Schnauzer has an instinctive desire to please. The key to training is repetition, repetition and more repetition - along with heaping lots of praise on them when they do something correctly."

What the Owners Say

Chloe: "Before I got my Schnauzer, I would browse online forums and people would joke that Miniature Schnauzers would do anything for a treat - to the point that "they will do your tax returns for a treat." I can for sure say I'm surprised by how true that saying is; treats are a huge motivator for Schnauzers when training.

"Oslo's motivation to learn new things is extremely treat-reliant. His treats include kibbles, store-bought training treats, and small carrot bits or blueberries in moderation."

Rebecca: "I believe that the Mini Schnauzer is the only dog in the Terrier Group listed in the Top 15 Most Intelligent Dog List - at number 12. Navy *(pictured here as a puppy)* is relentless when she wants something; she can be a very determined Schnauzer. I had to remove the "string of bells" from the door. If she wanted outside, she would continually "hit the bells" until I removed them or let her out...who is training who?!

"The most important training tip is to keep it FUN - make all training a game. Be consistent and reward the desired behavior."

Chris: "Betsy went to puppy training and we learned a few tips from them. However, she is bright and a simple food reward system seems very effective. Lots of praise and celebrating her success have been the key to obedience, which we would describe as pretty good. The key seems to be being kind, calm but firm."

Leah: "Our three have been very easy to teach; Minis are very intelligent. All our dogs enjoy squeaky toys - Freddie has a squeaky duck that he loves."

Yolande: "Mayzy loves her training sessions and is eager to learn, both with me, the agility trainer, the puppy classes and socialisation classes. Since she was spayed last September, she has become more focused on food, so small treats are a great encouragement to learn."

Vivian: "My husband and I are advocates of early and adult dog training from professionals. We believe that positive reinforcement is the best dog training method, especially for Miniature Schnauzers, who seem to be sensitive little souls.

"Like every other dog we've owned, we took Bogart to puppy classes and later to a basic obedience class. We found him to be extremely bright and, since he is also food-motivated, easy to train. He performs a few tricks. Because Bogart occasionally howls, one of the tricks we taught him is to howl on command. Our breeder wanted us to extinguish that behaviour but we think it's cute and now Bogart strictly howls only when asked!

"At mealtimes, Bogart is trained to sit and give his paw on command (we consider him far too dignified to be expected to "beg" for his food!). After his bowl is placed in his crate, he continues to look at us and waits patiently to eat until he is given the "Okay" command. We have similar expectations for him to wait for permission before he goes outside; bolting outside is never allowed.

"We invested in some puzzle games for our dogs, since both Bogart and Rabies, our Standard Poodle *(pictured)* are highly intelligent and need a variety of mental stimulation."

Gary: "I have been quite surprised by their strong will and desire to be in charge; also how cheeky they are and how much energy they have for a small dog.

"Start training on Day One, they are never too young to learn the basics. Be patient, that said Minis learn quickly as they are intelligent little dogs. Use treats to reward their good efforts and praise them with a happy voice; scold with a gruff voice.

"Remember they are strong-willed little dogs and will challenge you, so stand up to them."

Simon and Yvonne: "Ours are very food motivated, so the training goes well in this house."

Lisa: "Minis are very smart and willing to please. They excel at obedience, but can become bored with repetitive training; so wise trainers will learn to switch things up to keep their Mini happy and engaged in learning!"

Photo courtesy of Lisa.

"They are very food and praise-oriented and love to learn and please their trainers. Excited praise will readily set in a response. Regarding bad behavior, my motto is simply to ignore or interrupt bad behaviors, and replace them with the wanted behavior by marking and rewarding it."

Common Training Mistakes

Here's a list of actions to avoid if you want to train your Mini speedily:

- ❧ **Repetition** - dogs hate repetition. They switch off after the first or second command!

- ❧ **Giving the reward too slowly** - one command equals one immediate treat or praise. Leave it longer and the dog doesn't know why he's being rewarded

- ❧ **Proceeding too quickly** - you want your Mini to excel at training, so don't move on to new commands until he's a dab hand (or paw) at the one you're working on

- ❧ **Domination** - Minis do NOT like to be dominated; it's stressful for them. Don't push or pull your dog around, don't shout. He won't like it and he'll learn nothing

- ❧ **Too many distractions in the early stages**. Make sure your Mini can obey a command fairly reliably before proceeding - and then only one distraction at a time, if possible

- ❧ **Reinforcing unwanted behaviour** - if your Mini is barking or whining, don't give him a treat as soon as he stops. Wait, so he realises he's getting it for being quiet, not noisy

- ❧ **Different commands from different people** - these confuse a dog. Make sure all the family is on the same page and specific words for the commands are agreed. Down is Down, so if you use that word, stick to it, don't use Lie, Lie Down, Off, Get Off, Get Down, etc.

- ❧ **Being boring** - Minis have a very short attention span and soon get bored. A few minutes at a time is plenty

- ❧ **Training on a full stomach** (the dog's, not yours!). A hungry dog is more likely to be motivated by food or treats

Collar and Leash Training

If you want to take your Mini away from the home, which hopefully you do, then you have to train them to get used to a collar and leash and to walk beside you. This can be challenging with young Schnauzers, who don't necessarily want to walk at the same pace as you - some puppies might even slump to the ground and refuse to move in the beginning!

All dogs will pull on a leash initially. It's not because they want to show you who's boss, it's simply that they are excited to be out and are forging ahead.

You will need a small collar to start with. Some puppies don't mind collars, some will try to fight them, while others will lie on the floor. Be patient and calm and proceed at a pace comfortable to your dog; don't fight him and don't force the collar on.

1. **Start with a lightweight collar** and give praise or a treat as soon as the collar is on - not once you have taken it off. Gradually increase the length of time you leave the collar on. If you leave your dog in a crate, or alone in the house, take off the collar and tags. They may get caught, causing panic or injury.

2. Put the collar on when other things will occupy him, like when he is going outside to be with you, when you are interacting with him, at mealtimes or when you are doing some basic training. Don't put it on too tight, you want him to forget it's there.

   TIP: You should be able to get two fingers underneath the collar.

   Most pups will scratch the collar, some may react as if you've hung a two-ton weight around their necks, while others will be more compliant. When he scratches the collar, get his attention by encouraging him to follow you or play with a toy to forget the irritation.

   Once your puppy is happy wearing the collar, **introduce the leash**. Some owners prefer an extending or retractable leash, but a fixed-length one is best for training. Begin in the house and yard or garden.

 Think of the leash as a safety device to stop him from running off, not something to drag him around with. You want a Schnauzer who doesn't pull, so don't start by pulling him around.

3. **Attach the leash and give a treat while you put it on.** Use the treats (instead of pulling on the leash) to lure him beside you, so that he gets used to walking with the collar and leash on. You can also make good use of toys to do exactly the same thing - especially if your dog has a favourite. Walk around the house with the leash on and lure him forward with the toy.

Act as though it's the most natural thing in the world for you to walk around the house with your dog on a leash - and just hope the neighbours aren't watching! Some dogs react the moment you attach the leash and they feel some tension - a bit like when a horse is being broken for the first time.

Drop the leash and allow him to run around the house or yard, dragging it behind, but be careful

he doesn't get tangled and hurt himself. Try to make him forget about it by playing or starting a short fun training routine with treats. While he is concentrating on the new task, occasionally pick up the leash and call him to you. Do it gently and in an encouraging tone.

4. **Don't yank on the leash.** If it gets tight, just lure him back beside you with a treat or a toy. Remember to keep the hand holding the treat or toy down, so your dog doesn't get into the habit of jumping up. If you feel he is getting stressed, try putting treats along the route you'll be taking to turn this into a rewarding game: good times are ahead... and he learns to focus on what's ahead of him with curiosity, not fear.

NOTE: UK law requires all dogs to wear a collar with an ID tag, containing the owner's contact details, outside the home.

 Take collar and leash training slowly. Let him gain confidence in you, the leash and himself. Some dogs sit and decide not to move! If this happens, walk a few steps away, go down on one knee and encourage him to come to you, then walk off again.

Some Miniatures are perfectly happy to walk alongside you off-leash, but behave differently when they have one on. Others may become more excitable or aggressive on a leash once they gain their confidence when their *Fight-or-Flight* instinct kicks in.

NOTE: A collar is essential for any Schnauzer who becomes nervous or aggressive in a veterinary clinic. You and the vet will have more control.

Harnesses

Opinions vary as to whether harnesses are a good thing for Miniature Schnauzers. Certainly, some owners do use them. Before deciding, here are some points to consider:

* If your Mini pulls, changing to a harness will not stop the pulling, nor otherwise improve his behaviour. Train your dog to walk correctly on a leash first - it is entirely possible to teach a Schnauzer not to pull using a normal collar and leash!

* Schnauzers have a keen sense of smell and will often pull towards interesting scents while out on a walk. This is natural and nothing personal against their owner. The ideal life for a Miniature Schnauzer is to have controlled exercise and some off-leash time to behave instinctually

* Harnesses were originally developed for big, working dogs in different roles. A harness is easier for tracking dogs like Bloodhounds to move freely without being distracted by the handler, who is still attached to the dog via a long line. Siberian Huskies pull sleds and harnesses allow them to exert more power, pull more weight or free a sled caught in ice

* Badly-fitting harnesses can be more detrimental than a traditional collar as they can impede the dog's natural movement

* When the right harness is fitted correctly, it can help take pressure away from the sensitive neck area and distribute it more evenly around the front of the body

 The consensus among our contributing breeders is that all Schnauzers should be trained on a collar and leash. They do not advocate the use of a harness - unless the dog has a neck or throat problem.

We also do not recommend a halter, headcollar or any form of choke collar on a Miniature Schnauzer.

If you do opt for a harness, avoid the heavy ones that wrap around the front of the dog, as these can prevent the shoulder joints from moving normally or put extra pressure on the back and neck.

The ideal type looks like two collars in parallel with a thin vertical strap or panel between the dog's front legs. Make sure it has a safe collar part that the dog cannot escape from - or attach the harness to a collar - and that it is tight enough elsewhere. Once you have fitted it, stretch out your dog's forelegs to make sure it doesn't affect his ability to walk normally.

 If you've never used a harness before, it's easy to get tangled up while your Schnauzer is bouncing around, excited at the prospect of a walk. It's a good idea to have a few "dry runs" without the dog!

Lay the harness on the floor and familiarise yourself with it. Learn which bits the legs go through, which parts fit where and how it fits together once the dog is in. If you can train your Schnauzer to step into the harness, even better...!

Walking on a Leash

There are different methods, but we have found the following one to be successful for quick results with a Mini. Initially, the leash should be kept fairly loose. Have a treat in your hand as you walk, it will encourage your dog to sniff the treat as he walks alongside. He will not pull ahead as he will want to remain near the treat.

Give him the command **"Walk"** or **"Heel"** and then proceed with treat in hand, giving him a treat every few steps initially, then gradually extend the time between treats. Eventually, you should be able to walk with your hand comfortably at your side, periodically (every minute or so) reaching into your pocket to grab a tiny treat to reward your dog.

If your Mini starts pulling ahead, give him a **"No"** or **"Steady"** warning. If he slows down, give him a treat. But if he continues to pull ahead so that your arm becomes fully extended, stop walking.

Wait for him to stop pulling and look up at you.

At this point reward him for good behaviour before carrying on. Be sure to reward or praise him **quickly** any time he doesn't pull and walks alongside you with some slack on the leash.

If you have a lively young pup who is dashing all over the place on the leash, start training sessions when he is already a little bit tired - after play or exercise - but not exhausted.

Another way is what dog trainer Victoria Stillwell describes as the "*Reverse Direction Technique.*" When your dog pulls, say **"Let's Go!"** in an encouraging manner, then turn away from him and walk off in the other direction, without jerking on the lead. When he is following you and the leash is slack, turn back and continue on your original way.

It may take a few repetitions, but your words and body language will make it clear that pulling will not get your dog anywhere, whereas walking calmly by your side - or even slightly in front of you - on a loose leash will get him where he wants to go.

Google "*Victoria Stillwell Loose Leash Walking*" for more detailed information.

FACT > If you allow your Mini to pull you in his direction, you are reinforcing his behaviour. In his mind, it works because he gets to go where he wants to go!

11. Next Training Steps

We all dream of having a perfectly-behaved Miniature Schnauzer we can take anywhere. But it doesn't happen overnight - and even when we spend time training our dogs, things don't always run smoothly.

Like small children, Mini Schnauzer puppies will get away with whatever they can; some are more wilful or independent by nature, and others learn then regress as teenagers - any time from around nine months until 'maturity' at 18 to 24 months.

This chapter gives you an insight into your dog's mind when training. Miniature Schnauzer breeders and professional dog trainer Lisa Cole outline positive strategies not only to cope with unwanted behaviour, but also to speed up everyday training.

Tips From A Trainer

Lisa Cole's life has always revolved around animals. She has worked with dogs for decades at kennels, veterinary practices, boarding kennels and Greyhound Rescue. While working in rescue, she saw the difference time and training could make to an individual dog and this set her on her path to professional dog training.

Here Lisa helps owners to understand and train their dogs and offers advice on dealing with some common behaviour problems.

I can quickly teach a dog to sit on a Monday with no problem, yet a different dog trained with the same technique on a Tuesday just does not understand what I am asking. This is not because the dog is stupid or untrainable; it's because he learns in a slightly different way.

All dogs can be taught at all ages, but the methods used to get different dogs to the same point can vary quite dramatically. Before we start, it helps to understand how dogs think, process information and communicate with us and other dogs.

Dogs cannot talk, but they do bark, which usually indicates excitement or a perceived threat. A bark can mean Go away, Someone is at the door, Mum's home, Leave me alone.

All of these are alert sounds, but there is so much more than the bark. Dogs' conversations are also done with posture, ear and tail placement, and even making the fur rise so they seem bigger when needed.

We can change how our dog acts with just a little understanding of how he or she thinks.

Factors Affecting Behaviour

Natural instincts affect behaviour, so when choosing a pet (non-working) dog, always research the breed and Breed Group. There are seven Breed Groups: Gundog, Pastoral, (Herding in the US), Working, Hound, Utility (Non-Sporting in the US), Terrier and Toy. Minis are in the Utility Group in the UK and the Terrier Group in the USA.

FACT ➤ The Miniature Schnauzer was bred down from the original Standard Schnauzer, whose job was to catch vermin and guard the home and wagon. So it's not surprising that, typically, most Minis will chase and all of them have a tendency to bark if not well-socialised.

Most Miniature Schnauzers are very loyal and people-loving, but can be harder to train or to call back when a squirrel or rabbit has just taken off across the field or park. There are some tips later on how to try and control this.

One extremely important factor affecting behaviour is *socialisation,* or dogs meeting other dogs of all sizes, shapes and colours, and people with different smells, colours and moods. Socialisation is so important for a dog's happiness and mental health.

If you buy a dog and he never goes out, never sees other dogs, cats, cars, bikes, people or buses, when he does go out he is very frightened by all these moving things.

Photo: Max meeting Lottie the Labradoodle for the first time. They went on to become good friends, although he generally preferred the company of humans to other dogs.

Your dog may walk quietly by your side, but if he's not socialised, there is an increased risk of him showing aggression if someone approaches.

Imagine you are born and everything is blue. You are blue, your mum is blue, all your brothers and sisters are blue, and you are all happy in a safe, warm, blue home. Then one day a pink person arrives and takes you away from your safe blue home.

You are thrust into a world of red, yellow, green, orange, pink — it's scary! But if you were introduced slowly to the other colours a little at a time, you'd be far less afraid.

Socialisation also helps your dog to speak *"Dog."* All day every day your dog is learning the sounds from his owners and trying to respond. When meeting other dogs, he also learns how to behave with them.

There is nothing worse than a dog trying to be friendly and, because he does not know what to do, getting the messages mixed up and the other dog takes it as a threat. Fights can happen.

If you become the owner of a dog that has had no socialisation and/or a bad experience, he will be full of fear. It's embarrassing on walks when he lunges and barks at almost everything. With you at home, he is happy, kind and placid, but taking him out is a nightmare.

Many owners stop walking their dogs completely or return the dog to the rescue. Sadly, many dogs are returned time and time again before they find the right home.

Common Scenarios

Before any training or behaviour work is done, try to understand some of the thought processes going through your dog's mind:

Scenario 1: A lovely, happy dog is put in his bed every morning. After the owner leaves the dog starts to bark. WOOF, WOOF, WOOF, this goes on all day every day - poor neighbours. As soon as the owner returns, the happy dog greets the owner and settles down quietly all evening. Why?

From the dog's point of view, the owner gets up and lets the dog out for a wee and leaves. The dog wants the owner to come back, so the only thing he can think of is to shout as loud as he can so the owner will hear him and return. So, WOOF, WOOF, WOOF! And, of course, the owner returns - only the owner knows he was coming back anyway.

In the dog's eyes it worked, so tomorrow when he is left alone, he barks all day again.

Scenario 2: The postman comes to the house and posts some letters through your letterbox. Your dog goes bananas, rushing to the front door and barking crazily. Then after a short time, your dog returns to being the happy calm dog he was before the postman arrived. Why?

In the dog's eyes, he's snoozing on the sofa loving life, then suddenly a man comes up to the house and is trying to get in through the hole in the door. WOOF, WOOF, WOOF! Then the man goes away. It worked, he has frightened the man away, so tomorrow guess what will happen...

Scenario 3: The owner is out for a walk with his dog on a lead. His neighbour is heading straight towards him with his dog on a lead.

The first dog becomes stiff, staring straight at the approaching dog. In a seemingly aggressive manner, he starts barking, lunging forward, pulling at the lead trying to get to the neighbour's dog. He only calms down after the neighbour and dog have passed by.

The following day both neighbours are in the park with their dogs off-lead. The dogs see each other, run over with tails wagging and start to play together.

This can happen for a few reasons, but the biggest cause of this type of on-lead behaviour is **us!** Having the dog on the lead means the dogs must greet face to face, which is an aggressive posture in the canine world, so the dog feels the need to protect himself and you.

He is feeling scared, excited and protective all at the same time - resulting in barking and lunging.

So, armed with a little knowledge about your dog's behaviour and why it might be happening, we can start training. Five to 10 minutes in a whole day is all that is needed, but these short training sessions are especially important.

Do a little bit every day, not 60 minutes one day and nothing for the rest of the week, otherwise your dog will learn a little but not achieve what you want.

....

Taking Control

The first step towards being in control of a dog is by training him to focus and listen to us.

The Clicker

I believe it's important to have a tool that bridges the language barrier of man and dog, and *the clicker* is a simple and highly effective way of letting your dog understand that what he has just done is *exactly* the thing you are asking for.

Dogs love to please using a clicker, and it enforces the fact that he is doing it right. The click must happen at the right moment as it means: Well done! He's done what you asked.

One example is teaching the Sit. With the clicker in your hand and treats in your pocket or a bowl out of reach, ask your dog for a Sit. The moment his bottom touches the floor, CLICK. After the click has happened, take out a treat and give your dog his prize.

If you are too slow, he will think you are praising him for getting up out of a Sit - or if it is too soon, you will be praising him for looking at you.

NOTE: If the clicker goes off randomly it can confuse your dog and the training will not be as effective. You can practise getting used to a clicker (out of your dog's hearing) by bouncing a ball and clicking every time it hits the floor.

Call My Name (Recall)

For no more than two minutes at a time and spread randomly through the day, practise the *Call My Name* game. With the clicker in your hand ready and treats in your pocket or nearby, wait until your dog is busy doing something or falling asleep. Then in a clear voice - but not shouting - just call your dog's name once.

If your dog shows any interest by moving his ear, looking over or even coming over, CLICK then throw a treat over to him. This is the start of good Recall; we want the dog to come so always throw the treat.

Tip: Don't get over-excited when your dog gets it right! We want him to be in control and not rushing around the room in excitement. Stay calm and give a "Good Boy."

Repeat and practise. Very soon your dog will hear you calling his name and come running every time. Perfect, just what we want - but take it one more step. When you have called your dog's name and your dog runs over, hold the treat and in your head count to 10. Your dog should sit nicely in front of you. When you get to 10, CLICK then treat. Good boy!

Instead of calling your dog's name, you can use a whistle in two short blasts. Then CLICK and throw the treat. The dog should very quickly understand if you follow the Call My Name instructions but blow the whistle instead, he should come to you and sit in front of you nicely.

Look at Me (Focus)

This next exercise also needs to be done randomly during the day. Now we are getting your dog to focus on you, and to do so on command if needed.

Hold a treat in your right hand and clicker in the left. Call your dog over and he should sit. Allow the dog the knowledge you have a treat in your right hand - the treat should be held between your thumb and middle finger leaving your index finger free.

Move your hand up towards your face and with your index finger point to the outside of your right eye (or left, if you are left-handed). Hold it there and use the command word "LOOK." If your dog is looking towards your face, CLICK and give the treat.

Once your dog understands what you are asking, repeat the exercise - but this time keep the treat in your pocket. Just raise your hand and point to the corner of your eye and say "LOOK." If your dog stays looking at you, CLICK and give the treat.

Your visual command for this exercise is to point to your eye while looking at your dog and the command word is "LOOK." Practise this indoors, in the garden and while on a walk. Repeat each day until your dog understands the exercise, and then do it only occasionally.

Once your dog has learned to focus on you and you have started to take control, you can teach him the commands outlined in the previous chapter on **Basic Training.**

 Training is teaching a dog to sit or give a paw, etc. Behaviour work is trying to change something the dog already does.

You cannot untrain a dog. Once you have taught him to sit, you cannot stop him from sitting - but you can change the Sit into something else. This is not straightforward and can take a little longer than regular training, but with dedication from the owner, it can be done. Here are a few of the common behavioural problems I come across:

How to Stop Your Dog Jumping Up

This common behaviour problem is something your dog has learned during puppyhood, and it can be the last thing in the world you want after a busy day at work. Dogs that do this are annoying to some and dangerous to others, such as small children, the elderly or people with disabilities.

So, you walk through the door and your dog, who has missed your company, goes manic and is leaping around the room. You are pushing him off, saying "Get down!"

You are trying to scold him, but the truth is that negative attention is better than no attention, so you are rewarding your dog for his behaviour every time this happens.

ATTENTION = REWARD, so the trick here is to give a bigger, better reward for keeping all four paws on the ground.

Unfortunately, for this exercise you need patience and persistence, so if you are not prepared to put the effort in, then stay with a dog who jumps up and leave it at that! However, if you want to put the time in and be consistent, your reward will be your best friend keeping all four paws firmly on the floor.

Part 1 - We stop giving attention - positive and negative - this is VERY important. As soon as your dog jumps up, turn your back. Cross your arms over your chest and do not speak to your dog or look at him.

If he runs around trying to get your attention and keeps jumping up, keep turning away from him. BUT DO NOT SAY ANYTHING OR LOOK AT HIM. Or, you could try leaving the room. Again, do not say anything or look at him, but as soon as he jumps up, you leave. Wait a moment, then step back inside and repeat until the dog is calm enough to stop jumping up.

Part 2 - **Reward good behaviour.** Make sure you always have High Value treats to hand (see **Chapter 10. Basic Training**). As soon as your dog is in front of you with all four paws on the ground, throw him a treat. You can praise him, but keep all speech and praise low-key; we do not want to excite him.

Then, practise, practise. Set up situations to practise with your dog. If jumping happens when you come home, spend a little time coming and going from the house. Do not make a big fuss and step outside if he jumps up. ONLY REWARD WHEN ALL FOUR PAWS ARE ON THE FLOOR.

Part 3 - Add the Sit. Once your dog is keeping his paws on the floor for a few seconds or more, ask for a sit. Walk into the room through the front door and say "SIT." As soon as the dog sits, give a treat (High Value). Practise with a lot of repetitions and your dog WILL start to sit when you walk through the door.

Part 4 - Practise with other people. Use friends, neighbours, family, in fact, anyone who is willing to help with training! If you do not, your dog may learn that it's not OK to jump on you, but it's OK to jump on other people. So, when anyone enters the room he must sit. This is your goal.

 We have replaced the Jump with the Sit. Your dog still knows how to jump up; we cannot delete this from his brain, but we can make him feel that doing something else is much better.

How Do I Stop My Dog Chasing?

Let's be honest, it's an uphill task to stop many Miniature Schnauzers from chasing! Practice, repetition and determination are all essential, and the regime must be stuck to, otherwise it won't work or will only partially work.

All dogs inherit certain behaviour traits, which give them *internal reinforcement.* An easy example of this is that dogs dig. Nobody teaches them to do it. They just do it and they enjoy doing it, so they keep on digging.

The strength of the inherited instinct varies from one bloodline to another and from one dog to the next. Chasing behaviour is part of what is inherited; it is genetically hard-wired into the dog - and many Miniature Schnauzers are hard-wired to chase.

We know that with inherited behaviour traits, the behaviour itself is rewarding and the reward is internal. Good endorphins are released and the dog feels good. So how on earth can we stop a dog chasing if he is rewarded just by doing it? Well, here is what to do...

We can use *external reinforcement,* such as treats, to train dogs. Some dog trainers will tell you the chase problem is due to the dog having poor Recall. Well, working on the Recall may help a little, but the chase urge is often a lot deeper set than that.

 Understanding the dog's motivation to chase is especially important. When changing a dog's behaviour pattern, you must try to understand what your dog is seeing and feeling.

There are several reasons a dog wants to chase. All of these motivations are quite different and any solution needs to be tailor-made for the individual dog. However, true chasing is a predatory behaviour. This checklist is a guide - if you tick two, plus the last one - your dog is a predatory chaser!

- The dog tries to chase more than one target – e.g. cars, bikes, runners, cats and birds
- The dog is always looking for the opportunity to chase
- The dog gets excited at the smell, sight or sound of the target
- The dog may show signs of stalking or searching
- The dog can do this anywhere
- The dog will want to chase if the target is moving; the faster the target, the more excited the dog becomes
- The dog appears to enjoy chasing more than anything

First Steps

Look at the environment you are in. Look for anything that could make your dog anxious and remove or reduce any background anxieties before looking at controlling his behaviour. Go somewhere where there are as few "targets" as possible and introduce as many *emotional improvers* as possible. Possible triggers are fear, noise, phobias, separation and social problems. Improvers are chew toys, praise and treats.

To stop your dog chasing, we may first have to address some things that may seem completely unrelated, e.g. fear. If your dog fears something, he will have very negative feelings and may chase to make himself feel a lot better. If all targets and problems cannot be removed, then add more positive actions to balance the negative emotions thereby reducing the need to chase.

Many owners make the mistake of trying to train their dog when he is chasing. DON'T DO THIS AS IT WON'T WORK! It only reinforces the behaviour. Start to gain control. The chasing behaviour arises because you have no control over his behaviour, so we are going to now control the dog's primary target.

We cannot control cats, rabbits, squirrels or birds, so we need to change the primary target to one we CAN control.

Start as you mean to go on. Your dog must not at any time get the opportunity to chase anything at all. This is essential, because every time he chases, he gets a brain boost. So, do not take your dog anywhere where they can continue their addictive behaviour.

Changing the Target

Buy your dog an exciting toy. It could squeak, have a bell, rustle, you could hide treats in it. It must not resemble anything your dog has chased, so no squeaky rabbits or ducks, or toys easily torn apart. Play in areas where there are none of the old 'targets.'

Many dogs will chase a ball, but some dogs may be so focused on their primary target that they ignore toys. This is the time for you to get inventive to make the new target inviting. If speed or movement is something your dog chases, a ball is perfect as it can be thrown and it moves quickly.

Many Mini Schnauzers prefer playing with soft toys, rather than repetitively chasing a ball, which they soon get bored with.

1. Play with the target (ball/toy) just a few steps away from your dog before starting to throw it further. This builds the neural connections between the Got to Chase and the new toy: "Play, play, play."

NOTE: All training bouts should be short but frequent with no other distractions. Most Miniature Schnauzers only concentrate for short periods. Also, they can have a stubborn streak and switch off if they are not challenged/entertained/getting a treat. Stop before your dog gets bored and always end the games with the toy in your possession.

2. Once you have your dog's attention, work on teaching retrieve. **Do not allow access to the toy at any other time than when you are training.** This is the special treat and chase ball or toy. Your dog will eventually become happy to play with this ball if you have banished all his old targets.

3. Practise, practise, practise with no distractions until your dog is desperate to play the game. This will make your dog's chase drive high, but now it will all be focused on the game.

4. Next we must use the command word, so let us call it "TOY." Say it in a high tone to make it clear and happy. Use it every time you throw the toy. Very quickly the dog will associate the word "TOY" with the actual toy you are throwing.

5. Now the dog is understanding that TOY = GAME. So, we need to move the new training up a notch. (Please remember to work in a place with no distractions).

6. Buy another identical toy. Take both identical toys with you when training. Ask your dog for a Sit Stay (if he won't, then hold the collar) and throw one of the balls as far as you can **without** using the verbal command "TOY."

7. Count to five in your head then give your dog the "FETCH" command and let go of the collar. Then immediately call "TOY" and throw the other toy past your dog, but not as far as the first toy. As the second toy is still moving, your dog should choose to chase it as it bounces past him.

8. Collect the toys and repeat. If your dog does go after the first ball and ignores the second one, change the first thing you throw to something much less interesting.

Don't worry if your dog goes in search of the first ball after they have retrieved the second. You will have already achieved your goal by getting your dog to focus on the second ball.

After a little while your dog will start waiting for the second ball to be thrown. If this happens call "TOY" for the first one thrown then start over again.

Next Steps

1. Throw the first and call "TOY," but do not throw it immediately. Wave the toy above your head for your dog to see and, when he comes back to you, reward him by throwing the toy. If your dog stops running for the first toy, remember to call "TOY" on occasions for that first throw. Even stop the retrieve and just play with the toy and your dog with no calling at all.

2. All play ends with the toy in your possession. Do not be manipulated by your dog. If he will not let you have the toy, the game ends.

3. Start to leave it a bit longer before you call "TOY!" The aim is to throw the first toy, immediately send your dog, wait until he is almost there and then call "TOY" and wait for him to come back before you throw the second toy.

You have worked extremely hard to get to this point and your dog will be doing well, now we need to start adding some distractions. We do not throw in cats, rabbits and so on just yet but we can add things like other dogs and people.

So, take your dog to a place where there is not much chance of a fluffy bunny turning up but does have dog walkers, and play the game while the distractions are there. If you are feeling nervous or you feel your dog might run off, buy a 10ft or 20ft lead. When you feel ready to progress you can undo the line, but remember to repeat, repeat, repeat. Try to do it once a day every day.

Eventually, the neural connections between *chase* and *toy* will be stronger than with *chase* and *old target.* The time it takes will vary with each dog and how much reinforcement, or inherited behaviour, they have received, but persistence will pay off.

When your dog is spinning around looking eagerly for a game every time you call "TOY," you are ready to test how well he is doing where there are rabbits, cats and birds. Look at your dog, watch him, as soon as he even looks in the direction of a cat or squirrel, immediately call "TOY" and play the game in the opposite direction from his old target.

Over time, very slowly edge closer and closer until your dog ignores his old targets. You will never be able to give up the reinforcement and the game, because if you do not satisfy your dog's chase needs, they will find their own targets.

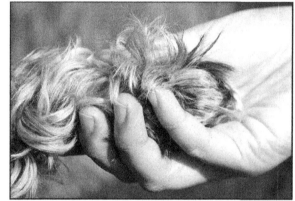

 Finally, whatever the issue, remember that without control you will have little chance of stopping any behaviour issues.

Training is not just about getting your dog to do what you want him to do or correcting unwanted behaviour; it is an important part of building a lifelong partnership.

Done properly with love and patience, training is a very rewarding experience for both dog and owner.

With thanks to Lisa for this article.

(Please note, the verb practice is spelled 'practise' in the UK!)

Puppy Biting and Chewing

Here we explain why young Schnauzers nip and chew so much - and what you can do to discourage it.

All puppies spend a great deal of time chewing, playing, and investigating objects; it's natural for them to explore the world with their mouths and needle-sharp teeth. When puppies play with people, they often bite, chew, nip and mouthe on people's hands, limbs and clothing.

Play-biting is normal for puppies; they do it all the time with their littermates. They also bite moving targets with their sharp teeth; it's a great game.

 All puppies are mouthy. Like babies, one of their first reactions to anything new is to put it in their mouths and bite it.

But when they arrive at your home, they have to be taught that human skin is sensitive and body parts are not suitable biting material. Biting is not acceptable - not even from a tiny Miniature Schnauzer puppy - and can be a real problem initially, especially if you have children.

When your puppy bites you or the kids, he is playing and investigating; he is NOT being aggressive. A lively young pup can easily get carried away with energy and excitement.

 Puppy biting should be dealt with from the get-go so it doesn't escalate into something more serious.

Every time you have a play session, have a soft toy nearby and when he starts to chew your hand or feet, clench your fingers (or toes!) to make it more difficult and distract him with a soft toy in your other hand.

Keep the game interesting by moving the toy around or rolling it around in front of him. (He may be too young to fetch it back if you throw it). He may continue to chew you, but will eventually realise that the toy is far more interesting and livelier than your boring hand.

 If he becomes over-excited and too aggressive with the toy, if he growls a lot, stop playing and walk away. When you walk away, don't say anything or make eye or physical contact with your puppy.

Simply ignore him, this is usually extremely effective and often works within a few days.

If your pup is more persistent and tries to bite your legs as you walk away, thinking this is another fantastic game, stand still and ignore him. If he persists, say *"No!"* in a very stern voice, then praise him when he lets go.

If you have to physically remove him from your trouser leg or shoe, leave him alone in the room for a while and ignore all demands for your attention.

 Try not to put your pup in a crate when he is being naughty, or he will associate the crate with punishment. Instead, remove yourself or the pup from the room - or put him in a pen. Wait until he has stopped being naughty before you put him in his crate.

As Lisa has already suggested, you may also think about keeping special toys you use to play with your puppy separate from other toys he chews alone.

That way he can associate certain toys with having fun with you and may work harder to please you. Miniature Schnauzers are playful and you can use this to your advantage by teaching yours how to play nicely with you and the toy, and then by using play time as a reward for good behaviour.

As well as biting, puppies also chew; it is a normal part of the teething process. Some adolescent and adult Minis chew because they are bored - often due to being left alone for too long, a lack of exercise and/or mental stimulation. If puppy chewing is a problem, it is because your pup is chewing something you don't want him to.

So, the trick is to keep him, his mouth and sharp little teeth occupied with something he CAN chew on, such as a durable toy – see **Chapter 6. Bringing Puppy Home** for suggestions.

You can also freeze peanut butter and/or a liquid inside a Kong toy. Put the Kong into a mug, plug the small end with peanut butter and fill it with gravy before putting it into the freezer. But don't leave the Kong and your Miniature Schnauzer on your precious Oriental rug! This will keep your pup occupied for quite a while.

It is also worth giving the dog a frozen Kong or Lickimat when you leave the house if he suffers from Separation Anxiety. There are lots of doggie recipes for Kongs and other treats online.

TIPS

❧ Puppies growl and bite more when they are excited. Don't allow things to escalate, so remove your pup from the situation **BEFORE** he gets too excited by putting him in a crate or pen

❧ Don't put your hand or finger into your pup's mouth to nibble on; this promotes puppy biting

❧ Don't leave anything lying around the house, such as shoes, socks, cables, remote controls, etc. that you don't want your dog to chew

❧ Limit your children's playtime with pup - and always supervise the sessions in the beginning. Teach them to gently play with and stroke your puppy, not to wind him up - excitable children and excitable Minis are a challenging combination!

❧ Don't let the kids (or adults) run around the house with the puppy chasing – this is an open invitation to nip at the ankles

❧ If your puppy does bite, remove him from the situation and people – never smack him

Although you might find it quite cute and funny if your puppy bites your fingers or toes, it should be discouraged at all costs. You don't want biting and nipping to get out of hand; as an adolescent or adult dog, he could inadvertently cause real injury, especially to children.

 Miniature Schnauzers are affectionate and most have empathy. Another tried and tested method is to make a sharp cry of "OUCH!" when your pup bites your hand - even when it doesn't hurt. This has worked very well for us.

Most Miniature Schnauzer pups will jump back in amazement, surprised to have hurt you. Divert your attention from your puppy to your hand. He will probably try to get your attention or lick you as a way of saying sorry.

Praise him for stopping biting and continue with the game. If he bites you again, repeat the process. A sensitive Mini should soon stop biting you.

Excessive Barking

There's no getting away from the fact that some Miniature Schnauzers can become too fond of the sound of their own voices.

They are naturally protective, and wary of strangers. You DO want your Miniature Schnauzer to bark to alert you to approaching strangers, often before you hear a thing. The trick is to get him to bark at the right times and then to stop - as incessant barking will drive you and your neighbours nuts.

FACT > The roots of unwanted barking often lie in a lack of socialisation. The importance of exposing a young Miniature Schnauzer to new people, places, animals, experiences, etc. in safe conditions cannot be over-emphasised.

See **Chapter 12. Exercise and Socialisation** for detailed information on how best to do this.

Dogs, especially youngsters, sometimes behave in ways you might not want them to until they learn that this type of unwanted behaviour doesn't earn any rewards. The problem may develop during adolescence when a dog becomes more confident.

Young Miniature Schnauzers can get carried away - until they learn that when they stop their indiscriminate barking, good things happen, such as treats, praise, a game.

Puppies teethe until about seven or eight months of age, so make sure yours has hardy chews, and perhaps a bone with supervision, to keep him occupied and gnawing. Give these when he's quiet, not when he is barking.

Photo: Oslo, aged eight months, with his first-ever Christmas present and favourite new toy! Courtesy of Chloe Dong and Jacky Zou.

Is your dog getting enough exercise and mental stimulation? Barking can be a way of letting off steam. Or he may be lonely, bored, attention-seeking, possessive or over-protective.

Sometimes it is the Miniature Schnauzer's alert system going into overdrive. Is he barking at people he can see through the window or coming to the door? You want an alert bark, but not a constant bark.

Your behaviour can also encourage excessive barking. If your dog barks his head off and you give him a treat to quieten down, he associates his barking with getting a nice treat.

Tip Tone of voice is very important. Do not use a high-pitched or semi-hysterical STOP!! or NO!! Use low, firm commands.

One method is to set up a situation where you know he is going to bark, such as somebody arriving at your house, and put him on a leash beforehand. When he has barked several times, give a short, sharp tug on the leash and the **"Quiet"** command - spoken, not shouted. Reward him when he **stops** barking, not before.

If he's barking to get your attention, ignore him. If that doesn't work, leave the room and don't allow him to follow, so you deprive him of your attention.

Do this as well if his barking and attention-seeking turn to nipping. Tell him to **"Stop"** in a firm voice, or use the **"ACK!"** sound, remove your hand or leg and, if necessary, leave the room.

NOTE: You may have heard about **sprays**, or **anti-bark collars** that emit a noise, electric shock or spray of citronella when the dog barks. We do not recommend them as Minis are sensitive souls and the best way to train one is undoubtedly WITH the dog's co-operation. If you are at your wit's end with uncontrolled barking and do buy an anti-bark collar, avoid ones that emit a noise or electric shock. Only use them or a water spray for a short time or you will lose the trust of your dog.

Schnauzer Language

FACT As humans, we use our voices in many different ways: to express happiness or anger, to scold, to shout a warning, and so on. Dogs are the same; different barks and whines give out different messages.

LISTEN to your dog and try and get an understanding of Miniature Schnauzer language. Here are a few sounds; all have different tones:

- Alert bark (when they hear or see something or the doorbell rings)
- Excited bark (I'm enjoying this, I want to play more)
- Demanding bark (STROKE ME! GIVE ME THE TREAT!, etc.)
- Fearful, high-pitched bark (Yikes, that's a big dog, I'll do my fierce bark)
- Aggressive bark (I'm not happy and might even bite if I think I've no other option)
- *"I'm barking 'coz I can bark"* bark!

Chris Lee has previously owned Boxers but is now the proud owner of Betsy, aged nearly two. He says: "Perhaps the biggest surprise about Mini Schnauzers is their 'language,' which is different from the bark. We get the 'roo-roos' when we return home, whether we've been out for five minutes or two days.

"If 'roo-roos' are returned by the recipient, then a 'roos-roos' conversation may follow. In addition, Betsy makes throaty/mumbling noises when waiting for food and sometimes just for the sake of it. I think the best word for her is 'conversational!'."

Speak and Shush!

The Speak and Shush technique teaches your dog or puppy to bark and be quiet on command. When your dog barks at an arrival at your house, gently praise him after the first few barks. If he persists, tell him **"Quiet."**

Get a friend to stand outside your front door, then you say **"Speak"** or **"Alert."** This is the cue for your accomplice to knock on the door or ring the bell - don't worry if you both feel like idiots, it will be worth the embarrassment!

When your dog barks, say **"Speak"** and praise him profusely. After a few good barks, say **"Shush"** or **"Quiet"** and then dangle a tasty treat in front of his nose. If he is food-motivated, he will stop barking as soon as he sniffs the treat, because it is **physically impossible for a dog to sniff and woof at the same time.**

Praise your dog again as he sniffs quietly and give him the treat. Repeat this routine a few times a day and your Mini will quickly learn to bark whenever the doorbell rings and you ask him to

"Speak." Eventually, your dog will bark AFTER your request but BEFORE the doorbell rings, meaning he has learned to bark on command. Even better, he will learn to anticipate the likelihood of getting a treat following your **"Shush"** request and will also be quiet on command. With Speak and Shush training, progressively increase the length of required shush time before offering a treat - at first just a couple of seconds, then three, five, 10, 20, and so on.

By alternating instructions to speak and shush, the dog is praised and rewarded for barking on request and also for stopping barking on request.

NOTE: In the unlikely event that you have a Miniature Schnauzer who is silent when somebody approaches the house, you can use the following method to get him to bark on the command of **"Speak."** This is also a useful command to teach if you walk your dog alone, especially at night; the bark will help keep you safe:

1. Have some treats at the ready, waiting for that rare bark.

2. Wait until he barks - for whatever reason - then say **"Speak"** or whatever word you want to use.

3. Praise him and give him a treat. At this stage, he won't know why he is receiving the treat.

4. Keep praising him every time he barks and give him a treat.

5. After you've done this for several days, hold a treat in your hand in front of his face and say **"Speak."**

6. Your dog will probably still not know what to do, but will eventually get so frustrated at not getting the treat that he will bark.

7. At this point, praise him and give him the treat.

We trained a quiet dog to do this in a week and then, like clockwork, he barked enthusiastically every time anybody came to the door or whenever we gave him the "Speak" command, knowing he would get a treat for stopping.

Breeders' Advice

Andrew Ray, Minnienoom Miniature Schnauzers, takes part in regular training activities with his dogs, including the Good Citizen Dog Training scheme: "Schnauzers of all three sizes are quick to learn. The first thing we teach at Minnienoom is Recall.

"As we enter the puppy room, we call the puppies in a high-pitched voice: "Puppy, puppy, puppy" and they usually come running towards us. Then it's straight out the door for toileting with a **"Gooooood Puppy"** as they complete the task.

"As puppies grow, they start to play-fight each other; this is normal behaviour and part of their survival trait. However, it can sometimes spill over into puppies nipping their human owners. The best advice is a firm NO.

"If this does not work, walk away or ignore the puppy for a short while - the puppy will soon learn this doesn't get their human's attention.

"All puppies "YAP" like a high-pitched bark when excited. This should not be encouraged; the puppy is trying to get your attention and by you shouting: "STOP!" at it, the dog has won. Our advice is to ignore and walk away or just stop and stare - this usually works after a few seconds.

"If a dog jumps up, place one of your feet forward and knee out - this will knock the dog off-balance - whilst giving a firm NO command. This usually stops it from happening again."

Photo: Meet the Gang. Andrew and Gaynor's Minnienoom Miniature Schnauzers, showing all four permitted UK colours (pepper and salt, black and silver, black, and white).

Steve Matthews, Silbertraum Miniature Schnauzers: "A stern 'No' is always good for dealing with bad behaviour, as is turning away and ignoring the dog when it behaves badly. Schnauzers like attention and the approval of their owners and don't like being ignored. Praise and rewarding good behaviours is the best training tip."

Lesley Myers, UK show judge and former breeder with the Ersmy prefix: "Miniature Schnauzers are very intelligent. I have found training them easy. I think it's important to talk to your Mini as it helps to build a bond. I talk to my dogs all day and Ulrich will sit, look me in the eye and listen as though he understands what I'm talking about, and then he talks back to me in his grunt language!

"Minis just love to please you, which I think is not only them being intelligent, but also the bond and trust you build up with them: 'Are you pleased with me mummy?' I used to line six up in a semi-circle and call each one out by their name for a treat, starting with the eldest. They would then go back in line in turn. Thinking this could just be a habit, I started calling them out by their name in a random order, it still worked.

"Give plenty of praise and have a treat ready. Wait a couple of seconds to make sure the dog is looking at you (a sign the dog has re-focused) then give the treat."

Photo: Lesley's Fritz (Jastalla Awethentic), two months, with Schultz (Ritzbeech Mood Swings With Ersmy), seven months.

Lesley added: "For the Recall, I've always used a clothes line tied to the lead. Let the pup go a distance you are happy with then get down on your haunches, call their name excitedly, clapping your hands and as soon as they've come back, praise and treat. Once you are confident, then let them off the lead.

"A good test in a safe space, if you are confident enough, is to let your dog off the lead and then, when he's not looking, hide behind a tree or bush. Don't call or whistle, don't say anything and wait for your dog to find you - when you have been found, praise and treat. The first day I did this with my two boys I was so, so proud of them!

"One boy when he passed the test had a look on his face as if to say: "Oh, where are you?' He turned back and found me. The look on the face of the other one, the very intelligent one, was: 'I know where you are, you can't kid me!' and he found me instantly. If your pup or dog barks and wants to chase a bicycle or a jogger, give the Wait or Stand command, wait until they pass, say 'Good dog' and walk the opposite way for a short distance, then carry on in the direction of the original walk."

Lesley agrees with trainer Lisa Cole on the importance of getting the dog to focus on you: "If nipping, say 'NO' in a stern voice whilst removing the pup from what he or she is nipping. Repeat if it continues. When pup stops and looks at you (re-focused), praise and treat. If nipping at your shoes, say 'NO' and move the pup away. Repeat if it continues. For jumping up, gently push the pup down with the command 'NO.' When the jumping stops and pup looks up at you (re-focused), praise and treat. Or say 'NO,' turn your back on the pup and when the jumping has stopped and he looks at you (re-focused), praise and treat.

"Growling if over-excited, which can happen when playing with a toy: say 'NO' and take the toy from the pup. After a minute give the toy back and, if needed, repeat your action. Don't forget to praise and treat when the naughty action has ceased. A great deal of patience and continuity is needed; people sometimes forget that - also that training a Mini can be FUN!"

Photo: Lesley's beautiful Rommey (Wundai Just a Rumour, JW Sh. CM), aged 14 months.

"Minis can be wilful little dogs, so owners must start as they mean to go on - otherwise they can wrap you around their little paw and they then become the boss! Also, they seem to get upset if they think you are not pleased with them. They can sulk if they have been told off, so you must make friends soon afterwards!"

You may have been told not to stare at a dog as this will be perceived as a challenge. However, Lesley, who has 38 years' experience as an owner, breeder and show judge, believes that it is important to LOOK AT your Mini.

She adds: "The Mini Schnauzer is a breed that loves eye contact and will look you in the eye. When I'm going over them during judging at dog shows, they make eye contact with you and you get all kinds of eye expressions, e.g. alert, mischievous, happy, the odd one a bit bland, coy, loving, etc."

Lesley's comment is a light bulb moment for me. I look at 10,000s of photos of dogs when writing The Canine Handbooks and what has struck me is how often the Minis are staring straight into the camera, compared with other breeds - and this was certainly true of our Mini, Max. Next time you photograph yours, call his or her name for a photo of them looking straight at you.

....

Training for Agility

Rebecca Makdad already owned eight-year-old Rosie when she decided to get another Mini to compete in Agility competitions. She got Navy (Sumerwynd Following Seas), a female, who excelled and now has a string of titles after her name: MX MXJ OF ACT2 CGC TKI. Minis do well at Agility for many reasons: they are athletic for their size with a compact conformation, they are intelligent, eager to please their owners, and love challenges, being rewarded and showing off!

Rebecca, who lives in Pennsylvania, says: "I started Agility after I retired. It looked fun and I was amazed at the dogs' abilities. I soon realized that Agility offers many benefits for both handler and dog, providing social, mental and physical stimulation to the **team**. Agility is definitely a team (Handler and Canine) companion sport. I purchased Navy with agility in mind. Mini Schnauzers are great little agility dogs, once trained and conditioned. When I initially spoke with our breeder Wade Bogart, I explained what I was looking for; most important was a structurally-sound dog. Over the course of their Agility life, they will take thousands of jumps, weave poles and A-frame climbs.

"A Mini Schnauzer of Breed Standard height and weight should have limited issues, if any. Most training comes with treats, and the owner must be attentive to the Mini's weight.

"The Mini's intelligence is well suited to agility. They master verbal commands, hand signals and handler body language quickly. If training is kept as a game, Minis are all in. I think they view it as chasing a handler around a playground, with a huge reward at the end! The reward may be a ball, toy or treat.

"I think Navy's success has been a combination of Nature and Nurture. It started with quality breeding followed by the amount of time I put into her training. We have a professional trainer. Navy is a very curious Mini, which leads to her being quite mischievous.

"Hence, her energies needed to be channeled in a positive direction, i.e. training. Fortunately, our trainers are ladies that understand the Terrier mentality and how to challenge an active Mini. The conclusion was to train her by playing games."

Rebecca has this advice for anyone considering Agility with their Mini: "Dogs, like humans, do not all like the same sports. Rosie, my 12-year-old, started agility at approximately four years of age and never loved the sport, so she was retired by eight. Navy started Foundation training at six months and loved it. Her favorite part was the rewards.

"Our training sessions were actually a game and kept under five minutes; a good instructor will guide you. Numerous training aides are available, from The Manners Minder to a margarine lid - even a cardboard box.

"I'd advise anyone to attend Agility trials to observe the different breeds running, the handlers' ability and interaction with their dog. If you see a team you'd like to emulate someday, talk with them - most 'Agility' people love talking about the sport.

"If you have a puppy, look out for Agility Foundation courses. In the US, most agility organizations (AKC, UKI, USDAA) require the Mini to be a certain age before trialling. Remember, Agility is a journey and the Mini is an athlete, and all athletes need conditioning and periods of rest."

Photos of Navy in action by photographer Richard Knecht.

"Finally, remember no Mini wakes up and says, "I want to go run a 20-obstacle agility course." They are doing it because they were asked to and because they want to PLEASE you. Mistakes are not made on purpose, so no matter how the session or trial goes, BE KIND TO YOUR DOG!"

12. Exercise and Socialisation

One thing all dogs have in common – including every Miniature Schnauzer ever born - is that they need daily exercise. Even if you are lucky enough to have a large back yard or garden where your dog can run free, there are still lots of benefits to getting out and about.

Mini Schnauzers are alert and curious little dogs that love going for walks and investigating new places, smells, people, etc. They are happy to lounge around at home as well, but don't think that because they like snuggling up on the sofa with you, they don't need regular exercise – THEY DO.

Daily exercise helps to keep your Schnauzer happy and healthy. It:

- ❧ Strengthens respiratory and circulatory systems
- ❧ Helps get oxygen to tissue cells
- ❧ Helps the heart to stay healthy
- ❧ Wards off obesity
- ❧ Keeps muscles toned and joints flexible
- ❧ Aids digestion
- ❧ Releases endorphins that trigger positive feelings
- ❧ Helps to keep dogs mentally stimulated and socialised

FACT ❯ Some Schnauzers - especially Giants from working bloodlines and some Standards - have considerable "drive," which requires physical and mental activity to stop them from becoming bored or mischievous.

If you have the time and interest, an excellent way of keeping your Schnauzer's mind and body exercised is to take part in the (Canine) Good Citizen Training scheme or an activity such as Agility - give your Mini a chance to shine!

Exercising Puppies

It's important not to over-exercise young pups. Until a puppy's growth plates close, they're soft and vulnerable to injury. Too much impact can cause permanent damage. Mini Schnauzers are physically mature at around one year old.

So, playing Fetch or Frisbee for hours on end with your young Mini is not a good plan, nor is allowing a pup to freely run up and down stairs in your home. You risk ending up with a pile of vet bills and an increased likelihood of joint problems developing later in life.

Just like babies, puppies have different temperaments and energy levels; some need more exercise than others. Start slowly and build it up. The worst combination is over-exercise and overweight.

Don't take your pup out of the yard or garden until the all-clear after the vaccinations, unless you carry her around to start the socialisation process. Begin with daily short walks outside the home environment - literally just a few minutes - so she can experience new situations and get used to on-leash walking. The general guideline for puppies is:

Five minutes of on-leash exercise every day per month of age

So, a total of 15 minutes per day when three months (13 weeks) old

30 minutes per day when six months (26 weeks) old, etc.

Slowly increase the time as she gets used to being exercised and this will gradually build up muscles, stamina and a strong frame.

 It is OK for your young pup to have free run of your garden or yard, provided the surface is soft, such as grass. This does not count in the five minutes per month rule.

If the yard is stone or concrete, limit the time your dog runs around on it, as the hard surface will impact joints. It's fine for your pup to run freely around the house to burn off energy - just not stairs.

If you have other dogs at home, make sure playtime does not get too rough and monitor the time the pup runs around with the other dogs – pups don't know their limits.

It is fine for your pup to run freely around the house to burn off energy.

One breeder added: "For the first year whilst the puppy's bones are soft and developing, it's best not to over-exert and put strain on the joints. Daily gentle walking is great, just not constant fast and hard running/chasing in the puppy stage, as too much is a big strain."

And when your little pup has grown into a beautiful adult Miniature Schnauzer with a skeleton capable of carrying her through a long and healthy life, it will have been worth all the effort:

A long, healthy life is best started slowly

How Much Exercise?

Speak to 10 different owners and you'll get 10 different answers as to how much exercise their Mini needs!

Minis are versatile. They can adapt to living in a small home in the suburbs, an apartment in the city, or a log cabin in the middle of nowhere. They are suitable for families, couples, older people and single people living alone. They are easy to please; some are happy running around the yard or garden, others love a hike. The key is to establish a routine. If you are intending going for long walks, build up slowly.

The amount of exercise each adult Mini needs varies tremendously from one dog to the next. Factors include:

- Temperament
- Energy levels
- Bloodline
- Your living conditions
- Whether your dog is kept with other dogs
- What she gets used to

Some of your dog's temperament and energy level will depend on the bloodline - ask the breeder how much exercise he or she recommends.

Owning more than one dog - or having friends with dogs - is a great way for them to get more exercise. A couple of dogs running around together get far more exercise than one on her own. Mini Schnauzers often do well with other Mini Schnauzers.

Look out online for Schnauzerfest, Mad About Schnauzers (both UK), Schnauzer Meet Up (USA) and similar gatherings, which are a great opportunity to socialise with other Schnauzers - and talk 'Schnauzer' all day with fellow owners!

A garden or yard with a secure, close-boarded fence is a great advantage. Make sure the fence is high enough - Minis can jump and scramble several feet.

Our Max was a dab hand at scrambling up and over five or six-foot drystone walls! Minis are curious and love investigating new scents and places, which is why you need to plug every little gap in your fence – or they'll be off!

Schnauzers like going for walks on the leash, but enjoy life much more when allowed to run free - even if some only want to meander around with their noses to the ground. If your dog is happy just to amble along beside you, think about playing some games to raise the heartbeat (hers and yours!), build muscle and get fit.

Minis have no road sense! You must make sure it's safe, away from traffic and other hazards, before letting them off the leash - and only after they have learned the Recall.

 Many have a strong instinct to chase - and when they spot a small furry critter or their noses latch on to a scent, their ears stop working! The Recall is the most important command you can teach your dog.

Never underestimate a Schnauzer's prey drive; keep them on a leash near livestock and wild animals - unless you have accustomed yours to livestock and trained them not to chase other animals.

 Schnauzers are known for being playful, they enjoy toys and games. A game such as Hide and Seek, training or an activity where they are using different senses can be just as tiring as a walk.

People contact our website to ask if the Miniature Schnauzer can go on a day-long hike or if they make suitable running partners. Other owners keep Minis as companions and their dogs are happy living in the home and garden with the occasional walk.

We used to take Max out three times a day, the late-night walk was shorter and the other two were a minimum of half an hour. Max was definitely happier going for a five or even 10-mile hike than staying in the garden because he had got used to a lot of daily exercise. Like many Schnauzers, he had an inbuilt clock. He'd start looking at us and pacing when he thought it was time for a walk or a meal!

 The trick is to get your Schnauzer into an exercise and feeding routine that fits into your lifestyle and keeps your dog content.

If you take your Mini out three times a day and then suddenly stop, she'll become restless and demanding because she's been used to more. Start with a schedule you know you can stick to.

Adult Minis can and do go on all-day hikes. But they are small dogs and need to gradually build up to it. We've taken Max on six-hour hikes in the hills and he'd still be running at the end of the day.

Although once back home he'd crash into his bed and snore all night. I think this is where the expression "dog tired" comes from!

Miniature Schnauzers are not ideal running partners. Firstly, they are small dogs with no great speed and secondly, they are ratters by nature with a keen sense of smell and are easily distracted by scents and small furry animals.

I tried jogging with Max, and even bought a special jogging lead, but to no avail. He insisted on stopping every few yards to sniff or pee! Females do not urinate as often, but, like males, they also have an incredible sense of smell and love to have their nose to the ground investigating.

Minimum 30 Minutes

Veterinarians advise that you take your Mini out for at least one walk of at least 30 minutes every day - more is better. Up to an hour a day is the Kennel Club recommended amount.

Mini Schnauzers are not slothful by nature, they are similar to Terriers and enjoy running around. They are also quite competitive, and their compact bodies lend themselves to a short stride and small turning circle, which is helping them gain success in Agility.

Breeder Wade Bogart says: "Miniatures from Sumerwynd lines have taken part in Agility, Barn Hunt, Canine Good Citizen, Earth Dog, Jumper, Obedience, Rally, Trick Dog and Versatility. Minis are extremely intelligent and have conformation as defined in the official AKC Breed Standard. They also have heart; all three are essential for success.

"The dogs enjoyed getting treats for positive accomplishments - the more they won, the more treats they received!"

Throwing a ball or a toy is a good way of burning off your dog's excess energy - although, you'll probably get more exercise than her. Don't expect your Mini to fetch it back every time - Minis have many qualities, but attention span is not one of them!

Schnauzer Exercise Tips

- Don't over-exercise puppies
- Don't allow them to run up and down stairs or jump on and off furniture
- Aim for at least one, preferably more, walks away from the house every day
- Vary your exercise route - it will be more interesting for both of you
- Triple check the fencing around your garden or yard to prevent The Great Escape
- Exercise within your dog's capabilities - Schnauzers have no sense of their own limitations

- Don't strenuously exercise your dog straight after or within an hour of a meal as this can cause Bloat. See **Chapter 8. Feeding a Mini** for details
- Some Schnauzers have "drive" and need play time as well as walk time to keep their creative minds engaged
- All love interaction with their owners

- In hot weather, exercise your dog early morning or in the evening

- Exercise old dogs more gently - especially in cold weather when it is harder to get their bodies moving. Have a cool-down period after exercise to reduce stiffness and soreness; it helps to remove lactic acids - Max absolutely loved a body massage

- Make sure your dog has constant access to fresh water. Dogs can only sweat a tiny amount through the pads of their paws, they need to drink water to cool down

Admittedly, when it is raining, freezing or scorching, the last thing you may want to do is to venture outdoors with your dog. But make the effort; the lows are more than compensated for by the highs.

 Don't let your Mini dictate if she doesn't want to go out, it will only make her lazier and less sociable with others.

Exercise helps you bond with your dog, keep fit, see different places and meet new companions - both canine and human. In short, it enhances both your lives. 1.

Water and Snow

Some Schnauzers enjoy paddling, but most are not keen on swimming out of their depth. If your dog is to be around water regularly, introduce her to the water in a positive manner; NEVER throw her in or entice her out of their depth. You don't want your dog to lose her nerve.

Although Schnauzers that want to swim can swim, a doggie life vest is an option that gives you peace of mind if yours spends a lot of time on or near water, for example, if you are regularly on boats. And in an emergency, you can use a boat hook to lift the dog out of the water.

★ **Swimming is a very strenuous activity for any dog, so keep any swim sessions SHORT. Don't repeatedly throw a ball or toy into water.**

Short swim sessions are an excellent form of exercise; many veterinary clinics now use water tanks not only for remedial and physical therapy, but also for canine recreation. **NOTE:** Remember to dry the inside of their ears afterwards to help prevent infections.

Most Schnauzers love snow - even though some hate rain!

Photo: Max loved the snow. It traps scents and he'd spend hours running and sniffing in the white stuff.

Snow and ice can clump on their paws, beards, legs and tummy. If your dog gets iced up, bathe paws and other affected areas in lukewarm - NOT HOT - water.

Salt or de-icing products on roads and pathways contain chemicals that can be poisonous to dogs and cause irritation – particularly if they try to lick the stuff off.

Routine

Dogs love routine. If you can, get your dog used to a walk or walks at similar times every day and gradually build that up as the puppy reaches adulthood. Start with a routine you know you can continue with, as your dog will come to expect it and will not be happy if the walks suddenly stop.

 If you haven't enough time to give your Schnauzer the exercise she needs, consider employing a daily dog walker, if you can afford it, or take her to doggie daycare once or twice a week. As well as exercise, she will enjoy the interaction with other dogs.

Older dogs still need exercise to keep their body, joints and systems functioning properly. They need a less strenuous regime - they are usually happier with shorter walks, but still need enough to keep them physically and mentally active.

If your old or sick dog is struggling, she'll show you she's not up to it by stopping and looking at you or sitting/lying down and refusing to move. If she's healthy and does this, she is just being lazy or stubborn!

Regular exercise can add months or even years to a dog's life.

Mental Stimulation

Schnauzers have lively minds which need to be exercised or this intelligence can turn to boredom and/or naughtiness.

NOTE: Sniffing exercises a dog's mind - another good reason for a daily walk away from the home where there are different scents.

If you return home to find your favourite cushions shredded or the contents of the kitchen bin strewn around the floor, ask yourself: *"Is she getting enough exercise/mental stimulation?"* and *"Am I leaving her alone for too long?"*

Have toys and chews, and factor in regular playtime with your Schnauzer – even gentle playtime for old dogs to help keep them interested in life.

There are also numerous toys and games to keep your dog occupied, such as canine puzzles and the Snuffle Mat.

 **Sticks can splinter in a dog's mouth or stomach, and jumping up for a Frisbee can cause back damage. Balls should be big enough not to choke.**

A Schnauzer at the heart of the family getting regular exercise and mental challenges is a happy dog and an affectionate snuggle bug second to none!

Schnauzer Circles

Also known as 'the Zoomies,' this is when your Mini just decides to take off and run circles at full speed. It could be around the living room, yard or garden, on the beach or in the woods.

It's whenever they are so full of beans and excited that they can't contain themselves - so Schnauzer circles are their chosen method of blowing off steam and celebrating life!

Photo: Max running Schnauzer circles around me on the Yorkshire Moors. He loved being up on the wild moorland with the wind whistling through his ears and did it every time we went.

He also did it around the house - especially after he'd just survived the 'near-death experience' (or so it seemed to him) of having a bath!

Owners' Exercise Regimes

Gary Blain, owner of Jamie, eight, and Evie, five: "I tend to walk them through the day. I only have a small garden and Jamie won't poo in the garden unless he's desperate in the middle of the night!

"On weekdays when I work, I walk them for 15 minutes first thing, then 30 minutes at lunchtime and usually 45 to 60 minutes in the evening, longer in spring, summer and autumn, and longer at weekends. I'm lucky, I can take my dogs to work every day if I wish, and I often do."

Chloe Dong and Jacky Zou, who live in an apartment with Oslo: "First thing in the morning, we let Oslo run on the rooftop for 10 to 15 minutes to stretch his legs and do his business. If one of us is working from home, we try to take him out every few hours throughout the day to let him relieve himself.

"If weather permits, we have him play fetch and run numerous laps on the rooftop. His energy seems endless."

Chris Lee: "Betsy is exercised at least twice a day and usually in a park for 30 minutes or so. She is lucky in that occasionally we go to the beach for a good run, but she draws the line at going in for a swim!"

Rebecca Makdad, owner of Rosie, 13, and Navy, four: "We do controlled exercise such as leash walking or Agility training approximately 30 minutes three or four times per week. I consider Navy, my Agility girl, an athlete and like most athletes, she needs down time and conditioning. My girls also have over an acre of yard to run in."

Photo: No worries Mom, I got it! As she exits the tunnel, Navy has her sights set on the next obstacle. Photographer: Richard Knecht.

Vivian Williams, owner of Mini Bogart and Rabies the Standard Poodle: "We own a 123-acre farm with 20 acres of woods and a three-acre pond. We use an invisible fence to keep the dogs close to the house for their safety. There are coyotes, foxes, whitetail deer, many hundreds of geese in the spring and fall, and all manner of critters that could pose a distraction or threat.

"The containment system keeps the dogs close to the house, but gives them plenty of space to run and play. When Bogart was a puppy, we leash-walked him every time he went outside. When he was about a year old, we trained him to the invisible fence.

"Usually we play Fetch with our dogs twice a day for about 10 to 15 minutes. From time to time, we play Hide-And-Seek with them (for kibble or to find one of us). In addition, they go outside to play together three or four times a day."

Yolande: "Mayzy has two on-lead walks early and late in the day with me, usually in the dark. My son takes her on a one-hour off-lead run in the woods.

"Mayzy and I play games in the garden with frisbee and balls or I take her into the adjacent fields. She has a one-hour Agility class once a week."

Photo: Mayzy as a puppy.

"Living next to pastureland, it is essential that Mayzy is under control around farm animals. Generally, she is respectful of any creature bigger than herself, but has a strong chase instinct. In our large garden she will continually hunt for rodents, which is what she was bred for, and loves digging up molehills; I have seen her chase a rabbit.

"Our Agility trainer has some very tame sheep and has given Mayzy the opportunity to come into close contact with them. Mayzy is the one to back off. I think it's important to try to introduce our dogs in a controlled manner to farm animals and horses."

Simon and Yvonne Sonsino, owners of Bu, 15, and puppy Wilf: "We don't go for walks as such, we tend to exercise them in our large garden. Bu is a bit old for long yomps and Wilf is a bit too young just yet and isn't quite lead-trained."

....

Socialisation

Socialisation is ESSENTIAL for Miniature Schnauzers. It's as important as exercise or feeding the right diet.

Your adult dog's character will depend largely on two things: inherited temperament and environment, or **NATURE AND NURTURE**. And one absolutely essential aspect of nurture for all Schnauzers is socialisation.

 Scientists now realise the importance that socialisation plays in a dog's life. A fairly small window is regarded as the optimum time for socialisation - up to the age of four to five months.

Socialisation means *"learning to be part of society,"* or *"integration."* This means helping dogs become comfortable within a human society by getting them used to different people,

environments, traffic, sights, noises, smells, animals, other dogs, etc.

It begins from the moment the puppy is born, and the importance of picking a good breeder cannot be over-emphasised.

Not only will he or she breed for good temperament and health, but the dam (puppy's mother) will be well-balanced, friendly and unstressed, and the pup will learn a lot in this positive environment.

Learning When Young Is Best

Most young animals, including dogs, are naturally able to get used to their everyday environment until they reach a certain age. When they reach this age, they become much more suspicious of things they haven't yet experienced. This is why it often takes longer to train an older dog.

When you think about it, humans are not so different. Babies and children have a tremendous capacity to learn, we call this early period the *"formative years."*

As we age we can still learn, but not at the same speed. Also, we often become less receptive to new ideas or new ways of doing things.

This age-specific natural development allows a puppy to get comfortable with the normal sights, sounds, people and animals that will be a part of her life. It ensures that she doesn't spend her life barking, growling or cowering at everything that moves.

The suspicion that dogs develop later also ensures that they react with a healthy dose of caution to new things that really could be dangerous - Mother Nature is clever!

It is essential that your dog's introductions to new things are all **positive**. Negative experiences lead to fear and mistrust.

Your dog may already have a wonderful temperament, but she still needs socialising to avoid thinking that the world is tiny and revolves around her. Minis can be very demanding – don't let yours become an attention-seeker!

 **FACT** ⟩ Good socialisation gives confidence and helps puppies - whether bold or timid - to learn their place in society. The ultimate goal is to have a happy, well-adjusted Miniature Schnauzer you can take anywhere.

Ever seen a therapy dog in action and noticed how incredibly well-adjusted they are? This is no coincidence.

These dogs have been extensively socialised and are ready and able to deal calmly with whatever situation they encounter.

They are relaxed and comfortable in their own skin - just like you want your dog to be.

✦ Socialisation should start as soon as you bring your puppy home and continue regularly until around 18 months old, then less often throughout life. If it is not practised, your dog will become less good at interacting.

Minis that have not been properly integrated are more likely to react with fear or aggression to unfamiliar people, animals and experiences, resulting in one or more of these:

- ❧ Unwanted barking
- ❧ Timidity
- ❧ Becoming too protective/territorial

FACT ⟩ Well-socialised dogs live more relaxed, peaceful and happy lives than dogs that are stressed by their environment.

The Puppy Rules of 12

The Puppy Rules of 12 was developed by dog trainer and behaviourist Margaret Hughes. By the time a puppy is 12 weeks old, it should have:

1. Experienced 12 different **SURFACES**: wood, woodchips, carpet tile, cement, linoleum, grass, wet grass, dirt, mud, puddles, grates, uneven surfaces, on a table, on a chair, etc.

2. Played with 12 different **OBJECTS**: fuzzy toys, big and small balls, hard toys, funny-sounding toys, wooden, paper or cardboard items, milk jugs, (all under supervision) etc.

3.   Experienced 12 different **LOCATIONS**: front yard, other people's homes, schoolyard, lake, pond, river, basement, elevator, car, moving car, garage, laundry room, hardware store, pet store, stairs, etc.

4.   Met and played with 12 **NEW PEOPLE**: (outside of family) including children, adults (male and female) elderly adults, people in wheelchairs, walkers, people with canes and umbrellas, crutches, hats, sunglasses, men with deep voices, people with dark skin, etc.

5.   Exposed to 12 different **NOISES**: (ALWAYS keep positive and watch puppy's comfort level - we don't want the puppy scared) garage door opening, doorbell, children playing, babies screaming, big trucks, motorcycles, skateboards, washing machine, shopping carts, clapping, pan dropping, vacuums, lawnmowers, etc.

6.   Exposed to 12 **FAST-MOVING OBJECTS**: (Don't allow to chase) skateboards, roller-blades, bikes, motorcycles, cars, people running, cats running, scooters, children running, squirrels, etc.

Tip Work at your puppy's own pace and don't worry if it takes longer. All experiences should be POSITIVE. An early bad experience can stay with a puppy for life.

Margaret Hughes added this advice: "Never force your pup to approach anyone or anything, let her explore on her terms, quietly praising and encouraging her when she boldly approaches by herself.

When your puppy seems uncertain, allow her to proceed at her own pace or to move away from that which worries her.

"Then encourage her to approach at her own rate again, such as having a 'scary' person kneel down to the side and not look at the puppy while holding out a treat for her. Keep in mind that you're not trying to overwhelm your puppy with new experiences - quantity is not better than quality!

"Make sure your puppy is confident, well-rested and having a good time whenever you introduce her to something new. Don't overdo it either!

"Puppies get tired very quickly and, most importantly, give your dog lots of downtime after a new experience to recuperate and rest in a safe, quiet place."

If your pup is frightened by a new experience, take a step back, introduce her to the scary situation much more gradually, and make a big effort to do something she loves during the situation or right afterwards.

For example, if your puppy seems to be frightened by noise and vehicles at a busy road, a good method would be to go to a quiet road, sit with the dog away from - but within sight of - the traffic.

Every time she looks towards the traffic say *"YES!"* and reward her with a treat.

If she is still stressed, you need to move further away. When your dog calmly takes the food, she is becoming more relaxed and getting used to traffic sounds, so you can edge a bit nearer - but still just for short periods until she becomes relaxed.

Keep each session short and **POSITIVE**.

Meeting Other Dogs

When you take your gorgeous and vulnerable little Mini out with other dogs for the first few times, you're bound to be a bit apprehensive, I know we were.

To begin with, introduce your puppy to just one other dog – one that you know to be friendly, rather than taking her straight to the park where there are lots of dogs of all sizes racing around, which might frighten the life out of your timid little darling.

On the other hand, your pup might be full of confidence right from the off, but you still need to approach things slowly.

If your puppy is too cocksure, she may get a warning bite from an older dog, which could make her more anxious when approaching new dogs in the future.

Always make initial introductions on neutral ground, so as not to trigger territorial behaviour. You want your Schnauzer to approach other dogs with friendliness, not fear.

From the first meeting, help both dogs experience good things when they're in each other's presence. Let them sniff each other briefly, which is normal canine greeting behaviour.

As they do, talk to them in a happy, friendly tone of voice; never use a threatening tone.

Don't allow them to sniff each other for too long as this may escalate to an aggressive response.

Photo: a young Mini with a friendly Giant Schnauzer.

After a short time, get the attention of both dogs and give each a treat in return for obeying a simple command, e.g. *"Sit"* or *"Stay."* Continue with the *"happy talk,"* and rewards.

Learn to spot the difference between normal rough-and-tumble play and interaction that may develop into fear or aggression.

Here are some signs of fear to look out for when your dog interacts with other canines:

- Running away or freezing on the spot
- Licking the lips or lips pulled back
- Trembling or panting, which can be a sign of stress or pain
- Frantic/nervous behaviour, e.g. excessive sniffing, drinking or playing frenetically with a toy
- A lowered body stance or crouching
- Lying on her back with paws in the air – this is submissive, as is submissive urination
- Lowering the head or turning the head away, when you may see the whites of the eyes as the dog tries to keep eyes on the perceived threat
- Growling and/or hair raised on her back (raised hackles)
- Tail lifted in the air or ears high on the head

Some of these responses are normal. A pup may well crouch on the ground or roll onto her back to show other dogs she's not a threat. If the situation looks like escalating, calmly distract the dogs or remove your puppy – don't shout or shriek. Dogs will pick up on your fear.

Another sign to look out for is *eyeballing.* In the canine world, staring a dog in the eyes is a challenge and may cause an aggressive response.

NOTE: whereas we might look someone in the eye when we are first introduced, it is normal for dogs to sniff the scent glands in another dog's bottom!

Tip **Your puppy has to learn to interact with other dogs. Don't be too quick to pick up your Mini; she will sense your anxiety and lose confidence.**

The same is true when walking on a leash – don't be nervous every time you see another dog – your Schnauzer will pick up on it and may react by barking, lunging or snapping.

Always follow up a socialisation experience with praise, petting, a fun game or a special treat.

One positive sign from a dog is the *"play bow" pictured,* when she goes down onto her front elbows but keeps her backside up in the air.

This is a sign that she's feeling friendly towards the other dog and wants to play. Relaxed ear and body position and wagging tail are other positive signs.

Miniature Schnauzers are not naturally aggressive dogs. It's highly unlikely they will attack another dog, but they can be very brave and many will fiercely defend themselves if attacked - which can be quite a frightening scene.

If you think a meeting or situation may result in aggression, calmly remove yourself and your dog from the scene - **without transferring your anxiety to your Mini**. Only pick them up as a last resort.

With Minis, aggression, such as high-pitched barking or lunging on the lead, is often grounded in fear, and a dog that mixes easily with other dogs is less likely to be combative.

Take your puppy everywhere you can - in the car, on the bus, to the café or pub, etc. You want her to feel relaxed in any noisy and crowded situation. Take treats with you and praise her when she reacts calmly to new situations.

Tip **An excellent way of getting your new puppy to meet other dogs in a safe environment is at a puppy class. We highly recommend this for all puppies.**

Ask around locally if any classes are being run. Some veterinary practices and dog trainers run classes for very junior pups who have had all their vaccinations. These help pups get used to other dogs of a similar age.

What the Breeders Say

Good Schnauzer breeders start the socialisation process right from the off. Every breeder involved in this book stresses the importance of socialising young Minis to develop a well-balanced adult dog.

Wade Bogart, Sumerwynd Miniature Schnauzers, New York State: "Socialization is vital for proper mental and social development in dogs. At Sumerwynd, socialization begins at birth.

"Pups are born and raised in my home and each one is handled so many times each day I lose count."

Photo: Wade's GrCh. Sumerwynd Stardust.

"When a litter arrives we have a line of well-wishers wanting to see the newborns! As they grow older, friends often want to take the pups for a "sleepover."

"This early socialization prevents constant barking, shyness, and aggression. Our dogs love everyone and everyone loves our dogs!"

Andrew and Gaynor Ray, breeders of all three sizes at Minnienoom Schnauzers, Derby, England: "By the time they leave, our puppies have been introduced to people of different ages and to a variety of household noises.

"New owners should continue to slowly introduce different encounters, gradually increasing the number as they are more able to cope. Meeting adults and children should be a priority.

"Don't forget to introduce your puppy to people wearing hats, uniforms, glasses, helmets, men with facial hair, umbrellas, joggers and delivery people. Be patient and let him or her decide when they feel secure enough to approach a new person.

"Try to arrange successful and rewarding experiences - if all early life is pleasant and positive, your puppy will grow up to feel safe and confident enough to deal with whatever life has in store.

"Your puppy needs to meet a variety of other animals including cats, small pets, ducks, livestock and horses. Ensure he or she is kept under control to prevent chasing.

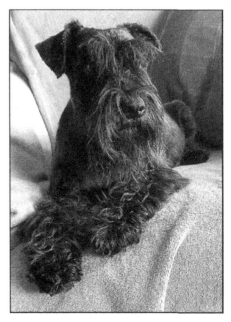

But until your puppy is fully protected by vaccination, they should not be allowed to mix with dogs of unknown vaccination status or be taken to parks or walked in areas that other dogs have fouled.

"He or she also needs to encounter different environments and situations in order to become familiar with a range of traffic, including bicycles, pushchairs and skateboards, the countryside and towns.

"Remember to *'think puppy'* and imagine how it feels to be that small, vulnerable and inexperienced - and try to make sure your puppy is enjoying the experience and not feeling overwhelmed."

Photo: Andrew and Gaynor's Freda (Minnienoom Dancing Freda), aged five, relaxing at home.

Steve, Matthews, of Silbertaum Miniature and Giant Schnauzers, Dorset, England: "Puppies are first socialised in the household with other dogs, visitors and household appliances (vacuums, washing machines, etc.). I always recommend joining puppy training classes as soon as they have had their full course of vaccination.

"The first few months of life set the socialisation standards and rules for the rest of the dog's life - it's very difficult to change the behaviour of an older dog that hasn't been socialised properly as a puppy, and some residual bad behaviours will always lie just under the surface."

Veterinarian and breeder of Beauideal Miniature Schnauzers, North Carolina, **Dr Lisa Sarvas**: "Socializing is critical during the first year.

"We follow the comprehensive program **Puppy Culture** to socialize and start early training.

"We expose them to age-appropriate sights, sounds, textures, grooming, wobble boards, play houses, and toys. Plus, of course, plenty of hugs, kisses and cuddles!"

Photo courtesy of Lisa

Show judge and former breeder **Lesley Myers**, Berkshire, England: "Socialisation is essential for Miniature Schnauzers.

"As soon as my puppies are on their legs there are soft toys in their 10ft pen and a mobile with bells, rings and small discs on it so that when they move and catch it, it makes a noise. I have this to get them used to sudden noises.

"New owners and any family are allowed to visit once a week if they wish, once pups are 4.5 weeks old. Their shoes are sprayed with Formula H and they have to wipe their hands and wrists with Milton antibacterial wipes, sit down and have a small covering on their knees if they want to hold a puppy. Any children visiting are carefully watched and are not allowed to pick the puppies up.

"The puppies I have kept have all been to puppy training or puppy socialisation classes. Even though they aren't allowed to run free to play and meet other puppies, they have at least been in an environment where there are other canines.

"I stand outside supermarket doors with the pup in my arms, take them on short walks around the town centre. At four months old I take them to a couple of outdoor dog shows, ideal places for different noises, loud noises, dogs barking, and masses of scents and other dogs.

"I advise new owners not to rush to take them outside in the big wide world two weeks after their final vaccination, proceed at a pace comfortable for your puppy.

"A good way to keep them safe and comfortable is to carry them in a body harness. This can also help as a comfort zone when walking alongside a road of busy traffic. Also if strangers approach to stroke the puppy (they should ask permission first), at least the small pup isn't way down on the floor watching this tall person's hand coming down towards their head.

"If people want to stroke the puppy, politely ask them to approach with the hand reaching for under their chin and not their head. Reaching to pat the pup on the head could frighten a pup."

13. Mini Schnauzer Health

Miniature Schnauzers are relatively robust, healthy dogs with a typical lifespan of double figures - into the teens if you're lucky. Unlike some other breeds, they also remain active until quite late in life.

Health should always be a major consideration when choosing and raising a dog. Firstly, select a puppy from a breeder who produces Schnauzers sound in both body AND temperament. Secondly, you can play your role in helping to keep your dog healthy throughout his or her life.

NOTE: This chapter is intended to be used as an encyclopaedia to help you to identify potential health issues and act promptly in the best interests of your dog. Please don't read it thinking your Mini Schnauzer will get lots of these ailments – he or she WON'T!

First, let's put things in perspective: the UK Kennel Club has a **Breed Watch Fit For Purpose** campaign that identifies potential faults that could lead to health issues. There are three categories:

1 Breeds with no current points of concern reported

2 Breeds with Breed Watch points of concern

3 Breeds where some dogs have visible conditions or exaggerations that can cause **pain** or discomfort

The good news is that all three types of Schnauzer are classed in Category 1.

Health Testing

It is becoming increasingly evident that genetics can have a huge influence on a person's health and even life expectancy, with lots of time and money currently being devoted to genetic research.

A human is more likely to suffer from a hereditary illness if the gene (or genes) for that disorder is passed on from parents or grandparents. That person is said to have a *"predisposition"* to the ailment if the gene is in the family's bloodline. Well, the same is true of dogs.

There is not a single breed without the potential for some genetic weakness. For example, many Cavalier King Charles Spaniels have heart problems and 25% of all West Highland White Terriers have a hereditary itchy skin disease.

Anyone thinking of getting a Miniature Schnauzer puppy can reduce the chance of their dog having a genetic disease by choosing a puppy from healthy bloodlines.

Tip If you're actively searching for a puppy, you might be considering a breeder based on the look or colour of her dogs or their success in the show ring, but consider the health of the puppy's parents and ancestors as well.

Could they have passed on unhealthy genes along with the good genes for all those features you are attracted to?

The way to reduce those hereditary diseases that can be screened for is for breeders to carry out DNA testing and NOT to mate an *Affected* dog with another *Affected* dog or *Carrier.*

Many inherited diseases are *"Autosomal Recessive,"* below are all possible outcomes – these are average results over thousands of litters. They are the same averages for all autosomal recessive genetic diseases.

PARENT CLEAR + PARENT CLEAR = pups clear

PARENT CLEAR + PARENT CARRIER = 50% will be carriers, 50% will be clear

PARENT CLEAR + PARENT AFFECTED = 100% will be carriers

PARENT CARRIER + PARENT CLEAR = 50% will be carriers, 50% will be clear

PARENT CARRIER + PARENT CARRIER = 25% clear, 25% affected and 50% carriers

PARENT CARRIER + PARENT AFFECTED = 50% affected and 50% carriers

PARENT AFFECTED + PARENT CLEAR = 100% will be carriers

PARENT AFFECTED + PARENT CARRIER = 50% affected and 50% carriers

PARENT AFFECTED + PARENT AFFECTED = 100% affected

As long as a *Carrier* is bred to a dog with a *Clear* result, no puppies will show signs of the disease (although half will be *Carriers* with no symptoms).

Carriers carry the faulty gene(s) but do not show signs of the disease. The reason breeders don't remove all *Carriers* from their breeding stock is that the gene pool would become too small, resulting in interbreeding.

And breeding two closely-related dogs can increase the risk of health issues. There is a factor called *COI (Coefficient of Inbreeding)* which measures how closely-related a dog's ancestors are.

For example, if a dam or sire (mother or father) were bred with one of their puppies, or if two siblings mated, the COI of the resulting puppies would be 25%. Breeding grandparent to grandchild, or mating half-siblings, results in 12.5%.

In the UK you can check COI on the Kennel Club website by typing the registered name of your puppy into their COI Calculator: www.thekennelclub.org.uk/search/inbreeding-co-efficient; the lower the number the better.

There's an excellent guide to COI at: www.dogbreedhealth.com/a-beginners-guide-to-coi

Health Certificates for Puppy Buyers

Anyone thinking of getting a Miniature Schnauzer puppy today can reduce the chances of their dog having a genetic disease by choosing a puppy from healthy bloodlines.

If you're actively searching for a puppy, you might be considering a breeder based on the look or colour of her dogs or their success in the show ring, but consider the health of the puppy's parents and ancestors as well. Could they have passed on unhealthy genes along with the good genes for all those features you are attracted to?

Which Tests?

In the UK, Kennel Club Assured Breeders must have all breeding Mini Schnauzers eye tested and screened for MAC (Mycobacterium Avium Complex) - more on this later. It is also highly recommended that all their puppies are eye screened.

In the USA, the OFA (Orthopedic Foundation for Animals) recommends the following basic health screening tests for all breeding stock. Dogs meeting these requirements qualify for Canine Health Information Center (CHIC) certification, which is the gold standard for health screening in the USA.

OFA says: "All results do not need to be normal, but they must all be in the public domain so that responsible breeders can make more informed breeding decisions. For potential puppy buyers, CHIC certification is a good indicator that the breeder responsibly factors good health into their selection criteria."

- ❖ ACVO Eye Exam
- ❖ Cardiac Evaluation
- ❖ MAC - Optional but recommended
- ❖ PRA Type B HIVEP3 DNA Test (an eye disease) - Optional but recommended

The most recent UK Breed Health Coordinators' Annual Health Report identified the following top health concerns for Minis:

1. Hereditary eye conditions
2. Mycobacterium Avium Complex (MAC)
3. Cancers

Below is the summary of health concerns that Miniature Schnauzer owners reported in the latest Breed Health Survey carried out by the four UK Schnauzer clubs:

Condition	Number Affected
Other	47
Gastrointestinal	46
Eye Conditions	19
Heart Problems	18
Bladder Problems	16
Epilepsy	14
Auto-immune Disease	11

Hypothyroid	11
Cancers	5
Kidney disorder	4
Spondylitis	1
Lymphoma	0

The Survey also revealed the most common reasons for Minis visiting the vet: dental problems (19.2%) digestive (13.7%), skin (12.7%), ears (10%) and obesity (8.2%) - more females than males. Other issues included blocked anal glands (5.8%) and heart murmur (4.2%).

 Wherever you live, check what DNA tests the parents have had and ask to see original certificates - a good breeder will be happy to provide them.

As well as asking to see health certificates, prospective buyers should always find out exactly what contract the breeder is offering with the puppy. Good breeders offer a Puppy Contract.

While Health Certificates are not a guarantee that your dog will remain healthy throughout his or her life, they DO give owners peace of mind knowing that your puppy is free from the most common hereditary diseases that can affect the breed.

FACT ❯ If a puppy is sold as "Vet Checked," it does not mean that the parents have been health screened. It means that a veterinarian has given the puppy a brief physical and visual examination, worming and vaccinations are up to date, and the pup appears to be in good health <u>on the day of the examination.</u>

And a pedigree certificate from the Kennel Club or AKC does NOT mean that the puppy or parents have been health screened. It simply guarantees that the puppy's parents can be traced back several generations and that the ancestors were registered purebred Schnauzers.

If you have already got your dog, don't worry! There is plenty of advice in this book on how to take the best care of your Mini. Being careful with your puppy's exercise, feeding a quality food, monitoring weight, regular grooming and check-overs, socialisation - and exercise for adult dogs - all help to keep your Schnauzer in tip-top condition. Good owners can certainly help to extend the life of their dog.

Schnauzer Insurance

Insurance is another point to consider for a new puppy or adult dog. Puppies from many reputable breeders in the UK come with five weeks' insurance that can be extended before it expires.

 USA breeders may or may not provide insurance, if not, ask if they can recommend a plan.

If you are getting an older Schnauzer, get insurance BEFORE any health issues develop, or you may find any pre-existing conditions are excluded. If you can afford it, take out life cover.

This may be more expensive but will cover your dog throughout his or her lifetime - including for chronic (recurring and/or long-term) ailments, such as joint, heart or eye problems, epilepsy and cancer.

Insuring a healthy puppy or adult dog is the only surefire way to ensure vets' bills are covered before anything unforeseen happens - and you'd be a rare owner if you didn't use your policy at least once during your dog's lifetime.

The average cost of dog insurance in the US is around $50 per month. This varies a lot, depending on location, the excess, and total coverage per year in dollars. With advances in veterinary science, there is so much more vets can do to help an ailing dog - but at a price.

Costs in the UK range from around £15 a month for Accident Only to around £30-£50 per month for Lifetime Cover, depending on where you live, how much excess you are willing to pay and the total in pounds covered per year. Surgical procedures can rack up bills of thousands of pounds or dollars. Below are Trupanion and www.PetInsuranceQuotes.com examples of insurance claims:

> Diabetes $10,496, Ingestion of foreign body $2,964, Parvo gastroenteritis $5,084, Cruciate ligament tear $5,439, Dental Problems $250 to $1,500, Epilepsy $200 to $15,000, Cancer $5,000 to $20,000. ($1.20 = approx. £1 at the time of writing).

Of course, if you make a claim your monthly premium will increase. But if you have a decent insurance policy BEFORE a recurring health problem starts, your dog should be covered if the ailment returns. You have to decide whether insurance is worth the money. On the plus side:

1. Peace of mind financially if your beloved Schnauzer falls ill, and

2. You know exactly how much hard cash to part with each month, so no nasty surprises.

Three Health Tips

1. **Buy a well-bred puppy** - Good Schnauzer breeders select their stock based on:

   a) General health and genetic health of the parents

   b) Conformation (physical structure)

   c) Temperament

   d) COI

Believe it or not, committed breeders are not in it for the money, often incurring high bills for stud fees, health screening, veterinary costs, specialised food, etc. Their main concern is to produce healthy, handsome puppies with good temperaments that are *"fit for function."*

2. **Get pet insurance as soon as you get your dog** - Don't wait until he has a health issue and needs to see a vet as most insurers exclude all pre-existing conditions on their policies. Check the small print to make sure all conditions are covered and that if the issue recurs, it will continue to be covered year after year. When working out the costs of a dog, factor in annual or monthly pet insurance fees and trips to a vet for check-ups, vaccinations, etc.

3. **Find a good vet** - Ask around, rather than just going to the first one you find. A vet that knows your dog from his or her puppy vaccinations and then right through their life is more likely to understand your dog and diagnose quickly and correctly when something is wrong. If you visit a big veterinary practice, ask for the vet by name when you make an appointment.

We all want our dogs to be healthy - so how can you tell if yours is? Well, here are some positive things to look for in a healthy Schnauzer:

Health Indicators

1. **Eyes** - Mini Schnauzers have black or dark eye rims (except 'no colour' white Minis; they have pink rims). Paleness around the eyeball (conjunctiva) could also be a sign of something amiss. A cloudy eye could be a sign of cataracts.

   Sometimes the dog's third eyelid (nictating membrane) is visible at the inside corner - this is normal. But there should be no thick, green or yellow discharge from the eyes.

2. **Movement** - Healthy dogs move at all speeds freely and without pain. Look out for warning signs of stiffness when getting up from lying, limping, a reluctance to move, get in the car or go up steps.

3. **Nose** - A dog's nose is an indicator of health. Schnauzer noses are black (except no colour whites). They should be free from clear, watery secretions. Any yellow, green or foul-smelling discharge is not normal - in younger dogs, this can be a sign of canine distemper. Schnauzer pups may have a pink nose or pink patches that normally turn black within a few months.

   NOTE: a *'snow nose'* or *'winter nose'* is one that turns lighter-coloured, often during colder months. Scientists are not sure what causes it; it may be a vitamin deficiency, but the nose often returns to black in warmer weather. Older dogs may also lose some black pigment in their noses.

4. **Ears** - If you are choosing a puppy, gently clap your hands behind the pup - not so loud as to frighten him - to see if he reacts. If not, this may be a sign of deafness. Ears should still be checked when grooming to make sure they are clean and not smelly, which is a sign of yeast infection.

5. **Mouth** - Schnauzer gums are usually pink or pink and black. Paleness or whiteness can be a sign of anaemia, Bloat or lack of oxygen due to heart or breathing problems. Blue gums or tongues are a sign that your dog is not breathing properly. Red, inflamed gums can be a sign of gingivitis or another dental disease.

   Like humans, young dogs have sparkling white teeth, whereas older ones have darker teeth, but they should not have any hard white, yellow, green or brown bits. Your dog's breath should not smell unpleasant.

6. **Energy** - Miniature Schnauzers are busy, alert dogs. Yours should have good energy levels with fluid movements. Lack of energy, lethargy or lack of interest in their surroundings could be a sign of an underlying problem.

7. **Coat and Skin** - These are easy-to-monitor indicators of a healthy dog. A healthy Schnauzer has a clean, double coat with a soft, dense undercoat and a harsher, wiry topcoat. A rinse or towel dry after a wet walk will help to keep the coat and skin healthy. Any dandruff, bald spots, a dull, lifeless, discoloured or oily coat, or one that loses excessive hair, can all be signs that something is amiss. The skin should be smooth without redness or rashes. If a dog is scratching, licking or biting a lot, he may have a condition that needs addressing.

   Open sores, scales, scabs, red patches or growths can be a sign of a skin issue or allergy. Signs of fleas, ticks and other external parasites should be treated immediately; check for small black or dark red specks, which may be fleas or flea poop, on the coat or bedding.

8. **Weight -** Obesity shortens a dog's life. Some Minis are very greedy and they ALL have lovable faces with pleading eyes that are hard to resist. **Be strong!** Don't give in to their attempts to scrounge extra treats and food; monitor their calories and make sure yours is getting plenty of exercise.

A Schnauzer's ribs should be well covered, but the stomach should be **above** the bottom of the rib cage when standing, *pictured,* and you should be able to see a visible waistline and feel the ribs beneath the coat without too much effort.

If the stomach is level or hangs below, your Schnauzer is overweight - or may have a pot belly, which can also be a symptom of other conditions.

9. **Temperature -** The normal temperature of a dog is 101°F to 102.5°F. (A human is 98.6°F). Excited or exercising dogs may run a slightly higher temperature. Anything above 103°F or below 100°F should be checked out. The exceptions are female dogs about to give birth that will often have a temperature of 99°F. If you take your dog's temperature, make sure he is relaxed and *always* use a purpose-made canine thermometer.

10. **Stools -** Poo, poop, business, faeces - call it what you will - it's the stuff that comes out of the less appealing end of your Schnauzer on a daily basis! It should be mostly firm and brown, not runny, with no signs of blood or worms. Watery stools or a dog not eliminating regularly are both signs of an upset stomach or other ailments. If it continues for a couple of days, consult your vet.

 If puppies have loose or runny poop, they need checking out much sooner as they can quickly dehydrate.

11. **Smell -** Schnauzers who are regularly groomed are clean dogs that don't smell – unless they have been rolling in something unmentionable (cow poop was a particular favourite of our Max, closely followed by the slightly less messy fox poop).

If yours has a musty, 'off' or generally unpleasant smell, it could be a sign of a yeast infection. This can be caused by several different triggers, including environmental or food allergies. Or your dog might have an anal sac issue, which may be accompanied by *'scooting'* (dragging the rear end across the floor). Whatever the cause, you need to get to the root of the problem quickly before it develops into something more serious.

12. **Attitude -** A generally positive attitude is a sign of good health. All three types of Schnauzer are alert dogs; they are interested in life and love to be engaged with their humans. Symptoms of illness may include one or all of the following: a general lack of interest in their surroundings, tail not wagging (if yours has one!), lethargy, not eating food and sleeping a lot more than normal.

The important thing is to look out for any behaviour that is out of the ordinary for YOUR Schnauzer.

Many different signs indicate your Best Friend isn't feeling great. If you don't yet know your Schnauzer, his habits, temperament and behaviour patterns, then spend some time getting acquainted with them.

What are his normal character and temperament? Lively or calm, playful or serious, a joker or an introvert, bold or nervous, happy to be left alone or loves to be with people?

How often does he empty his bowels, does he ever vomit? (Dogs will often eat grass to make themselves sick, this is perfectly normal and a natural way of cleansing the digestive system).

 **You may not think your Schnauzer can talk, but he most certainly can!**

If you really know your dog, his character and his habits, then he CAN tell you when he's not well. He does this by changing his patterns. Some symptoms are physical, some emotional and others are behavioural. It's important to be able to recognise these changes, as early treatment can be the key to keeping a simple problem from snowballing into something more serious.

If you think your dog is unwell, it is useful to keep an accurate and detailed account of his symptoms to give to the vet, and perhaps even take a video of him on your mobile phone. This will help the vet to correctly diagnose and effectively treat your dog.

Three Vital Signs of Illness

1. **Temperature** - A newborn puppy has a temperature of 94-97°F (34.4-36.1°C). This reaches the normal adult body temperature of around 101°F (38.3°C) at four weeks old. A vet takes a dog's temperature reading via the rectum. If you do this, only do it with a special thermometer, like this electronic rectal one *pictured*. Infrared forehead thermometers (which may be slightly less accurate but are less invasive) are also widely available.

   NOTE: Exercise or excitement can cause the temperature to rise by 2°F to 3°F (1-1.5°C) when your dog is actually in good health, so wait until he is relaxed before taking his temperature. If it is above or below the norms and the dog seems under par, give your vet a call.

2. **Respiratory Rate** - Another symptom of illness is a change in breathing patterns. This varies a lot depending on the size and weight of the dog.

   - Big dogs like Giant Schnauzers have a normal rate of 70 to 120 beats per minute
   - Medium dogs like Standard Schnauzers have a normal rate of 80 to 120 beats per minute
   - Small dogs like Miniature Schnauzers have a normal rate of 90 to 140 beats per minute

   To check your dog's heart rate, put your hand on the inside of his rear leg at the mid-thigh, where you should be able to feel the femoral artery pulsing near the surface. It's easiest to find if your dog is standing. Count the number of beats over 15 seconds and multiply by four to get the beats per minute. (Don't do it when he is panting).

3. **Behaviour Changes** - Classic symptoms of illness are any inexplicable behaviour changes. If there has NOT been a change in the household atmosphere, such as another new pet, a new baby, moving home, the absence of a family member or the loss of another dog, then the following symptoms may well be a sign that all is not well:

- Depression or lethargy
- Tiredness - sleeping more than normal or not wanting to exercise
- Lack of interest in his surroundings
- Loss of appetite
- Being more vocal - grunting, whining or whimpering
- Abnormal posture
- Restlessness, not settling, walking in circles, etc.
- Aggression
- Anxiety and/or shivering, which can be a sign of pain
- Falling or stumbling

If any of them appear for the first time or worse than usual, you need to keep him under close watch for a few hours or even days. Quite often he will return to normal of his own accord. Like humans, dogs have off days too.

If he is showing any of the above symptoms, then don't over-exercise him, and avoid stressful situations and hot or cold places. Make sure he has access to clean water. Keep a record and it may be useful to take a fresh stool sample to your vet. If your dog does need professional medical attention, most vets will want to know:

WHEN the symptoms first appeared in your dog

WHETHER they are getting better or worse, and

HOW FREQUENT the symptoms are - intermittent, continuous or increasing?

Eyes

Several eye diseases can affect Schnauzers. Here are some of the main ones.

Hereditary Cataracts

These are known to occur slightly more often than average in Miniature and Giant Schnauzers, compared with other breeds. Two types affect Minis; the first is **Congenital Hereditary Cataracts** (meaning a puppy is born with them).

In the UK, Kennel Club Assured Breeders must test Miniature Schnauzer puppies before they go to their new homes.

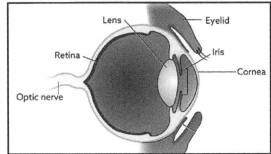

The second type is **Hereditary Cataracts,** which is the type affecting Giants as well. These can only be diagnosed from around six months or older. It is recommended that breeding dogs undergo an annual eye test.

The purpose of the lens, which should be transparent, is to focus the rays of light to form an image on the retina.

A cataract occurs when the lens becomes cloudy. Less light enters the eye, images become blurry and the dog's sight worsens as the cataract becomes larger. One or both eyes may be affected and the cataracts may not appear at the same time. Untreated, it can result in blindness.

Hereditary Cataracts are different from Late Onset Cataracts, which can develop in any breed later in life – much the same as elderly humans who develop cataracts.

Diagnosis and Treatment

An owner may realise something is wrong when they notice their dog's pupils are cloudy or have changed colour, or when the dog starts bumping into things. The middle of the pupil may have a white spot or area. Take a photo with a flash or shine a flashlight in your dog's eyes, you should see a coloured reflection. If you see something grey or dull white, your puppy may have a cataract.

Cataracts are not usually painful, but the loss of vision and eventual blindness can cause confusion and anxiety in some dogs and may make them more prone to injury.

If you think your Schnauzer has cataracts, get him to a vet as soon as possible. Sometimes, if the puppy's cataracts are small, they can be watched and may not need treatment. They won't go away, but they may not get bigger quickly. Discuss this with your vet and, if you choose this option, you have to be vigilant and monitor your puppy's eyes for any signs of change.

Some puppies born with congenital cataracts can even improve as they mature. That's because the lens inside the puppy's eye grows along with the dog, but the cloudy area remains the same size, so by the time the puppy is an adult, the affected area is relatively small. By adulthood, some dogs born with cataracts can compensate and "see around" the cloudiness.

Early removal of more serious cataracts can restore vision and provide a dramatic improvement in the quality of a dog's life. The only treatment for severe cataracts is surgery (unless the cataracts are caused by another condition like Diabetes).

Left: eye with cataracts. Right: same eye with an artificial lens

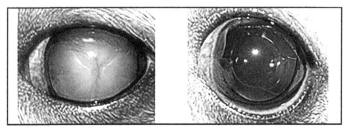

Surgery costs thousands of dollars and the dog is anaesthetised, but the good news is that the success rate is around 90%. The procedure is similar to small incision cataract surgery in people, and once a cataract has been removed, it does not recur.

An artificial lens is implanted in the dog's eye to replace the cataract lens. (Dogs can see without an artificial lens, but the image will not be in focus). Discuss with the vet or ophthalmologist whether your dog would benefit from an artificial lens and the risks of surgery.

After the procedure, the dog usually stays with the vet for one or two nights and then has to wear a protective E collar (also called an Elizabethan collar or the Cone of Shame!) for a week or two while the eye is healing.

 Miniature Schnauzers hate the E collar; they look depressed and bang into doorways and furniture. Don't be tempted to take it off; it only takes a couple of seconds for a dog to scratch and damage the eye.

Our Max was a nightmare when he returned from the vet with one on a couple of occasions. He felt very sorry for himself and kept slumping to the ground! Fortunately, his body had good healing properties and he didn't have to wear one for more than a few days.

The owner plays a big part in recovery. Firstly, by making sure that the dog does not damage the eye. Then you have to keep him quiet and calm, no chasing, tug-o-war or any game where he might shake his head.

And finally, you'll have to give him eye drops, several times a day for the first week and then less frequently after that.

He'll also need regular check-ups with the vet to make sure there are no complications.

 The success of cataract surgery depends very much on the owner doing all the right things. But all the effort is worth it when the dog regains his sight.

PRA (Progressive Retinal Atrophy)

PRA is the name for several progressive diseases that lead to blindness. First recognised at the beginning of the 20th century in Gordon Setters, this inherited condition has been documented in over 100 breeds, including Miniature Schnauzers.

Minis born with normal eyesight can develop PRA any time from as early as one year old, although affected dogs often don't show any signs until they are three to five years old, or older.

If your dog has PRA, you may first notice that he lacks confidence in low light; perhaps reluctant to go downstairs or along a dark hallway. If you look closely into his eyes, you may see the pupils dilating (becoming bigger) and/or the reflection of greenish light from the back of his eyes.

As the condition worsens, he might then start bumping into things, first at night and then in the daytime too. The condition is not painful and the eyes often appear normal - without redness, tearing or squinting. The lenses may become opaque or cloudy in some dogs.

Two types affect Minis and DNA tests are available for both. Ask to see certificates for both parents of your chosen puppy. In addition to the DNA test certificate for PRA, it is recommended that prospective owners of all sizes of Schnauzer ask to see the parents' annual eye exam results.

Retinal Dysplasia

This is a hereditary disease present from birth that can affect Minis and Giants. The retina's layers don't form or attach properly when the puppy is in the womb, although the severity ranges from minor to completely detached retinas that cause blindness. Even if the dog isn't badly affected, the retina can become detached as he ages.

Other eye disorders, including Glaucoma and Cataracts, often develop in dogs with Retinal Dysplasia. Moderately affected dogs might benefit from laser surgery.

Eyelash Disorders

These can affect dogs of all breeds, but it's useful to be able to recognise the signs:

Entropion

This occurs when the edge of the lower eyelid rolls inward, causing the dog's fur to rub the surface of the eyeball, or cornea. In rare cases, the upper lid can also be affected, and one or both eyes may be involved. This painful condition may have a hereditary link.

The affected dog scratches at his painful eye with his paws and this can lead to further injury. If your Schnauzer suffers from it, he will usually show signs at or before his first birthday. You will notice that his eyes are red and inflamed and they will produce tears. He will probably squint.

The tears typically start clear and can progress to a thick yellow or green mucus. If left untreated, Entropion causes corneal ulcers and you might also notice a milky-white colour develop. This is caused by increased fluid which affects the clarity of the cornea.

For your poor dog, the irritation is constant. Imagine how painful and uncomfortable it would be if you had permanent hairs touching your eyes. It makes my eyes water just thinking about it.

 It's important to get your dog to the vet as soon as you suspect Entropion before your dog scratches his cornea and worsens the problem.

A vet will make the diagnosis after a painless and relatively simple inspection of your dog's eyes. He or she will first have to rule out other issues, such as allergies. In mild cases, the vet may successfully prescribe eye drops, ointment or other medication.

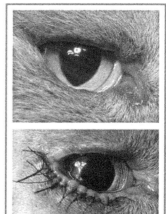

However, the most common treatment for more severe cases is a fairly straightforward surgical procedure to pin back the lower eyelid, *pictured.*

Some vets may delay surgery in affected young dogs and treat the condition with medication until the dog's face is fully grown. This avoids having to repeat the procedure later.

Ectropion

This is a condition where the lower lids turn outwards, causing the eyelids to appear droopy. One or both eyes may be involved and it can occur in any breed, but certain breeds, including Bulldogs, Saint Bernards, Bassett Hounds and Bloodhounds are more susceptible.

When the lower eyelid droops it exposes the conjunctiva and creates a pocket where pollens, grasses and dust can collect and rub against the sensitive conjunctiva. This is a consistent source of irritation and leads to increased redness of the conjunctiva and tears which flow over the lower lid and face, often causing a brownish staining of the fur below the eyes.

A thick mucus discharge may appear along the eyelid margin and the dog may rub or scratch his eyes if it becomes uncomfortable. Vets normally make a diagnosis during a physical examination.

Blood and urine tests may be performed on older dogs to search for an underlying cause. The vet may also perform corneal staining to see if any ulcers are present.

Many dogs live normal lives with Ectropion. However, some develop repeated eye infections due to the collection of dirt and dust within the eye. Therefore, the risks are minor except in the most severe cases.

Some dogs require no treatment. But you should visit your vet if the eye is irritated. Mild cases can be treated with eye drops and ointments that prevent the cornea and conjunctiva from drying out. Special eye (ophthalmic) antibiotics are used to combat any corneal ulcers. In severe cases surgery can remove excess tissue to tighten the lids and remove the abnormal pocket - the procedure has a high success rate.

Dry Eye (Keratoconjunctivitis sicca)

Keratoconjunctivitis sicca is the technical term for *Dry Eye*, which is caused by not enough tears being produced and can affect dogs of all breeds. With insufficient tears, a dog's eyes can become irritated and the conjunctiva appears red. It's estimated that as many as one in five dogs can suffer from Dry Eye at one time or another in their lives.

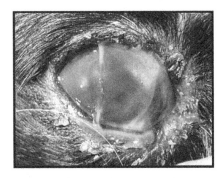

Dry Eye causes a dog to blink a lot, the eye or eyes typically develop a thick, yellowy discharge and the cornea develops a film.

Infections are common as tears also have anti-bacterial and cleansing properties, and inadequate lubrication allows dust, pollen and other debris to accumulate. The nerves of these glands may also become damaged.

FACT Dry Eye is often associated with skin disorders, it may be due to increased rubbing and secondary infection in the eyes, or it could be part of an immune disorder. It may also be caused by injuries to the tear glands, eye infections, diseases such as distemper or reactions to drugs.

Left untreated, a dog will suffer painful eye infections, and repeated irritation of the cornea results in severe scarring - and even ulcers, which can lead to blindness.

Early treatment is essential and usually involves drugs: cyclosporine, ophthalmic ointment or drops. In some cases, another eye preparation - Tacrolimus - is also used. Sometimes artificial tear drops are also prescribed.

Treating Dry Eye involves commitment from the owner. Gently cleaning the eyes several times a day with a warm, wet cloth helps a dog feel better and may also help stimulate tear production. In very severe and rare cases, an operation can be performed to transplant a salivary duct into the upper eyelid, causing saliva to drain into and lubricate the eye.

 Any eye condition can be worsened by irritants and injury. Remove or fence off low, spiky plants in your garden or yard. And although your Schnauzer may look like the canine version of Easy Rider with his head stuck out of the car window and ears flapping in the breeze, bear in mind that dust, insects and dirt particles can hit and damage those beautiful eyes!

Pancreatitis

The pancreas is a V-shaped organ located behind the stomach and the first section of the small intestine, the duodenum. It has two main functions: it aids in the metabolism of sugar in the body through the production of insulin, and it produces a pancreatic enzyme which helps digest and absorb nutrients from food.

The Miniature Schnauzer is a breed which may have a moderate risk of developing Pancreatitis. **Acute Pancreatitis** is a sudden onset of pancreatic inflammation, while **Chronic Pancreatitis** is a long-term condition.

This is a complicated illness. Many factors can trigger this illness, including a high-fat diet or meal, steroids and genetics may also play a role. At its worst, or left untreated, it can be life-threatening, while mild cases may be managed with a special diet.

Symptoms of Acute Pancreatitis (the dog may have one or more of these) can range from mild to severe and are similar to those of several other ailments:

- Swollen or painful abdomen

- Hunched back

- Lack of appetite

- Dehydration

- Vomiting

- Diarrhoea

- Fever

During an episode, a dog may also lower his head and shoulders onto the floor and raise his rear end.

To diagnose Pancreatitis, a complete history is taken by the vet, along with a thorough physical exam, a blood count, chemistry panel and urine analysis. X-rays and ultrasounds can also help in making the diagnosis. Then other causes of the symptoms must be ruled out, which isn't always straightforward.

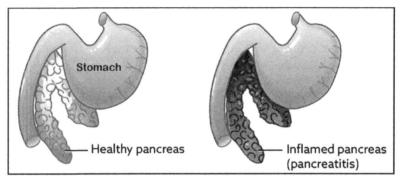

Early diagnosis and treatment lead to more successful outcomes. Treatment is geared towards:

- Correct dehydration

- Pain relief

- Controlling vomiting

- Providing nutritional support

- Preventing complications

Dehydration and electrolyte imbalances are common in dogs with Acute Pancreatitis, so supplemental fluids are given either by injection or intravenously, depending upon the severity of the condition.

Dogs that are experiencing pain will be treated with pain relievers, and if the dog is vomiting, he will be fasted and given anti-vomiting medication.

Depending upon the dog's response, food intake can be started again after a day or more. The dog is generally fed small meals of bland, easily digestible, high-carbohydrate and low-fat food. In some severe cases, it may be necessary to use tube feeding to provide proper nutrition.

If the Pancreatitis was caused by a medication, this should be stopped. If it was caused by a toxin, infection or other condition, the vet should start the appropriate treatment for the underlying condition. In rare instances where there are intestinal complications or the development of a pancreatic abscess, surgery may be necessary.

Prognosis (Outlook)

Pancreatitis can be unpredictable. Often, if the Pancreatitis was mild and the dog only had one episode, the chances of recovery are good. Keeping the dog on a low-fat diet may be all that is necessary. In other cases, what appears to be a mild case may progress, or may be treated successfully only to have recurrences, sometimes severe.

Some dogs develop Chronic Pancreatitis, which can lead to Diabetes and/or Pancreatic Insufficiency, also called 'Maldigestion Syndrome.' Treatment for this is lifelong and expensive, but possible.

 Good habits can help to prevent Pancreatitis, which commonly occurs in dogs after having eaten high-fat foods. Lower your dog's risk by feeding him a healthy, low-fat diet in the right quantities – and avoid giving lots of treats. Since overweight dogs are at risk, regular exercise is important as well.

Hyperlipidaemia

Hyperlipidaemia is not an uncommon problem seen in Minis (and Beagles). It's caused by excess lipids (fats) in the blood - the two most common fats being cholesterol and triglycerides. It's normal to have a surge of fats in the bloodstream after eating, but this normally clears in six to 10 hours.

In dogs with hyperlipidaemia, the fat levels in the blood remain high and this is a problem because it can cause them to become susceptible to other diseases such as Pancreatitis, eye diseases and Diabetes in later life. The causes are not understood, but it's thought to be a hereditary connection.

Science Direct says: "A recent investigation of the prevalence of hypertriglyceridemia in Miniature Schnauzers found that nearly a third (32.8%) had triglyceride concentrations that were higher than the reference range for healthy dogs.

"Only 5.4% of control dogs from the general population have Hyperlipidaemia, which does suggest a genetic predisposition in this breed."

Males and females are equally affected and it's usually first seen in Minis over four years of age. Affected dogs are either asymptomatic (they have no symptoms) or show some or all of these:

- Vomiting
- Diarrhoea
- Stomach pain
- Bloating
- Loss of appetite

These are similar to the symptoms of Acute Pancreatitis, which is why Hyperlipidaemia is sometimes referred to as *"Pseudopancreatitis."*

The good news is that dogs can be screened for Hyperlipidaemia and with lifestyle management changes, which involve switching to a low-fat diet, the symptoms can usually be managed or avoided completely.

Some veterinarians recommend that all older Miniature Schnauzers have an annual fasting blood test.

NOTE: Hyperlipidaemia can be triggered by another disease, such as Cushing's or an underactive thyroid gland. If these primary diseases are treated, the Hyperlipidaemia normally resolves itself.

Bladder Stones

Urolithiasis is the technical name given to a condition in which mineral crystals in urine combine to form stones anywhere in the urinary tract, including the bladder, kidneys and urethra, causing irritation and infection.

The Miniature Schnauzer is considered to be more at risk of bladder stones (which take weeks or months to form) than other breeds. One study of dogs of all breeds found that the typical age of onset was six to 11 years of age.

The causes are not fully understood, there may be a genetic connection, but UFAW also states: "Miniature Schnauzers may be more likely to form such stones than other breeds as they are found to urinate less often and produce a smaller, more concentrated volume of urine containing more calcium" - I don't think they ever met our Mini, Max, whose record was 43 pees on a 45-minute walk!

More often than not, bladder stones can be passed with urine and only become a problem once one of them blocks the flow of urine. At this point, your dog won't be able to pee properly and needs prompt veterinary attention. A complete blockage is a medical emergency, as the bladder can rupture. Signs are:

- ❖ Blood in the urine
- ❖ Straining to urinate
- ❖ Increased urination
- ❖ The urine may be cloudy or have an unpleasant smell
- ❖ Loss of appetite or energy

Diagnosis is made by urine analysis and X-ray or ultrasound. Treatment usually follows one of three courses, depending on the number and size of the stones:

- ❖ A special diet
- ❖ Removing the stones via a catheter, or
- ❖ Surgery, which is quite common - often the dog can return home the same day with antibiotics and painkillers

Bladder stones are caused by too many minerals in the blood, so it is important not to overfeed your Mini - a magnesium supplement may help to prevent bladder stones from forming. Apple cider vinegar is a recommended remedy for dogs that suffer from recurring bladder stones (which is not uncommon) as they help to regulate the acidity levels in the stomach.

Make sure your Schnauzer has access to water 100% of the time. This will help to naturally flush out excess minerals and unwanted waste products before they start to solidify.

Cushing's Disease

This complex ailment, also known as **Hyperadrenocorticism or HAC,** is best described as a set of symptoms caused when a dog produces too much of a hormone called Cortisol. It develops over time, which is why it is more often seen in middle-aged or senior dogs. Mini Schnauzers are more susceptible to the disease than many other breeds.

Cortisol is released by the adrenal gland located near the kidneys. Normally it is produced during times of stress to prepare the body for strenuous activity. It alters the metabolism, allowing the body to draw energy from stored fats and sugars while retaining sodium and water - think of an adrenaline rush.

While this hormone is essential for the effective functioning of cells and organs, too much of it can be dangerous, and when the body is constantly producing Cortisol it is, in effect, in a persistent state of breakdown.

Symptoms

The most common signs of Cushing's are similar to those of old age, making it hard to diagnose and then monitor. Your dog may display one or more of them.

 If you can, keep a note or diary of any changes you notice in your dog's habits, behaviour and appearance and take these notes with you to the vet. They will help to get a correct diagnosis. The most noticeable include:

* Drinking excessive amounts of water
* Urinating frequently and possible urinary incontinence
* A ravenous appetite
* Hair loss or recurring skin problems
* Pot belly
* Thin skin
* Muscle wastage
* Insomnia
* Lack of energy, general lethargy
* Panting a lot

There are three types of Cushing's, but 80-85% of cases are caused by a tumour on the pituitary gland at the base of the brain.

This type is called PD or PDA. Usually benign and often pea-sized, this tumour puts pressure on the gland, causing an increase in pituitary secretion. This in turn causes the adrenal gland to release additional cortisol.

A small percentage of dogs have ADH, where one of the adrenal glands themselves has developed a tumour that is directly producing too much cortisol. The third type is called **iatrogenic** and is the result of the chronic use of steroids.

In the early stages of Cushing's, the impact is minor, but symptoms gradually progress and become more severe if the dog doesn't receive the correct treatment.

As muscle wastage increases, it reduces the dog's ability to behave normally and exercise, and dogs with more advanced stages of the disease will feel ill, with infections and blood clots causing discomfort and pain.

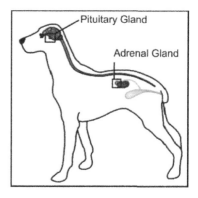

Diagnosis and treatment usually require multiple visits to the vet, several tests and possibly hospitalisation, all of which can be stressful for a Mini Schnauzer – our Max hated the vet and would start high-pitch barking in the car when we were a few hundred yards away.

Cushing's disease cannot be cured, but it can be managed and controlled with medication, usually giving your dog a longer, happier life. Some dogs with mild symptoms do not require immediate treatment, but should be closely monitored for signs of the condition worsening.

Treatment usually requires lifelong medication with drugs. Lysodren (mitotane) or Vetoryl (trilostane) are usually prescribed by vets to treat the most common pituitary-dependent Cushing's disease. Both have several side effects, so the dog needs monitoring. If you suspect your dog has Cushing's disease, don't delay in contacting your vet.

....

Hypothyroidism

Hypothyroidism (underactive thyroid) is a hormonal disorder that can affect many breeds, including some Miniature Schnauzers. According to UFAW (Universities Federation for Animal Welfare): "The cause is unclear, but is thought, at least partly, to have a genetic basis. The welfare consequences may be relatively mild if the disease is diagnosed and successfully treated, but diagnosis (and sometimes treatment) can be difficult.

"Thyroid hormone insufficiency has widespread effects in the body and, in cases where the disease progresses, welfare effects can be severe and prolonged; for example, due to increased susceptibility to infections and to effects on various organs including brain and kidneys."

The thyroid is a gland located on either side of the windpipe in the dog's throat, and Hypothyroidism occurs when it does not produce enough of the hormone thyroid, which controls the speed of the metabolism.

Dogs with very low thyroid levels have a slow metabolic rate.

Hypothyroidism occurs in both males and females, usually over five years old. The symptoms are often non-specific and quite gradual; they vary depending on breed and age. Most forms of Hypothyroidism are diagnosed with a blood test.

Symptoms - listed in order, with the most common ones being at the top of the list:

- High blood cholesterol
- Lethargy, reluctance to exercise
- Weight gain
- Skin problems - hair loss, dry coat or excessive shedding
- Wounds not healing
- Hyperpigmentation or darkening of the skin, seen in 25% of cases
- Intolerance to cold, seen in 15% of dogs with the condition

Treatment

Although Hypothyroidism is a type of auto-immune disease and cannot be prevented, as you have read, symptoms can often be easily diagnosed and treated **if diagnosed early.**

Many affected dogs are well-managed on oral thyroid hormone replacement therapy (tablets), often a daily dose of a synthetic thyroid hormone called thyroxine (levothyroxine). A dog is usually given a standard dose for his weight and then blood samples are taken periodically to check his response and the dose is adjusted accordingly.

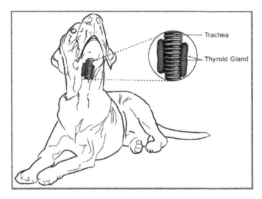

The medication can also be given in liquid form or as a gel that can be rubbed into the ears. Once treatment has started, the dog will be on it for life. In some less common cases, surgery may be required to remove part or all of the thyroid gland.

Another treatment is radioiodine, where radioactive iodine is used to kill the overactive cells of the thyroid. While this is considered one of the most effective treatments, not all animals are suitable for the procedure and a lengthy hospitalisation is often required.

 Some dogs may suffer from **Hyper**thyroidism (as opposed to **Hypo**thyroidism). This is caused by the thyroid gland producing **too much** thyroid hormone. It is quite rare in dogs, being more often seen in cats. A common symptom is the dog being ravenously hungry all the time, but actually losing weight.

....

Mycobacterium Avian Complex (MAC)

MAC is a genetic disorder of the immune system, similar to Tuberculosis, that first appeared in North American Miniature Schnauzers a few decades ago and has now spread to other countries. No other breeds are affected.

It is compulsory for all UK Kennel Club Assured Breeders of Miniature Schnauzers to screen their breeding dogs for this disease and recommended for the USA's CHIC certificate for Minis.

Minis with MAC are at risk of catching or developing a serious form of mycobacterial infection that other dogs are usually able to successfully fight off. It affects males and females equally, usually between 10 months and three years of age.

It is the infection, known as Mycobacterium Avium Infection, rather than MAC itself that attacks the dog. Sadly, affected dogs die young.

The first symptom is enlarged lymph nodes (located in the neck, chest, armpits, groin and behind the knees), which are not very easy to spot with a wiry topcoat like the Mini Schnauzer's. The bacterial infection goes on to infect the spleen and liver, causing both organs to become enlarged.

Other early signs that may be easier for an owner to detect are:

- High temperature
- Pale mucous membranes
- Loss of appetite
- Frequent vomiting
- Reluctance to exercise or play

Some dogs will also suffer from diarrhoea, bloody stools and potentially, a discharge from the eyes and nose. A vet will diagnose MAC with a fine needle aspirate (where a thin needle is inserted into abnormal-looking tissue or body fluid) or a biopsy of the lymph nodes. Sometimes MAC can be misdiagnosed as lymphoma; make sure your vet is aware of the possibility of MAC.

MAC is a type of Tuberculosis, and research into the disease indicates that it could be '**zoonotic,**' i.e. it can potentially be passed from one species of mammal to another species. However, as yet there have been no recorded cases of infections being transmitted from a dog to a human.

 If you are buying a Mini Schnauzer puppy, ask to see the MAC DNA health test for the puppy's parents. A dog will be graded as Clear, Carrier or Affected. A full list of UK-tested dogs can be seen by Googling *'Northern Schnauzer Club MAC DNA results.'*

The Heart

Just as with humans, heart issues are relatively common among the canine population in general.

The heart is a mechanical pump. It receives blood in one half and forces it through the lungs, then the other half pumps the blood through the entire body. Heart failure, or **Congestive Heart Failure (CHF),** occurs when the heart is not able to pump blood around the dog's body properly.

In people, heart disease usually involves the arteries (that supply blood to the heart muscles) becoming hardened over time, causing the heart muscles to receive less blood than they need. Starved of oxygen, the result is often a heart attack.

 In dogs, hardening of the arteries (arteriosclerosis) and heart attacks are very rare. However, heart disease is quite common, and in dogs it is often seen as heart failure, which means that the muscles "give out."

This is usually caused by one chamber or side of the heart being required to do more than it is physically able to do. It may be that excessive force is required to pump blood through an area and over time the muscles fail.

Unlike a heart attack in humans, **heart failure in a dog is a slow process** that occurs over months or years. Once symptoms appear, they usually worsen over time until the dog requires treatment.

Symptoms

- Tiredness and decreased activity levels
- Restlessness, pacing around instead of settling down to sleep
- Intermittent coughing - during exertion or excitement, at night or when he wakes up in the morning - in an attempt to clear the lungs

As the condition progresses, other symptoms may appear:

- Lack of appetite
- Rapid breathing
- Abdominal swelling (due to fluid)
- Noticeable loss of weight
- Fainting (syncope)

Paleness

Mitral Valve Disease

Mitral Valve Disease (MVD) is a very common heart disease. Studies show that about 10% of older dogs of all breeds are affected and the Miniature Schnauzer has a higher risk than average of getting MVD.

While DCM (Dilated Cardiomyopathy) more commonly affects larger breeds like the Giant Schnauzer, MVD usually affects smaller breeds.

The heart is a muscle that pumps blood through the four chambers via a one-way system. The valves between the chambers form a tight seal that prevents the blood from flowing backwards into the chamber it has just come from, so the blood is always flowing forwards.

When the valves degenerate over time, they become thickened and deformed, losing their tight seal and causing some blood to seep backwards.

When the valve between the left atrium and left ventricle, **the mitral valve,** no longer forms a tight seal, blood flows back into the left atrium.

This backflow means that the heart has to work extra hard to pump the required volume of blood the body needs.

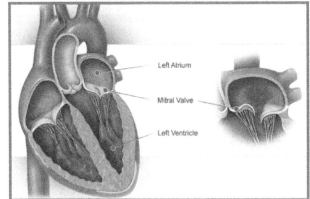

If your dog is showing some of the typical signs of heart failure, get him to the vet. If the vet suspects a heart problem, he or she may refer you to a cardiologist, who will carry out further tests.

These may include listening to the heart, chest X-rays, blood tests, electrocardiogram (a record of your dog's heartbeat) or an echocardiogram.

A specialist cardiologist will be familiar with the condition and the wide range of medications and other available options - and when and how to adjust them to best suit your dog.

As with DCM and any type of congestive heart failure, there is no cure. However, the vast majority of dogs with MVD don't require any treatment at all until they show symptoms - and then they generally do well on medication. Only in very severe cases do dogs die from the disease.

Treatment

Treatment for MVD, DCM and other heart issues focuses on managing the symptoms with various medications. Diuretics may be prescribed to reduce fluid around the lungs and coughing – these will make your dog pee a lot. A special low-salt diet may also be prescribed, as sodium (found in salt) determines the amount of water in the blood.

Your dog's exercise has will have to be managed; it could be controlled exercise or complete rest. The treatment and medication may change as the condition develops. There is some evidence that vitamins and other supplements may be beneficial, discuss this with your vet or cardiologist.

It is ESSENTIAL that the dog does not become overweight, as this places increased stress on the heart.

The prognosis (outlook) for dogs with heart problems depends on the cause and severity, as well as their response to treatment. Once diagnosed, many dogs live a long, comfortable life with the right medication and regular check-ups.

Heart Murmurs

Heart murmurs are not uncommon in dogs and are one of the first signs that something may be amiss.

Our Max was diagnosed with a Grade 2 murmur when he was five or six years old and, of course, your heart sinks when the vet gives you the terrible news.

But once the shock is over, it's important to realise that there are several different severities of the condition and, at its mildest, it is no great cause for concern. Max went on to have many more active years and died of old age at 13.

A heart murmur is a specific sound heard through a stethoscope, which results from the blood flowing faster than normal within the heart itself or in one of the two major arteries. Instead of the normal *lub dub* noise, an additional sound can be heard that can vary from a mild *"pshhh"* to a loud *whoosh.*

The different grades are:

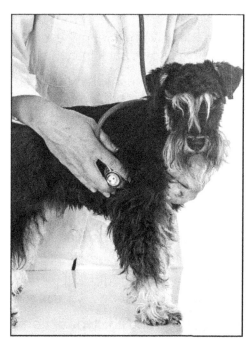

- ❧ **Grade 1 -** barely audible

- ❧ **Grade 2** - soft, but easily heard with a stethoscope

- ❧ **Grade 3** - intermediate loudness; most murmurs that are related to the mechanics of blood circulation are at least Grade 3

- ❧ **Grade 4** - loud murmur that radiates widely, often including the opposite side of the chest

- ❧ **Grade 5 and Grade 6** - very loud, audible with the stethoscope barely touching the chest; the vibration is strong enough to be felt through the dog's chest wall

Murmurs are caused by a number of factors; it may be a problem with the heart valves or could be due to some other condition, such as anaemia or heartworm.

In puppies, there are two major types of heart murmurs, often detected by a vet at the first or second vaccination visit. The most common type is called an innocent **"flow murmur."**

This type is soft - typically Grade 2 or less. It is not caused by underlying heart disease and typically disappears by four to five months of age.

However, if a puppy has a loud murmur - Grade 3 or louder - or if it is still easily heard with a stethoscope after four or five months of age, it's more likely that the pup has an underlying heart problem.

The thought of a puppy having congenital heart disease is worrying, but it is important to remember that the disease will not affect all puppies' life expectancy or quality of life.

Tip **Pay attention to your Schnauzer's weight and teeth, as obesity and dental problems can increase the risk of heart disease.**

NOTE: There is some evidence that fatty acids and other supplements may be beneficial for a heart condition; discuss this with your vet.

Diabetes

Diabetes can affect dogs of all breeds, sizes and both genders, and obese dogs are particularly prone to it. There are two types:

Diabetes insipidus is caused by a lack of vasopressin, a hormone that controls the kidneys' absorption of water

Diabetes mellitus occurs when the dog's body does not produce enough insulin and therefore cannot successfully process sugars

Dogs, like us, get their energy by converting the food they eat into sugars, mainly glucose. This travels in the bloodstream and then, using a protein called *insulin*, cells remove some of the glucose from the blood to use for energy.

Most diabetic dogs have Type 1 Diabetes; their pancreas does not produce any insulin. Without it, the cells can't use the glucose that is in the bloodstream, so they *"starve"* while the glucose level in the blood rises.

Diabetes mellitus (Sugar Diabetes) is the most common form and affects mostly middle-aged and older dogs. Both males and females can develop it, although unspayed females have a slightly higher risk. Vets take blood and urine samples to diagnose Diabetes. Early treatment helps to prevent further complications from developing.

FACT ❯ **Diabetes mellitus is treatable and need not shorten a dog's lifespan or interfere greatly with quality of life. Due to advances in veterinary science, diabetic dogs undergoing treatment now have the same life expectancy as non-diabetic dogs of the same age and gender.**

Symptoms of Diabetes Mellitus:

- Extreme thirst
- Excessive urination
- Weight loss
- Increased appetite
- Coat in poor condition
- Lethargy
- Vision problems due to cataracts

If left untreated, Diabetes can lead to cataracts or other ailments.

Schnauzers mustn't be allowed to get overweight, as obesity is a major trigger for Diabetes.

FACT ❯ **Many cases of canine Diabetes can be successfully treated with a combination of a diet low in sugar, fat and carbs (a raw diet may be worth considering), alongside a moderate and consistent exercise routine and medication. More severe cases may require insulin injections.**

In the newly-diagnosed dog, insulin therapy begins at home after a vet has explained how to prepare and inject insulin. Normally, after a week of treatment, you return to the vet for a series of blood sugar tests over a 12 to 14-hour period to see when the blood glucose peaks and troughs.

Adjustments are made to the dosage and timing of the injections. You may also be asked to collect urine samples using a test strip of paper that indicates the glucose levels.

Tip If your dog is already having insulin injections, beware of a "miracle cure" offered on the internet. It does not exist. No diet or vitamin supplement can reduce a dog's dependence on insulin injections, because vitamins and minerals cannot do what insulin does in the dog's body.

If you think that your dog needs a supplement, discuss it with your vet first to make sure that it does not interfere with any other medication.

Exercise burns up blood glucose the same way that insulin does. If your dog is on insulin, any active exercise on top of the insulin might cause him to have a severe low blood glucose episode, called **"Hypoglycaemia."**

Keep your dog on a reasonably consistent exercise routine. Your usual insulin dose will take that amount of exercise into account. If you plan to take your dog out for some demanding exercise, such as running around with other dogs, you may need to reduce his usual insulin dose.

Tips

- Specially-formulated diabetes dog food is available from most vets

- Feed the same type and amount of food at the same times every day

- Most vets recommend twice-a-day feeding for diabetic pets (it's OK if your dog prefers to eat more often)

- Help your dog to achieve the best possible blood glucose control by NOT feeding table scraps or treats between meals

- Watch for signs that your dog is starting to drink more water than usual. Call the vet if you see this happening, as it may mean that the insulin dose needs adjusting

Food raises blood glucose - Insulin and exercise lower blood glucose - Keep them in balance

For more information visit www.caninediabetes.org

Epilepsy

Epilepsy means repeated seizures (also called fits or convulsions) due to abnormal electrical activity in the brain. Epilepsy affects around four or five dogs in every 100 across the dog population as a whole.

Epilepsy can be classified as **structural,** when an underlying cause can be identified in the brain, or **idiopathic,** when the cause is unknown. The type of epilepsy affecting most dogs of all breeds is **idiopathic epilepsy.**

In some cases, the gap between seizures is relatively constant, in others it can be very irregular with several occurring over a short period, but with long intervals between **"clusters."**

Affected dogs behave normally between seizures. If they occur because of a problem somewhere else in the body, such as heart disease (which stops oxygen from reaching the brain), this is not epilepsy.

Seizures are not uncommon; however, many dogs only ever have one. If your dog has had more than one, it may be that he is epileptic.

Anyone who has witnessed their dog having a seizure knows how frightening it can be. The good news is that, just as with people, there are medications to control epilepsy in dogs, allowing them to live happy lives with normal lifespans.

Symptoms

Some dogs seem to know when they are about to have a seizure and may behave in a certain way. You will come to recognise these signs as meaning that an episode is likely. Often dogs just seek out their owner's company and come to sit beside them. There are two main types of seizure:

- ❧ **Petit Mal**, also called a Focal or Partial Seizure, which is the lesser of the two as it only affects one half of the brain. This may involve facial twitching, staring into space with a fixed glaze and/or upward eye movement, walking as if drunk, snapping at imaginary flies, and/or running or hiding for no reason. Sometimes this is accompanied by urination. The dog is conscious throughout

- ❧ **Grand Mal,** or Generalised Seizure, affects both hemispheres of the brain and is more often what we think of when we talk about a seizure. Most dogs become stiff, fall onto their side and make running movements with their legs. Sometimes they will cry out and may lose control of their bowels, bladder or both

 With Grand Mal the dog is unconscious once the seizure starts - he cannot hear or respond to you. While it is distressing to watch, the dog is not in any pain - even if howling.

It's not uncommon for an episode to begin as Petit Mal, but progress into Grand Mal. Sometimes, the progression is pretty clear - there may be twitching or jerking of one body part that gradually increases in intensity and progresses to include the entire body - other times the progression happens very fast.

 Most seizures last between one and three minutes - it is worth making a note of the time the seizure starts and ends - or recording it on your phone because it often seems to go on for a lot longer than it actually does.

If you are not sure whether or not your dog has had a seizure, look on YouTube, where there are many videos of dogs having epileptic seizures.

Dogs behave in different ways afterwards. Some just get up and carry on with what they were doing, while others appear dazed and confused for up to 24 hours afterwards. Most commonly, dogs will be disorientated for only 10 to 15 minutes before returning to their old self.

 Most seizures occur while the dog is relaxed and resting quietly, often in the evening or at night; it rarely happens during exercise. In a few dogs, seizures can be triggered by particular events or stress.

They often have a set pattern of behaviour that they follow - for example going for a drink of water or asking to go outside to the toilet. If your dog has had more than one seizure, you may well start to notice a pattern of behaviour that is typically repeated.

The most important thing is to **STAY CALM**. Remember that your dog is unconscious during the seizure and is not in pain or distress. It is probably more distressing for you than for him. Make sure that he is not in a position to injure himself, for example by falling down the stairs, but otherwise do not try to interfere with him.

NEVER try to put your hand inside his mouth during a seizure or you are very likely to get bitten.

It is very rare for dogs to injure themselves during a seizure. Occasionally, they may bite their tongue and there may seem to be a lot of blood, but it's unlikely to be serious; your dog will not swallow his tongue.

If it goes on for a very long time (more than 10 minutes), his body temperature will rise, which can cause damage to the liver, kidneys or brain. In very extreme cases, some dogs may be left in a coma after severe seizures. Repeated seizures can cause cumulative brain damage, which can result in early senility (with loss of learned behaviour and housetraining, or behavioural changes).

When Should I Contact the Vet?

Generally, if your dog has a seizure lasting more than five minutes or is having them regularly, you should contact your vet. When your dog starts fitting, make a note of the time.

If he comes out of it within five minutes, allow him time to recover quietly before contacting your vet. It is far better for him to recover quietly at home rather than be bundled into the car right away.

If your dog does not come out of the seizure within five minutes, or has repeated seizures close together, contact your vet immediately, as he or she will want to see your dog as soon as possible.

Call the vet before setting off to make sure there is someone who can help when you arrive.

The vet may need to run a range of tests to ensure that there is no other cause of the seizures. These may include blood tests, X-rays or an MRI scan of your dog's brain. If no other cause can be found, then a diagnosis of epilepsy may be made.

If your Schnauzer already has epilepsy, remember these key points:

* Don't change or stop any medication without consulting your vet

* See your vet at least once a year for follow-up visits

* Be sceptical of *"magic cure"* treatments

Treatment

As yet, it is not possible to cure epilepsy, so medication is used to control seizures – in some cases, even a well-controlled epileptic may have occasional fits. There are many drugs available. There are also several holistic remedies advertised, but we have no experience with them or any idea if any are effective.

 Factors that have proved useful in some cases are: avoiding dog food containing preservatives, adding vitamins, minerals and/or enzymes to the diet and ensuring drinking water is free of fluoride.

Each epileptic dog is an individual and a treatment plan will be designed specifically for yours, based on the severity and frequency of seizures and how he responds to different medications. Many epileptic dogs require a combination of one or more types of drugs for best results.

Keep a record of events in your dog's life, note down dates and times of episodes and record when you have given medication. Each time you visit your vet, take this diary along with you so he or she can see how your dog has been since his last check-up.

If seizures are becoming more frequent, it may be necessary to change the medication.

 Owners of epileptic dogs need patience and vigilance. Treatment success often depends on owners keeping a close eye on the dog and reporting any physical or behavioural changes to the vet.

It is also important that medication is given at the same time each day, as the dog becomes dependent on the levels of a drug in his blood to control seizures. If a single dose of treatment is missed, blood levels can drop, which may be enough to trigger a seizure.

It is not common for epileptic dogs to stop having seizures altogether. However, provided your dog is checked regularly by your vet, *there is a good chance that he'll live a full and happy life; most epileptic dogs have far more good days than bad ones.*

LIVE *WITH* EPILEPSY NOT *FOR* EPILEPSY

....

Canine Cancer

This is the biggest single killer and will claim the lives of one in four dogs, regardless of breed. It is the cause of nearly half the deaths of all dogs aged 10 years and older, according to the American Veterinary Medical Association, and 27% of all deaths in the UK's Pedigree Dog Health Survey were attributable to cancer.

Schnauzers live longer than many other breeds, so they may be more prone to cancer in their golden years. As with all breeds, many different types of cancer have been reported in Schnauzers. Some of the more common include: Hemangiosarcoma, Lymphoma, Mast Cell Tumours and Carcinoma.

Hemangiosarcoma is an aggressive cancer of the blood vessel walls, most commonly found in the spleen, heart or liver, and can affect dogs of any age. Symptoms include:

- Pale gums
- Disorientation, tiredness or collapse
- Lack of appetite
- Rapid breathing
- Extreme thirst

Unfortunately, Hemangiosarcoma has a high mortality rate. Affected dogs can die from internal bleeding or the cancer spreading to other parts of the body. However, in some cases, if the cancer is in the spleen and discovered early, the spleen may be removed before the malignant cells spread to other organs.

Lymphoma is one of the more common canine cancers. It is a blanket term used to describe more than 30 types of canine cancer that stem from *lymphocytes,* a type of white blood cell that helps the immune system fight infection.

They are highly concentrated in organs that play a role in the immune system, like the lymph nodes, spleen and bone marrow. While lymphoma can affect any organ in the body, these organs tend to be where most lymphoma cancers are found.

Multicentric lymphoma is by far the most common of these types: 80-85% of all lymphomas. This type causes swelling of the lymph nodes, which are located under the chin, on either side of the neck, behind the knees on the back legs, armpits, chest and groin.

Other symptoms are lethargy, fever, anorexia, weakness and dehydration, and diagnosis is usually made by doing a biopsy (taking a tiny sample) of the affected organ.

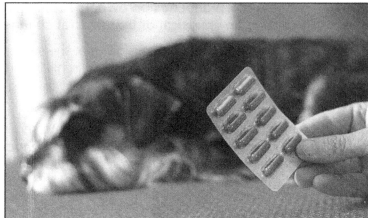

Treatment normally involves chemotherapy and the prognosis (outlook) varies from one dog to another: which organs are affected, and how far the disease has progressed are two factors.

It is true to say that outcomes have improved dramatically with the advancement of veterinary science.

Mast Cell Tumours (MCTs) are one of the most common types of cancer and are found on or under the skin, showing as raised, round masses.

Unfortunately, they often look just like other kinds of skin lumps and bumps, some of which are harmful and others not. Suspicious lumps should be tested and any questionable lump should be surgically removed as soon as possible.

MCTs often affect older dogs, although all ages can be affected. Malignant mast cell tumours can spread to the lymph nodes, spleen, liver and bone marrow if left untreated. However, the good news is that if the tumour is spotted early and completely surgically removed, the dog often has an excellent chance of recovery. Dogs that are tumour-free after six months are unlikely to have a recurrence.

Many cancers are curable by surgical removal, so early detection and removal are critical.

Carcinoma is cancer that forms in epithelial tissue which lines most of the organs and the internal passageways in the body and skin.

Other Cancers

Typical symptoms of other types of cancer include:

- Swellings anywhere on the body or around the anus
- Sores that don't heal
- Weight loss
- Lameness, which may be a sign of bone cancer, with or without a visible lump
- Laboured breathing
- Changes in exercise or stamina level
- Change in bowel or bladder habits
- Increased drinking or urination

- Bad breath, which can be a sign of oral cancer
- Poor appetite, difficulty swallowing or excessive drooling
- Vomiting

FACT There is evidence that the risk of mammary, testicular and uterine cancers decreases after neutering and spaying. However, recent studies also show that EARLY neutering may affect development in some breeds. See Chapter 16. The Facts of Life for more detailed information.

Just because your dog has a skin growth doesn't always mean that it's serious. Many older dogs develop fatty lumps *(lipomas)* which are often harmless, but it's still advisable to have the first one checked.

Reducing the Risk

We have all become aware of the risk factors for human cancer: stopping smoking, protecting ourselves from over-exposure to strong sunlight and eating a healthy, balanced diet all help to reduce cancer rates.

We know to keep a close eye on ourselves, go for regular health checks and report any lumps to our doctors as soon as they appear.

The same is true with your dog.

The outcome depends on the type of cancer, the treatment used and, importantly, how early the tumour is found. The sooner treatment begins, the greater the chances of success. While it is impossible to completely prevent cancer, the following points can help to reduce the risk:

- Feed a healthy diet with few or no preservatives
- Don't let your Schnauzer get overweight
- Consider dietary supplements, such as antioxidants, Vitamins A, C, E, beta carotene, lycopene or selenium, or coconut oil – check compatibility with any other treatments

- Give pure, filtered or bottled water (fluoride-free) for drinking
- Give your dog regular daily exercise
- Keep your dog away from chemicals, pesticides, cleaning products, etc. around the garden and home
- Avoid passive smoking
- Consider natural flea remedies (check they are working) and avoid unnecessary vaccinations
- Know your dog and keep an eye out for any physical or behavioural changes
- If you are buying a puppy, ask whether there is any history of cancer among the ancestors

 Every time you groom your dog, get into the habit of checking his body for lumps and bumps, and lift his top lip to check for signs of pale gums. Early detection often leads to a better outcome.

Our Happy Ending

We know from experience that canine cancer can be successfully treated if it is diagnosed early.

Our Max was diagnosed with T-cell lymphoma when he was four years old. We had noticed a very small black lump on his anus which grew to the size of a small grape literally within a few days.

We didn't hang around. We took him straight off to the vet (this was still within a few days of first noticing the bump). After a test, Max was diagnosed with the dreaded T-Cell Lymphoma. This is a particularly nasty and aggressive form of cancer which can spread to the lymph system and is often fatal for dogs.

As soon as the diagnosis was confirmed, our vet Graham operated on Max the following day and removed the lump. He also had to remove one of his anal glands, but as dogs have two, this was not a serious worry. Afterwards, we were on tenterhooks, not knowing if another lump would grow or if the cancer had already spread to his lymph system.

We had some blood tests done afterwards and the 'markers' for the disease were still in his blood, which was bad news. So, for a couple of months, Max was waited on hand and foot like the Royal Family.

He did, however, seem to be remarkably fit and active for a dying dog... and with a particularly healthy appetite.

After a few more weeks, we had another blood test and he was finally given the all-clear. Phew! Huge sigh of relief after a stressful few months. The first test had shown a 'false positive.'

Max went on to live another nine happy, healthy and event-filled years.

Photo: Me with Max, aged seven - I love the way he's staring right into the camera lens!

We were very lucky. I would strongly advise anyone who suspects that their dog has cancer to get him or her to your local vet as soon as possible.

As I write, canine cancer research is being conducted all over the world, and medical advances are producing a steady flow of new tests and treatments to significantly improve survival rates and cancer care.

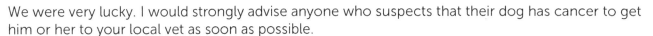

NOTE: Vaccinations, dental issues, parasites, allergies, skin problems, food sensitivities, Pyometra, spaying and neutering are covered in other chapters.

14. Schnauzer Skin & Allergies

Visit any busy veterinary clinic these days – especially in spring and summer – and you'll see itchy dogs. Skin conditions, allergies and intolerances are on the increase in the canine world as well as the human one - and anecdotal evidence seems to show that Miniature Schnauzers can be more susceptible than some other breeds.

It's certainly a subject that generates lots of questions from Mini owners on our website.

....

How many children did you hear of having asthma or a peanut allergy when you were at school? Not too many, I'll bet. Yet allergies and adverse reactions are now relatively common – and it's the same with dogs. The reasons are not clear; they could be connected to genetics, diet, environment, over-vaccination, or a combination. As yet, there is no clear scientific evidence.

Canine skin disorders are a complex topic. A whole book could be written on this subject alone. Some dogs suffer from sensitive, itchy, dry or oily skin, hot spots, bald spots, yeast infections or other skin disorders, causing them to scratch, bite or lick themselves excessively. Symptoms vary from mild itchiness to a chronic reaction.

They may be the result of one or more of a wide range of causes - and the list of potential remedies and treatments is even longer!

It's by no means possible to cover all of them in this chapter. What we hope to do is give you a broad outline of the main categories and causes of Miniature Schnauzer skin issues.

We have also included remedies tried with some success by ourselves and other Schnauzer owners and advice from a holistic specialist.

 Most skin conditions affecting Minis can be well-managed if caught early.

Before he or she can do that, you'll have to tell the vet all about your dog's diet, exercise regime and habits, medical history and local environment. The vet will then carry out a thorough physical examination, possibly followed by further tests, before prescribing the correct treatment.

Canine Skin

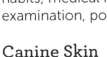 The skin is the dog's largest organ. It acts as the protective barrier between your dog's internal organs and the outside world; it also regulates temperature and provides the sense of touch.

Surprisingly, a dog's skin is thinner than ours, and it is made up of three layers:

1. **Epidermis** or outer layer. This bears the brunt of your dog's contact with the outside world.

2. **Dermis** is the extremely tough layer mostly made up of collagen, a strong and fibrous protein. This is where blood vessels deliver nutrients and oxygen to the skin, and it also acts as your dog's thermostat by allowing his body to release or retain heat, depending on the outside temperature and your dog's activity level.

3. **Hypodermis** is a dense layer of fatty tissue that allows your dog's skin to move independently from the muscle layers below it, as well as providing insulation and support for the skin.

 Human allergies often trigger a reaction within the respiratory system, causing us to wheeze or sneeze, whereas allergies or hypersensitivities in a dog often cause a reaction in their SKIN.

✓ Skin can be affected from the **INSIDE** by things that your dog eats or drinks

✓ Skin can be affected from the **OUTSIDE** by fleas, parasites, or inhaled and contact allergies triggered by grass, pollen, man-made chemicals, dust, mould, etc.

Most Minis can run through fields, woodland and scrub and roll around in the grass with no after-effects - except for a muddy or tangled coat.

A few others may spend more time indoors and have an excellent diet, but still experience itching, hot spots, bald patches or recurring ear infections. Some can eat anything and everything with no issues at all, while owners of others spend a lot of time trying to find the magic bullet – the ideal food for their Schnauzer's sensitive stomach.

NOTE: This information is not intended to take the place of professional help; always contact your vet if your dog appears physically unwell or uncomfortable. This is particularly true with skin conditions:

 SEEK TREATMENT AS SOON AS POSSIBLE. If you can find the cause(s) early, you reduce the chances of it taking hold and causing secondary issues and recurring infections.

One of the difficulties with skin ailments is that the exact cause is often difficult to diagnose as the symptoms are similar to other ailments.

If environmental allergies are involved, specific and expensive tests are available. You'll have to take your vet's advice on this as the tests are not always conclusive. And if the answer is pollen, it can be difficult - if not downright impossible - to keep your Schnauzer away from the triggers.

There's no way you can keep a Schnauzer permanently indoors, so it's often a question of managing rather than curing the condition.

There are many things you as an owner can do to reduce the allergen load – and many natural remedies and supplements that can help, as well as veterinary medications.

NOTE: Food allergies and intolerances are dealt with in <u>Chapter 8. Feeding a Mini.</u>

Types of Allergies

"Canine dermatitis" means inflammation of a dog's skin and it can be triggered by numerous things, but the most common is allergies. Vets estimate that as many as one in four dogs they see has some kind of allergy. Symptoms are (your dog may have one or more of these):

❧ Chewing, most commonly the feet or belly

❧ Itchy ears, head shaking

❧ Rubbing their face on the floor

❧ Scratching

❧ Scratching or biting the anus

❧ Hair loss

❧ Flaky or greasy skin, perhaps with sore or discoloured patches or hot spots

❧ The skin can smell of corn (tortilla) chips

Miniature Schnauzers who are allergic to something show it through skin problems and itching; your vet may call this *"pruritus."*

It may seem logical that if dogs are allergic to something inhaled, like certain pollen grains, their nose will run; if allergic to something eaten, they may vomit, or if allergic to an insect bite, they may develop a swelling. But in practice this is seldom the case.

Dogs with allergies often chew their feet until they are sore and red. You may see yours rubbing his face on the carpet or couch, or scratching his belly and flanks.

 The ear glands then produce too much wax in response to the allergy, causing ear infections. Bacteria and yeast (which is a fungus) thrive in the excessive wax and debris.

Digestive health can play an important role. US holistic vet Dr Jodie Gruenstern says: "It's estimated that up to 80% of the immune system resides within the gastrointestinal system; building a healthy gut supports a more appropriate immune response.

The importance of choosing fresh proteins and healthy fats over processed, starchy diets (such as kibble) can't be overemphasized.

"Grains and other starches have a negative impact on gut health, creating insulin resistance and inflammation."

Allergic dogs may cause skin lesions or *hot spots* by constant chewing and scratching. Sometimes they will lose hair, which can be patchy, leaving a mottled appearance, or the coat may change colour. The skin itself may be dry and crusty, reddened, swollen or oily, depending on the dog. It is common to get secondary bacterial skin infections due to these self-inflicted wounds.

An allergic dog's body is reacting to certain molecules called *allergens.* These may come from:

- Tree, grass or plant pollens

- Flea bites

- Grain mites

- Specific food or food additives, such as cooked or raw meat or poultry, grains, colourings or preservatives

- Milk products

- Fabrics, such as wool or nylon

- Rubber and plastics

- House dust and dust mites

- Mould

- Chemical products used around the home or garden

 **These allergens may be INHALED as the dog breathes, INGESTED as the dog eats, or caused by CONTACT with the dog's body when walking or rolling.**

Regardless of how they arrive, they all cause the immune system to produce a protein called IgE, which releases irritating chemicals like histamine inside the skin, hence the scratching.

Inhalant Allergies (Atopy)

Some of the most common allergies affecting Minis are inhalant and seasonal - at least at first; some allergies may develop and worsen. Look at the timing of the reaction. Does it happen all year round? If so, this may be mould, dust or some other permanent trigger. If the reaction is seasonal, then pollens may well be the culprit.

There is a serum test called *VARL Liquid Gold* widely used in the USA. A simple blood sample is taken and tested for reactions to different types of pollen in your area, other environmental triggers and food. VARL claims it's at least as effective (around 75%), as the more intrusive *intradermal skin testing (see photo below)* which involves sedating the dog, injecting a small amount of antigen into the skin and then inspecting it for an allergic reaction.

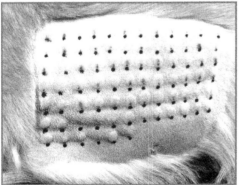

They say a further advantage is that it does not give false positives. Depending on the results, treatment may involve avoidance or an immunotherapy programme consisting of a series of injections or tablets. A similar serum test called *Avacta* is used by vets in the UK.

Photo: A Golden Retriever after intradermal skin testing for over 70 allergens (which is a lot!). The injections are in kits. If you consider this option, ask the vet or specialist how many allergens are in the kit.

Other blood tests work by checking for antibodies caused by antigens. The two standard tests are *RAST* and *ELISA*. Many vets feel that the ELISA test gives more accurate results, although both can give false positives.

Some owners of dogs with allergies consider changing to an unprocessed diet (raw or cooked) and natural alternatives to long-term use of steroids, which can cause other health issues.

 Dealing with allergies is all about REDUCING THE ALLERGEN LOAD. So it may be that you have to employ several tactics to manage the reaction.

These may include: switching to a less processed and more natural diet, rinsing your Schnauzer's feet and belly after a walk, regular ear cleaning, avoiding high pollen areas in spring and summer, reducing chemicals around the house and garden, and possibly giving your Schnauzer medication for part of the year if the allergies are seasonal (as our Mini's were).

Environmental or Contact Irritations

These are direct reactions to something the dog physically comes into contact with, and the triggers are similar to inhalant allergies. If grass or pollen is the issue, the allergies are often seasonal.

An affected dog may be given treatments such as tablets, shampoo or localised cortisone spray for spring and summer – with a steroid injection to control a flare-up - but be perfectly fine the rest of the year.

It's a bit of a nightmare if your dog does develop environmental or contact allergies as there's nothing many Schnauzers love more than running full tilt through the pollen-laden Great Outdoors. However, there's plenty you can do to reduce the symptoms.

 If you suspect your Schnauzer has outdoor contact allergies, hose him down after walks. Washing his feet and belly will get rid of some of the pollen and other allergens, which in turn reduces scratching and biting. And try him on a less processed or unprocessed diet.

The problem may be localised - such as the paws or belly. Symptoms are a general skin irritation or specific hotspots - itching (pruritus) and sometimes hair loss. Some visitors to our website report that their Schnauzer will incessantly lick one part of the body, often the paws, anus, belly or back.

Flea Bite Allergy

This is a common allergy affecting lots of dogs. It's typically seasonal, worse during summer and autumn - peak time for fleas - and in warmer climates where fleas are prevalent. Unfortunately, some dogs with flea bite allergies also have inhalant allergies.

This allergy is not to the flea itself, but to proteins in flea saliva left under the dog's skin when the insect feeds. Just one bite to an allergic dog will cause red, crusty bumps *(pictured)* and intense itching.

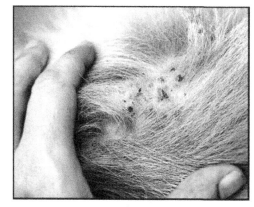

Affected dogs usually have a rash at the base of their tails and rear legs, and will bite and scratch the area. Much of the skin damage is done by the dog's scratching, rather than the flea bite, and can result in hair falling out or skin abrasions.

Some dogs also develop hot spots, often along the base of the tail and back.

A vet can make a diagnosis with a simple blood test. If fleas are the cause, you'll also have to make sure your dog's bedding and your home are flea-free zones.

Most flea bite allergies can be treated with medication, but they can only be totally prevented by keeping all fleas away from the dog. Various flea prevention treatments are available – see the section on **Parasites**.

Acute Moist Dermatitis (Hot Spots)

A hot spot can appear suddenly and is a raw, inflamed and often bleeding area of skin. The area becomes moist and painful and begins spreading due to continual licking and chewing. They can become large, red, irritated lesions in a short space of time. The cause is often a local reaction to an insect bite.

 Cleanse hot spots, interdigital cysts and other skin irritations with hibiscrub and then spray with iodine, which is an antiseptic. Iodine is not suitable for deep or puncture wounds, but is very good generally for cuts and sores; wipe off the excess.

Once diagnosed and with the right treatment for the underlying cause, hot spots often disappear as soon as they appeared. Treatments may come in the form of injections, tablets or creams – or a combination of all three. The affected area is first clipped and cleaned by the vet.

Bacterial infection (Pyoderma)

Pyoderma literally means *pus in the skin* (yuk)! The offending bacteria is staphylococcus, and the condition may also be referred to as a *staph infection.* Early signs are itchy red spots filled with yellow pus, similar to pimples or spots in humans. They can sometimes develop into red, ulcerated skin with dry and crusty patches. Fortunately, the condition is not contagious.

Pyoderma is caused by several things: a broken skin surface, a skin wound due to chronic exposure to moisture, altered skin bacteria, or poor blood flow to the skin.

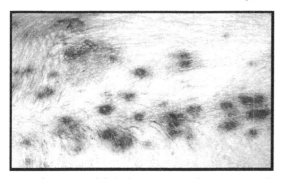 Allergies to fleas, food, parasites, yeast or fungal skin infections, thyroid disease, hormonal imbalances, heredity and some medications can all increase the risk. One of the biggest causes of infection is a dog with a skin disorder excessively licking or biting an itchy patch.

Puppies can develop *puppy pyoderma* in thinly-haired areas, such as the groin and underarms. If you notice symptoms, get to the vet quickly before the condition develops from *superficial pyoderma* into *severe pyoderma*, which is very unpleasant and takes a lot longer to treat.

Fortunately, superficial and puppy pyoderma is usually successfully treated with a two to six-week course of antibiotic tablets or ointment.

Severe or recurring pyoderma looks awful, causes your dog some distress and can take months to completely cure.

Medicated shampoos and regular bathing, as instructed by your vet, are also part of the treatment. It's also important to ensure your dog has clean, dry, padded bedding. Bacterial infection, no matter how bad it may look, usually responds well to medical treatment.

Sebaceous Cysts

Sebum is an oily substance secreted from the sebaceous glands, which are sac-shaped glands in the dermis layer of the skin, usually near hair follicles. Their purpose is to keep the skin and fur waterproof and to protect them from drying out.

Sebaceous Cysts can affect some Schnauzers - Standards in particular - it's thought there may be a genetic predisposition to them. They are caused by clogged glands, either when the gland produces too much sebum or the sebum become trapped. However, injuries, dirt and infections can also cause them, so it pays to keep your Schnauzer's coat clean.

A Sebaceous Cyst is a white, pink or slightly blue lump that usually develops on the head, neck, body or upper legs. It can be anything from a quarter inch to two inches wide and may bleed or give off a light-coloured discharge if it bursts.

If the cyst is smelly, it is probably infected and needs veterinary attention. A vet may carry out a biopsy to rule out cancer and if a cyst is the diagnosis, treatment may vary. If it hasn't burst, the vet may suggest no action other than monitoring the bump. Sometimes they can be drained and, if not, a simple surgical procedure can be undertaken to remove the gland.

If the cyst is bleeding, infected, or simply won't go away, the vet will probably recommend removal – either by incision or laser surgery. Although the cyst won't come back again, this does not rule out others appearing in different areas.

 Run your hands over your Schnauzer when grooming to check for cysts. If you find one, DON'T be tempted to squeeze it! It can force the cyst inside the body, cause infection if it pops, or even trigger an allergic reaction. See your vet instead.

Schnauzer Bumps (Comedone Syndrome)

If I had a pound or dollar for every email to our website about Schnauzer Bumps on Miniature Schnauzers, I'd be a rich woman indeed!

A comedone is a blackhead. Blackheads form when the hair follicles become blocked with too much keratin (a skin protein) and sebum. The definition of a blackhead, or open comedo, is "a plug of keratin and sebum within a hair follicle that is blackened at the surface."

Symptoms of Schnauzer Bumps, *pictured,* are normally fairly easy to detect and are often first noticed when the Mini has just returned from the grooming salon after a short trim.

You may see small black bumps, or crusts, usually on the back. Often falsely blamed on bad grooming, it is the normal trimming of the dog's hair that makes the bumps more visible.

Professional groomer and Standard Schnauzer breeder Beth Railton has done some research into this:

"Schnauzers, especially Minis, can get 'Schnauzer spots' (or bumps). Through my own research I believe that it may be due to not hand-stripping, or at least carding (removing the dead hair and undercoat from) the dog.

"Because the coat is left in and only falls out with time - rather than being stripped regularly - hair follicles can become blocked and cause blackhead-type spots. Not all Schnauzer spots are caused by this and it's worth visiting a vet in the first instance, but also not all vets are aware of this."

Schnauzer Bumps don't usually affect a dog's health unless they become infected. However, once infected with dirt or pus, they can become itchy and may even develop into abscesses or bumps. Some Minis have them all the time, while others have an occasional flare-up.

Schnauzer Comedone Syndrome is not a serious or life-threatening condition. Mild symptoms do not need any treatment and even in more severe cases, the worst outcome is irritation and itching - unless infection takes hold.

There is no cure for them and if your dog does have Schnauzer Bumps, they will probably stay for life. The good news, however, is that they can be well managed.

Get your Mini to the vet to rule out allergies and other skin conditions. He or she will be able to assess the severity of the condition and prescribe the correct treatment, which is usually a medicated shampoo and/or ointment – and antibiotics if there is an infection.

Prevention/Management

Here are some causes and remedies that Miniature Schnauzer owners have told us they've found useful to help either reduce the symptoms or get rid of them completely. These include:

- ❧ **Bathing** - This may be necessary for affected dogs. Anything from twice a week to once every two weeks using an ***antiseborrheic shampoo*** that breaks down oils that plug the hair follicles. One example is SulfOxyDex shampoo *(pictured)*, which can be followed by a cream rinse such as Epi-Soothe Rinse afterwards to prevent the skin from drying out

- ❧ **Dabbing** - Using an astringent such as witch hazel or alcohol to encourage the bumps to dry out

- ❧ **Grooming** - Keeping your Schnauzer's coat short and the hairs inside his ears regularly plucked or trimmed

- ❧ **Sunshine** - Some owners have found that Schnauzer Bumps are not as bad during summer. Try and get your dog regularly out into the sunshine

- ❧ **Fleas** - Sometimes Minis with flea allergies also have Schnauzer Bumps

- ❧ **Food** - A reaction to food can sometimes be the issue. Try changing food and avoid foods containing corn or grain

- ❧ **Daily supplements** - Vitamin E, vitamin A, zinc and omega oils all help to make a dog's skin healthy. Feed a daily supplement which contains some of these, such as fish oil, which provides omega

- ❧ **Medication** - Some Minis with a persistent problem respond well to the drug **isotretinoin (Accutane Rx),** but this is an expensive treatment and only works in a small percentage of dogs. Discuss with your vet

....

Yeast Infections

Yeast Infection/Dermatitis is an extremely common skin disease in dogs of all breeds and can affect Schnauzers, particularly in their ears. Yeast is a fungus.

A dog's skin is naturally host to numerous bacteria and fungi (try not to think about that!). In normal circumstances they are kept under control by the immune system and don't cause a problem. However, if the skin conditions change or the immune system is compromised, these bacteria and fungi can cause infection.

Yeast infections love humid conditions - and especially warm, damp areas on a dog's body like ear canals where air doesn't circulate - particularly on Minis with natural, floppy ears.

Pricked-up ears, *pictured,* are less likely to suffer yeast infections as air circulates inside them much better, keeping the inside of the ear cooler and drier. Skin folds such as the armpits are another target area as, again, these areas are warm with little airflow. Saliva can also be a trigger for yeast, especially when a dog repetitively licks - which explains why feet are sometimes stained red or brown and itchy.

 Dogs that already have poor skin condition, allergies, a hormonal disorder or immune system under stress are more prone to yeast infections.

Symptoms of a yeast infection are:

* Recurring ear infections
* Reddish tear stains (could be yeast or could be natural)
* Itchy, flaky skin at inflamed areas around the lips, ear canals, neck and armpits, between the toes and in skin folds on the face
* Reddish-brown discolouration around the feet
* Greasy or flaky skin
* Unpleasant smell
* In long-term cases, the skin may become thicker and darker

The condition is easily diagnosed with an examination and/or skin scraping and is often effectively treated with anti-fungal shampoos, wipes and creams, or tablets NOTE: A course of antibiotics may temporarily help but is usually not a long-term solution; the underlying cause needs to be identified and treated.

Ear Infections

The inside of a Miniature Schnauzer's ear is VERY hairy! And some Schnauzers can be more prone to ear infections than short-haired dogs with pricked-up ears. Signs of an ear infection are:

* Rubbing or scratching the ears
* Shaking or tilting the head a lot
* A brown waxy substance inside the ear(s)
* Smelly ears
* Scaly or inflamed skin

Like toothache, ear infections are painful and this may cause your beloved Schnauzer to become irritable

 Recurring ear infections do NOT necessarily mean that the ears are the problem - although they might be. Ask your vet to not only treat the yeast infection but to try and determine if there is an underlying cause, otherwise the yeast will come back.

Dogs can have ear problems for many different reasons, including:

* Allergies, such as environmental or food allergies
* Ear mites or other parasites
* Bacteria or yeast infections

- Injury, often due to excessive scratching

- Hormonal abnormalities, e.g. hypothyroidism

- The ear anatomy and environment, e.g. excess moisture

- Hereditary or immune conditions and tumours

In reality, many Schnauzers have ear infections due to the structure of their ear. The ear canal is narrow, and underneath the ear flap is very hairy. It's also warm and sometimes moist, an ideal breeding ground for fungus (yeast) and bacteria.

The amount of hair varies from one Mini to the next, but Schnauzers are very low-shedding, so it will not fall out naturally.

 Keeping your Mini's ears clean, and regularly plucking or trimming excess hair inside the ear flaps will reduce the chance of your dog getting an ear infection. If you don't want to pluck or trim yourself, make sure your groomer does it on every visit.

Treatment for ear infections depends on the cause – is it the ear itself, allergies or another problem?

Antibiotics are used for bacterial infections and antifungals for yeast infections. Glucocorticoids such as *dexamethasone* are often included in these medications to reduce inflammation.

Your vet may also flush out and clean the ear with special drops, something you may have to do daily at home until the infection clears. A dog's ear canal is L-shaped, which means it can be difficult to get medication into the lower (horizontal) part of the ear.

The best method is to hold the dog's ear flap with one hand and put the ointment or drops in with the other, if possible tilting the dog's head away from you so the liquid flows downwards **with gravity.**

Make sure you then hold the ear flap down and massage the medication into the horizontal canal before letting go of your dog, as the first thing he will do is shake his head – and if the ointment or drops aren't massaged in, they will fly out.

 When cleaning, plucking or trimming your Schnauzer's ears, be very careful not to put anything too far down inside. Visit YouTube to see videos of how to correctly clean without damaging them. DO NOT use cotton buds, they are too small.

Canine ear cleaning solution is widely available, or you can use a 50/50 mixture of water and white vinegar.

If you can nip a first infection in the bud, you reduce the risk of it returning. Recurring deep ear infections can damage or rupture the eardrum, causing an internal ear infection and even permanent hearing loss. Closing of the ear canal *(hyperplasia* or *stenosis)* is another sign of severe infection.

Most extreme cases of hyperplasia will eventually require surgery as a last resort; the most common procedure is called a 'lateral ear resection.' This is an extremely painful procedure for a dog and should only be considered as a very last resort to stop the dog from going deaf.

Ear infections are notoriously difficult to get rid of once your Mini has had one, so prevention is better than cure. Check your Schnauzer's ears weekly when grooming, dry them after bathing and get the vet to check inside on routine visits.

Interdigital Cysts

If your Schnauzer gets a fleshy red lump between the toes that looks like an ulcerated sore or a hairless bump, then it's probably an interdigital cyst - or *interdigital furuncle*. These can be very difficult to cure as they are often not the main problem, but a symptom of some other ailment.

They are not cysts, but the result of *furunculosis*, a skin condition that clogs hair follicles and creates chronic infection. Causes include allergies, obesity, poor foot conformation, mites, yeast infections, ingrowing hairs or other foreign bodies.

FACT ⟩ Bulldogs are the most susceptible breed, but any dog can get them - often the dog also has allergies.

These nasty-looking bumps are painful, will probably cause a limp and can be a nightmare to get rid of. Vets might recommend a whole range of treatments to get to the root cause, and it can be very expensive to have a barrage of tests or biopsies - even then you're not guaranteed to find the underlying cause.

Here are some remedies your vet may suggest:

❧ Antibiotics and/or steroids and/or mite killers

❧ Soaking the feet in Epsom salts, *pictured*

❧ Testing for allergies or thyroid problems

❧ Starting a food trial if food allergies are suspected

❧ Shampooing the feet

❧ Cleaning between the toes with medicated (benzoyl peroxide) wipes

❧ A referral to a veterinary dermatologist

❧ Surgery (this is a last-resort option)

If you suspect your Schnauzer has an interdigital cyst, visit the vet as soon as possible for a correct diagnosis and to discuss the various options. A course of antibiotics may be suggested initially, along with switching to a hypoallergenic diet if a food allergy is suspected. If the condition persists, many owners get discouraged, especially when treatment continues for several weeks.

 Be wary of agreeing to a series of steroid injections or repeated courses of antibiotics, as this means that the underlying cause has not been diagnosed. In this case it is worth exploring natural diets and remedies and trying to lower the overall allergen load on your dog.

Before you resort to any drastic action, first try soaking your Schnauzer's affected paw in Epsom salts for five or 10 minutes twice a day. After the soaking, clean the area with medicated wipes, which are antiseptic and control inflammation.

Surgery is a drastic option. Although it can be effective in solving the immediate issue it doesn't deal with the underlying problem. Interdigital cysts are not simple to deal with and it's important to *get the right diagnosis as soon as possible.*

Parasites

Demodectic Mange (Demodex)

Also known as *red mange, follicular mange* or *puppy mange,* this skin disease is caused by the tiny mite Demodex canis, *pictured.* The mites live inside the hair follicles on the bodies of virtually every adult dog and most humans without causing any harm or irritation.

In humans, the mites are found in the skin, eyelids and the creases of the nose...try not to think about that!

The mite spends its entire life on the host dog. Eggs hatch and mature from larvae to nymphs to adults in 20 to 35 days and the mites are transferred directly from the mother to the puppies within the first week of life by direct physical contact.

Demodectic mange is not a disease of poorly-kept or dirty dogs or kennels. It is generally a disease of young dogs with inadequate or poorly-developed immune systems - or older dogs suffering from a suppressed immune system.

Virtually every mother carries and transfers mites to her puppies, and most are immune to the mite's effects, but a few puppies are not and they develop full-blown mange. They may have a few (less than five) isolated lesions and this is known as *localised mange* – often around the head.

Puppy Mange is quite common, usually mild and often disappears on its own.

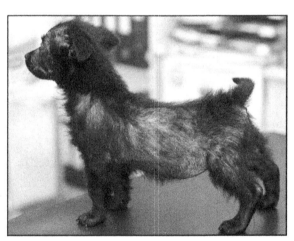

Generalised Mange is more serious and covers the entire body or region of the body, *shown here on a small mixed-breed puppy.*

Bald patches are usually the first sign, usually accompanied by crusty, red skin which sometimes appears greasy or wet. Usually, hair loss begins around the muzzle, eyes and other areas on the head. The sores may or may not itch.

In localised mange, a few circular crusty areas appear, most frequently on the head and front legs of three to six-month-old puppies. Most self-heal as the puppy becomes older and develops their own immunity, but a persistent problem should be treated.

With generalised mange, there are bald patches over the entire coat, including the head, neck, body, legs, and feet. The skin on the head, side and back is crusty, often inflamed and oozes a clear fluid.

The skin itself will often be oily to the touch and there is usually a secondary bacterial infection. Some puppies can become quite ill and can develop a fever, lose their appetites and become lethargic.

If you suspect your puppy has generalised demodectic mange, get him to a vet straight away.

There is also a condition called *pododermatitis*, when the mange affects a puppy's paws. It can cause bacterial infections and be uncomfortable, even painful. Symptoms include hair loss on the paws, swelling of the paws (especially around the nail beds) and red, hot or inflamed areas which are often infected.

Treatment is always recommended and can take several rounds to clear it up.

Diagnosis and Treatment

The vet will make a diagnosis after he or she has taken a skin scraping or biopsy, in which case the mites can be seen with a microscope. As these mites are present on every dog, they do not mean that the dog necessarily has mange.

Only when they are coupled with lesions will a diagnosis of mange be made. Treatment usually involves topical (on the skin) medication and sometimes tablets.

 **Some of the tablets, such as Mitaban, can have side effects. Toy breeds in particular may become nauseous. Discuss treatment and other options fully with your vet.**

One UK veterinarian added: "One very effective treatment for Demodex is *Bravecto,* recently licensed for this, and now the best one available."

Bravecto, *pictured,* is given in chewable tablets according to weight. It not only gets rid of the mites, but also remains effective for 12 weeks following treatment. A bonus is that it's also effective against ticks and fleas during those 12 weeks.

Dogs with generalised mange may have underlying skin infections, so antibiotics are often given for the first several weeks of treatment.

Because the mite flourishes on dogs with suppressed immune systems, try to get to the root cause of immune system disease, especially if your Schnauzer is older when she develops demodectic mange.

Sarcoptic Mange (Scabies)

Also known as *canine scabies*, this is caused by the parasite *Sarcoptes scabiei.* This microscopic mite can cause a range of skin problems, the most common of which is hair loss and severe itching.

The mites can infect other animals such as foxes, cats and even humans, but prefer to live their short lives on dogs. Fortunately, there are several good treatments and it can be easily controlled.

In cool, moist environments, the mites live for up to 22 days. At normal room temperature they live from two to six days, preferring to live on parts of the dog with less hair.

Diagnosing canine scabies can be somewhat difficult, and it is often mistaken for inhalant allergies.

The vet will take a skin scraping to make a diagnosis and there are several effective treatments, including selamectin (Revolution – again, some dogs can have a reaction to this), an on-the-skin solution applied once a month which also provides heartworm prevention, flea control and some tick protection.

Various Frontline products are also effective – check with your vet for the correct ones.

One product used by some breeders whose dogs are outdoors a lot is the **Seresto Flea Collar,** *pictured,* which provides full body protection for up to eight months against all fleas, ticks, sarcoptic mange, lice and other bloodsucking critters! There are also holistic remedies for many skin conditions.

Because your dog does not have to come into direct contact with an infected dog to catch scabies, it is difficult to completely protect him. Foxes and their environment can also transmit the mite.

Fleas

Miniature Schnauzers are active dogs and most spend time outdoors every day, so are more likely to pick up parasites such as fleas and ticks than couch potato breeds.

When you see your Mini scratching and biting, your first thought is probably: *"He's got fleas!"* and you may well be right. Fleas don't fly, but they do have very strong back legs and they will take any opportunity to jump from the ground or another animal into your Schnauzer's lovely, warm coat. You can sometimes see the fleas if you part your dog's hair.

 And for every flea that you see on your dog, there is the stomach-churning prospect of hundreds of eggs and larvae in your home! So, if your dog gets fleas, you'll have to treat your environment as well as the dog to completely get rid of them. **The best form of cure is prevention.**

Vets recommend giving dogs a preventative flea treatment every four to eight weeks – although the Seresto Flea Collar lasts for eight months. If you do give a regular skin treatment, the frequency depends on your climate, the season - fleas do not breed as quickly in the cold - and how much time your Schnauzer spends outdoors.

To apply topical insecticides like Frontline and Advantix, part the skin and apply drops of the liquid onto a small area on your dog's back, usually near the neck. Some kill fleas and ticks, and others just kill fleas - check the details.

 It is worth buying a quality treatment, as inferior brands may not rid your Schnauzer completely of fleas, ticks and other parasites. Also, some Minis can have a bad reaction to cheap chemical products. There are also holistic and natural alternatives to insecticides, discussed later in this chapter.

Some breeders are opposed to chemical flea treatments. One added that when she found a flea, she simply washes all of her dogs, one after the other, and then washes every last piece of bedding.

Ticks

A tick is not an insect, but a member of the arachnid family, like the spider. There are over 850 types, some have a hard shell and some a soft one. Ticks don't have wings, they crawl. They have a sensor called Haller's organ that detects smell, heat and humidity to help them locate food - which in some cases is a Schnauzer!

A tick's diet consists of one thing and one thing only - blood! They climb up onto tall grass and when they sense an animal is close, crawl on. Ticks can pass on several diseases to animals and humans, the most well-known of which is **Lyme Disease**.

 This is a bacterial illness passed on to dogs by ticks once they have been on the dog's body for one to two days. The ticks that carry Lyme Disease are most likely to be found in woods, tall grasses, thick brush and marshy ground.

In the UK, Lyme Disease is more prevalent in wooded areas, and in the US almost all cases are from the Northeast, Upper Midwest and Pacific coast. Typical symptoms include fever, loss of appetite and energy, possible lameness, stiffness, pain or swelling.

Treatment includes antibiotics, usually for at least 30 days, which often resolve the symptoms. But in severe cases, Lyme Disease can progress to fatal kidney failure, and serious cardiac and neurological effects can also occur. Your dog can't pass Lyme Disease on to you or other pets, but a carrier tick could come into your house on your dog's fur and get on to you. If your Schnauzer spends a lot of time outdoors in high-risk areas consider having them vaccinated against Lime Disease. One breeder added: "If ticks are removed quickly, they're not harmful. We use a tick tool *(pictured)*, which has instructions in the packet. You put the forked end on either side of the tick and twist it till it comes out."

 If you do find a tick on your Schnauzer's coat and are not sure how to get it out, have it removed by a vet or other expert. Inexpertly pulling it out yourself can leave a bit of the tick behind.

Here's a cautionary tale: recently a friend of ours removed a tick from the top of her dog's head, but accidentally left a bit in. This quickly developed into a big sore lump which then had to be surgically removed by the vet.

Once back home, the dog scratched the wound and split the stitches (the vet hadn't said to use or supplied an E-collar), resulting in another trip to the clinic for restitching - and an E-collar. The total bill was in the high hundreds and the poor dog was miserable for over a week.

Heartworm

Although heartworm does not affect the skin, it's included here as it is a parasite. Heartworm is a serious and potentially fatal disease affecting pets in North America (all states) and many other parts of the world, but not the UK. It's active in Mediterranean countries, so check with your vet if you're intending taking your dog there from the UK. *Leishmaniasis* is another parasitic disease that dogs can pick up in Europe, transmitted by a biting sand flea and causes skin lesions or organ infection.

The foot-long heartworms live in the heart, lungs and blood vessels of affected animals, causing severe lung disease, heart failure and damage to organs. It looks like strands of cooked spaghetti.

The dog is a natural host for heartworms, enabling the worms living inside a dog to mature into adults, mate and produce offspring. If untreated, their numbers can increase; dogs have been known to harbour several hundred worms in their bodies.

Untreated heartworm disease causes lasting damage to the heart, lungs and arteries, and can affect the dog's health and quality of life long after the parasites are gone. For this reason, **prevention is by far the best option** and treatment - when needed - should be administered as early as possible.

When a mosquito bites and takes a blood meal from an infected dog, it picks up baby worms that develop and mature into *infective-stage* larvae over 10 to 14 days. Then, when it bites another dog, it spreads the disease.

Once inside a dog, it takes about six months for the larvae to develop into adult heartworms, which can then live for five to seven years in a dog. In the early stages, many dogs show few or no symptoms. The longer the infection persists, the more likely symptoms will develop, including:

- ❖ A mild persistent cough
- ❖ Reluctance to exercise
- ❖ Tiredness after normal activity
- ❖ Decreased appetite and weight loss

As the disease progresses, dogs can develop a swollen belly due to excess fluid in the abdomen and heart failure. Dogs with large numbers of heartworms can develop the life-threatening caval syndrome, which, without prompt surgery, is often fatal.

The American Heartworm Society recommends that you get your dog tested every year and give your dog heartworm preventive treatment for all 12 months of the year. If you live in a risk area, check that your tick and flea medication also prevents heartworm. In the UK, heartworm has only been found in imported dogs.

Ringworm

This is not a worm, but a fungus and is most commonly seen in puppies and young dogs. It is highly infectious and often found on the face, ears, paws or tail. This fungus is most prevalent in hot, humid climates but, surprisingly, most cases occur in autumn and winter. But it is not that common; in one study of dogs with active skin problems, less than 3% had ringworm.

Ringworm, *pictured,* is transmitted by spores in the soil and by contact with the infected hair of dogs and cats, typically found on carpets, brushes, combs, toys and furniture.

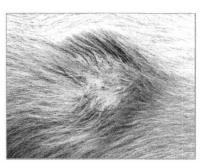

Spores from infected animals can be shed into the environment and live for over 18 months, but most healthy adult dogs have some resistance and never develop symptoms. The fungi live in dead skin, hairs and nails - and the head and legs are the most common areas affected.

Tell-tale signs are bald patches with a roughly circular shape. Ringworm is relatively easy to treat with fungicidal shampoos or antibiotics from a vet.

FACT ❯ Humans can catch ringworm from pets, and vice versa. Children are especially susceptible, as are adults with suppressed immune systems and those undergoing chemotherapy. Hygiene is extremely important.

If your dog has ringworm, wear gloves when handling them and wash your hands well afterwards. And if a member of your family catches ringworm, make sure they use separate towels from everyone else or the fungus may spread.

As a teenager, I caught ringworm from horses at the local stables - much to my mother's horror - and was treated like a leper by the rest of the family until it cleared up!

Warning!

Chemical flea and parasite treatments, such as *Seresto, Bravecto, Comfortis, Nexgard, Frontline, Advantix,* etc. can trigger epilepsy, other disorders or strange behaviour in a very small percentage of dogs – often toy or small breeds.

Our website has a page dedicated to US Miniature Schnauzer owners' reports of *Trifexis,* a once-a-month tablet given to kill fleas, prevent heartworm and treat and control adult hookworm, roundworm and whipworm infections.

DISCLAIMER: We have never used Trifexis and have no way of verifying these personal accounts. We encourage all owners to do your research, talk to your vet and consider all options, including natural alternatives.

Trifexis, *pictured,* combines two powerful active ingredients: spinosad and milbemycin oxime. Spinosad is a biologic product, an ultra-fast flea-killing tablet. It is classified as 'slightly toxic' by the USDA.

Milbemycin is a strong drug able to interfere with a parasite's nerve transmission, causing the death of many forms of parasites.

Here are a couple of stories from Mini owners: "My advice is not to use Trifexis. I gave my Mini Schnauzer one dose and within two hours he became so lethargic he could not keep his head up. He was totally fine and energetic up to that point. He would not eat or drink. My vet told me to give it 24 hours and it should be out of his system.

"After 24 hours, he was still the same. So, I started researching the internet and saw lots of people with the same experience in all breeds and sizes of dogs. I then contacted my Vet and told him about what I had been reading. At 11pm, my vet called me and ask me to please bring my dog in so we could start fluids and flush that drug out of his system. After a day of fluids, he finally started to be himself again.

"That was five months ago and I have had no problems since. I now give him Heartgard and use Advantix II for flea/tick problems."

Here's another: "My two male Schnauzer brothers, 1.5 years old, have had six doses of Trifexis. Each time I have noticed strange behavior, some diarrhea, and a lack of interest in food. It was hard for me to explain to the vet what I meant by "strange behavior."

"And I still can't really describe it but they act differently for about two days after each dose. Def. will be going back to a different med for next month."

And this very sad story: "I am so sad to say that we lost one of our three Schnauzers today. I had a very traumatic experience yesterday with her. She vomited really bad, then about one hour later she started having seizures. Rushed her to the vet, first thing I told him was she had Trifexis the day before.

"All vets should warn their patients about these side effects, nothing was ever told to me, and now I have lost a beloved pet."

Some Allergy Treatments

Treatments and success rates vary tremendously from dog to dog and from one allergy to another. However, one factor is common: earlier diagnosis is more likely to lead to a successful treatment.

Some owners of dogs with **recurring skin issues** find that a course of antibiotics or steroids works wonders for their dog's sore skin and itching. However, the scratching starts all over again shortly after the treatment stops.

Food allergies require patience, a change or several changes of diet and maybe even a food trial, and the specific trigger is notoriously difficult to isolate – unless you are lucky and hit on the culprit straight away.

With **inhalant and contact allergies,** blood and skin tests are available, followed by hyposensitisation treatment. However, these are expensive and often the specific trigger for many dogs remains unknown. So, the reality for many owners of Minis with allergies is that they manage the condition, rather than curing it completely.

FACT ▶ While a single steroid injection is often highly effective in calming down symptoms almost immediately, frequent or long-term steroid use is not a good option as it can lead to serious side effects.

Our Journey

According to our vet, Graham, more and more dogs are appearing in his waiting room with various types of allergies. Whether this is connected to how we breed or feed our dogs remains to be seen.

Our Mini Schnauzer Max was perfectly fine until he was about two years old when he began to scratch a lot. He scratched more in spring and summer, which meant that his allergies were almost certainly inhalant or contact-based and related to pollens, grasses or other outdoor triggers.

We decided not to have a lot of tests, not because of the cost (although they were not cheap), but because the vet said it was highly likely that he was allergic to pollens. Max was an active dog and if we'd had a pollen allergy confirmed, we were not going to stop walking him two or three times a day and going on occasional all-day hikes in the hills.

Treatments

Regarding medications, Max *(pictured),* was at first put on a tiny dose of Piriton a cheap antihistamine manufactured in the millions for canine and human hay fever sufferers. For the first few springs and summers, this worked well.

Allergies can change and a dog can build up a tolerance to a treatment, which is why they can be so difficult to treat.

Max's symptoms changed from season to season, although the main ones were: general scratching, paw biting and ear infections.

One year he bit the skin under his tail a lot – he would jump around like he had been stung by a bee and bite frenetically. This was treated effectively with a single steroid injection, followed by spraying the area with cortisone once a day at home for a period.

Localised spray can be very effective if the itchy area is small, but no good for spraying all over a dog's body.

Over the years we tried a number of treatments, all of which worked for a while, before he came off the medication every October when pollen levels fell. He was perfectly fine the rest of the year without any treatment at all.

Not every owner wants to treat his or her dog with chemicals, nor feed a diet that includes preservatives, which is why this book includes alternatives. Also, when we were starting on the *"Allergy Trail,"* there were far fewer options than there are now.

We fed Max a high-quality hypoallergenic dry food. If we were starting again from scratch, knowing what we know now, I'd look into a raw or home-cooked diet (which is what we fed him as he neared the end of his life) if necessary, in combination with holistic remedies.

One spring the vet put him on a short course of steroids, which were effective for a season, but steroids are not a long-term solution. Another year we were prescribed the non-steroid Atopica. The active ingredient is *cyclosporine,* which suppresses the immune system - some dogs can get side effects, although ours didn't.

The daily tablet was expensive, but initially extremely effective – so much so that we thought we had cured the problem completely. However, after a couple of seasons on cyclosporine he developed a tolerance to the drug and started scratching again.

He then went back on to Piriton, a higher dose than when he was two years old, and this was effective.

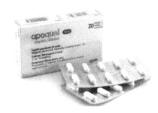

In 2013 the FDA approved **Apoquel** (oclacitinib), ***pictured,*** to control itching and inflammation in allergic dogs. Like most allergy drugs, it acts by suppressing the immune system, rather than addressing the root cause.

It has, however, proved to be highly effective in treating countless thousands of dogs with allergies. We used Apoquel with excellent results. There was some initial tweaking to get the daily dose right, the tablets are administered according to body weight, but it did the trick.

 Side effects have been reported in some dogs (although ours didn't have any), and holistic practitioners, Dogs Naturally magazine and others believe it can be harmful to the dog. Do your research.

Cytopoint, pictured, is a more recent option that's proved to be the magic bullet for many dogs. It is given as an injection every four to eight weeks and starts working almost immediately. Dogs with seasonal allergies may only need the injections for part of the year.

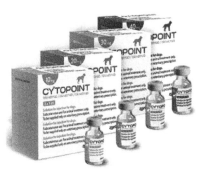

One big advantage of Cytopoint is that it is a biological therapy, not pharmaceutical, and does not suppress the dog's immune system. It contains engineered antibodies, similar to a dog's natural antibodies.

These antibodies have been specifically designed to target and neutralise a protein that sends itch signals to a dog's brain. This helps to minimise scratching, giving the irritated skin chance to heal.

All dogs are different. If Cytopoint works for your dog, it is a good choice as it doesn't have the side effects reported with Apoquel.

Suggestions

 Add fish oils, which contain Omega-3 fatty acids, to a daily feed to keep your dog's skin and coat healthy all year round – whether or not she has problems.

A liquid supplement called Yuderm, ***pictured,*** (formerly Yumove Itchy Dog), which contains Omegas 3 and 6, golden flax and borage, is a good choice to add to your dog's daily feeds.

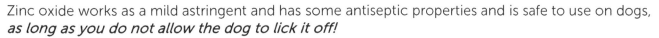

When the scratching got particularly bad, we also bathed Max in an antiseborrheic shampoo twice a week for a limited time. This helped, although was not necessary once on Apoquel. Here are some other suggestions from Mini Schnauzer owners:

Use an astringent such as witch hazel or alcohol on affected areas. We have heard of zinc oxide cream being used to some effect on dogs as well as babies' bottoms! In the human world, this is rubbed on to mild skin abrasions and acts as a protective coating."

Zinc oxide works as a mild astringent and has some antiseptic properties and is safe to use on dogs, *as long as you do not allow the dog to lick it off!*

Vitamins A and E also help to make a dog's skin healthy, and one breeder added: "A couple of mine tend to have itchy legs and feet. I feed them grain-free food and use anti-itch herbal remedies."

 Coconut oil was widely recommended for dogs, but the latest research shows that it may contribute to inflammation and a leaky gut.

The Holistic Approach

Many owners of dogs with sensitivities find that their dog does well for a time with steroid injections or medication, but then the symptoms slowly start to reappear. More owners are now considering natural foods and remedies. A holistic practitioner looks at finding and treating the root cause of the problem, rather than just treating the symptoms.

Dr Sara Skiwski is an American holistic vet. She writes here about canine environmental allergies: "Here in California, with our mild weather and no hard freeze in Winter, environmental allergens can build up and cause nearly year-round issues for our beloved pets.

"Also, seasonal allergies, when left unaddressed, can lead to year-round allergies. Unlike humans, whose allergy symptoms seem to affect mostly the respiratory tract, seasonal allergies in dogs often take the form of skin irritation/inflammation."

Recurring Problems

"Allergic reactions are produced by the immune system. The way the immune system functions is a result of both genetics and the environment: Nature versus Nurture. Let's look at a typical case.

"A puppy starts showing mild seasonal allergy symptoms, for instance, a red tummy and mild itching in Spring. Off to the vet!

"The treatment prescribed is symptomatic to provide relief, such as a topical spray. The next year when the weather warms up, the patient is back again - same symptoms but more severe this time.

"This time the dog has very itchy skin. Again, the treatment is symptomatic - antibiotics, topical spray (hopefully no steroids), until the symptoms resolve with the season change.

"Fast forward to another Spring...on the third year, the patient is back again but this time the symptoms last longer, (not just Spring but also through most of Summer and into Fall).

"By Year Five, all the symptoms are significantly worse and are occurring year-round. This is what happens with seasonal environmental allergies. The more your pet is exposed to the allergens they are sensitive to, the more the immune system over-reacts and the more intense and long-lasting the allergic response becomes. What to do?"

Root Cause

"In my practice, I like to address the potential root cause at the very first sign of an allergic response, which is normally seen between the ages of six to nine months old. I do this to circumvent the escalating response year after year.

"Since the allergen load your environmentally-sensitive dog is most susceptible to is much heavier outdoors, I recommend two essential steps in managing the condition. They are vigilant in foot care as well as hair care. What does this mean? A wipe down of feet and hair, especially the tummy, to remove any pollens or allergens is key.

This can be done with a damp cloth, but my favorite method is to get a spray bottle filled with Witch Hazel *(pictured)* and spray these areas.

"First, spray the feet then wipe them off with a cloth, and then spray and wipe down the tummy and sides. This is best done right after the pup has been outside playing or walking. This will help keep your pet from tracking the environmental allergens into the home and into their beds. If the feet end up still being itchy, I suggest adding foot soaks in Epsom salts."

Dr Sara also stresses the importance of keeping the immune system healthy by avoiding unnecessary vaccinations or drugs: "The vaccine stimulates the immune system, which is the last thing your pet with seasonal environmental allergies needs.

"I also will move the pet to an anti-inflammatory diet. Foods that create or worsen inflammation are high in carbohydrates. An allergic pet's diet should be very low in carbohydrates, especially grains. Research has shown that 'leaky gut,' or dysbiosis, is a root cause of immune system overreactions in both dogs and cats (and some humans).

"Feed a diet that is not processed, or minimally processed; one that doesn't have grain and takes a little longer to get absorbed and assimilated through the gut. Slowing the assimilation assures that there are no large spikes of nutrients and proteins that come into the body all at once and overtax the pancreas and liver, creating inflammation.

"A lot of commercial diets are too high in grains and carbohydrates. These foods create inflammation that overtaxes the body and leads not just to skin inflammation, but also to other inflammatory conditions, such as colitis, pancreatitis, arthritis, inflammatory bowel disease and ear infections.

"Also, these diets are too low in protein, which is needed to make blood. This causes a decreased blood reserve in the body and in some of these animals this can lead to the skin not being properly nourished, starting a cycle of chronic skin infections which produce more itching."

Supplements

"After looking at diet, check that your dog is free from fleas and then these are some of Dr Sara's suggested supplements:

✓ **Raw (Unpasteurised) Local Honey** - an alkaline-forming food containing natural vitamins, enzymes, powerful antioxidants and other important natural nutrients, which are destroyed during the heating and pasteurisation processes.

Raw honey has anti-viral, anti-bacterial and anti-fungal properties. It promotes body and digestive health, is a powerful antioxidant, strengthens the immune system, eliminates allergies, and is an excellent remedy for skin wounds and all types of infections.

Bees collect pollen from local plants and their honey often acts as an immune booster for dogs living in the locality.

Dr Sara says: "It may seem odd that straight exposure to pollen often triggers allergies, but that exposure to pollen in the honey usually has the opposite effect. But this is typically what we see.

"In honey, the allergens are delivered in small, manageable doses and the effect over time is very much like that from undergoing a whole series of allergy immunology injections."

✓ **Mushrooms -** make sure you choose the non-poisonous ones! Dogs don't like the taste, so you may have to mask it with another food. Medicinal mushrooms are used to treat and prevent a wide array of illnesses through their use as immune stimulants and modulators, and antioxidants.

The most well-known and researched are reishi *(pictured)*, maitake, cordyceps, blazei, split-gill, turkey tail and shiitake.

Histamine is what causes much of the inflammation, redness and irritation in allergies. By helping to control histamine production, the mushrooms can moderate the effects of inflammation and even help prevent allergies in the first place.

WARNING! Mushrooms can interact with some over-the-counter and prescription drugs, so do your research as well as checking with your vet first.

- ✓ **Stinging Nettles** - contain biologically active compounds that reduce inflammation. Nettles can reduce the amount of histamine the body produces in response to an allergen. Nettle tea or extract can help with itching. Nettles not only help directly to decrease the itch, but also work overtime to desensitise the body to allergens.

- ✓ **Quercetin** - is an over-the-counter supplement with anti-inflammatory properties. It is a strong antioxidant and reduces the body's production of histamines.

- ✓ **Omega-3 Fatty Acids** - help decrease inflammation throughout the body. Adding them into the diet of all pets - particularly those struggling with seasonal environmental allergies - is very beneficial. If your dog has more itching along the top of her back and on her sides, add in a fish oil supplement. Fish oil helps to decrease the itch and heal skin lesions.

- ✓ The best sources of Omega 3s are krill oil, salmon oil, tuna oil, anchovy oil and other fish body oils, as well as raw organic egg yolks. If using an oil alone, it is important to give a vitamin B complex supplement.

Dr Sara adds: "Above are but a few of the over-the-counter remedies I like. In non-responsive cases, Chinese herbs can be used to work with the body to help to decrease the allergy threshold even more than with diet and supplements alone. Most of the animals I work with are on a program of Chinese herbs, diet change and acupuncture.

"So, the next time your dog is showing symptoms of seasonal allergies, consider rethinking your strategy to treat the root cause instead of the symptom."

With thanks to Dr Sara Skiwski, of the Western Dragon Integrated Veterinary Services, San Jose, California, for her kind permission to use her writings as the basis for *The Holistic Approach*.

....

Remember:

- ❧ A high-quality diet
- ❧ Maintaining a healthy weight
- ❧ Regular grooming and check-overs, and
- ❧ Attention to cleanliness

all go a long way in preventing or managing skin problems in Miniature Schnauzers.

Photo: Max tackling our neighbour's showjumping course.

....

15. The Coat and Grooming

One of the many wonderful things about Schnauzers is that they shed very little hair.

The reason for all three sizes being classed as *hypoallergenic* ("less likely to cause an allergic reaction") - and why most allergy sufferers are NOT allergic to Schnauzers - is that their coat is made up of two layers. The top coat is hard and wiry, while the undercoat is soft and dense.

It is the dander (like dandruff) that most allergy sufferers react to and in the case of the Schnauzer, this is trapped between the layers.

 **NO dog is 100% non-shedding, but the Schnauzer's double coat normally sheds, or 'casts,' less than other coats. NOTE: If you're allergic to dog urine or saliva, you're probably still allergic to a Schnauzer.**

You may see a very occasional fur ball, but you'll find very few loose hairs around the house. Another great advantage of a Schnauzer is that they do not have a doggy smell when bathed and groomed regularly. In fact, they smell very nice - perfect for snuggling up to!

The downside of having a low-shedder is that the Schnauzer coat is relatively high maintenance, compared with breeds whose hair falls out more. So they need grooming at home at least once or twice a week and trips to a professional groomer every few weeks. This can work out quite expensive unless you learn how to machine clip or hand strip (pull out the hairs by hand).

If you want to show your Mini Schnauzer in AKC or Kennel Club events, your dog has to be hand-stripped and entire (not castrated or spayed). Trimming with clippers destroys the wiriness and colour bands of the outer coat.

In the case of salt and pepper Schnauzers, the dark pepper hairs lie on top of the light on the outer wiry coat. If a salt and pepper Mini is regularly machine-clipped, (as opposed to hand-stripped), the banded hairs will gradually disappear and your Mini will just be grey. Some black Schnauzers may lose a bit of sheen to their coat, while others become dilute and grey. Also, all coats become soft and wavy.

Despite all of this, most pet owners have their Miniature Schnauzers clipped (also called clippered).

Photo: Left: a beautifully groomed hand-stripped Miniature Schnauzer with the wiry outer coat and pepper banding clearly visible. Right: Our Max, aged five on a hike! Regular trips to the groomer for clipper trims changed his coat to soft, grey and wavy.

It does not matter at all if your dog is clipper-trimmed if you enter him in the community dog show in your local park. Miniature Schnauzers are extremely handsome and undeniably cute, so yours may well come away with the prize for "Judge's Favourite" or "Most Attractive Dog." They can also compete in other canine events such as Agility, Canine Good Citizen and Obedience.

Coat Colours

Despite all the colours you may have seen advertised, the number of Schnauzer colours accepted by the Kennel Clubs is extremely limited:

Salt and Pepper, Black, Black and Silver. The UK accepted **White** in 2015, but the North American Kennel Clubs do not.

NOTE: Salt and pepper is also called pepper and salt.

A small white mark is permitted on the chest of black Schnauzers in the USA, but is considered 'undesirable' by the UK Kennel Club.

You may see Miniature Schnauzer puppies, advertised in different colours, e.g. wheaten, platinum, platinum silver, liver, liver pepper, liver tan, chocolate, chocolate phantom or parti (white and one other colour). **NONE** of these colours is accepted by the AKC or UK Kennel Club. They have probably been crossed with other breeds and are highly unlikely to be true pedigrees.

 **Strangely, Schnauzers in non-acceptable colours can have AKC or Kennel Club pedigree papers if both their parents have pedigree papers.**

But even if a coloured Schnauzer has Kennel Club papers, he or she may not be entered into conformation shows under KC, AKC, or AMSC (American Miniature Schnauzer Club) rules. You might ask: "If people love the look of a parti, chocolate, merle or any other colour of Mini Schnauzer, what's the problem?"

Well, one of the main aims of the AKC, KC and Schnauzer breed clubs is to protect the integrity of the breed by laying down a set of definitions called the **Breed Standard.** Good breeders produce dogs in line with this definition, which ensures that a Miniature Schnauzer looks and acts like a Miniature Schnauzer.

The rise of demand for different coloured pups has led to people with little knowledge of Schnauzers cashing in on the craze and breeding Mini Schnauzers for (money and) colour, rather than for conformation, health or temperament.

Bear in mind that Schnauzers are not naturally parti-coloured (**pictured),** or any of the other strange colours, so a different breed has been introduced somewhere along the line. All of this is detrimental to the Miniature Schnauzer.

AKC Licensed Show Judge Marcia Feld says: "It is not up to each of us to decide that we would like to change each of these breeds because we like it or find it appealing. Adhering to these definitions is what retains the individuality of the breed. Breeding to the definition is the challenge for the breeder.

"A brown Dalmatian might be cute - but he is no longer a Dal; a tiny Great Dane would be more easily kept - but he is no longer a Great Dane, and a hard-coated Poodle would be easier to groom, but he wouldn't be a Poodle. And in that same light, a white (or coloured) Schnauzer is no longer a Schnauzer; he is disqualified because he does not meet the definition of that breed."

The White Schnauzer

White is the exception, as many experts claim that white occurs naturally in the Miniature Schnauzer - although still not accepted in North America.

One of the original colours in Germany, where Schnauzers originate, was "gelb" (yellow), but more commonly taken to mean white. In the early German Miniature Schnauzer studbooks, pepper and salt was actually recorded less often than other colours, including yellow.

Interestingly, black and silver Miniature Schnauzers were originally classified as pepper and salt and, by the time the mistake was discovered, it was too late to take back all of their registration papers.

When breeders saw that this colour bred "true," (black and silver parents consistently produced black and silver puppies), the colour became accepted by the breed societies.

For those interested in the technical reason for whites, they are Schnauzers who carry the double recessive e/e gene. They are not albinos, as their skin has pigment. There are quite a few different types of white -

* **A no-colour** is a dog with a pure white coat. They are born with pink lips, pads and noses which later turn the base colour. The usual base colour of Schnauzers is black or brown.

* **A true white** is also known as black-nosed white, no prizes for guessing why, *pictured.*

* **A white chocolate** is also called a brown-nosed white (the clue is in the name again!) This is genetically the same coat as the black-nosed white, only the base colour is brown, not black.

A white Schnauzer with a light skin or nose may need sun cream. Like pale-skinned horses and other animals, white Schnauzers can suffer from sunburn.

And just as with humans, lighter skin has less of the pigment melanin to protect against the sun's harmful rays, so sunbathing time should be limited.

 If you do have your heart set on a parti Schnauzer, or one of the other "illegal" colours, make sure that all the other boxes related to finding a good breeder and health testing are checked.

Dog Groomers

Unless you learn how to groom to a professional standard, a trip to the groomer every few weeks is a must for a Miniature Schnauzer. Here in Yorkshire in the North of England, we pay anything from £35 to £60 for a full wash and trim with a professional groomer, and the going rate for hand stripping is £80 or more.

In the USA, prices vary even more according to location and level of service offered. Basic grooming may start at $60, but you can pay a lot more.

 Don't leave it too long between visits. About every eight weeks is about right for a pet (non-show) Miniature Schnauzer – perhaps every six if you don't brush your dog regularly, as knots can occur very easily in beards and leg hair.

The dense, wiry coat, which they are usually unable to shed when it gets hot, can become uncomfortable and itchy for your dog, and during the summer you may find that your Schnauzer starts to scratch more.

And bear in mind that central heating can have the same effect. Some Minis can be prone to skin complaints (our Max was), **see Chapter 14. Schnauzer Skin and Allergies** for more information. Keeping the coat clean and trimmed helps the skin to stay healthy.

When you are choosing a groomer, don't just go for the cheapest; ask around other dog owners to see who is recommended and take your time to find a good one.

First Trim

We highly recommend getting your Schnauzer used to a little gentle grooming early on - both at home and at a professional groomer's. Many groomers do a "puppy clip" for puppies – a pup can be professionally groomed as soon as it's safe to go out after vaccinations.

 When taking your Mini to a groomer for the first time, be very specific about whether you want to have your dog hand-stripped or clippered (clipped).

We have had very upset owners contact our website after their puppy has been returned with a machine clip, which affects the coat forever, rather than the hand strip they had intended. Also, if you want your dog hand-stripped, make sure the groomer knows how to do it properly - ask to see previous photos.

Photo: This four-year-old Miniature Schnauzer is overdue a trip to the groomer! Leaving the coat too long leads to knots, matting, dirty beards, etc.

Good grooming is especially important in a hot climate or warm weather. Schnauzers' coats have an inbuilt cooling system; the removal of some undercoat will help to keep the dog cool and the harsh top coat will protect the dog from the elements: rain, sun, etc. A matted or pelted coat prevents cooling

Dogs can also cool through panting, and sweating through the pads of their paws, but not very much, which is why they can overheat amazingly quickly.

Hand-stripping is the removal of dead hair from the hair root or follicle. This method keeps the natural coarse, wiry texture of the outer 'jacket' of the Schnauzer's distinctive coat. Only a very small amount at a time should be done with young puppies - and gently - by someone who knows what they are doing.

 You may want to consider having yours gently hand-stripped until the full adult coat has grown naturally. Then you can decide how to proceed. Occasionally, a Schnauzer may be unsuitable for hand stripping, for example, if he has a naturally fluffy coat or sensitive skin.

If you are not showing your Schnauzer under Kennel Club rules, there are no major reasons - other than aesthetics - why you should not have your dog trimmed with electric clippers *(pictured)*.

The wiry topcoat will disappear, along with an element of waterproofing, but electric clippers are an easy way to maintain a neat-looking pet Schnauzer, unless you know how to hand strip.

Expert Advice

Beth Railton has been involved with Schnauzers for decades and breeds (Standard) Schnauzers with the Lefenix prefix. Beth's Schnauzers are her passion - along with grooming which, she believes, is an art.

She started showing at 19, when she also began her career as a professional groomer. A few years later she set up K9 Cuts, which ran successfully for over 17 years. During that time Beth trained and employed a small team of dedicated groomers and lectured on the subject at colleges.

She specialises in all three types of Schnauzer and has groomed dogs from all over England for both pet owners and show people, having taken top honours in the show world. Since Covid, she operates on a smaller scale, with Schnauzer owners travelling from far and wide for her specialised grooming services.

Here Beth describes the Schnauzer coat and shares her in-depth knowledge on how best to care for and present your Schnauzer:

The Schnauzer Coat

A Schnauzer's coat should be practical and functional. From the beginning I was mentored to understand that a good coat is the icing on the cake of a well-constructed dog.

The coat is both wiry and double-coated. It comes in two colours for Standards and Giants: solid black and pepper and salt, with black and silver being the third colour for Miniatures. Black is the most common colour for Giants, while it's pepper and salt for Standards and Miniatures.

Pepper and salt is unique in the fact that the coat is banded; each hair is black, white, black. The pepper and salt ranges from dark iron grey to light grey with unique markings, and their faces should have a dark mask.

The undercoat is thick and dense and the topcoat should be harsh and crisp. All dogs' coats are designed for the job at hand. The wire coat is easily brushed clean, keeping the Schnauzer warm and dry. But the coat also has a cooling system, ensuring that the dog is suited for its daily purpose.

A well-presented Schnauzer, while it takes time and effort to achieve, can be fairly easy to maintain once established.

A proper hand-stripped Schnauzer coat is self-cleaning and rarely smells. Brushing the coat will remove any loose soil and debris, plus if the coat is 'rolled' (more about this later), you'll constantly be refreshing the coat with new fur.

Beards should be washed regularly and kept knot-free. Leg hair can be bathed too.

The Personal Touch

Grooming is very personal and each groomer brings different skills and ideas to the table. The Schnauzer is a groomed breed; this gives the advantage of being able to hide faults and emphasise a dog's good points. For me, grooming is an extension of my artistic side.

A good groomer understands construction and how to show the dog off at its best. A good coat doesn't need products to enhance it and a coat's condition is only ever as good as the health of the dog. Dull, dry coats and skin issues may relate to the inner health of the dog, and nutrition may need addressing.

Photo: Beth with her best friend, Standard Schnauzer Agi (Okera Born to be Wild)

Bad grooming can give a dog faults which can be a disadvantage in the show ring. For example, you can make a Schnauzer appear short in the leg by leaving too much hair underneath.

Too much hair on the chest can draw attention to a lack of forechest, or make the dog look heavy in front.

A Schnauzer in essence is square and cobby (stocky) with a slight touch of elegance; this should be the go-to appearance in every owner's mind.

To make sure a Schnauzer is happy and confident being groomed, it helps to start the process early. My puppies are always clipped and groomed at six weeks, and again before they leave for their new homes.

They are introduced to the grooming table early in the hope that they enjoy the process. In fact, my dogs always enjoy their grooms and jump up onto the tables.

Schnauzers love the one-to-one time spent with just them. Grooming should be a natural, kind process, even when it can be stressful for some dogs. Introducing dogs early and making it an enjoyable event will go a long way further down the line. I find putting the puppies on the table as often as possible to do bits little and often is a good way of making it a great bonding experience.

I'd recommend you do a few minutes of brushing and handling a Schnauzer puppy from the very beginning. If you have a table you can put them on, use it. It not only gets them used to being on a table at the groomer's, but it also takes them out of their environment into yours, where they are likely to be more cooperative. But don't leave them unattended on a grooming table.

Hand Stripping

My dogs are stripped from eight weeks old, although my older ones are clipped, as it is less stressful for them. How often a Schnauzer needs hand stripping varies from one dog to the next; diets are different, as are seasons - and age, castration or spaying all make a difference too. No two dogs are the same.

Typically, a pet Schnauzer may come in every three to six months for hand stripping. It also depends on how the owners want the dog to look, or what lifestyle the dog has. It takes time for a groomer to understand an individual dog's needs and an owner's preferences.

The Schnauzer coat should be stripped to maintain its texture and weather resistance. Clipping the coat will leave it soft as you shave off the topcoat and leave the dense undercoat, and eventually the coat will lose its colour and lustre.

Stripping the coat is the removal of dead hair to allow new coat growth, and there are different methods and tools. I personally feel that the traditional method of stripping using finger and thumb is best - finger cots, *pictured,* are helpful when pulling the coat. Hair should be pulled out in the direction in which it lies, and chalk can be used to help grip the fur. This ensures that the coat is not broken, which can happen when using tools.

Tools include stripping knives, which come in many different brands, shapes and for different coat types. While a Schnauzer's coat should be wiry, there are many different textures within the breeds and finding the correct knife that works on a specific coat is trial and error. You also need to find one that fits comfortably in your hand and is personal to you.

The undercoat should be kept to a minimum, especially in summer, so the dog can regulate its temperature better. This can be done by either using a wide-toothed comb with a wide elastic band woven between the teeth *(pictured, above)* or a stripping knife *(pictured)*.

Both should be laid flat on the body and dragged through the coat, which should remove a sufficient amount of soft, fluffy undercoat. However, it should be kept in mind that a certain amount of undercoat is required in the show ring.

I find a Furminator works well on a short-maintained coat. It should be noted that tools such as knives and undercoat rakes can be sharp when new and easily cut the coat. I always advise to blunt them on an old bit of carpet before using. *Photo: A Furminator undercoat rake.*

A hand-stripped Schnauzer is also clipped in certain areas: the chest, neck, cheeks, ear leathers, inside the back legs, hygiene areas and bum. These are parts of the dog deemed sensitive to be stripped. The top of the head is either stripped or clipped, this is a personal preference. Clipping for show is normally done on a #10 blade or, if a black with a finer coat, #7f can be used, always shave **against** the direction of the coat.

The 'Flashy' Parts

Furnishings are the eyebrows, beard and 'feathers' on a Schnauzer's legs, and these should be harsh, bristly and dense. Fluffy hair is no good for a day's work and can attract all kinds of vegetation outdoors. Keep them combed and knot-free at home with a good slicker brush and a metal comb. I always both strip and trim leg hair with scissors and thinning scissors.

A dog with plenty of furnishings can be sculptured to appear perfect, whereas one with less flashy furnishings seems to not do so well in the show ring, even if their construction is exactly the same.

Photo: Beth trimming the eyebrow. DO NOT try this at home! You could injure your Schnauzer if he suddenly moves - leave it to the professionals.

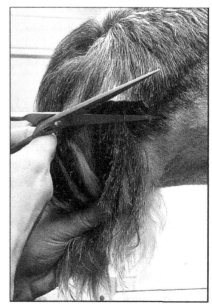

The Schnauzer head should be strong and brick-like and the eyebrow should emphasise the keen expression. Too much beard may distract from the brick shape or create a top-heavy look.

Tails come in all different shapes and sizes. I like the tail stripped on the upper side and the underside clipped with a #7f blade, blending in. But this will depend on the tail.

My pet hate is bushy tails! We do not have bushy tails as a Breed Standard, but some people request it. It's like leaving fluffy heads on Cocker Spaniels; it's not supposed to be there! I protest a bit, but we always have a laugh about it and I have a great customer base. At the end of the day, it's your dog!

Any stripped-to-clipped areas should be blended to show no obvious lines. It is vital that a Schnauzer should be flowing and natural in shape, with no sharp edges.

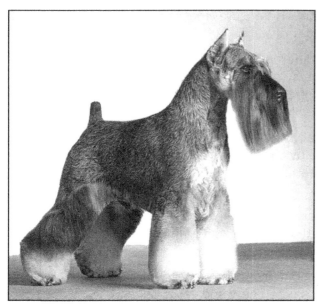

Skirts are a tricky task and deciding the length depends on the natural shape of the dog - a dog lacking in depth will need more skirt.

Photo: A North American show Miniature Schnauzer with beautiful furnishings and a short skirt. He also has cropped ears and a docked tail (not allowed in the UK and Europe).

I strip down into the skirt leaving little that requires scissoring, so the hair stays thick and textured throughout. I feel this gives a stronger-looking dog and is less of a mud magnet when out on a walk.

The key is not to distract from good points nor emphasise bad points. Black Schnauzers have the advantage when grooming because it really doesn't matter whether you take too much or too little out in any area, and there will be no 'tide lines,' as can be the case with the banded salt and pepper coat.

Rolling The Coat

'Rolling' the coat is a constant removal of hair; I do my Schnauzers about every three weeks. This is also done with a lot of Terriers. The aim is to keep the dog permanently in coat, rather than pulling the entire coat down to the undercoat in one go when 'blown' (when the entire jacket is dead and ready to be stripped).

Because of the different growth stages of the coat when rolling, it can change the colour of a banded pepper and salt coat. Rolling is a skill learned over time when you develop an eye for it. When you brush the coat backwards, the coat that stands up is dead, while the shorter new coat stays flat. Only the dead coat needs to be removed.

For example, in one square centimetre you may have 12 hairs, and you pull four hairs every two or three weeks. By the time you get to the last four hairs a few weeks later, the first four have grown back enough to leave a covering of coat... That's the theory! I find rolling the coat is sufficient to keep the dog looking smart, and it only takes about 20 minutes once you know how to do it.

Clipping

While I prefer a stripped coat - and if the coat is suitable to strip, I will encourage the owner to have this done for at least the first year - clipping is a cheaper alternative. Sometimes it's difficult to get a nice, smooth finish with a clipped coat, especially when transitioning from stripped to clipped.

From a groomer's point of view, Schnauzers have harsh coats and can take their toll on equipment, and a pepper and salt coat is harder to leave with a good finish because of the banding, unlike a solid black, which is more even. However, a week after clipping, the coat will look tidy.

I advise owners to brush and comb their Schnauzer after every walk, inspecting for ticks, grass seeds and sticky burrs, etc. Combing should be done every week as a minimum with a metal comb to ensure all knots are removed.

As a groomer, I see many owners who just brush their dogs and forget about the comb. While brushing helps to stimulate the skin and pulls essential oils down the shaft of the hairs, unfortunately, you can brush a dog and the coat will remain knotty.

If you don't comb thoroughly to the skin this can lead to knotting, mats and eventually 'pelting,' which is when the fur is so matted and tangled that it has to be shaved off to a 'short back and sides' for the health of the dog.

Photo: Beth combing the legs with a metal comb.

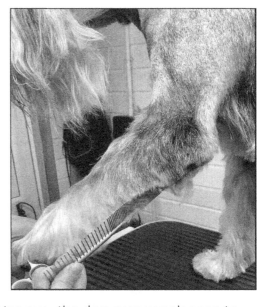

Some owners prefer a short back and sides-type of clip so they don't have to brush their dogs, and they opt for a short beard and eyebrows.

Most older dogs generally end up with a short back and sides with clippers when they age and start to find the grooming process too stressful. Some older dogs can't cope with bathing anymore so we change the process to suit the dog and vanity is no longer involved.

A clipped coat will still cast (shed) some hair. All dog breeds cast coat, just not all in the same way - and some individual dogs drop hair more than others. I'd suggest using a Furminator over the dog every week or so to help stimulate this.

A clipped coat generally casts a lot less than a stripped coat, purely because the hair is shorter so it's not noticed as much.

There are several types of trim; I always start with the Breed Standard and work my way down. Easily-knotted areas like armpits, groin and hygiene areas are shaved short. Skirts are optional - some clients opt for no-skirt for easy maintenance, and some prefer a full show-style trim.

A clipped coat loses some weather resistance, so you may need to get your dog a coat for bad weather... rain and cold. However, you should also brush and comb your dog each time after a coat has been worn. Dog coats cause friction and static, which cause knotting - as does a harness. Be vigilant and brush all high-friction areas.

Bathing

Ideally, a stripped coat does not really need washing at all and once the mud is dry it can be brushed off. Clippered coats can absorb moisture and mud if the coat texture is lost, so sometimes a brush or rub isn't enough. You can try a damp shammy (chamois) or towel to remove any dirt.

A Schnauzer's coat doesn't need bathing often, I'd say no more often than every four weeks - that should work out at one bath in between every eight-weekly groom. However, in the real world, Schnauzers have beards and stick their faces in everything!

Photo: The author's Max being bathed at home - note the colour of the water! After chasing squirrels, Max's second favourite pastime was rolling in cow dung...

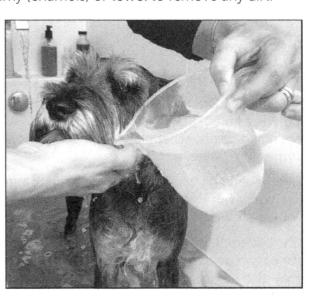

Leg hair, undercarriage and beards can be rinsed off once back from a muddy, wet walk and towel dried. Then brush and comb through. You can use an anti-tangle spray to help with brushing the knots out. I don't like dry shampoos, as I don't like the idea of leaving them on a dog's natural coat.

If they are incredibly dirty and have rolled in something bad and/or dead, then shampooing is your only option. Please try to use a quality canine shampoo recommended by your dog groomer. There are lots on the market, some are better than others.

My Schnauzers hate being bathed and it becomes a game of cat and mouse! I feel that they'd prefer to take a bath in the muddy field or paddling pool than clean running water and dog shampoo.

At the moment it's wet outdoors and mine are getting their legs and beards washed daily. That's because I walk them three or four miles, much of it in fields where they usually find something dead or horrible to roll in! I also give them a good scrub for Christmas - much to their annoyance!

Avoid bathing body coats regularly - especially if you are showing. If I have to bath the dog near the day of the show, I try and use a drying coat or a cool coat to encourage the coat to lie flat.

Photo: Before and after. Stella aged 20 weeks looks a bit grumpy, but a lot tidier, after her first clip! Beth used a No.7f clipper blade. Photo with the kind permission of owner Claire Carson.

Whether you have your Schnauzer hand-stripped or clippered, there's no denying that all three sizes are without doubt one of the most handsome of all the breeds and I, for one, wouldn't be without mine. They drive me crazy at times and constantly keep me on my toes, but they are my passion, my life.

With sincere thanks to Beth for writing this article for The Canine Handbooks.

Personal Experiences

Veterinarian **Dr Lisa Sarvas** has been involved with Miniature Schnauzers since 1985, she shows and breeds with the Beauideal prefix. Lisa says: "We bath at least once weekly, trimming their non-shedding coat is scheduled monthly. This schedule keeps their beards clean and fresh, and their furnishings white.

"Non-shedding coats require regular grooming, otherwise their hair can tangle and if left long enough, even matt. In addition to this home care, professional grooming may be scheduled every four to six weeks."

She added: "Mini coats may get stripped to maintain their harsh weather-resistant coat, or clippered for easy regular grooming. Legs and beard mesh be left long and trimmed into classic trim. Legs may also be clipped short for ease of grooming. If started early and gently, they will love their grooming time."

Photo of the stunning Nyo (GChB Kaos Black is King), courtesy of Lisa. Nyo also won the American Miniature Schnauzer Club National Specialty Show, Macungie, PA.

Show judge **Lesley Myers** also got her first Mini in 1985: "When I was showing, mine were groomed every week to keep leg furnishings free of knots and to keep their wiry jacket (body coat) in good condition.

"Of course, they were also bathed every week or two to go to a dog show. Since I stopped showing, I groom them every six to eight weeks.

"Beware of knots in their leg hair and beard which, if not teased out, eventually become matted clumps and have to be cut out. I find bathing their legs, bottoms, chest, tummies and beards (not jackets) every two weeks makes it easier to comb through the leg hair and beards."

Photo of Schultz looking extremely smart, courtesy of Lesley.

Leah Dummer, owner of Freddie, Leelo and Lily: "I try and brush our dogs once a day, especially their beards and legs as they can get matted.

"This only takes a couple of minutes per dog. Luckily for us, a member of the family is trained in dog clipping, so we get them clipped as and when it's needed."

Chris Lee: "Betsy goes to a professional groomer about once every six weeks, but often needs her legs and beard groomed, probably every other day."

Chloe Dong and Jacky Zou: "We do basic grooming (brushing Oslo's wire coat, checking for knots, cleaning eye boogers) every two to four days. Basic grooming usually takes no more than 20 minutes.

"On recommendation from our breeder, we also bought equipment to give him a full haircut. This is done every one to one-and-a-half months, depending on coat length and season. Full grooming takes about two hours."

Vivian Williams: "Bogart is professionally groomed every five weeks. Between grooming appointments, his beard needs an occasional brushing, in addition to wiping wet or muddy paws."

Yolande: "This may upset traditionalists, but I now have Mayzy clipped all over. This is because with Agility training, I need to see her face and she mine and her 'furnishings' got in the way of this.

"We live next to fields and woods, and she loves rootling about in the leaf litter and she likes to dig holes and pulls up clumps of grass if allowed.

"Her soft 'furnishings' are like Velcro, (incidentally, I know of a Mini Schnauzer called Velcro!) and rather than have to subject her to endless combing to get the seeds, twigs and burrs out of her coat, which could otherwise cause her harm by working into her skin, we have her fully clipped.

"Every time she goes out (four times a day), we may have to wash her paws and towel dry her if necessary and give a brief brush. She has a regular appointment with the groomer every six weeks.

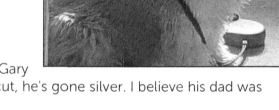

"Every night, I use a tooth pad and paste and gently clean her teeth and give her a five-minute brush down before bed, which she accedes to with grudging tolerance."

Gary Blain: "I don't spend long enough on grooming. Jamie hates being groomed. I've tried so many different types of combs and brushes, but never found one he will readily accept, while Evie is happy to be brushed.

"They go to the same groomer every six to eight weeks. I tend to leave them looking natural, I don't have them groomed like typical Minis."

Photo of Evie (at the back, aged five) and Jamie (aged eight) with their 'natural' look.

Evie is a white Schnauzer and Jamie is, unusually, silver. Gary adds: "Jamie was salt and pepper, but since his first haircut, he's gone silver. I believe his dad was white, which could explain his transformation in colour."

....

Ear Cleaning

Many Miniatures have narrow ear canals with very furry ears. These conditions can lead to the ears becoming an ideal breeding ground for infection-causing bacteria *(otitis externa)*. Typical signs of an ear infection are:

- The dog shaking his head a lot
- Scratching his ears
- Rubbing his ears on the floor
- An unpleasant smell coming from the ears, which is a sign of a yeast or other infection
- Redness and/or inflammation inside the ears
- Lots of wax inside the ears - black wax smells

If your dog has any of these signs, consult your vet ASAP, as simple routine cleaning won't solve the problem. When you take your Schnauzer to the groomer, ask for the hairs inside the ears to be plucked out. This should be done carefully by hand, as the loud noise of the clippers inside the ear can be distressing for the dog. It is also impossible for the clippers to get right down to the hairs inside a narrow ear channel.

Beth adds: "Owners should be encouraged to pull the hair out themselves, little and often. This is much kinder than the groomer doing it all in one go, which is can be most distressing for dogs.

"Some dogs can get awkward and bite the groomer, who then can't remove all the hair. In bad cases, the dog ends up at the vet's and sometimes sedation is required."

Ear infections are painful for your dog and notorious for recurring once they have taken hold. In very severe cases they can cause deafness, so it pays to check your dog's ears regularly while grooming – both at home and professionally.

Our photo shows a lot of hair and a build-up of wax under the ear flap, an unwelcome but all-too-common sight with Miniature Schnauzers.

Beth: "Ear canals should be kept clear of hair and ear wax. Never clean the ear by putting anything deep into the ear canal. The expression 'never put anything smaller than your elbow in your ear' also springs to mind. Forceps can be used to remove ear hair and ear powder to help grip."

 Use small balls of warm, damp cotton wool to clean the ears. NEVER use cotton buds or tips as these are too small and can damage the ear if they go too deep or your Mini suddenly moves. Check and clean the inside of your Schnauzer's ears regularly - once every week or two.

From time to time you can also consider using an ear cleansing solution, which will also soften any wax, making it easier to remove with damp cotton wool balls. Squeeze a few drops of cleanser into the ear canal. If you can, tilt your dog's head so the ear canal is pointing downwards, allowing gravity to help distribute the solution. Beth recommends Otodex, *pictured*, which kills mites too.

Massage the base of the ear for 15 seconds before allowing him to shake his head. Then dry the inside of the ear flap with cotton wool and gently wipe out any dirt and waxy build-up in the ear canal with cotton wool.

Keep your dog's ears clean and free from too much hair right from puppyhood and hopefully he will never get an ear infection.

....

Teeth Cleaning

Veterinary studies show that by the age of three, 80% of dogs show signs of gum or dental disease. Symptoms include a yellow and brown build-up of tartar along the gum line, red inflamed gums and persistent bad breath (halitosis). And if your dog suddenly stops eating his food, check his mouth and teeth.

 **Small breeds like Miniature Schnauzers are more prone to dental issues than large breeds as their teeth are crammed into a smaller space.**

Regular dental care greatly reduces the onset of gum and tooth decay and infection. Plaque coats teeth and within a few days this starts to harden into tartar, often turning into gingivitis (inflammation of the gums). Gingivitis is regularly accompanied by periodontal disease (infections around the teeth).

In the worst cases, it can even lead to infections of vital organs, such as the heart, liver and kidneys. Even if the infection doesn't spread beyond the mouth, bad teeth or gums cause painful toothache and difficulty chewing.

If your Mini Schnauzer needs a deep clean, remedial work or teeth removing, he will have to be anaesthetised. Prevention is better than cure.

If your Mini has to be anaesthetised for another procedure, ask the vet to check and clean your dog's teeth while he's under.

Many owners keep their dogs' teeth clean by giving them an occasional raw bone (not cooked chicken as it splinters, but raw chicken bones are OK; knuckle bones are better) or regularly feeding bully sticks, Nylabones, Dentastix, etc. – although these man-made options are high in calories.

One product recommended by many vets and breeders is *Plaque Off, pictured.* This is a powder supplement which, when added to one daily meal can help to keep a dog's teeth clean by reducing plaque, tartar and bad breath.

Lesley (Myers) added this advice: "Mini Schnauzers have what is called a *'scissor bite;'* the top front teeth just overlap the bottom front teeth. Avoid using pull toys as pulling can distort the pup's mouth and your dog could end up being undershot, where the bottom front teeth overlap the top front teeth, e.g. like a Bulldog.

"A chew toy will help to clean teeth and exercise the jaws. Select toys carefully as too small a toy can choke a dog. Miniature Schnauzers seem to prefer soft toys to play and cuddle up with."

Another option is to brush your dog's teeth. Start while still a puppy and take things slowly in the beginning, giving lots of praise.

Various brushes, sponges and pads are available - the choice depends on factors such as the health of your dog's gums, the size of his mouth and how good you are at teeth cleaning. Use a pet toothpaste, as the human variety can upset a dog's stomach.

Get him used to the toothpaste by letting him lick some off your finger when he is young. If he doesn't like the flavour, try a different one. Continue this until he enjoys licking the paste - it might be instant or it might take days.

Gently rub it on one of the big canine teeth at the front of his mouth. Then get him used to the toothbrush or dental sponge for several days - praise him when he licks it – before you start brushing.

Lift his upper lip gently and place the brush at 45° to the gum line. Gently move the brush backwards and forwards. Start just with his top front teeth and then gradually do a few more.

Once used to the process, many Schnauzers love the attention - especially if they like the flavour of the toothpaste!

Regular brushing shouldn't take more than five minutes - well worth the time and effort when it spares your Schnauzer the pain and misery of serious dental or gum disease.

Nail Trimming

If you can hear the nails clicking on a hard surface, they're too long. If your Schnauzer is regularly exercised on grass or other soft surfaces, his nails may not be getting worn down enough, and foot shape can also have a big impact on nail wear. Nail trimming is another task you can ask your groomer to do.

Overly-long nails interfere with a dog's gait, making walking awkward or painful, and putting stress on elbows, shoulders and back. They can also break easily, usually at the base of the nail where blood vessels and nerves are located. The longer the nail, the longer the quick - and older dogs have longer quicks

 Get your dog used to having his paws inspected from puppyhood; it's also a good opportunity to check for, cracked pads, interdigital cysts, etc.

To trim your dog's nails yourself, use a specially designed clipper - most have safety guards to stop you from cutting the nails too short. Clip only the hook-like part of the nail that turns down. Start trimming gently, a nail or two at a time, and your dog will learn that you're not going to hurt him. If you accidentally cut the quick, stop the bleeding with some styptic powder.

Trim only the ends, before the *'quick,'* which is a blood vessel inside the nail (hence the expression 'cut to the quick'). You can see where the quick ends on a white nail but, unfortunately, not on a black nail like the Schnauzer's, so be careful.

You can also use a nail grinder tool (*'Dremel,' pictured).* Some dogs have tough nails that are harder to trim and this may be less stressful with less chance of cutting the quick. The Dremel is like an electric nail file, some dogs prefer them to a clipper, although others don't like the noise.

Beth, *pictured,* added: "Schnauzer feet should be cat-like and trimmed accordingly. Pads should be clear of hair to help prevent knotting and the gathering of debris. Nails should be trimmed and black."

Anal Glands

While you might spend a long time gazing at your Schnauzer's beautiful face and deep brown eyes, it's important not to forget his less-appealing end! So, let's dive straight in and talk about anal sacs.

Sometimes called scent glands, these are a pair of glands located inside your dog's anus that give off a scent when he has a bowel movement. You won't want to hear this, but problems with impacted anal glands are not uncommon!

When a dog passes firm stools, the glands normally empty themselves. But watery poop can mean there's not enough pressure to empty the glands, causing discomfort. They become swollen and painful once infected. In extreme cases, one or both anal glands can be removed - our Max lived happily for many years with one anal gland.

If your dog is dragging himself along on his rear end (*'scooting'*) or trying to lick or scratch his anus, he could well have impacted anal glands that need squeezing, or 'expressing.' (Scooting can also be a sign of worms).

Some groomers will express the glands if asked, but if you think your Mini is straining to poop or has another problem with his rear end, go and see the vet. Either way, it pays to keep an eye on both ends of your dog!

16. The Facts of Life

Judging by the number of questions our Max the Schnauzer website receives, there is a lot of confusion about the canine facts of life. Some owners ask if, and at what age, they should have their Mini Schnauzer spayed or neutered, while others want to know whether they should breed their dog.

Owners of females ask when and how often she will come on heat and how long this will last. Sometimes they want to know how you can tell if a female is pregnant or how long a pregnancy lasts. So here, in a nutshell, is a chapter on the birds and bees as far as Schnauzers are concerned.

Females and Heat

The female Schnauzer has an oestrus *(estrus* in the US) cycle. This is when she is ready (and willing!) for mating and is more commonly called *heat*, being *in heat*, *on heat* or *in season*.

Schnauzers usually have their first cycle any time between six months and one year old. Each dog is an individual and so the exact time varies.

 Smaller breeds like the Miniature Schnauzer mature quicker than larger breeds like the Giant Schnauzer. Typically, a Mini has her first heat cycle at around six to eight months old.

Here's what some of our breeders said, starting with **Steve Matthews,** of Silbertraum Miniature and Giant Schnauzers, Dorset: "Most of my Mini Schnauzer girls have their first season at six months and regularly at six months thereafter. The Giants tend to have their first season slightly later at around nine months and then repeated at six-monthly intervals.

Lesley Myers, show judge and former UK hobby breeder (Lesley bred occasional litters and kept one of the puppies to show) has been involved with Minis for nearly 40 years. She says:

"Rommey's first season was at nearly eight months old and she had them every five to six-and-a-half months. They lasted 21 to 22 days.

"Ziska's first season was at nine months old, and they were anything from every four-and-a-half to five-and-a-half months, also lasting 21 to 22 days."

Photo: Ziska (Ersmy Miss Congeniality JW Sh.CM) aged 15 months, courtesy of Lesley.

Andrew and Gaynor Ray, breeders of 40 years' standing who breed all three types of Schnauzer at Minnienoom Schnauzers, Derbyshire:

"In our experience, Miniature Schnauzers have their first season any time from six to nine months of age, and then usually every six months, more or less to the last date going forward. We have experienced one Miniature Schnauzer here at Minnienoom who had her first season at six months of age and then all ongoing seasons every three months.

A few years later one of her offspring that we had kept back for our ongoing breeding programme also had her seasons every three months. This is the only time we have experienced this behaviour in all of our many years of breeding Miniature Schnauzers."

AKC Breeder of **Merit Wade Bogart,** of Sumerwynd Miniature Schnauzers, New York State, has bred Minis since 1979 and is an Approved Breed Mentor. He says: "Our females typically have their first season at six to eight months and then every six to eight months after that."

Tip Females often follow the patterns of their mother, so ask the breeder at what age the dam had her first season and how often they occur.

No time of the year corresponds to a breeding season, so heat could occur during any month.

When a young bitch comes in season, it is normal for her cycles to be somewhat irregular - it can take up to two years for regular cycles to develop. The timescale also becomes more erratic with older, unspayed females.

A heat cycle normally lasts 18 to 21 days, the last days might be lighter in terms of blood loss - you might not even know that she is still in heat.

FACT > Unlike with women, the reproductive cycle does not stop when dogs reach middle age, although the heat becomes shorter and lighter. However, a litter takes a heavy toll on older females. NOTE: Women cannot get pregnant during their period, while female dogs can ONLY get pregnant during their heat.

Here are some typical physical signs of heat:

- 🐾 The pink bit under her tail (external sex organ called the vulva) becomes swollen and sometimes darker
- 🐾 She loses some blood - the amount of blood varies from one dog to another - from "spotting," which is very light, to heavier bleeds
- 🐾 She tries to lick the area under her tail
- 🐾 She may urinate more frequently

The canine heat cycle is a complex mix of physical, hormonal and behavioural changes. Here are some behaviour changes to look out for - your Schnauzer may display none, one or several of these:

- 🐾 Some dogs become needier around you - or irritable, e.g. being less tolerant of other dogs and people, or more possessive with toys or food
- 🐾 She may go off her food
- 🐾 Some shed more hair when on heat
- 🐾 Others seem a little depressed and retire to their beds
- 🐾 Her hormones are raging and she may try to mount you, other dogs or even the furniture!

Some dogs clean themselves regularly, while others are less scrupulous on the personal hygiene front.

If your girl has "heavy days" and is constantly on and off your furniture, put covers on your sofa (if she's allowed on there) during her heat – or you could invest in a couple of pairs of washable doggie pants for her heaviest days.

Check the sizing, which is usually based on waist measurement. Some dogs can get out of them pretty quickly, and even with pants on leakages occasionally occur.

....

The Cycle

There are four stages of the heat cycle (a female's season is **proestrus** plus **oestrus**):

Proestrus - this is when the bleeding starts and lasts around nine days. Male dogs are attracted to her, but she is not yet interested, so she may hold her tail close to her body. Her vulva becomes swollen. The blood is usually light red or brown, turning more straw-coloured or even colourless when she's ready to mate.

(Tip) If you're not sure if she's in heat, hold a tissue against her vulva or put a white sheet or cloth underneath when she lies down. Does any of it turn pink or red?

Oestrus - when eggs are released from ovaries and the optimum time for breeding. Males are extremely interested in her and the feelings are often very much reciprocated - her hormones are raging! If there is a male around she may stand for him and *"flag"* her tail (or move it to one side) to allow him to mount her. Oestrus is the time when a female CAN get pregnant and usually lasts around nine days, so roughly from Day 10-19.

Dioestrus - the two-month stage when her body produces the hormone progesterone whether or not she is pregnant. During this stage she is no longer interested in males. These hormones can sometimes lead to what is known as a *"false pregnancy."*

Anoestrus - period of rest when reproductive organs are inactive. It is the longest stage of the cycle and lasts around five-and-a-half months. If she normally lives with a male dog, they can return to living together again - neither will be interested in mating and she cannot get pregnant.

FACT When a female is on heat, she produces pheromones that attract male dogs. Because dogs have a sense of smell several hundred times stronger than ours, your girl on heat is a magnet for all the neighbourhood males. It is believed that they can detect the scent of a female on heat up to two miles away!

They may congregate around your house or follow you around the park (if you are brave or foolish enough to venture out there while she is in season), waiting for their chance to prove their manhood – or mutthood in their case.

Don't expect your precious little princess to be fussy. Her hormones are raging when she is on heat and, during her most fertile days, she is ready, able and ... VERY willing!

As she approaches the optimum time for mating you may notice her tail bending slightly to one side. She will also start to urinate more frequently. This is her signal to all those virile male dogs out there that she is ready for mating.

Although breeding requires specialised knowledge on the part of the owner, it does not stop a female on heat from being extremely interested in attention from any old mutt!

To avoid an unwanted pregnancy, you must keep a close eye on her throughout her heat and not allow her to wander unsupervised.

Keep her on a lead if you go out on walks and whatever you do, don't let her run free anywhere that you might come across other dogs. If you have a large garden or yard, you may wish to restrict her to that during her heat – but only if you 100% know it is safe. Determined male dogs can jump and scramble over high fences.

You can compensate for the restrictions by playing more games at home to keep her mentally and physically active.

It is amazing the lengths to which some entire (uncastrated) males will go to impregnate a female on heat. Travelling great distances to follow her scent, digging under fences, jumping over barriers, chewing through doors or walls and sneaking through hedges are just some of the tactics employed by canine Casanovas on the loose.

 Her hormones are raging and during her most fertile days (the oestrus), your female's instinct to mate will trump all of her training.

If you do have an entire male Schnauzer, you need to physically keep him in a separate place, perhaps with an understanding friend or even boarding kennels. His desire to mate is all-consuming and can be accompanied by howling or 'marking' (urinating) indoors.

A dog living in the same house as a bitch in season has even been known to mate with her through the bars of a crate!

You can buy sprays that mask the natural oestrus scent. Marketed under such attractive names as "*Bitch Spray,*" these lessen but don't eliminate, the scent. They may reduce the amount of unwanted attention, but are not a complete deterrent.

There is no canine contraceptive, so if your female is unspayed, you need to keep her under supervision during her heat cycle - which may be up to three or even four weeks.

If your female is accidentally mated (a *"mismating")*, there is an injection available in the UK called *Alizin* which blocks progesterone production. It is used any time from the end of the season up to 45 days after the mismating. It is given as two injections 24 hours apart and has a low risk if used early on. If used late it causes abortion.

NOTE: Females tend to come back into season quite soon after the Alizin injections - usually one to three months, so take care not to get "caught out" at the next season. Alizin is also quite a painful injection for your girl.

....

Pregnancy

A canine pregnancy lasts for 58 to 65 days; 63 days is average. This is true of all breeds of dog of all sizes, from the Chihuahua to the Great Dane, and the Mini to the Giant Schnauzer. Sometimes pregnancy is referred to as *"the gestation period."*

A female should have a pre-natal check-up after mating. The vet should answer any questions about the type of food, supplements and extra care needed, as well as informing the owner about any physical changes likely to occur in your female.

There is a blood test available that measures levels of *relaxin*. This is a hormone produced by the ovary and the developing placenta, and pregnancy can be detected by monitoring relaxin levels as early as 22 to 27 days after mating. The levels are high throughout pregnancy and then decline rapidly after the female has given birth.

A vet can usually see the puppies (but not how many) using ultrasound from around the same time.

Signs of Pregnancy

- After mating, many females become more affectionate. However, a few may become uncharacteristically irritable and maybe even a little aggressive!

- She may produce a slight mucous-like discharge from her vagina one month after mating

- Three or four weeks after mating, some females experience morning sickness – if this is the case, feed little and often. She may seem more tired than usual

- She may seem slightly depressed or show a drop in appetite. These signs can also mean there are other problems, so you should consult your vet

- Her teats will become more prominent, pink and erect 25 to 30 days into the pregnancy. Later on, you may notice fluid coming from them. This first milk (colostrum) is the most important milk a puppy gets on Day One as it contains the mother's immunity

- Her body weight will start to increase about 35 days after mating

- Abdominal swelling may be just about noticeable from Day 40 and becomes more obvious from around Day 50, although first-time mums and females carrying few puppies may not show as much

- Many pregnant females' appetites will increase in the second half of pregnancy

- Her nesting instincts will kick in as the delivery date approaches. She may seem restless or scratch her bed or the floor - she may even rip and shred items like your comforter, curtains or carpeting!

- During the last week of pregnancy, females often start to look for a safe place for whelping. Some seem to become confused, wanting to be with their owners and at the same time wanting to prepare their nest.

(If the female is having a C-section (Caesarean section), she should still be allowed to nest in a whelping box with layers of newspaper, which she will scratch and dig as the time approaches)

 If your Schnauzer becomes pregnant - either by design or accident - your first step should be to consult a vet.

Litter Size

The size of Miniature Schnauzer litters varies a great deal. The number of puppies can be affected by factors such as bloodlines, the age of the dam and sire (young and older dogs have smaller litters), the health and diet of the dam, Mother Nature, and the size of the gene pool; the lower the genetic diversity, the smaller the litter.

Wade: "In our 40-plus years of breeding, we have found that the age of the bitch plays a significant factor in determining litter size. That said, six pups is the typical litter size for bitches one to three years old, then four pups for bitches four to six years old. With bitches older than six years, one is lucky if a single puppy is born."

Steve: "Mini litters tend to be around four or five, although we have had 11 on one occasion. My Giant litters are usually 10 to 12, but I have heard up to 16 pups being born."

Andrew and Gaynor: "The usual Miniature Schnauzer litter size is five to seven pups. However, we personally have had as few as one and as many as 11. In our opinion, any more than eight in a litter can be challenging both for the mother of the pups and the owner, who has to ensure that all puppies get sufficient milk."

Lesley: "Their litters were usually between five and seven pups, although Ziska's last litter was three."

False Pregnancies

Occasionally, unspayed females may display signs of a false pregnancy. Before dogs were domesticated, it was common for female dogs to have false pregnancies and to lactate (produce milk). She would then nourish puppies of the Alpha bitch or puppies who had lost their mother in the pack.

False pregnancies occur 60 to 80 days after the female was in season - about the time she would have given birth - and are generally nothing to worry about for an owner. The exact cause is unknown; however, hormonal imbalances are thought to play an important role. Some dogs have shown symptoms within three to four days of spaying; these include:

- Making a nest
- Producing milk (lactating)
- Appetite fluctuations
- Barking or whining a lot
- Restlessness, depression or anxiety
- Mothering or adopting toys and other objects
- Swollen abdomen
- She might even appear to go into labour

 Under no circumstances should you restrict your Schnauzer's water supply to try and prevent her from producing milk. This is dangerous as she can become dehydrated.

Occasionally, an unspayed female may have a false pregnancy with each heat cycle. Spaying during a false pregnancy may actually prolong the condition, so better to wait until it is over to have her spayed.

False pregnancy is not a disease, but an exaggerated response to normal hormonal changes. Even if left untreated, it almost always resolves itself.

However, if your dog appears physically ill or the behavioural changes are severe enough to worry about, visit your vet. He or she may prescribe *Galastop*, which stops milk production and quickly returns the hormones to normal. In rare cases, hormone treatment may be necessary.

Generally, dogs experiencing false pregnancies do not have serious long-term problems, as the behaviour disappears when the hormones return to their normal levels in two to three weeks.

Pyometra

One exception is *Pyometra,* a serious and potentially deadly infection of the womb, caused by a hormonal abnormality.

It normally follows a heat cycle in which fertilisation did not occur and the dog typically starts showing symptoms within two to four months. It occurs most often in middle-aged females. Commonly referred to as *"pyo,"* there are *open* and *closed* forms of the disease. Open pyo is usually easy to identify with a smelly discharge, so prompt treatment is easy.

Closed pyo is often harder to identify and you may not even notice anything until your girl becomes feverish and lethargic. When this happens, it is very serious and time is of the essence.

Typical signs of Pyometra are: excessive drinking and urination, vomiting and depression, with the female trying to lick a white discharge from her vagina. She may also have a temperature.

If the condition becomes severe, her back legs will become weak, possibly to the point where she can no longer get up without help.

Pyometra can be fatal and needs to be dealt with promptly by a vet.

Standard treatment is emergency spay soon after starting intravenous fluids and antibiotics. In some milder cases, the vet may recommend Alizin injections plus antibiotics and (if needed) IV fluids, then spay as soon as possible after the pyo resolves.

Should I Breed My Schnauzer?

The short and very simple answer is: NO! Not unless you do a lot of research, find a mentor for expert advice and then a good vet, preferably one experienced with Schnauzers. Breeding healthy Schnauzer puppies with good temperaments is a messy, complex, time-consuming and expensive process and should not be approached lightly.

Unfortunately, lots of people with little or scant knowledge of Schnauzers have been tempted to breed their dogs to cash in on the rise in dog ownership and the high price of puppies.

This can often lead to heartbreak for owners when the puppy has a temperament issue or later develops a disease or structural problem.

Ultimately, it leads to badly-bred dogs entering the Schnauzer population and bringing unwanted traits with them.

The risk of breeding puppies with health issues is very real if you don't know what you are doing. Today's responsible breeders are continually looking at ways of improving the health of the Schnauzer and Schnauzer through selective breeding. See <u>Chapter 13. Mini Schnauzer Health</u> for more information on health tests and ailments that can affect Schnauzers. Another major consideration is that not all Schnauzers are easy whelpers - meaning that birth is not always straightforward - and some cannot manage without veterinary help.

 According to a study published in the Journal of Small Animal Practice, 21.5% of Mini Schnauzer litters and 11.8% of Giant litters were born by C-Section. No figures were published for Standards.

Typical veterinary fees for a C-section are in four figures and are not covered by normal pet insurance - and even then, a good outcome is not guaranteed. We know of several breeders of different breeds who have lost beloved dogs during or following C-sections.

Photo: A veterinarian performing a C-Section.

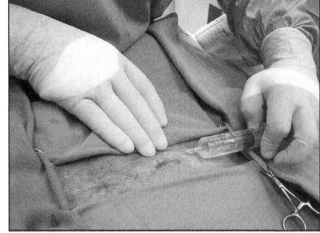

Schnauzer genetics is a complicated business that covers a multitude of traits, including structure, health, coat and colour, temperament and instinct.

Well-bred Miniature Schnauzer puppies fetch a high price. But despite this, you may be surprised to hear that many dedicated breeders make little or no money from the practice, due to the high costs of veterinary fees, health screening, stud fees and expensive special nutrition and care for the female and her pups.

Responsible breeding is backed up by genetic information and screening as well as a thorough knowledge of the desired traits of the Schnauzer. It is definitely not an occupation for the casual hobbyist.

 Breeding is not just about the look or colour of the puppies; health and temperament are just as important.

Many dog lovers do not realise that the single most important factor governing health and certain temperament traits is genetics. Good breeders have years of experience in selecting the right pair for mating after they have considered the ancestry, health, temperament and physical characteristics of the two dogs involved.

They may travel hundreds of miles to find the right mate for their dog. Some of them also show or take part in other canine activities with their Schnauzers.

Anyone considering mating their dog should first ask themselves these questions:

❖ **Did you get your Miniature Schnauzer from a good, ethical breeder?** Dogs sold on general sales websites are seldom good specimens and can be unhealthy

❖ **Does your dog conform to the Breed Standard?** Do not breed from a Mini Schnauzer that is not an excellent specimen in all respects, hoping that somehow the puppies will turn out better. They won't! Talk with experienced breeders and ask them for an honest assessment of your dog

❖ **Do you understand COI and its implications?** COI stands for Coefficient of Inbreeding. It measures the common ancestors of a dam and sire and indicates the probability of how genetically similar they are. This cannot be overlooked when breeding Schnauzers, due to the relatively small gene pool.

❖ **Have your dog and her or his mate both been screened** for genetic Schnauzer health issues that can be passed on to the puppies?

❖ **Have you researched his or her lineage** to make sure no problems are lurking in the background? Puppies inherit traits from their grandparents and great-grandparents as well as from their mother and father

❖ **Are you 100% sure that your Mini Schnauzer has no temperament issues** which could be inherited by the puppies?

❖ **Are you positive that the same can be said for the dog you are planning on breeding yours with?**

❖ **Do you have the finances** to keep the mother healthy through pregnancy, whelping, and care of her and the puppies after birth – even if complications occur?

❖ **Is your female two years old or older and at least in her second heat cycle?** Female Schnauzers should not be bred until they are physically mature, and robust enough to whelp and care for a litter. Even then, not all females are suitable

❖ **Giving birth takes a lot out of a female - are you prepared to put yours through that?** And, as you've read, it's not without risk

❖ **Some females are poor mothers,** which means that you have to look after the puppies 24/7. Even if they are not, they need daily help from the owner to rear their young

❖ **Can you care for lots of lively puppies if you can't find homes for them?**

❖ **Will you be able to find good homes for all the puppies?** Good breeders do not let their precious puppies go to just any home. They want to be sure that the new owners will take good care of their dogs for their lifetime

❖ **Would you take back, or help to rehome, one of your dogs if circumstances change?**

Breeders' Advice:

Wade: "READ, READ AND DO MORE READING! A great source would be the American Kennel Club's Guide to Responsible Dog Breeding."

Steve: "My advice on breeding would be don't do it if you think you are going to make money from it. The costs of doing it properly can outweigh any potential gain and numerous things can go wrong, i.e. having to call a vet to do an emergency Caesarean at three o'clock in the morning, loss of the bitch and having to hand-rear the puppies.

"Also, you need the time and space to do it correctly - and if you are unable to sell them, they may be with you for several months."

"You also need to be with a Giant mum and her litter 24 hours a day for the first few days to prevent her from sitting on them and squashing them. Also, with the advent of recent animal breeding legislation in the UK, it has become difficult for many unlicensed breeders to advertise litters."

Schnauzer Groomer and Standard Schnauzer breeder **Beth Railton:** "My advice would be to start by reading *'The Book of the Bitch'*. Then be prepared to lose your bitch or a whole litter, have at least £3,000 ($3,500) in a bank account or on a credit card and be prepared to lose money.

"Do it for the love of the breed, not for your pocket. Research health test requirements, etc. etc. I was always told that where there is livestock there is dead stock, which can be heartbreaking."

Andrew and Gaynor are prepared to act as mentors if they think the conditions are right for one of their puppies later to be bred and lots of criteria have been met:

"We discourage everyone from wanting to 'JUST' have a litter from their girl, expressing the pitfalls of what could go wrong during pregnancy and birthing - not to mention all the hard work and time that goes into rearing a successful litter of puppies.

"However, for someone who can prove to us that breeding from their girl is the correct thing to do we, of course, will provide as much support and advice as possible ensuring that our baby that we took time and care in breeding ourselves gets the best support required to ensure all her requirements are met, i.e health tests required for that breed, choosing the best male to sire the puppies, ongoing health and welfare concerns for the pregnant dam, providing the best birthing programme, rearing of the puppies and providing help and support if things go wrong."

Research Tools

Having read all of that, it's also true to say that experts are not born, they learn their trade over many years. Anyone who is seriously considering getting into the specialised art of breeding Schnauzers should first spend time researching the breed and its genetics.

Tip **Make sure you are going into breeding for the right reasons and not primarily to make money - ask yourself how you intend to improve the breed.**

Make contact with established breeders, visit dog shows or talk to owners and breeders of Schnauzers. Find yourself a mentor, somebody who is already very familiar with the breed. To find a good breeder/mentor:

USA - The American Mini Schnauzer Club https://amsc.us

You can also Google *'AKC Find a Puppy'* where you'll be taken to the AKC marketplace and can then find breeders in your area.

UK - The Miniature Schnauzer Club www.theminiatureschnauzerclub.co.uk

All three types - The Schnauzer Club of Great Britain www.schnauzerclub.co.uk and

Northern Schnauzer Club at http://northernschnauzerclub.co.uk

You can also visit the Kennel Club website, click on the relevant Schnauzer breed, scroll down to **'Find a Puppy'** at the bottom of the page and find breeders near you.

Photo: Ziska's puppies feeding, courtesy of Lesley Myers.

If you are determined to breed from your Schnauzer - and breed properly - do your research. Read as much as you can and, like Beth, I also recommend reading *'The Book of the Bitch'* by J. M. Evans and Kay White, available on Amazon.

You may have the most wonderful Miniature Schnauzer in the world, but don't enter the world of dog breeding without knowledge and ethics. Don't do it for the money, the cute factor, to show the kids "The Miracle of Birth" or because you want to breed the best show Schnauzer ever - you won't!

Breeding poor examples only brings heartache in the long run. Our strong advice is:

When it comes to breeding Schnauzers, leave it to the experts - or set out to become one yourself.

Neutering - Pros and Cons

There is a lot to think about before you make a decision on what's best for your Schnauzer. Show and most working dogs are not spayed or neutered, whereas dogs kept purely as pets often are. There is already too much indiscriminate breeding of dogs in the world.

However, there's mounting scientific evidence that spaying or neutering young dogs while they are still growing can have a detrimental effect on their future health (particularly with large breeds like the Giant Schnauzer, no studies have yet been done on small breeds).

Then there is the very real threat of mammary cancer, as well as the life-threatening Pyometra in unspayed middle-aged females of all breeds.

As you will read in **Chapter 17. Schnauzer Rescue**, it is estimated that 1,000 dogs are put to sleep every hour in the USA alone. Rescue organisations in North America, the UK and Australia routinely neuter all dogs that they rehome. The RSPCA, along with most UK vets, also promotes the benefits of neutering; it's estimated that more than half of all dogs in the UK are spayed or castrated.

Another point is that you may not have a choice. Some breeders' Puppy Contracts may have a Spay/Neuter clause as a Condition of Sale. Others may state that you need the breeder's permission to breed your dog.

While early spay/neuter has been traditionally recommended, there is emerging scientific evidence that it is better to wait until the dog is through puberty before making the decision – whatever your vet might recommend.

The Science

It takes at least a full 12 months before a Miniature Schnauzer is fully grown; i.e. skeletons mature and their growth plates close.

 The latest scientific studies show that sex hormones play an important role in normal growth and development. We recommend waiting until your Mini is 12 months or older before spaying or neutering.

Veterinarian Dr Samantha Goldberg, says: "Testosterone and oestrogen are involved in some of the long bone formations in the body, so removing this too early can affect correct growth leading to prolonged growth and poorer quality bone with abnormal mechanical behaviours of the joints.

"Early neutering - i.e. before skeletal growth has finished - results in taller, leggier dogs as the closure of the plates in the long bones is helped by the release of puberty hormones. There is also an increased risk of cranial cruciate rupture, intervertebral disc disease (IVDD), hip dysplasia and patella luxation being cited in some breeds. The number of breeds listed as affected is likely to increase as we know more.

"Bitches may be sexually mature before the body has finished developing physically and mentally. Although they may be able to come into season, they have not finished growing if under 12 months and will certainly not have finished maturing mentally. Many vets will try to influence owners to spay their bitch at six months and often before a season. It is best to be patient and not just neuter to suit the human family."

Dr Goldberg added: "There is a lot of work looking at behavioural issues with dogs in rescues and when they were neutered. So far it seems likely that more dogs ending up in rescue with behavioural issues were neutered early – i.e. under 12 months.

"Neutering reduces metabolic rate and this means they need fewer calories or more exercise to balance it. Often neutering is carried out without the vet warning the owner of this. Thus we hear: 'She is overweight because she is spayed.' Not true - being overweight is caused by eating more calories than are expended.

"Overweight dogs have higher risks from many health conditions, e.g. Diabetes Mellitus and joint issues...and obvious things such as heart disease due to increased workload.

"Neutering male dogs directly reduces risks of increased prostate size due to testosterone (not the same as tumours) and in bitches removes the risk of Pyometra, a life-threatening uterine condition, and ovarian cancers. These effects are very positive.

"To summarise: Neutering should be carried out at the correct time to maximise health in your dog and afterwards their lifestyle may be changed a little, e.g. calorie control. Neuter to reduce risks of many health conditions, but do it at the right time to maximize the lifespan of your dog."

Spaying and Options

Spaying is the term traditionally used to describe the sterilisation of a female dog so that she cannot become pregnant.

* ✤ The most widespread procedure is an *"ovariohysterectomy,"* which involves the removal of the ovaries and uterus (womb). Although this is a routine operation, it is major abdominal surgery and she has to be anaesthetised. There are other alternatives.

* ✤ One less-invasive option offered by some vets is an *"ovariectomy,"* which removes the ovaries, but leaves the womb intact. It requires only a small incision and can even be carried out by laparoscopy, or keyhole surgery.

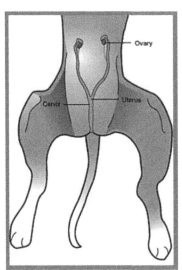

The dog is anaesthetised for a shorter time and there is less risk of infection or excessive bleeding during surgery. One major reason often given for not opting for an ovariectomy is that the female still runs the risk of *Pyometra* later in life.

However, there is currently little or no scientific evidence of females that have undergone an ovariectomy contracting Pyometra afterwards.

 Unspayed middle-aged (over six years old) Schnauzer bitches have a higher risk of getting *mammary cancer* (the equivalent of breast cancer in humans) than spayed bitches.

FACT > Spaying is a much more serious operation for females than neutering is for males. It involves an internal abdominal operation, whereas the neutering procedure is carried out on the male's testicles, which are outside his abdomen. Both procedures require a full general anaesthetic.

As with any major procedure, there are pros and cons.

Pros:

❖ Spaying eliminates the risk of Pyometra and significantly reduces the risk of mammary cancer. It also reduces hormonal changes that can interfere with the treatment of diseases like diabetes or epilepsy

❖ Spaying also prevents infections and diseases in ovaries and (with an ovariohysterectomy) the uterus

❖ You no longer have to cope with any potential mess caused by bleeding inside the house during heat cycles

❖ You don't have to guard your female against unwanted attention from males

❖ Spaying can reduce behaviour problems, such as roaming, aggression towards other dogs, anxiety or fear (not all canine experts agree)

❖ A spayed dog does not contribute to the pet overpopulation problem

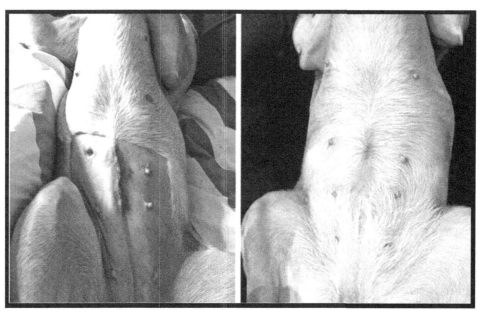

These photographs are reproduced courtesy of Guy Bunce and Chloe Spencer, of Dizzywaltz Labrador Retrievers, Berkshire, England. The left image shows four-year-old Disney shortly after a full spay (ovariohysterectomy). The right one shows Disney several weeks later.

Cons:

❖ Early spay (before the dog has finished growing) can lead to an increased risk of joint and other diseases

❖ Complications can occur, including an abnormal reaction to the anaesthetic, bleeding, stitches breaking and infections; these are not common

❖ Occasionally there can be long-term effects connected to hormonal changes. These include weight gain or less stamina, which can occur years after spaying

❖ Cost. This can range from £100 to £250 in the UK, more for keyhole spaying, and anything from $150 to over $1,000 at a vet's clinic in the USA, or from around $50 at a low-cost clinic, for those that qualify

❖ Urinary incontinence is more common in neutered females, especially if spayed early. One study found that urinary incontinence was not diagnosed in intact females, but was present in 7% of females neutered before one year old

NOTE: Spaying **during** a heat cycle results in a lot of bleeding during the operation, which makes things messy for the vet and can make the operation riskier for the female.

There is also a third option. Veterinarian and Miniature Schnauzer breeder **Dr Lisa Sarvas** says: "We recommend *ovary-sparing spays* at one year for girls. While, with appropriate prevention medicine, boys may be left intact their entire lives."

An *Ovary-Sparing Spay (OSS)* is a relatively new procedure that involves the removal of the womb and cervix (neck of the womb) while leaving one or both ovaries. Unlike the other two procedures, an OSS leaves the dog's sex hormones intact.

A female's ovaries are the main way she produces oestrogen and progesterone and when the ovaries are removed, the dog effectively goes into menopause. There can be negative consequences to a dog being without these hormones from an early age.

Although the female can't get pregnant, she continues to have heat cycles. A small amount of discharge may occur, but she will not bleed heavily. She will, however, still attract unwanted attention from males.

 By no means do all veterinarians offer all three procedures. Do your research, speak to your vet and then decide what's best for your girl - but wait until after she's one year old before any procedure.

Neutering

Neutering male dogs involves castration, or the removal of the testicles. This can be a difficult decision for some owners, as it causes a drop in the pet's testosterone levels, which some humans - men in particular! - feel affects the quality of their dog's life. Fortunately, dogs do not think like people, and male dogs do not miss their testicles or the loss of sex.

FACT ▷ Dogs working in the Services or for charities are often neutered and this does not impair their ability to perform any of their duties. NOTE: All male show Miniature Schnauzers are unneutered ('entire' or 'intact').

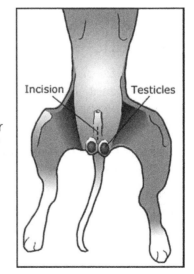

Technically, neutering can be carried out at any age over eight weeks provided both testicles have descended. However, as you've read, **recent scientific studies are undoubtedly coming down on the side of waiting until the dog is one year or older.**

Surgery is relatively straightforward, and complications are less common and less severe than with spaying. Although he will feel tender afterwards, your dog should return to his normal self within a couple of days.

When a dog comes out of surgery, his scrotum, or sacs that held the testicles, will be swollen and it may look like nothing has been done. It is normal for these to shrink slowly in the days following surgery.

Here are the main pros and cons:

Pros:

* ❖ Castration is a relatively straightforward procedure
* ❖ Unwanted sexual behaviour, such as mounting people or objects, is usually reduced or eliminated
* ❖ You cannot have an uncastrated male and unspayed female together when the female is on heat. A castrated male can live alongside a female all year round – although be aware he can still get a female pregnant up to three or four weeks after castration due to residual sperm in his tubes!
* ❖ Behaviour problems such as aggression, marking and roaming can be reduced
* ❖ Testicular problems such as infections, cancer and torsion (painful rotation of the testicle) are eradicated
* ❖ Benign prostatic hyperplasia (prostate gland enlargement) is much less likely after castration
* ❖ A neutered dog is not fathering unwanted puppies

Cons:

* ❖ Studies indicate that males neutered before one year old may be more susceptible to joint problems later in life compared with those neutered after two years old
* ❖ As with any surgery, there can be swelling and redness around the wound. It's fairly routine for dogs to need 10 days of anti-inflammatory medication and to have to wear an E-collar afterwards
* ❖ Some prostate cancers are more likely after neutering
* ❖ In some cases castration can make behaviour problems worse. Pain, trips to the clinic and having testosterone removed can lead to a reduction in the dog's confidence
* ❖ There is evidence that some dogs' coats may be affected; this also applies to spaying
* ❖ Cost - this starts at around £120 in the UK. In the USA this might cost anything from $150 to $1,000 at a private veterinary clinic, depending on your state, or less at a low-cost or Humane Society clinic

Dr Sarvas added: "With appropriate prevention medicine, boys may be left intact their entire lives."

Urban Myths

Neutering or spaying will spoil the dog's character - There is no evidence that any of the positive characteristics of your dog will be altered. He or she will be just as obedient, playful and loyal as before. Neutering may reduce aggression or roaming in male dogs, because they are no longer competing to mate with a female.

We had Max, our Mini, neutered when he was about four years old as he kept running off on walks after the scent of various bitches. We were very lucky that he got brought back home from miles away on two or three occasions and so we decided not to risk it again. Apart from the fact that he stopped disappearing after a scent, there were no other noticeable character changes.

A female needs to have at least one litter - There is no proven physical or mental benefit to a female having a litter.

Mating is natural and necessary - We tend to ascribe human emotions to our dogs, but they do not think emotionally about sex or having and raising a family. Unlike humans, their desire to mate or breed is entirely physical, triggered by the chemicals called hormones within their bodies.

Without these hormones – i.e. after neutering or spaying – the desire disappears or is greatly reduced.

Male dogs will behave better if they can mate - This is simply not true; sex does not make a dog behave better. In fact, it can have the opposite effect. Having mated once, a male may show an increased interest in females. He may also consider his status elevated, which may make him harder to control or call back.

Wade Bogart, AKC Breed Mentor and Miniature Schnauzer Breeder of Merit, added: "I wouldn't recommend spaying before 12 months of age. There is little actual data concerning the correct age to spay and neuter pets, but there is emerging research.

"For example, cancer, orthopedic disease, behavioral problems, endocrine disorders, obesity, and urinary incontinence may be linked to sterilization status and the age at which the procedure is performed."

Photo: Wade's intact Bolt jumping for joy outside the United Nations Building in New York.

"The University of California, Davis, conducted a study on Golden Retrievers in 2013 that turned the world of veterinary medicine on its head concerning early spaying and neutering.

"Early sterilization prevented many issues, according to the study, but also appeared to increase the risk of other diseases, such as cranial cruciate ligament rupture, hemangiosarcoma, mast cell tumors, lymphosarcoma, and hip dysplasia.

"More research is needed, especially with different canine breeds, to help us understand the cause and effect of sterilization and the relationship between spay/neuter status and disease. Armed with these facts the decision about when to spay or neuter your pet is one you should make with your veterinarian."

The link to the Golden Retriever early neuter study is at:
https://journals.plos.org/plosone/article?id=10.1371/journal.pone.0055937

17. Schnauzer Rescue

Not everyone who wants a Schnauzer gets one as a puppy from a breeder. Some people prefer to give a rescue dog a second chance for a happy life.

What could be kinder and more rewarding than adopting a poor, abandoned Schnauzer and giving her a happy, loving home for the rest of her life?

Not much really; adoption saves lives and gives unfortunate dogs a second chance of happiness.

....

Reasons for Rescue

The problem of homeless dogs is truly depressing. It's a big issue in Britain, but even worse in the US, where the sheer numbers in kill shelters are hard to comprehend. In "Don't Dump The Dog," Randy Grim states that 1,000 dogs are being put to sleep every hour in the States.

The internet is full of photos of cute Schnauzers, especially puppies. Those gorgeous little bundles of fluff with the funny whiskers, melt-your-heart eyes and cheeky expressions look so cute.

And people rush out in their droves to buy them, with scant regard for the nature or health of the puppy they are buying, or the decade-long commitment that dog ownership involves.

Many expect a lapdog and realise too late what they've actually got is a smart dog with some working instinct and a lively mind, who demands your attention and is not content to be left in a corner to amuse herself.

If you don't provide an activity or a challenge for a Schnauzer, they will certainly provide a challenge for you!

Behaviour is a common reason for dogs ending up in rescue. They may have become too vocal, demanding, anxious or badly behaved. This is almost always due to a lack of socialisation, training or exercise, or all three - all of which are part of the bargain when you decide to get an engaged, people-loving breed like the Miniature Schnauzer.

Other reasons for Schnauzers being put into rescue include:

- 🐾 The dog or owner develops health issues
- 🐾 A change in work patterns, so the dog is left alone for long periods
- 🐾 The dog has way too much energy and needs a lot more exercise and attention than the owner is able or prepared to give
- 🐾 A change in family circumstance, such as divorce or a new baby
- 🐾 Moving into smaller or rented accommodation

- The dog barks too much - Minis can be too vocal if bored or under-socialised

- She is growling, chewing things she shouldn't or nipping

- She makes a mess in the house - housetraining requires time and patience from the owner

- Keeping a dog costs more than people expect

There is, however, a ray of sunshine for some of these dogs. Every year many thousands of people in North America, Europe and countries all around the world adopt a rescue dog and the story usually has a happy ending.

....

The Dog's Point of View...

If you are serious about adopting a Mini Schnauzer, do so with the right motives and with your eyes wide open. If you're expecting a perfect dog, you could be in for a shock. Rescue Schnauzers can and do become wonderful companions, but much depends on you and how much effort you are prepared to put in.

If you can, look for a rescue group specialising in Schnauzers – and preferably one where the dog has been fostered out. They are more likely to be able to assess the dog and give you an idea of what you might be letting yourself in for. And if a dog has bad habits, the foster parents have probably already started working on some of them.

Schnauzers are extremely loyal to their owners. Sometimes those that end up in rescue centres are traumatised, others may have behaviour or health problems.

They don't understand why they have been abandoned, neglected or badly treated by their owners and may arrive at your home with 'baggage' of their own until they adjust to being part of a loving family again.

This may take time. Patience is the key to helping the dog to adjust to new surroundings and family and to learn to love and trust again.

Ask yourself a few questions before you take the plunge and fill in the adoption forms:

- Are you prepared to accept and deal with any problems - such as bad behaviour, unwanted barking, aggression, timidity, chewing, jumping up or eliminating in the house - that a rescue dog may display when initially arriving in your home?

- Just how much time do you have to spend with your new dog to help her integrate back into normal family life?

- Schnauzers are long-lived breeds. Are you prepared to take on a new addition to your family who may live for another decade?

- Will you guarantee that dog a home for life - even if she develops health issues later?

What could be worse for the unlucky dog than to be abandoned again if things don't work out between you?

Other Considerations

Adopting a rescue dog is a big commitment for all involved. It is not a cheap way of getting a Schnauzer. It could cost you several hundred dollars or pounds.

Depending on the adoption centre, you may have to pay adoption fees, vaccination and veterinary bills, as well as worm and flea medication and spaying or neutering. Make sure you're aware of the full cost before committing.

Many rescue dogs are older and some may have health or temperament issues. You may even have to wait a while until a suitable dog comes up. One way of finding out if you are suitable is to become a foster home for a rescue centre. Fosters offer temporary homes until a forever home comes along. It's shorter-term, but still requires commitment and patience.

And it's not just the dogs that are screened! Rescue groups make sure that prospective adopters are suitable. They also want to make the right match. Placing a high-energy dog with an elderly couple or an anxious dog in a noisy household could be storing up trouble; it would be a tragedy for the dog if things did not work out.

Most rescue groups ask a raft of personal questions - some of which may seem intrusive. But you'll have to answer them if you are serious about adopting. Here are some typical questions:

- Name, address, age
- Details, including ages, of all people living in your home
- Type of property you live in
- Size of your garden or yard and height of the fence around it
- Extensive details of any other pets
- Your work hours and amount of time spent away from the home each day

- Whether you have any previous experience with dogs or Schnauzers
- Your reasons for wanting to adopt
- Whether you have any experience dealing with canine behaviour or health issues
- Details of your vet
- If you are prepared for aggression/destructive behaviour/chewing/fear and timidity/soiling inside the house/medical issues
- Whether you are willing to housetrain and obedience train the dog
- Your views on dog training methods
- Whether you are prepared for the financial costs of dog ownership
- Where your dog will sleep at night
- Whether you are prepared to accept a Schnauzer cross
- Two personal references

If you go out to work, it is useful to know that UK rescue organisations will not place dogs in homes where they will be left alone for more than four to five hours at a stretch.

After you've filled in the adoption form, a chat with someone from the charity usually follows and usually a home inspection visit - even your vet may be vetted! If all goes well, you'll be approved to adopt and when the right match comes along, a meeting will be arranged with all family members and the dog. You then pay the adoption fee and become the proud new owner of a Schnauzer.

It might seem like a lot of red tape, but the rescue groups have to be as sure as they can that you will provide a loving, forever home for the dog. It would be terrible if things didn't work out and the dog had to be placed back in rescue again.

All rescue organisations will neuter the dog or, if he or she is too young, specify in the adoption contract that the dog must be neutered and may not be used for breeding. Some Schnauzer rescue organisations have a lifetime rescue back-up policy, which means that if things don't work out, the dog must be returned to them.

Training a Rescue Dog

Some Mini Schnauzers may be in rescue because of behavioural problems; how this manifests itself varies from one dog to another. Minis are people-loving attention-seeking dogs, so when problems develop it's often due to a lack of time and attention from the owner. These dogs can, however, be retrained - even when older.

As one rescue group put it: **"Rescue dogs are not damaged dogs; they have just been let down by humans, so take a little while to unpack their bags and get familiar with their new owners and surroundings before they settle in."**

If you approach rescue with your eyes wide open, if you're prepared to be patient and devote plenty of time to your new arrival, then rescuing a Mini Schnauzer is incredibly rewarding. They are such affectionate and loyal dogs, you'll have a friend for life.

 Ask as many questions as you can about the background of the dog, her natural temperament and any issues likely to arise.
You are better off having an honest appraisal than simply being told the dog is wonderful and in need of a home.

Training methods for a rescue Schnauzer are similar to those for any adult Schnauzer, but it may take longer as the dog first has to unlearn any bad habits.

If the dog you are interested in has a particular issue, such as indiscriminate barking, lunging at other dogs while on the leash or lack of housetraining, it is best to start right back at the beginning with training.

 Don't presume the dog knows anything and take each step slowly. See Chapter 10. Basic Training for more information.

Rescue Training Tips

- ❖ Start training the day you arrive home, not once the dog has settled in
- ❖ She needs your attention, but, importantly, she also needs her own space where she can chill out. Put the bed or crate in a quiet place; you want your dog to learn to relax. The more relaxed she is, the fewer hang-ups she will have

- Show her the sleeping and feeding areas, but allow her to explore these and the rest of her space in her own time

- Using a crate may help speed up training, but it's important she first learns to regard the crate as a safe place, and not a prison. See **Chapter 7. Crate and Housetraining** for the best way to achieve this

- If you have children or other animals, introduce them quietly and **NEVER** leave them alone with the dog for the first few months – you don't know what her triggers are

- Maintain a calm environment at home

- Never shout at the dog - even if she has made a mess in the house - it will only stress her and make things worse

- Don't give treats because you feel sorry for her. Only give a treat when she has carried out a command. This will help her to learn quickly and you to establish leadership

- Set her up to **SUCCEED** and build confidence – don't ask her to do things she can't yet do

- Socialisation is extremely important – introduce new places and situations gradually and don't over-face her. All new experiences should be positive or you may reinforce insecurities. You want her to grow in confidence, not be frightened by new things. Talk reassuringly throughout any new experience

- Mental stimulation as well as physical exercise is important for Schnauzers, so have games, toys or challenges to keep your new dog's mind occupied

- Don't introduce her to other dogs until you are confident she will behave well - and then not while on a lead (leash), when the *'fight or flight'* instinct might kick in

- Getting an understanding of your dog will help to train her quicker - is she by nature submissive or dominant, anxious or outgoing, fearful or bold, aggressive or timid? If she shows aggressive tendencies, such as barking, growling or even nipping, she is not necessarily bold. The aggression may be rooted in fear, anxiety or lack of confidence

 The aim of training a rescue Mini is to have a relaxed dog, comfortable in her surroundings, who loves and respects you and who responds well to your positive training methods.

Still Interested?

If we haven't managed to put you off with all of the above..... Congratulations, you may be just the family or person that poor abandoned Schnauzer is looking for!

If you can't spare the time to adopt - and remember - **adoption means forever**, you might want to help rescue dogs in other ways. Many rescue groups foster the Schnauzers until a suitable home can be found. This is a shorter-term arrangement than adopting for life - but still needs your commitment and patience.

Or you could be a fundraiser and help to generate cash to keep these very worthy rescue groups providing such a wonderful service.

However you decide to get involved, Good Luck!

Saving one dog will not change the world,

But it will change the world for one dog

North American Schnauzer Rescue Groups

There are a large number of Schnauzer rescue groups in the USA and these are usually manned by volunteers. We've done a lot of research and contacted many USA Schnauzer rescue groups and are now able to provide the most comprehensive up-to-date list of Schnauzer rescue organisations in the USA.

ALABAMA - Schnauzer Love Rescue Inc - https://schnauzerloverescue.net

ALASKA - Alaska Schnauzer Rescue - https://schnauzer.rescueme.org/Alaska

ARIZONA - Arizona Schnauzer Rescue - http://www.azschnauzer.org/
Photo: Stitch, rescued in Arizona.

ARKANSAS - Rescue Me - https://schnauzer.rescueme.org/Arkansas

CALIFORNIA - Miniature Schnauzer Club of Northern California - www.mscnc.us

COLORADO - Vintage Dog Rescue - http://www.cominischnauzerrescue.com/

DELAWARE - Schnauzer Rescue Cincinnati - www.schnauzerrescuecincinnati.org/
Schnauzer Rescue of the Mid Atlantic - http://www.schnauzerrescue.net/

FLORIDA - Schnauzer Love Rescue Inc - https://schnauzerloverescue.net
Schnauzer Rescue Cincinnati and Florida - www.schnauzerrescuecincinnati.org/

GEORGIA - Schnauzer Love Rescue Inc - https://schnauzerloverescue.net
Rescue Me - https://schnauzer.rescueme.org/Georgia

HAWAII - Rescue Me - https://schnauzer.rescueme.org/Hawaii

IDAHO - Maple Creek Miniature Schnauzer Rescue - https://www.maplecreekmsr.org/

ILLINOIS & IOWA - Miniature Schnauzer Rescue of Illinois & Midwest - http://schnauzerrescue.com

INDIANA - Schnauzer Friends for Rescue and Adoption - http://www.sfra.net/
Schnauzer Rescue Cincinnati - www.schnauzerrescuecincinnati.org/
Almost Home - https://ahsr.ngo/

KANSAS - Kansas Furever - http://www.petfinder.com/shelters/KS133.html

KENTUCKY - Schnauzer Friends for Rescue and Adoption - http://www.sfra.net/
Schnauzer Rescue Cincinnati - http://www.schnauzerrescuecincinnati.org/

LOUISIANA - Rescue Me - https://schnauzer.rescueme.org/Louisiana
Schnauzer Rescue of Louisiana - www.chewy.com/g/schnauzer-rescue-of-louisiana_b65808531

MARYLAND - Schnauzer Rescue of the Mid Atlantic - http://www.schnauzerrescue.net/

MICHIGAN - Schnauzer Friends for Rescue and Adoption - http://www.sfra.net/
Great Lake Miniature Schnauzer Rescue - http://members.petfinder.com/~MI71/

MINNEAPOLIS - Minneapolis/St Paul Miniature Schnauzer Rescue - http://www.mspmsr.org/

MISSISSIPPI - Schnauzer love Rescue Inc - https://schnauzerloverescue.net/2015/

MISSOURI - Boxer-Schnauzer Rescue of the Ozarks - http://www.bsro.org/

MONTANA - Rescue Me - http://schnauzer.rescueme.org/Montana

NEBRASKA - Rescue Me - https://schnauzer.rescueme.org/Nebraska

NEVADA - Southern Nevada Schnauzer Rescue - http://www.petfinder.com/shelters/NV87.html

NEW ENGLAND - Connecticut Rescue Me - https://schnauzer.rescueme.org/Connecticut
Maine Rescue Me - https://schnauzer.rescueme.org/Maine
New Hampshire Rescue Me - https://schnauzer.rescueme.org/NewHampshire
Rhode Island Rescue Me - https://schnauzer.rescueme.org/RhodeIsland
Vermont Rescue Me - https://schnauzer.rescueme.org/Vermont

NEW JERSEY - New Jersey Schnauzer Rescue Network Inc - http://www.njsrn.org/
also covers parts of NJ/PA/NY/CT/DE/MD/WV/VA

NEW MEXICO - New Mexico Schnauzers - https://schnauzer.rescueme.org/NewMexico

NORTH CAROLINA - Schnauzer Rescue - www.schnauzerrescueofthecarolinas.org

NORTH DAKOTA - Rescue Me - https://schnauzer.rescueme.org/NorthDakota

OHIO - Schnauzer Friends for Rescue and Adoption - http://www.sfra.net/
Schnauzer Rescue Cincinnati - http://www.schnauzerrescuecincinnati.org/

OKLAHOMA - Oklahoma Schnauzers - https://schnauzerrescueofthecarolinas.org
Miniature Schnauzer Rescue - https://www.msrnorthwest.org/

OREGON - Maple Creek Miniature Schnauzer Rescue - http://www.maplecreekmsr.org/
Miniature Schnauzer Rescue Inc - http://www.msrnorthwest.org/

PENNSYLVANIA - Rescue Me - https://schnauzer.rescueme.org/Pennsylvania
Schnauzer Rescue of the Mid Atlantic - http://www.schnauzerrescue.net/

SOUTH CAROLINA - Schnauzer Love Rescue Inc - https://schnauzerloverescue.net/2015/
Schnauzer Rescue of the Carolinas - https://schnauzerrescueofthecarolinas.org/

SOUTH DAKOTA - Rescue Me - https://schnauzer.rescueme.org/SouthDakota

TENNESSEE - Schnauzer Love Rescue Inc - https://schnauzerloverescue.net/2015/

TEXAS - Miniature Schnauzer Rescue of Houston - http://www.msrh.org/
Miniature Schnauzer Rescue of North Texas - http://www.msrnt.com/

UTAH - Rescue Me - https://schnauzer.rescueme.org/Utah

VIRGINIA - Schnauzer Rescue of the Mid Atlantic -http://www.schnauzerrescue.net/

WASHINGTON - Maple Creek Miniature Schnauzer Rescue - http://www.maplecreekmsr.org/
Schnauzer Rescue of the Mid Atlantic - http://www.schnauzerrescue.net/

WEST VIRGINIA - Rescue Me - https://schnauzer.rescueme.org/WestVirginia

WISCONSIN - Miniature Schnauzer Rescue of Illinois & Midwest - http://schnauzerrescue.com

WYOMING - Schnauzer Rescue of the Mid Atlantic - www.schnauzerrescue.net
American Miniature Schnauzer Club - local rescue co-ordinators and advice: rescue@amsc.us

This website has more rescue organisations:
http://members.petfinder.com/~CA1070/rescueboard/rescuecontacts2.html

CANADA

MINIATURE SCHNAUZER RESCUE OF ALBERTA - Ferne Gudnason tazaras@telus.net

STANDARD SCHNAUZER CLUB OF CANADA - Lori Elvin dinsdale@eagle.ca

UK

Miniature Schnauzer Club Re-Home and Rescue Trust
www.facebook.com/groups/431244500953804/about

Northern Schnauzer Club Rescue (all three sizes) - Pam Ciceri - Pamela.ciceri@btinternet.com

Since 2008, our website Max the Schnauzer has helped to rehome many Schnauzers with
experienced owners www.max-the-schnauzer.com/uk-schnauzer-rescue.html

18. Caring for Older Minis

When it comes to getting old, most Miniature Schnauzers enjoy longer lives than lots of other breeds. A typical lifespan might be 12 to 15 years - maybe even a year or so longer if you're lucky. The Mini is regarded as a robust and healthy breed and often stays fitter, more active and more playful than many other breeds in her twilight years.

Lifespan can be influenced by genetics; and how you feed, exercise and generally look after your dog will also have an impact on her quality and length of life. But eventually, all of them slow down to some extent.

....

Approaching Old Age

After having got up at the crack of dawn as a puppy, you may find your old Schnauzer now enjoys a lie-in in the morning. She may be a bit slower on her walks, stopping to sniff every blade of grass, and may not want to go quite as far.

Some Schnauzers seem to continue just as before, while others get slightly stiffer joints and sometimes organs, such as the heart, kidneys or liver, may not function quite as effectively. They will probably sleep more and may seek out a place in the sunshine to rest their old bones.

Your faithful companion might even become a bit grumpier, stubborn or less tolerant of lively dogs and children. You may also notice that she doesn't see or hear as well as she used to.

Photo: Bertie (Rhymes Good Boy) still enjoying life aged 15 years and one month, courtesy of Andrew and Gaynor Ray.

On the other hand, your old friend might not be hard of hearing at all. She might have developed that affliction common to many older dogs of *"selective hearing."*

When our Max was 12 years old, he had bionic hearing when it came to the word *"Dinnertime"* whispered from 20 paces, yet seemed strangely unable to hear the commands *"Come"* or *"Down"* when we were right in front of him!

FACT ▶ We normally talk about dogs being old when they are in the last third of their life. Dogs are classed as "Veterans" at seven years old in the show ring - however fit they are.

Ageing varies greatly from dog to dog and bloodline to bloodline. The consensus from our breeders was that a Miniature may start to show signs of ageing anywhere from eight to 10 years old.

You can help ease a mature dog into old age gracefully by keeping an eye on them, noticing the changes and adapting their lifestyle. This might involve:

- Slowly reducing the amount or intensity of daily exercise
- A change of diet
- Modifying your dog's environment – perhaps with an extra blanket, a warmer place and thicker bed for those old joints
- A visit to the vet for supplements and/or medications

It's very important to keep all Schnauzers at an optimum weight as they get older. Their metabolisms slow down, making it easier for them to pile on the pounds. Extra weight places additional, unwanted stress on their joints, back and organs, making them all have to work harder than they should.

Physical Signs of Ageing

Here are some signs of Schnauzers feeling their age - a Mini may show one or more of these:

- ❧ Grey hairs appear, particularly around the muzzle, and coat colour fades. This is especially noticeable with black Schnauzers

- ❧ They get up from lying down and move more slowly

- ❧ They slow down and some are not as keen to go for long walks - and perhaps a bit less keen to go out in bad weather

- ❧ They put on a bit of weight - or lose weight

- ❧ They may drink more water and/or pee more frequently

- ❧ They shed more hair

- ❧ Hearing deteriorates

- ❧ The foot pads thicken and nails may become more brittle

- ❧ One or more lumps or fatty deposits (lipomas) develop on the body

Photo: Max enjoying a trip to the Norfolk coast, aged 11.

One of our old dogs developed two small bumps on the top of his head aged 10 and we took him straight to the vet, who performed minor surgery to remove them. They were benign (harmless), but always get the first one checked out ASAP in case they are an early form of cancer - they can also grow quite rapidly, even if benign.

- ❧ Old dogs often can't regulate body temperature quite as well as they used to and may feel the cold and heat more easily

- ❧ Bad breath (halitosis), which could be a sign of dental or gum disease. If the bad breath persists, get it checked out by a vet

- ❧ If inactive, they may develop callouses on the elbows, especially if lying on hard surfaces

- ❧ Eyesight may also deteriorate – if eyes appear cloudy they may be developing cataracts, so see your vet if you notice the signs. Most older dogs live quite well with failing eyesight, particularly as Schnauzers have an incredible sense of smell

Mental Signs of Ageing

It's not just dogs' bodies that may slow down; their minds may too. It's normal for a dog's memory, ability to learn and awareness to start to dim - although one of Mini Schnauzers' many assets is that they often remain engaged and interested in life, their owners and surroundings right to the end.

If your dog's mind is starting to lose its sharpness, here are some signs to look out for; it's officially called *Canine Cognitive Dysfunction:*

- Sleep patterns change; older dogs may be more restless at night and sleepy during the day. They may start wandering around the house at odd times, causing you sleepless nights
- They bark more, sometimes at nothing or open spaces
- Forgetting or ignoring commands or habits they once knew well, such as the Recall and sometimes toilet training
- They stare at objects, such as walls, hide in a corner, or wander aimlessly around the house or garden (this could be a sign of a mini-stroke)
- Increased anxiety or aggression
- Some Minis may become clingier and more dependent, resulting in Separation Anxiety. They may seek reassurance that you are near as faculties fade and they become less confident and independent. Others can become a bit disengaged

Understanding the changes happening to your Mini and acting on them compassionately and effectively will help ease your dog's passage through her senior years. Your dog has given you so much pleasure over the years, now she needs you to give that bit of extra care for a happy, healthy old age.

 If your Mini Schnauzer is starting to show signs of slowing down or disengaging, you can help her to stay mentally active by playing gentle games and getting new toys to stimulate interest.

Helping Your Dog To Age Gracefully

There are many things you can do to ease your dog's passage into her declining years. As dogs age they need fewer calories and less protein, so some owners feeding kibble switch to one specially formulated for older dogs. These are labelled *Senior, Ageing* or *Mature.*

Check the labelling; some are specifically for dogs aged over 10, others may be for 12-year-olds. If you are not sure if a Senior diet is necessary for your Schnauzer, talk to your vet on your next visit. Remember, if you do change the brand or switch to a wet food, do it gradually.

Some old dogs go off their food. If you feed a dry food, try mixing it with gravy. When Max went off his food, we fed a morning feed of kibble with gravy and an afternoon/evening feed of home-cooked rice with boiled chicken or fish. Rice, white fish and chicken - all cooked - can be good for old dogs with sensitive stomachs.

Photo: Bu looking very alert aged 14.5, courtesy of Simon and Yvonne Sonsino.

Omega-3 fatty acids are good for the brain and coat, and glucosamine and various other supplements help joints, e.g. Yumega Omega 3, Yumove and Joint Aid.

 One of the most important things throughout your Schnauzer's life is dental care: regular tooth brushing and the occasional bone, bully stick or antler, etc. to gnaw on.

Some dogs can become more sensitive to noise as they age. The lead up to Bonfire Night was a nightmare for us (November 5th in the UK, when the skies are filled with fireworks and loud bangs). Other dogs become more stressed by grooming or trips to the vet as they age. Clippering an old Schnauzer is less stressful than hand stripping.

There are medications, homeopathic remedies such as melatonin, and various DAP (dog-appeasing pheromone) products that can help relieve anxiety. Check with your vet before introducing anything new.

 If your old friend has started to ignore your verbal commands when out on a walk - either through *"switching off"* **or deafness - try a whistle to attract her attention and then use an exaggerated hand signal for the Recall.**

Once your dog is looking at you, hold your arm out, palm down, at 90 degrees to your body and bring it down, keeping your arm straight, until your fingers point to your toes. Hand signals worked very effectively with our old Max. He looked, understood ... and then decided if he was going to come or not - but at least he knew what he should be doing! More often than not he did come back, especially if the visual signal was repeated while he was still making up his mind.

Weight - no matter how old your Schnauzer is, they still need a waist! Maintaining a healthy weight with a balanced diet and regular, gentler exercise are two of the most important things you can do for an old dog. Some dogs can also lose weight when they get older.

 **If your dog rapidly loses or gains weight without any obvious reason, consult your vet promptly to rule out any underlying medical issues.**

Environment - Make sure your dog has a nice soft place to rest, which may mean adding extra padding to her bed. This should be in a place that is not too hot or cold, as they may not be able to regulate their body temperature as well as they used to.

Photo of Rosie (Silver Paws Makdad's Rosebud RAE OAP OJP CGC) in her favourite ortho bed on her 13th birthday, courtesy of Rebecca Makdad.

They also need plenty of undisturbed sleep and should not be pestered and/or bullied by younger dogs, other animals or young children.

No jumping on and off furniture or in or out of the car, It's high impact for old joints and bones. She may need a helping hand to get onto the couch (if allowed on there) or a ramp.

We bought an expensive plastic ramp to get Max into the car, but it proved to be a complete waste of money as dogs are tactile and he didn't like the feel of the non-slip surface under his paws.

After a few tentative attempts, he steadfastly refused to set a paw on it and we donated the ramp to a canine charity! I've heard of breeders carpeting ramps to (successfully) persuade their dogs to use them.

If eyesight is failing, move obstacles out of their way or use pet barriers to reduce the chance of injuries.

Exercise - Take the lead from your dog, if she doesn't want to walk as far, then don't force her to go further. But if your dog doesn't want to go out at all, you will have to coax her out. ALL old dogs need exercise, not only to keep their joints moving, but also to keep their heart, lungs and joints exercised, and their minds engaged with different places, scents, etc.

Ears - Sometimes older dogs produce more ear wax, so keep checking that the insides of your Schnauzer's ears are clean and not dirty or smelly.

Coat - Some Schnauzers' coats thicken with age and they require grooming more often.

Time to Get Checked Out

If your dog is showing any of these signs, get them checked out by a vet:

- ❧ Cloudy eyes, possibly cataracts
- ❧ Drinking and/or peeing far more frequently than normal, which could be a sign of diabetes, Cushing's disease or a kidney complaint
- ❧ Constipation or not peeing regularly, a possible symptom of a digestive system or organ problem
- ❧ Watery poo(p) or vomiting
- ❧ Decreased appetite - this is often one of the first signs of an underlying problem
- ❧ Incontinence, which could be a sign of mental or physical deterioration
- ❧ Lumps or bumps on the body - often benign, but can occasionally be malignant (cancerous)
- ❧ Excessive sleeping or a lack of interest in you and her surroundings
- ❧ A darkening and dryness of skin that never seems to get any better, which can be a sign of hypothyroidism
- ❧ Any other out-of-the-ordinary behaviour for your dog. A change in patterns or behaviour is often your dog's way of telling you that all is not well

Expert Opinion

Our own Mini, Max, was fit and active until about 12 years of age, when he slowed down and went off his hypoallergenic kibble. He wasn't as keen to walk as far during the last year of his life (he lived to 13) and spent more time sleeping.

On walks he would sometimes just stop and turn around to go home after he had done his 'business.' He was still getting out on much-shortened walks three times a day, so we took the lead from him on distance.

Steve Matthews, of Silbertraum Miniature and Giant Schnauzers, Dorset: "Miniatures become seniors at around ten years old. As they age they tend to slow down, gain weight and may be reluctant to walk as far as previously. As this happens I tend to move to a Senior complete diet or look for a food with a lower protein level.

"Mini Schnauzers can remain healthy into old age, providing their weight is monitored. I have noticed that some seem to suffer tooth loss as they reach double figures, so it's important to keep their teeth healthy throughout their life.

"Older Schnauzers tend to get lots of lumps and bumps in their skin as they age, but these are normally just benign fatty tissue. All Schnauzers have lots of internal ear hair which should be plucked regularly allowing air to circulate inside the ear. This is something that many dog groomers fail to address and, if left, can allow dirt to accumulate and harbour infection."

Wade Bogart, of Sumerwynd Miniature Schnauzers, New York State, doesn't notice any great changes within his dogs and sticks with an Adult food that is approved for all life stages.

Andrew Ray, Minnienoom Schnauzers, Derbyshire: "I'd say the typical lifespan for a Miniature is 12 to 15 years (our oldest are 15 and 16). They become officially seniors over the age of eight years but, as with humans, all dogs age differently.

"It is noticeable, though, that this is the age when most dogs do appear to slow down a little, sleep more, eat less and put on weight.

"We do change the feed to Senior or Weight Control if a dog appears to be getting overweight, some of our stud dogs continue with their usual feeds. We only feed food supplements or multivitamins to older dogs if they require it, and pain relief if prescribed by our vet.

"In my experience, the health issues that affect older Schnauzers are bad breath, reduced eyesight, reduced hearing, becoming fussy eaters, arthritis, joint pain, urine incontinence and body odour - and they often become more stubborn!

"The coat condition appears to fade, it sometimes looks greasy, becomes curlier and loses its lustre. We tend to groom less but may bath more.

"As dogs get older we try and keep exercise the same unless the dog in question is struggling with movement or shows any sign of pain. Complementary therapies used have been herbal medications for joint pain or movement. On occasion, we have given a gentle massage to some of our very elderly dogs if and when they begin to get joint pain and stiffness.

"However, we must emphasise that, unfortunately, this is usually a turning point in the dog's life and difficult decisions have to be made in consultation with our vets. We would never let an elderly dog suffer. My advice for caring for the elderly Schnauzer is to respect the dog's age and adjust how you look after him or her accordingly."

Show judge and former breeder **Lesley Myers'** dogs have lived to between 14 and 16 years of age. She says: "Mini Schnauzers seem to grow old gracefully, none of mine has had any signs of arthritis. Some did lose a bit of weight in their final 12 months.

"Towards the end of my dogs' lives, cataracts, stomach problems and bladder stones were issues that required veterinary attention. Rommey was healthy until the last day of her life, aged 14 years and nine months, as was Kaizer, who passed away two weeks before his 15th birthday."

Photo: Proud as punch! Lesley's Schultz was possibly the first Mini to win his very first Challenge Certificate (Best in Breed) as an 8.5-year-old veteran.

Lesley added: "I used to feed my dogs on Royal Canin, then when Rommey was eight I put her on their Senior food. But it didn't suit her (according to her poops), so I put her back on to the Adult one.

"Later I changed all my dogs to Platinum and they are all healthy with good coats and happy on it.

"If your Mini is showing signs they are old - there may be not much interest in anything, they may be in a deep, sound sleep more often, and possibly take longer to eat their meals - keep them comfortable, cosy and warm.

"Cuddle them, let them know you are there to support them, read their body language to realise when they are in discomfort or pain, as they won't let you know until the very end."

Specialist Schnauzer groomer and Standard Schnauzer breeder **Beth Railton** says: "Change in coat happens after spay or neuter, sometimes age can make the coat grow more sparse, with bald patches, etc. and any meds the dog is on for age-related issues can also cause coat change.

"Once my dogs hit old age, I no longer hand strip them. I shave them down all over with a small beard so they do not require brushing and don't need grooming so often. I don't bath on the same day as grooming either, as this could be too much for the dog.

"My advice to owners is please don't keep them alive for your own personal emotional sake."

Owners' Experiences

Simon and Yvonne Sonsino, UK: "We started to notice a subtle change when Bu was about 13, he was sleeping more often and trotting instead of running. There were no behaviour changes, other than he slowed down and we went on shorter walks. We stuck to wet and dry food suitable for a senior with no extra supplements.

"He started to go grey around the face and his coat looked like he had a light dusting of icing sugar, but the frequency of grooming stayed the same. For the last few years, Bu had Cushing's, but it was easily controlled using medication."

Les Chant, UK, owner of Heidi and Merlin, both aged 12 and *pictured here*: "We noticed changes at around the age of eight years. Signs are similar to humans when they get older: slowing down, more sleepy, not so agile, some can suffer from arthritis or poor eyesight.

"Heidi *(left)* has thyroid problems and is on a daily tablet to keep it in check and annual blood tests.

"Other issues that might crop up are putting on weight - Senior food helps to reduce this problem. Also, their teeth might need cleaning or even some extracted. Their teeth should be checked for this yearly throughout their lives; dental sticks and bones help to prevent and remove plaque build-up.

"There are no real changes in behaviour, except they may not want to go so far on walkies, and Heidi sometimes needs help when trying to jump up onto the sofa.

"All dogs are different in their requirements so, if you're concerned about your old Mini, I'd advise anyone always to seek your vet's advice."

Rebecca Makdad, USA: "They slow down at about 10 to 12 years old, I think it depends on what you are doing with them. My senior dogs are switched to a Senior/less active kibble with glucosamine/chondroitin and fish oil supplements and I watch their weight.

"We have shorter walks and not in harsh weather. Rosie (aged 13) is still the Alpha dog, so no change there! My advice is to shower them with love, they deserve it."

The Last Lap

Huge advances in veterinary science have meant that countless procedures and medications can prolong the life of your dog, and this is a good thing. But there comes a time when you do have to let go.

If your dog is showing all the signs of ageing, has an ongoing medical condition from which she cannot recover, is showing signs of pain, anxiety or distress and there is no hope of improvement, then the dreaded time has come to say goodbye. You owe it to your Schnauzer.

There is no point in keeping an old dog alive if all that lies ahead is pain and death. We have their lives in our hands and we can give them the gift of passing away peacefully and humanely at the end when the time is right.

Losing our beloved companion, our best friend, a member of the family, is truly heartbreaking. But one of the things we realise at the back of our minds when we got that gorgeous, lively little Mini Schnauzer puppy that bounded up to meet us like we were the best person in the whole wide world is the pain that comes with it.

We know we will live longer than them and that we'll probably have to make this most painful of decisions at some time in the future. It's the worst thing about being a dog owner.

If your Schnauzer has had a long and happy life, then you could not have done any more. You were a great owner and your dog was lucky to have you. Remember all the good times you had together.

Try not to rush out and buy another dog straight away. Assess your current lifestyle and, if your situation is right, only then consider getting another dog and all that that entails in terms of time, commitment, exercise and expense over the next decade and more.

Whatever you decide to do, put the dog first.

....

This chapter is dedicated to Bu who passed away at the age of 15-and-a-half during the writing of this book, and who is missed terribly by Simon and Yvonne.

Breeder Contributors

Wade Bogart, Sumerwynd Miniature Schnauzers, Akron, New York State, USA

www.sumerwyndminiatureschnauzer.com

Dr Lisa Sarvas DVM BSA, Beauideal Schnauzers, North Carolina, USA

www.facebook.com/people/Beauideal-Schnauzers/100064675152671

Steve Matthews, Silbertraum Miniature & Giant Schnauzers, Dorchester, England

www.facebook.com/steve.matthews.9041

Andrew & Gaynor Ray, Minnienoom Miniature, Standard & Giant Schnauzers, Derby, England

www.facebook.com/groups/373004923418057 email: andrewmarkray@hotmail.com

Beth Railton, Lefenix Standard Schnauzers, Derbyshire, England www.lefenixschnauzers.co.uk

www.facebook.com/profile.php?id=100055227463756

Disclaimer

This book has been written to provide helpful information on Miniature Schnauzers. It is not meant to be used, nor should it be used, to diagnose or treat any medical condition. For diagnosis or treatment of any animal medical problem, consult a qualified veterinarian.

The author is not responsible for any specific health or allergy conditions that may require medical supervision and is not liable for any damages or negative consequences from any treatment, action, application or preparation, to any animal or to any person reading or following the information in this book.

The views expressed by contributors to this book are solely personal and do not necessarily represent those of the author. References are provided for informational purposes only and do not constitute an endorsement of any websites or other sources.

Useful Contacts

Miniature Schnauzer Club of America www.standardschnauzer.org

American Miniature Schnauzer Club https://amsc.us

AKC (American Kennel Club) www.akc.org/dog-breeds/miniature-schnauzer

The Schnauzer Club of Great Britain (all three sizes) www.schnauzerclub.co.uk

The Northern Schnauzer Club (UK) http://northernschnauzerclub.co.uk

Kennel Club (UK) Assured Breeders www.thekennelclub.org.uk/search/find-an-assured-breeder

AKC Preparing a Puppy Contract www.akc.org/expert-advice/dog-breeding/preparing-a-contract-for-puppy-buyers

RSPCA Puppy Contract https://puppycontract.rspca.org.uk/home

AKC Canine Good Citizen www.akc.org/products-services/training-programs/canine-good-citizen

KC Good Citizen Scheme www.thekennelclub.org.uk/training/good-citizen-dog-training-scheme

Association of Pet Dog Trainers UK www.apdt.co.uk

Association of Pet Dog Trainers US www.apdt.com

Canadian Association of Professional Pet Dog Trainers www.cappdt.ca

Useful info on dog foods (US) www.dogfoodadvisor.com (UK) www.allaboutdogfood.co.uk

Helps find lost or stolen dogs in the US: register your dog's microchip at www.akcreunite.org and www.petmicrochiplookup.com to trace a registered microchip

Schnauzer internet forums and Facebook groups are also a good source of information from other owners.

Index

Made in the USA
Las Vegas, NV
22 November 2024

12394595R00149